Equal Opportunity Peacekeeping

OXFORD STUDIES IN GENDER AND INTERNATIONAL RELATIONS

Series editors: J. Ann Tickner, University of Southern California, and Laura Sjoberg, University of Florida

Equal Opportunity Peacekeeping

Women, Peace, and Security in Post-Conflict States

Sabrina Karim and Kyle Beardsley

OXFORD
UNIVERSITY PRESS

OXFORD
UNIVERSITY PRESS

Oxford University Press is a department of the University of Oxford. It furthers
the University's objective of excellence in research, scholarship, and education
by publishing worldwide. Oxford is a registered trade mark of Oxford University
Press in the UK and certain other countries.

Published in the United States of America by Oxford University Press
198 Madison Avenue, New York, NY 10016, United States of America.

© Oxford University Press 2017

First issued as an Oxford University Press paperback, 2020

Library of Congress Cataloging-in-Publication Data
Names: Karim, Sabrina, author. | Beardsley, Kyle, 1979– author.
Title: Equal opportunity peacekeeping : women, peace, and security
in post-conflict states / Sabrina Karim and Kyle Beardsley.
Description: Oxford ; New York, NY : Oxford University Press, 2017. |
Series: Oxford studies in gender and international relations |
Includes bibliographical references and index.
Identifiers: LCCN 2016033646 (print) | LCCN 2016051887 (ebook) |
ISBN 9780190602420 (hardback) | ISBN 9780190093532 (paperback) |
ISBN 9780190602437 (Updf)
Subjects: LCSH: United Nations—Peacekeeping forces. |
United Nations. Security Council. Resolution 1325. | Peacekeeping forces—Women. |
Women and peace. | BISAC: POLITICAL SCIENCE / International Relations / Diplomacy. |
POLITICAL SCIENCE / Peace. | SOCIAL SCIENCE / Gender Studies.
Classification: LCC JZ6374 .K36 2017 (print) | LCC JZ6374 (ebook) |
DDC 341.5/8—dc23
LC record available at https://lccn.loc.gov/2016033646

For the man who always saved me the last sip of Scotch, my friend and source of solace,
"now until the end," James Kyle Doyle
April 5, 1985–June 24, 2011

—SK

To Esther and Hazel, that you might have the opportunity to pursue peace with a ferocity that knows no bounds.

—KB

From the bosom of the devastated earth a voice goes up with our own. It says: Disarm, disarm! The sword of murder is not the balance of justice. Blood does not wipe out dishonor, nor violence vindicate possession. As men have often forsaken the plough and the anvil at the summons of war, let women now leave all that may be left of home for a great and earnest day of council.

—*Julia Ward Howe, "Appeal to Womanhood throughout the World," 1870*

CONTENTS

ACKNOWLEDGMENTS

The individuals who made this book possible span several continents and countries. There were many members of the UN Mission in Liberia (UNMIL) who gave us their time and energy during 2012 and 2013. We appreciate the assistance of both the UN Department of Peacekeeping Operations (DPKO) and UNMIL in being able to observe the activities of peacekeepers and also interview them. Special and heartfelt thanks are in order to Clare Hutchinson, Jane Rhodes, Lola Aduke Oyediran-Ugbodaga, Deborah Addison-Cambell, Dabashish Barua, Andre Bouchard, César Montoya Villafuerte, Orlando Ugaz, Valentine Okoro, Eric Puls, Candice Rose Vera Flores, and Aerith Aivy Tina. We are also indebted to the soldiers and police officers from the following countries that served in UNMIL in June and July of 2012 and who participated in our interviews and focus groups: Philippines, Bangladesh, Nigeria, Sweden, Ghana, Norway, Uganda, Kenya, Jordan, Zimbabwe, India, Pakistan, Bosnia, Turkey, Denmark, Nepal, Switzerland, Gambia, Peru, and the United States. In addition, we are thankful for a meeting with Sade Uddin Ahmed Sohel in Dhaka, Bangladesh, which provided much more insight into how peacekeepers are selected to deploy to peacekeeping missions.

In addition to the help of UN DPKO and UNMIL, we received an enormous amount of support and assistance from the Liberian National Police (LNP). Many friendships were forged during the research process with the LNP. In particular, we are especially thankful for the help of William K. Mulbah, Abraham S. Kromah, Dao R. Freeman, John G. Kemoh, Karson Zubah, G. William Forkpa, Adolphus H. Yah Jr., Weah B. Goll, Margaret Forh, and Hazel Quaye, as well as C. Clarence Massaquoi, in giving us unique and deep insight into the inner workings of the LNP and for allowing for a partnership with the police in the name of research. Having spent nearly five years working in close contact with the LNP, we are extremely appreciative for the access and subsequent ability to tell the story of the experiences of police officers in Liberia.

Words cannot express the gratitude we have toward the many dedicated research assistants who worked diligently on various parts of this project. The many members of the Center for Applied Research and Training (CART) in Liberia must be acknowledged for providing excellent research support. In particular, this book would not have been possible without the leadership and passion of Kou M. Gbaintor-Johnson, the director of CART, who has made researching Liberia an absolute joy. Her friendship and collaboration are the foundation on which this book stands, as her dedication to us and the research has never subsided. In addition, Isaac Chear Wesseh, Finah Varney Bottomley, and James Vululleh have been invaluable in conducting field surveys that have yielded fruitful data for our project. Outside Liberia, the meticulous research assistantship and data collection of Sweta Maturu, Arianna Robbins, Ryan Gorman, and Joanna Satterwhite contributed significantly to the book.

In Liberia, more broadly, we are especially thankful to Felicia Howard, Lorpu Howard, Ballah Sannoh, Rufus N. Zerlee, and Nellie Cooper, who allowed us to conduct surveys in their communities, and Alex Kendima, who has clocked many hours driving Sabrina around Monrovia and telling her about his aspirations for creating Liberia's "Lollywood."

The initial trip to Liberia in 2012 that started the field research there would not have been possible without the immeasurable support and help of Pamela Scully. Erin Bernstein and Rosalyn Schroeder provided enormous emotional support in Liberia on that first trip. They were wonderful travel companions and field research partners.

The project received generous financial support from the Folke Bernadotte Academy, especially with the help of Louise Olsson and Christian Altpeter. In addition, Sita Ranchod-Nilsson, director of Emory University's Institute for Developing Nations, and Tom Crick at the Carter Center were instrumental in funding assistance to conduct initial research in the summer of 2012. Financial support was also provided by the British Research Council, thanks to the help of Theodora-Ismene Gizelis.

We are also indebted to those that read our manuscript and provided comments, including Dan Reiter, Ismene Gizelis, Louise Olsson, and Beth Reingold. We are also especially thankful to the anonymous reviewers and the editorial team at Oxford University Press, including Angela Chnapko. The book is much improved as a result of their input.

A number of coauthors on projects that also stemmed from the research in Liberia are worth noting, in particular Rob Blair, Michael Gilligan, Bernd Beber, and Jenny Guardado. These coauthored projects added to the richness of our book. We also received very helpful feedback from Dara Cohen, Ragnhild Nordås, Jacob Kathman, Ana Arjona, Isak Svensson, Mathilda Lindgren, Desirée Nilsson, William Durch, Marsha Henry, and participants at workshops at the Department of Peace and Conflict Research at Uppsala University and Folke Bernadotte Academy working groups on UNSC 1325 and Peacekeeping. Additionally, faculty at The University of Georgia's School of Public and International Affairs Department of Public Administration and Policy, where Sabrina was invited to give a talk about the book by Cas Mudde, also provided helpful comments.

In addition, we are grateful to Chantal de Jonge Oudraat at Women in International Security and Kathleen Kuehnas and Steve Steiner at the US Institute for Peace for sponsoring workshops and conferences that only added to the richness of the ideas for the book. In Liberia, encouragement has come from the US embassy.

Laura Sjoberg provided constant encouragement to pursue this project. From the onset, her enthusiasm for the project kept the vision alive, and we are grateful not only for her comments but also her guidance along the way.

There is absolutely no way this book would have been possible without the help and support of Joshua Riggins. Between 2012 and 2014, he put an immeasurable amount of time, dedication, and passion into making the many research aspects described in the book possible, including but not limited to helping to arrange interviews with peacekeepers in UNMIL, helping to implement the lab-in-the-field experiments, facilitating interviews with LNP officers, and providing emotional support in Liberia when the field research was most difficult. He was an integral part of the project, and there are not enough ways to thank him for all that he did for us.

We are also indebted to our friends and family members who gave us the love and patience to work on this project even before the idea for it emerged, including but not limited to Nazmul Karim, Selina Karim, Sohana Arni, Ryan Arni, Kaelen Arni, Malea Arni, Jessica Beardsley, Katherine Beardsley, and Robert Beardsley. Friends of Sabrina who deserve recognition and who have encouraged Sabrina from the early stages of her career to now include Jonathan Gingerich, Jonathan Dingel, Michelle Moon, Ines Marques Da Silva, Carrie Gladstone, Kelly Nieves, Anne Bellows, Maya Wilson, Penny Siqueiros, and Joshua Eli Smith.

Finally, in 2011, Sabrina came to Emory University as a graduate student wanting to do a project on female peacekeepers—her graduate school application statement mentioned the project idea. The inspiration behind those ideas as well as the support to pursue them stemmed from many late-night discussions and e-mail chains with Kyle Doyle. Kyle Doyle passed away on June 24, 2011, but his memory and the memory of those conversations lives on through this book.

ABBREVIATIONS

AFL	Armed Forces of Liberia
BINUB	UN Integrated Office in Burundi
BINUCA	UN Integrated Peacebuilding Office in the Central African Republic
CART	Center for Action, Research, and Training
CIMIC	civil military coordination
DAW	Division for the Advancement of Women
DDR	disarmament, demobilization and reintegration
DDRR	disarmament, demobilization, reintegration, and repatriation
DFS	Department of Field Support
DPKO	Department of Peacekeeping Operations
DRC	Democratic Republic of the Congo
ECOMOG	Economic Monitoring Group
FPU	Formed Police Unit
INSTRAW	International Research and Training Institute for the Advancement of Women
LNP	Liberian National Police
MINURCAT	UN Mission in the Central African Republic and Chad
MINURSO	UN Mission for the Referendum in Western Sahara
MINUSMA	UN Multidimensional Integrated Stabilization Mission in Mali
MINUSTAH	UN Stabilization Mission in Haiti
MONUC	UN Organization Mission in the Democratic Republic of the Congo
MONUSCO	UN Organization Stabilization Mission in the Democratic Republic of the Congo
NAP	National Action Plan
OIOS	Office of Internal Oversight Services
ONUB	UN Operation in Burundi
OSAGI	Office of the Special Adviser on Gender Issues and Advancement of Women
PKO	peacekeeping operation
PRIO	Peace Research Institute Oslo
PSU	Police Support Unit
SEA	sexual exploitation and abuse
SEAHV	sexual exploitation, abuse, harassment, and violence

SGBV	sexual and gender-based violence
SRSG	special representative of the secretary-general
SSR	security sector reform
UCDP	Uppsala Conflict Data Program
UNAMA	UN Assistance Mission in Afghanistan
UNAMID	UN-African Union Mission in Darfur
UNDOF	UN Disengagement Observer Force
UNDP	United Nations Development Programme
UNICEF	The United Nations International Children's Emergency Fund
UNIFEM	United Nations Development Fund for Women
UNFICYP	UN Peacekeeping Force in Cyprus
UNIFIL	UN Interim Force in Lebanon
UNIOSIL	UN Integrated Office in Sierra Leone
UNISFA	UN Interim Security Force for Abyei
UNMEE	UN Mission in Ethiopia and Eritrea
UNMIK	UN Mission in Kosovo
UNMIL	UN Mission in Liberia
UNMIN	UN Mission in Nepal
UNMIS	UN Mission in Sudan
UNMISS	UN Mission in the Republic of South Sudan
UNMIT	UN Integrated Mission in Timor-Leste
UNMOGIP	UN Military Observer Group in India and Pakistan
UNOCI	UN Operation in Côte d'Ivoire
UNOMIG	UN Observer Mission in Georgia
UNPOL	UN Police
UNSCR	United Nations Security Council Resolution
UNSMIL	UN Support Mission in Libya
UNTAC	UN Transitional Authority in Cambodia
UNTSO	United Nations Truce Supervision Organization
WPS	women, peace and security

Equal Opportunity Peacekeeping

CHAPTER 1

Introduction

Are Blue Helmets Just for Boys?

In 2014, Swedish Foreign Minister Margot Wallström made international head-lines when she announced that the Swedish government would pursue a "feminist foreign policy." The resulting doctrine affirms that "ensuring that women and girls can enjoy their fundamental human rights is both a duty within the framework of our international commitments, and a prerequisite for Sweden's broader foreign policy goals on development, democracy, peace and security."[1]

Several years before this announcement, former U.S. Secretary of State Hillary Clinton outlined the "Hillary Doctrine," in 2009, in which she proclaimed: "The United States has made empowering women and girls a cornerstone of our foreign policy because women's equality is not just a moral issue, it's not just a humanitarian issue, it is not just a fairness issue. It is a security issue. . . . Give women equal rights and entire nations are more stable and secure. Deny women equal rights and the instability of nations is almost certain" (Hudson and Leidl, 2015: 1).

Not only have some countries included a "feminist" orientation in their foreign policy, but many countries have begun implementing reforms to make their defense forces more gender equal as well. In December 2015, Secretary of Defense Ashton Carter announced that the U.S. military would let women serve in all combat roles.[2] The announcement came after Captain Kristen Griest and First Lieutenant Shaye Haver graduated from the army's famously rigorous Ranger School at Fort Benning, Georgia, four months earlier. These recent developments have propelled gender equality to the forefront of discussions on international security and politics.

On the academic front, the research of many scholars demonstrates that Margot Wallström and Hillary Clinton's approaches to foreign policy may actually help miti-gate conflict and violence globally. Research consistently shows that gender equality contributes to peace or the cessation of violence and human rights violations.[3] When societies are more gender equal, they are more peaceful, which means that promot-ing gender equality is a step toward ensuring long-term peace globally.

While developments that place gender equality at the forefront of foreign policy in Sweden and the United States are novel and radical, the United Nations (UN), particularly through its Department of Peacekeeping Operations (DPKO), has been paving new ground when it comes to gender equality in conflict-ridden and postconflict countries for decades.[4] In 2000, the UN Security Council passed Resolution 1325 (UNSCR 1325), which institutionalized the Women, Peace, and Security (WPS) agenda at the international level. The Resolution's adoption is considered by many to be a historic milestone since it marked the first time that the UNSCR dealt specifically with gender issues and women's experiences in conflict and postconflict situations and recognized women's contribution to conflict resolution and prevention.[5] The Resolution legally mandates peacekeeping operations (PKOs) to include women in decision-making roles in all aspects of the peacekeeping and peace-building processes. In this way, for nearly two decades, and long before Sweden and the United States formally made gender equality an integral part of foreign policy, the UN DPKO has been one of the main promoters of gender equality in international politics. If peacekeeping missions have a historic advantage in issues related to gender equality, one must ask to what extent have they achieved gender equality in PKOs and been vehicles for promoting gender equality in postconflict states?

In general, the UN DPKO and other stakeholders in the WPS agenda have taken two approaches to implementing gender reforms in PKOs.[6] They have undertaken an ambitious agenda to increase the participation of women in their peacekeeping forces in both military and police contingents, and they have sought to increase the protection of women by mitigating sexual and gender-based violence (SGBV), including exploitation, abuse, and harassment perpetrated by peacekeepers. To date, the results have been somewhat successful.[7] The number of women in PKOs has increased since the first peacekeeping mission in 1948, and there is an increased awareness in peacekeeping missions about the pernicious problem of sexual exploitation, abuse, harassment, and violence (SEAHV).[8] Gender reforms in peacekeeping missions additionally help to promote gender equality in host countries, as peacekeeping missions have been increasingly involved in consulting with and directly assisting domestic institutional reforms. To achieve these goals, UN peacekeeping missions have introduced the concept of gender mainstreaming—the constant assessment of how policies affect women and men—into operations.

While there have been advancements in promoting gender equality in and through PKOs, daunting challenges remain. The 2015 report to the General Assembly from the High-Level Independent Panel on Peace Operations notes a number of areas in which PKOs are falling short. The report specifically acknowledges that "15 years on [since the adoption of UNSCR 1325] there remains a poor understanding of the potential of both integrating a gendered perspective and increasing the participation of women at all levels of political and civil life, most especially at the leadership level" (UN, 2015: 23). Moreover, related to SEAHV, the report admonishes: "sexual exploitation and abuse in PKOs is continuing, to the enduring shame of the Organization, its personnel and the countries which provide the peacekeepers who abuse" (UN, 2015: 14).[9]

The culture of PKOs still too often prevents women and men from equal participation and perpetuates discrimination and violence. In particular, *gender power imbalances* between the sexes and among genders place restrictions on the participation of women in peacekeeping missions, both in terms of the proportions of women and how women are employed relative to men. These restrictions ensure continued discrimination, especially with respect to women's roles in PKOs. And they all but guarantee that SEAHV continues to be a problem both in missions and outside them. In the context of broader peacekeeping mandates, overcoming these imbalances is imperative for ensuring that gender equality is and continues to be a cornerstone of PKOs globally.

The international community is undertaking an ambitious effort to address gender inequality in postconflict security provision. There is tremendous opportunity in this endeavor, but there are also tremendous headwinds. Going forward, an understanding of the current state of peacekeeping with regard to gender reforms is crucial to make the most of the present opportunity to shape how peacekeeping is implemented and how gender is construed in the security sectors of the contributing countries, in multinational missions, and in the domestic institutions of the host countries. Moreover, by understanding the peacekeeping model, which arguably has an institutional comparative advantage in the promotion of gender equality globally, one is better able to understand the opportunities and challenges facing broader gender equality initiatives in foreign policy and other areas of international politics.

OUR ARGUMENT

This book explores the extent to which reforms that relate to gender equality in peacekeeping missions have been successful both in and through peacekeeping missions. We argue that there have been successes but that they are tempered by institutional barriers. The foundation for our main argument starts with an understanding of the origins and consequences of unbalanced power relations between the sexes and among genders—gender power imbalances. We contend that military and police institutions, of which peacekeeping missions are composed, are gendered institutions in that they project and replicate structures of power that privilege men and certain forms of masculinity.

The imbalance or inequality between the sexes and the genders creates and perpetuates particular gendered problems in PKOs. Power imbalances in PKOs can lead to the privileging of rigid gender roles for men and women. One source of gender power imbalance is the widespread perception that men are natural warriors and women are natural peacemakers. This has the consequence of outright discrimination against women (and men) in the security sector—women are subject to particular roles in the institution and therefore not seen as eligible to partake in or be promoted in areas that are traditionally considered masculine work.[10] Another source of imbalance is the entrenched norm that men are protectors and women are in need of protection. This "gendered protection norm" pervades many PKOs and thereby limits the number and full agency of female peacekeepers, specifically in terms of relegating them to "safe spaces." Finally, we argue that militarization processes tend to cultivate the potential for SEAHV, a particularly pernicious manifestation of gender power imbalances. As we explain in chapter 3, these problems are not mutually exclusive, as they often occur simultaneously.

In light of these challenges, we identify and examine how particular gender reforms, through increasing the representation of women in peacekeeping forces (as a policy lever—female ratio balancing) and, even more important, through enhancing a more holistic value for "equal opportunity," can enable peacekeeping to overcome the challenges posed by power imbalances and be more of an example of and vehicle for gender equality. By "equal opportunity" we mean much more than the equal opportunity for women and men to serve as peacekeepers. We mean that there is equal opportunity for the more marginalized identities and characteristics associated with nondominant forms of masculinity to be valued. We also mean that beliefs about women and men's contributions, in addition to actual contributions, are respected. The hope is that there will then be equal opportunity for women and men to have power and leadership in peacekeeping missions and equal opportunity for women and men to be part of the solution in identifying and resolving discriminatory practices and instances of SEAHV. These arguments are not new and have been and are the subject of research by many feminist scholars. Thus, we use this foundational work and apply it in the context of PKOs to better understand to what extent PKOs promote gender equality both in missions and through them.

We divide the book into three parts. The first part provides an account of the evolution of gender reforms in PKOs and an overview of current peacekeeping successes with regard to such reforms. We then provide an analysis of the overarching problem of gender power imbalances in security institutions, resulting in the challenges that PKOs face in promoting gender equality. In the second part, we conduct empirical analyses that explore some of the implications of our theoretical framework related to the prevalence of discrimination, a gendered protection norm, and SEAHV. In addition to confirming that these are problems confronting the contemporary peacekeeping landscape, the analyses shed light on the variation of their severity. The results suggest that contributing countries are unlikely to deploy women to missions when they lack the participation of women in their domestic security forces, when the mission environments have a history of brutal violence, and when the contributing countries do not have strong records of gender equality. We also find that the prevalence of SEAHV in peacekeeping missions marginally decreases as the representation of women increases and more robustly decreases as the proportion of troops from contributing countries with relatively strong records of gender equality increases.

The third part of the book uses the UN Mission in Liberia (UNMIL) as a case study. Specifically, we analyze the experiences of mostly female peacekeepers in the mission through interviews and focus group discussions, gauging the extent to which discrimination, the gendered protection norm, and SEAHV impede activities in the mission. We then use household surveys and lab-in-the-field experiments to understand how local interactions with female peacekeepers or local policewomen affect perceptions of the security sector, and how the introduction of reforms initiated by international peacekeepers has affected gender dynamics within the Liberian National Police (LNP). In these chapters, we find that the protection norm in mission cultures and discrimination often impede the efforts of many female peacekeepers in helping the local population and supporting one another within the mission. We also discuss first-hand accounts of sexual harassment against female peacekeepers.

From analysis of both the global data and the Liberian case, we draw conclusions about how peacekeeping missions can improve gender equality both in and through missions. While one approach has been to increase the proportion of female peacekeepers (and to introduce mostly female civilian gender advisers, units, and focal points) to improve the quality of missions, we posit that such a policy lever is likely to only yield limited fruit, given both practical constraints—if restrictions on female participation is one of the key problems to address, then simply planning to increase the representation of women does not tell us how the underlying problems are addressed—and theoretical concerns: a focus on increasing the representation of women might not sufficiently shape the dysfunctional institutional cultures at the root of the problems. As such, a more holistic approach, one that favors supporting a norm of "equal opportunity" through framing; leadership; recruitment and standards; promotion, demotion, and discipline; training and professionalism; access and accountability; women's representation; and gender mainstreaming (broadly defined) should be more fruitful. If successful, attempts to address the challenges that stem from power imbalances in peacekeeping missions will help advance gender equality globally.

OUR APPROACH AND CONTRIBUTION

Our approach to understanding the origins and consequences of gender power imbalances related to the provision of peacekeeping is theoretically driven by existing scholarship on gender and international relations. At the same time, our approach is empirically positivist in the sense that we identify and test for the expected manifestations of gender power imbalances in and through peacekeeping missions, using a combination of evidence from quantitative measures, qualitative interviews and focus groups, and surveys. In doing so, we recognize that this particular way of accruing knowledge differs from critical approaches to studying the role of gender in international institutions.[11] These alternative normative and critical approaches have provided a rich foundation for understanding the weight of gender in international politics and security affairs. Our positivist approach fills a gap by demonstrating how well observations from different types of data comport with our theoretical expectations, when so much of the existing empirical literature on peacekeeping has ignored the relevance of gender.

Indeed, much of the existing peacekeeping literature has explored whether PKOs contribute to a wide range of outcomes associated with peace, with the emerging consensus being that peacekeeping has generally played a constructive, if uneven, role—whether in preventing conflict relapse (Fortna, 2008), protecting civilians (Hultman, Kathman, and Shannon, 2013), containing conflict (Beardsley, 2011), or promoting human rights (Murdie and Davis, 2010).[12] Notably absent from this literature is any discussion on gender or gender equality. Yet gender inequality is inimical to human security and touches all aspects of society, which means that improvements in peacekeeping's record as a model for and catalyst of gender equality has direct implications for the cultivation of peace in host countries. Evaluations of peacekeeping efficacy without first understanding that PKOs are gendered institutions are incomplete. Years of scholarship by prominent feminist international relations scholars have pointed to the importance of gender in understanding international institutions, particularly the role gender power imbalances play in shaping the ways security institutions function.[13] Our goal is to bring these theories to the forefront of the literature on peacekeeping and demonstrate that a comprehensive approach to understanding peacekeeping efficacy must consider the role of gender.

Our empirical approach recognizes that a discussion of the challenges facing peacekeeping missions in nurturing gender equality needs to incorporate observations at different levels, including the individual, institutional, societal, and state levels. We thus use a variety of approaches, including surveys, interviews, focus groups, cross-national data, and lab-in-the-field experiments to triangulate the inferences we draw. We provide rich, multimethod empirical evidence to test our claims and to evaluate the current state of gender equality in peacekeeping missions in two forms—by analyzing all UN missions from 2006 to 2013 (with both a military and police focus) and by using the UNMIL mission in Liberia as a case study. The data include quantitative analysis of observational mission data at the yearly level, a household survey conducted in two internally displaced and ex-combatant communities in Monrovia, data from a lab-in-the-field experiment conducted with the Liberian National Police (LNP), and a series of interviews, participant observations, and focus group discussions with female and male peacekeepers in the UNMIL mission. Each of these sources provides us with a view from a different angle of how gender dynamics are playing out within and through peacekeeping missions.

In our work, unlike much of the previous work on peacekeeping missions, we opt to tell part of our story by highlighting the voices of those who are potentially most affected by gender reforms: female peacekeepers and locals. Part of understanding the extent to which gender reforms have worked is to ask those whom the reforms have affected. This means asking female peacekeepers about their experiences in peacekeeping missions. It also means gauging the locals' perceptions of peacekeeping missions, particularly whether or not there are positive or adverse consequences from the gender reforms that peacekeeping missions spearhead. One of the critiques of the scholarship on peacekeeping missions is that it often ignores the voices of those whom peacekeeping is supposed to help (Pouligny, 2006). In this way, through the interviews and focus groups that we study, we use "feminist" methodology by trying to understand women's roles in UNMIL through the perspective and experiences of the women on mission and through the perceptions of locals.[14]

As a more secondary objective, our approach provides much-needed nuance to the policy and media dialogue on gender and peacekeeping. Many policy-makers and media outlets have tended to unequivocally affirm that female peacekeepers make a strong impact in fostering peace and improving gender equality. We posit, however, that the story has more layers and caution against tropes that reduce gender to one-dimensional characterizations—for example, by emphasizing the peaceful nature of women—that can often reify the very stereotypes that undergird gender hierarchies. We consider both the strengths and limitations of using female ratio balancing as a policy lever to address the problems of institutional power imbalances in PKOs. We contend that meaningful progress in addressing the root problems requires more holistic approaches to peacekeeping reforms—approaches that include increasing the number of women in peacekeeping but, more important, also promote a value for "equal opportunity" across all personnel.

In interviewing the many men and women in UNMIL, the men frequently asked why we were not writing a book about male peacekeepers. The short answer is that, in a sense, there are many books about male peacekeepers. That is, as noted, much of the existing literature on peacekeeping is at best neutral toward gender, and because security forces are constructed as activity associated with masculinity, this supposedly gender-neutral approach has more accurately described the experiences of male peacekeepers. In explaining mission evolution and effectiveness, many existing studies rely on the views and narratives of male peacekeepers, often ignoring the specific experiences of female peacekeepers and local women that provide more detailed information about mission deployment and effectiveness. Among other elements, such accounts miss the stories of SEAHV by peacekeepers. Moreover, there has never been a conscious effort on the part of the international community to increase the number of male peacekeepers. In contrast, there has been a concerted effort to increase the ratios of women to men in peacekeeping missions because men vastly outnumber women in them.

Thus, we opt to tell a different story from other books on peacekeeping. In part, this is a book that describes the state of gender reforms in peacekeeping missions. In part, this is also a book that expands what we mean by "peacekeeping efficacy" to include equal opportunity for men and women. Most important, this is a book that highlights the challenges and opportunities facing the potential for peacekeeping missions to both facilitate and embody gender equality worldwide.

OUTLINE OF THE BOOK

Chapter 2 lays the historical foundations for the book by providing an account of gender reforms in PKOs. It explains how implementing gender reforms became a part of international peacekeeping mandates and highlights the success of current gender reforms, including those related to participation, protection, and gender mainstreaming.

Chapter 3 provides the theoretical foundations for the rest of the book. It begins by outlining our main theoretical argument: that gender power imbalances have led to particular problems in PKOs, mainly discrimination against female peacekeepers, a gendered protection norm that relegates female peacekeepers to safe spaces, and SEAHV. We then move on to address potential solutions to power imbalances. We start by critically analyzing the potential for female ratio balancing to work as a policy lever and conclude by suggesting that a more holistic approach is necessary, one that leads to "equal opportunity" peacekeeping.

In part II, we analyze discrimination, the protection norm, and SEAHV cross-nationally, specifically looking at missions from 2006 to 2013. Chapter 4 assesses how exclusion, discrimination, and the gendered protection norm contribute to the low participation rate of female peacekeepers globally. The scope of the analysis focuses on the willingness of contributing countries to send women to peacekeeping missions, as a function of the characteristics of both the contributing country and the target country. Chapter 5 turns to the relationship between gender power imbalances and SEAHV. The scope of the analysis focuses on mission-level variations in SEAHV offenses, as a function of the representation of women as well as the practice of gender equality in the contributing countries.

In Part III, we analyze the challenges that gender power imbalances pose for peacekeeping missions through our case study in Liberia. Chapter 6 focuses on the experiences of UNMIL peacekeeping personnel with regard to discrimination, the gendered norm of protection, and SEAHV in their day-to-day activities. Chapter 7 considers whether UNMIL has contributed to a culture of power imbalance or of equal opportunity in local contexts.

Chapter 8 summarizes the main findings, provides a comprehensive explanation of "equal opportunity" peacekeeping as a strategy to improve gender equality in and through peacekeeping missions, and concludes with a series of concrete policy changes that domestic countries and peacekeeping missions can use to ensure that gender equality in PKOs and local security institutions is achieved, while also high-lighting the potential challenges to implementing some of these recommendations.

PART I

History and Theory

CHAPTER 2

The Evolution of Gender Reforms in UN Peacekeeping Missions

On January 31, 2007, India deployed 105 Indian policewomen to the UN Mission in Liberia (UNMIL), becoming the first country in the world to deploy an all-female unit to a peacekeeping mission.[1] Even before the unit arrived on the ground, they became a global media sensation and were heralded as a major success for PKOs. In 2010, then Secretary of State Hillary Clinton called the unit "an example that must be repeated in UN peacekeeping missions all over the world."[2] All-female formed police units (FPUs) have deployed to UNMIL from 2007 until 2016 and have inspired all-female FPUs from Bangladesh to deploy to Haiti and the Democratic Republic of Congo (DRC).

The inclusion of the all-female FPU exemplifies a change in how peacekeeping is done. Peacekeeping missions now include broader mandates to address issues ranging from institution building to human rights to gender equality—the latter especially due to UN Security Council Resolution (UNSCR) 1325, adopted in 2000. It both ushered in and institutionalized a new focus on gender in conflict, moving women's participation and rights to the forefront of international politics, including in the practice of peacekeeping. Peacekeeping is no longer just about men observing and monitoring peace in conflict-ridden countries, it is also about changing local institutions and ensuring that different norms, such as gender equality, permeate them. The deployment of the all-female FPU from India was a major step toward this new goal, and more broadly, increasing the representation of women in peacekeeping missions is one tangible way the international community has strived to address gender inequality issues in postconflict states.

This chapter describes how we got to this point in time—a time when gender equality is an important component of PKOs—and describes the successes thus far in terms of gender equality in UN peacekeeping missions. It starts out by describing major reforms in missions more broadly and then shifts to the evolution of the "Women, Peace, and Security" agenda (WPS), which was the main stimulus for activity on gender equality at UN DPKO. We then describe the two main types of gender reform that have been implemented both within peacekeeping missions and also through them: enhancing the participation of women in processes related to conflict resolution and protecting women from violence.[3] We conclude by examining the role of and potential for gender mainstreaming to achieve gender reform goals in PKOs.

THE EVOLVING NATURE OF PEACEKEEPING

Since the end of the Cold War, traditional peacekeeping has gradually been replaced by broader, multidimensional PKOs. Boutros Boutros-Ghali's "Agenda for Peace" in 1992 laid the foundation for expanding the mandates of peacekeeping missions, as it emphasized the importance of peace-building activities as part of a more holistic accounting of how international missions can stabilize peace.[4] The Brahimi Report (the report of the Panel on UN Peace Operations) of 2000 called for further reforms in the implementation of peacekeeping and peace-building missions (UN, 2000). The use of the term "peace operations" makes it clear that the lines between peacemaking, peacekeeping, and peace-building are typically blurred in modern UN missions. Traditional missions focus on observation, where military observers monitor cease-fires and peace agreements.[5] In contrast, multidimensional peacekeeping missions are characterized by complex military, police, and civilian components that play a role not only in monitoring and enforcing peace agreements but also in peace- and state-building efforts that help reconstruct vital political and security institutions.

The emphasis on multidimensional mandates for peacekeeping missions has changed the composition of the forces deployed. Multidimensional forces now include troop contingents, military observers, and police (UN Police [UNPOL]), which all play different roles in the mission. In particular, the development of the FPUs demonstrates reform in the composition of deployed personnel. The first FPU was deployed to the UN Mission in Kosovo (UNMIK) in 1999. They are designed to be rapidly deployable, more heavily armed than regular UNPOL units and more capable of independent operations (Anderholt, 2012). They are intended to respond to a wide range of contingencies they have more flexibility in terms of response than traditional military contingents, and they are self-sufficient. They are also able to operate in "high-risk" environments and are deployed to accomplish policing duties such as crowd control rather than to respond to military threats.[6]

In addition, as one of the first missions to take on a more multidimensional approach to peacekeeping, the UN Transitional Authority in Cambodia (UNTAC), established in 1992, is a good example of peacekeeping reforms that have become the norm (Fréchette, 2012), and that mission has been noted as a relatively successful peacekeeping case (Paris, 2004). In Cambodia, UNTAC was responsible for maintaining a secure environment, disarming combatants and reintegrating them into civilian life, overseeing national elections, providing support to returning refugees, helping to reconstruct the economy, and overseeing the operations of five key ministries. Since UNTAC, many more tasks, such as training, monitoring, and reforming security and judiciary institutions, have been added to the mandates of UN peacekeeping missions.

As a follow-up to the Brahimi Report, in 2014 Secretary-General Ban Ki-moon established The Review by the High-Level Independent Panel on Peace Operations to conduct a comprehensive assessment of the current state of UN peace operations and the emerging needs for the future. The panel's report (High-Level Report), released in June 2015, further emphasizes the multidimensional nature of PKOs and highlights several areas in need of continued reform: (1) conflict prevention; (2) protection of civilians; and (3) rebuilding domestic institutions (UN, 2015: 10–13). The report goes on to recommend specific institutional changes that would achieve these goals and provide the foundation for the next generation of peacekeeping.

The changes in mission mandate and composition since 1948—the year of the deployment of the first peacekeeping mission—reflect the international community's attempt to be more innovative in how it addresses the sources of insecurity in postconflict countries. One of these innovations, explored in detail below, includes prioritizing gender equality in mandate construction, in mission composition, and in each host country's domestic security sector. Much of the existing literature that has assessed the efficacy of multidimensional peacekeeping and peace-building activities across multiple cases, however, has defined success in mostly gender-neutral terms. For example, Paul F. Diehl and Daniel Druckman (2010) have considered a number of ways to evaluate peacekeeping efficacy, but even they do not much consider the legacy of peacekeeping missions with regard to gender equality. Work by scholars such as Page Fortna (2008) has defined success in terms of no recurrence of conflict, which misses assessing the quality of the peace for large swaths of the societies involved. Michael Doyle and Nicolas Sambanis (2006) include progress toward democratization along with the absence of conflict in their definition of success. Multicase qualitative studies, such as those by Lise Howard (2008) and Roland Paris (2004), are better able to build the mandate objectives into their measurements of success and also comment on the quality of the peace, if any, attained. Recent quantitative work by Lisa Hultman and her colleagues (2013, 2014) has found that larger peacekeeping forces tend to do better in reducing levels of one-sided violence and battlefield fatalities. But such measures miss other forms of violence that are more prone to affect women.[7] Kyle Beardsley (2011), meanwhile, finds that peacekeeping can mitigate the potential for conflict to spread from one state to the next. Amanda Murdie and David Davis (2010) have also found that peacekeeping missions with a mandate for humanitarian assistance and with mediation mandates improve human rights. While these are all outcomes important to evaluate, missing is a sense of whether the missions are able to do much in terms of addressing gender inequality in destination countries and in the missions themselves, especially as there has been an increased emphasis in mandates to take gender equality seriously.

THE EVOLUTION OF THE WOMEN, PEACE, AND SECURITY AGENDA

The WPS agenda places gender equality at the forefront of international politics, particularly in the realm of conflict resolution. It first started with the 1995 Beijing

Platform for Action, which contained an entire chapter focused on WPS. During the 1990s, the NGO community was increasingly concerned about the negative impacts of war on women, particularly the widespread sexual violence seen in the civil wars in Bosnia and Rwanda. Activists were also upset that women faced significant barriers to entering peace talks and that the negative impacts that women experienced after the conflict were ignored in peace negotiations.[8] The Beijing Conference's fifth anniversary (Beijing + 5) provided critical momentum for progress on WPS issues at the UN and paved the way for the UNSCR 1325 movement.

The first major document integrating the WPS agenda into PKOs was the Windhoek Declaration and the Namibia Plan of Action on Mainstreaming a Gender Perspective in Multidimensional Peace Support Operations, which stressed the importance of gender mainstreaming and gender balancing in UN peace operations.[9] The Windhoek Declaration and Namibia Plan of Action were based on a comprehensive study, "Mainstreaming a Gender Perspective in Multidimensional Peace Operations," from peacekeeping missions in Bosnia, Cambodia, El Salvador, Namibia, and South Africa, conducted by the UN DPKO in cooperation with the Division for the Advancement of Women. The study concluded that "women's presence improves access and support for local women; it makes men peacekeepers more reflective and responsible; and it broadens the repertoire of skills and styles available within the mission, often with the effect of reducing conflict and confrontation" (UN DPKO, 2000).

Building on the momentum from Beijing and the Windhoek Declaration, the WPS agenda was institutionalized in 2000, with the adoption of UNSCR 1325—the product of a broad coalition of NGOs, social movements, and states that worked together to convince Member States that "women as victims of war" and "women as creators of peace" should be systematically involved in peacemaking, peacekeeping, and peacebuilding operations.[10] The Resolution's adoption is considered by many to be a historic milestone since it marked the first time that the UN Security Council dealt specifically with gender issues and women's experiences in conflict and postconflict situations and it recognized women's contribution to conflict resolution and prevention.[11]

Since its adoption, the WPS agenda has been an integral part of the UN DPKO. UNSCR 1325 mandates peace operations to include women in decision-making roles in all aspects of the peacekeeping and peace-building processes. With regard to the incorporation of a gender perspective in PKOs, the Resolution also contains the following (UN Security Council, Security Council Resolution 1325, 2000: 2–3):

- "The urgent need to mainstream a gender perspective into peacekeeping operations"
- The "need for specialized training for all peacekeeping personnel on the protection, special needs and human rights of women and children in conflict situations"
- The "willingness to incorporate a gender perspective into peacekeeping operations"

The Resolution also

- "[Urges] the Secretary-General to ensure that, where appropriate, field operations include a gender component"

- "Requests the Secretary-General to provide to Member States training guidelines and materials on the protection, rights and the particular needs of women, as well as on the importance of involving women in all peacekeeping and peace-building measures"
- "Invites Member States to incorporate these elements as well as HIV/AIDS awareness training into their national training programmes for military and civilian police personnel in preparation for deployment"
- "Further requests the Secretary-General to ensure that civilian personnel of peacekeeping operations receive similar training"

Subsequent resolutions since UNSCR 1325, such as UNSCR 1820 (2008), UNSCR 1888 (2009), UNSCR 1889 (2009), UNSCR 1960 (2010), UNSCR 2106 (2013), UNSCR 2122 (2013), and UNSCR 2242 (2015), also affirm that gender equality should be an integral part of PKOs globally.[12] Due to UNSCR 1325 and the subsequent resolutions, gender is now mentioned in almost every mandate authorizing peacekeeping missions (Karim and Beardsley, 2013). However, the mandates vary in their scope of mentioning gender, as some only prohibit the SEAHV of peacekeepers, while others mention specific objectives, such as promoting women's participation in politics or preventing sexual violence. It is also important to note that there have been numerous critiques of UNSCR 1325—particularly that it does not treat gender as a critical concept and has not been implemented as a part of a critical approach to security.[13] With the mixed views of the WPS agenda in mind, we assess in later chapters how UNSCR 1325 has driven the gender equality agenda in PKOs and whether there are notable and observable successes and failures in implementation.

Since UNSCR 1325, several major reports have assessed its implementation. According to a report titled *Ten-year Impact Study on Implementation of UN Security Council Resolution 1325 (2000) on Women, Peace and Security in Peacekeeping*,[14] missions have achieved little success in turning around the limited participation of women in peace negotiations and peace agreements, but more progress has been made in women's participation in politics. Missions have also experienced varying degrees of success, mostly modest, in integrating a gender perspective into disarmament, demobilization, and reintegration (DDR) programs and in supporting gender-sensitive security sector reforms (SSRs). Improvements have been more substantial in the implementation of legal and judicial reforms, as missions have supported the adoption of gender equality provisions in national constitutions and relevant national laws. In addition, the report states that peacekeeping missions are helping to implement policies on the ground that promote the UNSCR 1325 agenda through gender focal points, and gender units have been established to help guide members of the military and police in implementing UNSCR 1325.

The High-Level Independent Panel on Peace Operations' report (High-Level Report) in 2015 represents a notable change from earlier comprehensive reports on peacekeeping in that it includes a special section on the WPS agenda.[15] It mainstreams gender, particularly mentioning women's participation in conflict resolution and mediation; the participation of women in UNPOL; sexual violence;

the participation of female peacekeepers more broadly; the appointment of women to senior mission leadership positions; and sexual exploitation and abuse (SEA) in peacekeeping missions. This report, however, notes the challenges that remain and states, "while that important [WPS] agenda is broadly acknowledged, 15 years on, there remains a poor understanding of the potential of both integrating a gendered perspective and increasing the participation of women at all levels of political and civil life, most especially at the leadership level" (UN, 2015: 23). The report also notes as concerns: the assumption that items in the agenda are "only women's" issues; impediments to fully integrating a gender perspective into operations; lack of resources, technical skills, and leadership on gender issues in the UN DPKO; and failure to conduct proper outreach. The report makes specific recommendations to address these challenges, to which we return at the conclusion of the book.

In addition to the High-Level Report, in October 2015 the Security Council convened a different high-level review to assess fifteen years of progress at the global, regional, and national levels following UNSCR 1325. The review culminated with the report *Preventing Conflict, Transforming Justice, Securing the Peace: A Global Study on the Implementation of UN Security Council Resolution 1325* (1325 Review) (UN Women, 2015). This review highlights major successes, such as the adoption of a comprehensive normative framework with regard to sexual violence in conflict, an increased focus on holistic justice, increases in referencing gender in peace negotiations, an increase in the number of senior women in UN leadership positions, and increases in bilateral aid for gender equality.

However, similar to the High-Level Report, the 1325 Review also finds that significant challenges remain in the implementation of UNSCR 1325. With regard to sexual violence, despite the comprehensive normative framework, there are very few actual prosecutions, particularly at the national level. Women's participation in formal negotiations and peacekeeping also remains limited. In addition, only fifty-four countries have adopted National Action Plans (NAPs) for UNSCR 1325, and funding for programs related to gender equality remains a challenge. Like the other reports, the 1325 Review also makes recommendations for better implementation, to which we return in the conclusion of the book.

On the academic front, there has been some headway in understanding the WPS agenda as it relates to PKOs. Most of the focus of this literature has been on evaluating the role of gender in peace operations. In an edited collection, Louise Olsson and Torrun L. Truggestad (2001) include chapters that suggest that gender has played an increasingly important role in PKOs through increases in women's participation and gender mainstreaming. Dyan Mazurana, Angela Raven-Roberts, and Jane Parpart (2005) also examine the importance of gender mainstreaming and trace its evolution in various postconflict contexts, such as political emergencies, international intervention, peacekeeping missions, international humanitarian and human rights law, and in peacemaking and peace-building. Louise Olsson (2009) uses the peacekeeping mission in Timor-Leste to analyze whether peacekeeping missions are vehicles for gender equality in host countries. Annica Kronsell (2012) explores what gender means in the context of postnational defense, or a military system where less attention is paid to the defense of territory and more to the security situation outside its borders, such as through peacekeeping missions. She concludes that gender has been mainstreamed in postnational military practices but at the same time reinterpreted as meaning "women" who are deployed to faraway places. Finally, Louise Olsson and Theodora-Ismene Gizelis (2015) bring together a collection of contributions that evaluate the implementation of USCSR 1325 on three themes: participation, protection, and gender mainstreaming.[16] Again, the tenor of the scholarship evaluating the progress of UNSCR 1325 recognizes nontrivial progress but also nontrivial barriers to full realization of the WPS agenda.

PARTICIPATION, PROTECTION, AND MAINSTREAMING IN PKOS

As the various reports and scholarship demonstrate, the WPS agenda paved the way for the integration of a number of gender reforms into PKOs. The UN resolutions and peacekeeping mandates require changes with respect to increasing women's representation (participation), reducing SEAHV (protection), and ensuring gender mainstreaming. Peacekeeping missions have made some headway when it comes to participation, protection, and mainstreaming, but as we argue later, these developments are often met with institutional challenges that impede further progress on these important issues.

Participation: Increasing Women's Representation

With the passing of UNSCR 1325, the proportion of women in peacekeeping missions has steadily increased. According to the UN, between 1957 and 1989 a total of only twenty women served as UN peacekeepers, but today, of the approximately 125,000 peacekeepers, women constitute 3 percent of military personnel and about 15 percent of police personnel. According to the High-Level Report, as of December 2014, women made up 29 percent of all professional staff in UN peace operations (UN, 2015). Out of the three types of individuals within missions—civilians, UN police, and military—the proportions of women are highest among civilian employees, followed by UN police, then military observers, and finally troop contingents, even though many peacekeeping missions are mostly composed of military personnel.

The UN started disaggregating data on peacekeeping deployments for military personnel in 2006 and police in 2009. While the overall proportions of women are still quite low, there is a positive trend in female peacekeeping for both military and police contributions since 2006 and 2009, respectively, and it is rather rare for missions to not have any female peacekeepers at all. Figure 2.1 depicts the rise in the monthly proportions of women in UN peacekeeping troop and individual police

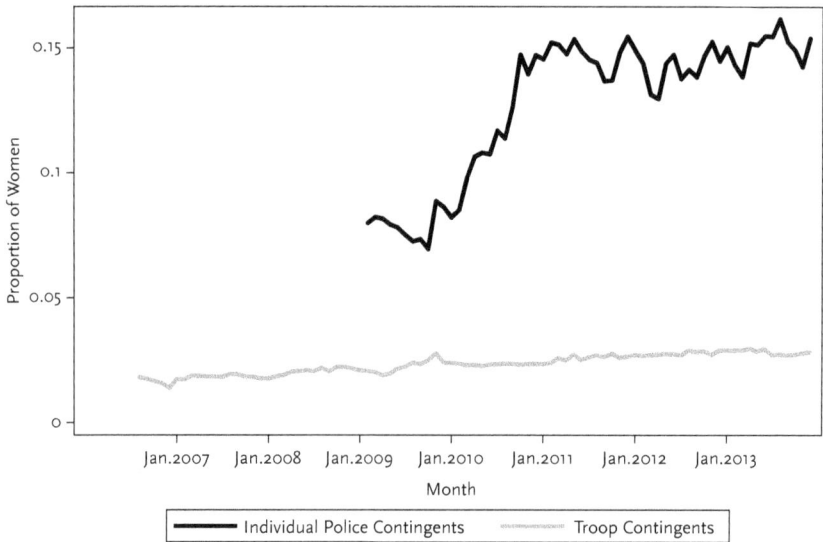

Figure 2.1. Proportions of women in UN peacekeeping troop and individual police contingents, by month.

contingents from late 2006 until the close of 2013. Since December 2006, the proportion of female troops has doubled, although it remains low at less than 3 percent of the total size of the troop contingents.

Since late 2009, the proportion of women in individual police roles has nearly doubled, and it is at a higher level than the proportion of female troops, although the upward trajectory has attenuated. From the end of 2010 to 2013, there was non-trending fluctuation in the proportions of women sent between approximately 12 and 16 percent across all missions. It is noteworthy that there has been little consistent increase in the proportions of individual female police in the last few years.

One of the main innovations for increasing women's representation in peacekeeping forces has been the all-female FPUs mentioned at the beginning of this chapter. All-female FPUs are an advancement from contributing countries—in this case India and Bangladesh. Scholars and policy-makers have argued that the all-female units deployed to Liberia, Haiti, and the DRC have made a substantive impact on promoting gender equality in the host countries (Pruitt, 2013, 2016; Kember, 2010; Onekali, 2013). The UN and other international actors have highlighted that the women in the FPUs have helped to improve the security of Liberian women, provided vital services to Liberian women, encouraged Liberian women to join the security services and challenge traditional gender norms, addressed sexual and gender-based violence (SGBV), and helped prevent SEA by male peacekeepers (Kember, 2010). Lea Angela Biason of the UN DPKO has said that the all-female FPU in Liberia made a substantial difference to the women victimized in sexual violence during the country's civil war and to conflict prevention initiatives in communities.[17]

While the successes of the all-female FPUs are notable, other scholars have argued that the women in the units have been evaluated based on gender stereotypes about appropriate women's behavior and not based on the skills for the job (Henry, 2012; Pruitt, 2013, 2016). For example, the media often highlight how the women from the FPUs have been active in the community, teaching young girls how to dance or cook, but has not highlighted how the women are engaged in protection roles, which is the mandate of the FPUs. Nevertheless, one of the benefits of all-female units is that they may provide an alternative or additional option for women wishing to pursue roles as peacekeepers yet not wishing to take on many of the burdens women in male-majority units have reportedly faced. In highlighting the potential for all-female FPUs to increase women's participation in peace operations, Pruitt (2016: 111) writes, "Given the problems that women peacekeepers encounter in male-majority units, the introduction of all-female units might assuage some of these concerns." This is a potential benefit that we return to in the conclusion of the book.

Despite the increase in attention to and in some cases numbers of women in peacekeeping missions, there is still much left to be desired with regard to the participation of women in peacekeeping. In 2009, in anticipation of the UNSCR 1325's ten-year anniversary, UN Secretary-General Ban Ki-moon launched a campaign to increase the share of female peacekeepers to 10 percent in military units and 20 percent in police units by 2014. The UN missions did not meet the deadline.

Moreover, when it comes to the composition of the senior ranks, women's representation is especially sparse. Although the UN deployed its first female force commander to the UN Peacekeeping Force in Cyprus (UNFICYP) in 2014, few senior-level peacekeepers, whether civilian, military, or police, are women. Table 2.1 displays the civilian professional staff at UN DPKO based on sex, from the 2015 High-Level Report. In chapter 4, we further explore the participation gap in depth, looking at

Table 2.1. STAFF IN THE PROFESSIONAL AND HIGHER CATEGORIES IN UN PEACE OPERATIONS, BY SEX (DECEMBER 31, 2014)

Grade	Number of women	Percentage of women
Under-secretary-general	5	28
Assistant secretary-general	5	13
D-2	8	16
D-1	30	24
P-5	93	25
P-4	248	28
P-3	352	31
P-2	95	41

Note: From UN, *Comprehensive Review of the Whole Question of Peacekeeping Operations in All Their Aspects* (June 17, 2015). General Assembly Security Council, A/70/95–S/2015/446, http://www.un.org/sg/pdf/HIPPO_Report_1_June_2015.pdf (December 10, 2015), 83.

not only the shortages in numbers but also whether there is a bias in where women deploy. We also explore participation biases within UNMIL in chapter 6.

The reforms targeting women's participation extend beyond the composition of peace operations. UN peacekeeping missions often help host countries rebuild institutions as a part of their expanded multidimensional mandates. The expanded mandates often include promoting domestic reforms that ensure gender equality, especially as they relate to increasing local women's representation in domestic institutions. For example, Sarah Bush (2011) finds that female legislative and party quotas are more likely in countries that have hosted PKOs. The potential influence of peacekeeping missions on the adoption of gender reforms related to women's participation extends to the security sectors of host countries. The UN DPKO Department of Field Support's "Policy on Gender Equality in Peacekeeping Operations" states that peacekeepers are to "facilitate the reforms of national military, police, and corrections structures in peacekeeping host countries, with appropriate gender policies and gender mainstreaming components in place."[18] As an example of UN peacekeeping reforms leading to changes in women's participation in the domestic security sector of host countries, the deployment of the all-female FPU in Liberia reportedly led to a noticeable uptick in women recruited into the LNP (Pruitt, 2016: 112).

There are at least two observable ways in which peacekeeping missions can follow the directive to help facilitate domestic reforms related to the participation of women in the security sector. First, peacekeeping missions might shape the types of UNSCR 1325 NAPs that states adopt. In 2005, the Security Council called on Member States to implement UNSCR 1325 through the development of NAPs or other national-level strategies.[19] The NAPs include outlines of policies to increase the number of women in national militaries and police. Some countries' NAPs focus on international reforms to provide aid to fund these policies in other countries, whereas other countries focus their NAPs on their own domestic institutions. Of the forty-three countries that have adopted NAPs by 2013, we identified twenty-one that emphasize domestic reforms.[20] We see that seven of the nineteen (37 percent) countries that experienced peacekeeping during this time period ended up with a domestic-oriented NAP, while less than 10 percent of the countries *without* peacekeeping missions ended up with an NAP that emphasizes domestic reforms.[21] Peacekeeping missions thus appear to encourage the creation of NAPs that focus on domestic gender reforms.

Second, in addition to helping host countries adopt NAPs, peacekeeping missions also help implement reforms geared toward increasing women's representation in the domestic security sector. Gender reforms that increase women's representation in the domestic security sector may include quotas for women in the police or military, female-focused recruitment campaigns, the removal of restricted gender roles in security institutions, and appointments of women to high-level security positions. Laura Huber and Sabrina Karim (2016) find that if a state has had a peacekeeping mission, then it is more likely to implement a domestic reform that increases the representation of women in the domestic security force of the country than if the state has not had a peacekeeping mission.

The observed association of UN PKOs with domestic-oriented NAP adoption and gender reforms in the security sector demonstrate that peacekeeping missions may be instrumental in promoting gender reforms in host countries.[22] This is an encouraging sign that peacekeeping efforts are helping domestic actors take seriously the goals championed by the UNSCR 1325 regime. We further explore this possibility and the downstream effects of such influence in chapter 7.

Protection: Reducing Sexual Exploitation, Abuse, Harassment, and Violence

Allegations about peacekeepers' involvement in widespread sexual misconduct initially emerged in the UN mission in Cambodia (1993) and were followed by reports from Bosnia and Herzegovina, Haiti, the DRC, East Timor, Liberia, and Sierra Leone. Despite the fact that many allegations emerged before 2000, it was not until 2003 that the UN secretary-general announced a zero tolerance policy that forbade peacekeepers from exchanging money, food, help, or anything of value for sex.[23] And it was not until 2005 that the UN DPKO established the Conduct and Discipline Team to train peacekeepers about the new policy, to enforce it, and to conduct investigations of violations of it.[24] In 2007 the policy was extended to all UN personnel (not just peacekeepers), and the Conduct and Discipline Team within the UN DPKO became the Conduct and Discipline Unit within the UN's Department of Field Support. Moreover, UNSCR 1820 specifically "requests the Secretary-General to continue and strengthen efforts to implement the policy of zero tolerance of sexual exploitation and abuse in UN PKOs; and urges troop and police contributing countries to take appropriate preventative action, including pre-deployment and in-theater awareness training, and other action to ensure full accountability in cases of such conduct involving their personnel "(UN Security Council, Security Council Resolution 1820, 2008: 3).

The UN defines sexual exploitation as "any actual or attempted abuse of a position of vulnerability, differential power, or trust, for sexual purposes, including, but not limited to, profiting monetarily, socially or politically from the sexual exploitation of another" and defines sexual abuse as "the actual or threatened physical intrusion of a sexual nature, whether by force or under unequal or coercive conditions" (UN, 2003). By these definitions, SEA actions include peacekeeper involvement in transactional sex and peacekeeper involvement in sexual violence (Csaky, 2008; Gilliard, 2012). Thus, we refer hereafter to SEA as sexual exploitation, abuse, harassment, and violence (SEAHV).

Despite the development of a framework for reducing SEAHV by mission personnel such as the UN's zero tolerance policy, figure 2.2, a chart of accusations of SEAHV in 2007–2013, demonstrates that it is still a problem, despite the UN's zero tolerance policy and despite numerous international legal reforms targeted at reducing it.[25] Although the numbers of reported SEAHV offenses in 2012 and 2013 were much lower than those from 2007–2009, the thirty reported military offenses in 2013 indicate that many peacekeepers are still sexually involved with individuals in the local population. Moreover, the count of military SEAHV allegations

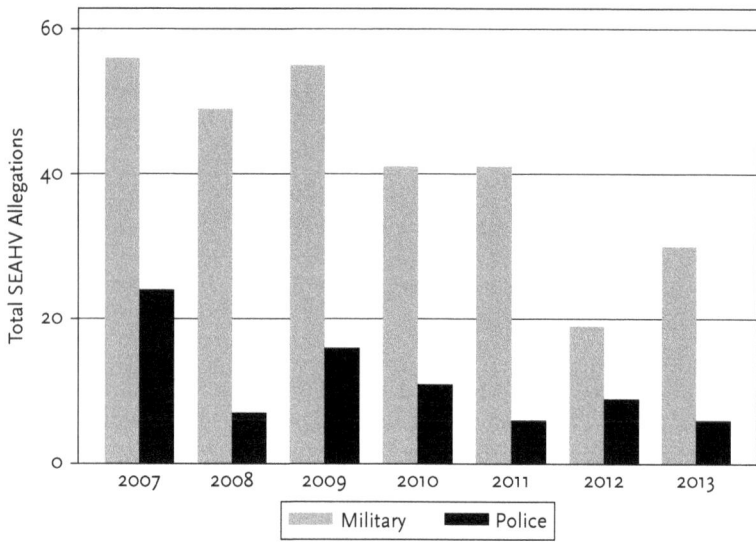

Figure 2.2. SEAHV allegations in military and police units.

increased by more than 50 percent from 2012 to 2013. And it is important to recall that SEAHV allegations are likely a drastic undercount of actual offenses because most victims do not feel comfortable reporting.[26]

While the UN DPKO has developed an infrastructure around mitigating SEAHV, there is much room for improvement, as it presents a major protection problem for the UN. Thus, we return to the problem of SEAHV in chapter 5, where we unpack potential causes of and solutions to it in PKOs.

Aside from concerns related to abuses by mission personnel, peace operations are increasingly tasked with protecting civilians from conflict-related sexual violence perpetrated by local actors. The UN defines "conflict-related sexual violence" as rape, sexual slavery, forced prostitution, forced pregnancy, forced sterilization, and any other form of sexual violence of comparable gravity perpetrated against women, men, or children with a direct or indirect (temporal, geographical, or causal) link to a conflict (UN, 2014). Conflict-related sexual violence is addressed in several UNSC resolutions, including UNSCR 1820, UNSCR 1888, and UNSCR 1960. Specifically, UNSCR 1820

- Requests the secretary-general, in consultation with the Security Council, the Special Committee on Peacekeeping Operations and its Working Group and relevant States, as appropriate, to develop and implement appropriate training programs for all peacekeeping and humanitarian personnel deployed by the United Nations in the context of missions as mandated by the Council to help them better prevent, recognize and respond to sexual violence and other forms of violence against civilians;
- Encourages troop and police contributing countries, in consultation with the secretary-general, to consider steps they could take to heighten awareness and the responsiveness of their personnel participating in UN peacekeeping operations to protect civilians, including women and children, and prevent sexual violence

against women and girls in conflict and post-conflict situations, including wherever possible the deployment of a higher percentage of women peacekeepers or police;

• Requests the secretary-general to develop effective guidelines and strategies to enhance the ability of relevant UN peacekeeping operations, consistent with their mandates, to protect civilians, including women and girls, from all forms of sexual violence and to systematically include in his written reports to the Council on conflict situations his observations concerning the protection of women and girls and recommendations in this regard (UN Security Council, Security Council Resolution 1820, 2008: 1–5).

UNSCR 1888, as a follow-up to UNSCR 1820, mandates that peacekeeping missions protect women and children from sexual violence during armed conflict and requests that the secretary-general appoint a special representative on sexual violence during armed conflict (Office of the Special Representative of the Secretary-General on Sexual Violence in Conflict) (UN Security Council, Security Council Resolution 1888, 2009). UNSCR 1960 instructs the UN to devise monitoring, analysis, and reporting arrangements on conflict-related sexual violence. Together, the resolutions require peacekeepers to respond to conflict-related sexual violence with as much determination as they would to any other atrocity (UN Security Council, Security Council Resolution 1960, 2010).

In order to address the problem, peacekeeping missions must actually deploy to countries that have experienced conflict-related sexual violence. Scholars have suggested that peacekeeping missions deploy to the most difficult conflict cases, such as those with higher fatality rates and greater intractability.[27] In a similar vein, we find, as shown in figure 2.3, evidence that many peacekeeping missions have deployed to

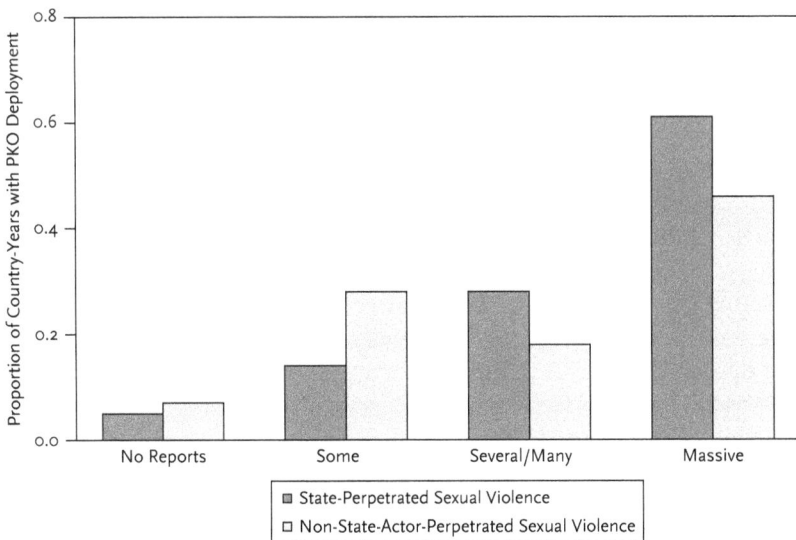

Figure 2.3. PKO deployments, by conflict-related sexual violence. Source: data from Cohen and Nordås (2014).

areas where there were reports of high levels of conflict-related sexual violence.[28] By deploying to the places of greatest concern, it appears that PKOs are well positioned to have an impact with regard to the protection of civilians. In chapter 4, we explore how the levels of conflict-related sexual violence in host countries relate to the deployment of *female* peacekeepers.

One of the main ways the UN DPKO has sought to address conflict-related sexual violence is through Women's Protection Advisers—mandated by the Security Council in 2009—who deploy to countries with evidence of the problem. Women's Protection Advisers focus specifically on the integration of conflict-related sexual violence considerations in the activities of the mission, including advocating for victims and highlighting to the parties of the conflict their obligations to prevent and address the problem. According to the High-Level Report, these protection advisers ensure better monitoring, analysis, and reporting on conflict-related sexual violence.[29]

While Women's Protection Advisers are a recent innovation in peacekeeping missions, PKOs have been active in promoting gender reforms that target SGBV in host countries even before missions included Women's Protection Advisers. Just as PKOs appear to influence the adoption of reforms to increase women's representation in domestic security sectors, peacekeeping missions may also be instrumental in ensuring that host countries adopt a framework for protection against SGBV. We explore this potentiality in chapters 6 and 7.

Gender Mainstreaming in Peacekeeping Operations

Although participation and protection have been major focus areas for gender reforms in PKOs, gender mainstreaming has been the cornerstone of the WPS agenda for PKOs. Gender mainstreaming is achieved when members of UN missions make a conscious effort to assess how their policies and decisions will impact women and men and adjust policies accordingly when the impact may have negative gender-related ramifications.[30] The UN's Economic and Social Council defined the concept of gender mainstreaming as follows: "Mainstreaming a gender perspective is the process of assessing the implications for women and men of any planned action, including legislation, policies or programmes, in any area and at all levels. It is a strategy for making the concerns and experiences of women as well as of men an integral part of the design, implementation, monitoring and evaluation of policies and programmes in all political, economic and societal spheres, so that women and men benefit equally, and inequality is not perpetuated. The ultimate goal of mainstreaming is to achieve gender equality" (UN, 2002).[31] The Office of the Special Adviser on Gender Issues at the UN states that "mainstreaming involves ensuring that gender perspectives and attention to the goal of gender equality are central to all activities—policy development, research, advocacy, dialogue, legislation, and resource allocation, as well as planning, implementation and monitoring of programs and projects" (UN, 2001).[32] According to the UN's online resources on gender, "using a gender mainstreaming strategy to achieve gender equality requires changes in awareness and capacity of all personnel, and implies strong management commitment."[33] UN Women suggests that "the long-term objective is that attention to gender equality will pervade all policies, strategies and activities so that women and men influence, participate in, and benefit equitably from all interventions."[34]

One of the main ways that gender has been mainstreamed in peacekeeping missions is through the appointment of gender advisers and the establishment of gender focal points and units. They aim to ensure a broad range of activities on gender both within the mission and with host populations. Within the mission these activities include systematic training of all peacekeeping personnel on the gender dimensions of their operations, the integration of gender perspectives in all standard operating procedures, and the planning, implementation and evaluation of gender activities in all functional areas. According to the DPKO'S Department of Field Support, the gender focal points "can provide ongoing advice to contingent commanders on how a gender perspective can enhance the efficiency and effectiveness of the contingent's operational tasks" (UN, 2010c).[35] These gender focal points offer targeted in-service gender training to members of the contingent. In 2010, there were gender advisers in ten multidimensional peacekeeping missions and gender focal points in six traditional peacekeeping missions. At present, all multidimensional peacekeeping missions have gender units and are also deploying women's protection advisers. The ten-year review of UNSCR 1325, however, notes that gender units in missions are generally understaffed and underresourced relative to the tasks they are expected to accomplish (UN, 2010a).

The focus on gender advisers and gender focal points in PKOs is an important innovation, as help may ensure that decisions are made with an eye toward gender balance in programming. Nevertheless, the use of gender advisers, units, and focal points as the main tools for gender mainstreaming relies on a narrow understanding of gender mainstreaming. In some ways, relying on such policies takes an "add women and stir" approach, as most advisers, focal points, and units are composed of women. Such a limited implementation strategy of gender mainstreaming may have little effect on larger structural changes that are needed in missions. A more holistic approach to gender mainstreaming may be better suited to change the culture of missions.

Indeed, the 1325 Review suggests that there have been a number of achievements in gender mainstreaming that include a broader range of policy levers.[36] The 1325 Review states that in the last few years, there have been numerous gender-sensitive innovations in peace operations, including the establishment of "monitoring, analysis, and reporting arrangements" on conflict-related sexual violence; scenario-based training, prosecution support cells, and mobile courts devoted to sexual and gender-based violence; an UNPOL best-practices toolkit of policing and training curricula that focus on preventing and investigating SGBV in postconflict settings; special police units solely addressing gender-based violence; and sex disaggregated statistics. In addition, the 1325 Review highlights the establishment of "Open Days" that have been organized for women's civil society groups to meet mission leadership alongside community alert networks; joint protection teams; firewood patrols and civil-military cooperation projects involving fuel-efficient stoves and rolling-water containers to spare women and girls a few dangerous trips out of camps to collect firewood or water; and quick-impact gender responsive projects that have included the construction of shelters, adequate latrines, and showers in camps (UN Women, 2015).

A broader set of policy levers to mainstream gender still may be required. In chapter 8, we suggest that gender mainstreaming is important for creating a culture of equal opportunity, but only so long as the interpretation of gender mainstreaming is more in line with the 1325 Review—much more broad than simply relying on gender focal points, units, and gender advisers in mission.

CONCLUSION

This chapter has highlighted the progress of PKOs in evolving to include gender reforms. The WPS agenda has provided a foundation through which peacekeeping missions can better make gender equality a priority in and through missions. Indeed, on this front, since 1948—the year of the deployment of the first peacekeeping mission—PKOs have made significant strides in addressing women's participation and representation, in addressing SEAHV, and in mainstreaming gender activities. Yet there is much room for growth. The proportion of women in peacekeeping missions is still very low, and discrimination and SEAHV are still major problems in missions.

The challenges that PKOs face are institutional in nature. While the WPS agenda has institutionalized gender equality through the various UNSC resolutions, compliance with these norms has been slow. The rest of the book is devoted to understanding the root causes of and the potential solutions to the challenges related to women's participation and the prevalence of SEAHV in and through PKOs—within missions and in the local communities served by the missions. We argue that peacekeeping missions are gendered institutions and that certain power imbalances exist that privilege men and certain masculinities. To overcome the institutional barriers, a holistic, cultural shift is necessary in PKOs to ensure that gender equality is fully achieved. This includes gender mainstreaming, as long as it is not limited to an "add women and stir" approach, and more broadly it means adopting an *equal opportunity* framework for peacekeeping.

CHAPTER 3

Gender Power Imbalances in Peacekeeping Missions

In order to explore the extent to which reforms that relate to gender equality in and through peacekeeping missions have been successful, we must first take a step back and investigate the sources of inequality that pervade PKOs. In this chapter, we outline the theoretical foundations of three challenges that impede gender equality in missions: the exclusion of and discrimination against female peacekeepers; the relegation of female peacekeepers to safe spaces; and SEAHV of female peacekeepers and local women.[1]

In the context of broader peacekeeping mandates, overcoming these challenges is imperative for ensuring that gender equality is and continues to be an essential element of PKOs globally. Thus, we also explore the potential for two broad, nonexclusive policy levers—improving the representation of women (female ratio balancing) and promoting equal opportunity peacekeeping—to help overcome the gender power imbalances that exist in missions. We believe that the first policy lever, while more straightforward and tangible, has inherent limitations in mitigating the challenges posed by gender hierarchies. Instead, we opt for equal opportunity peacekeeping as a more holistic framework for promoting gender equality in and through PKOs because it focuses more on deconstructing the underlying structures that perpetuate gender power imbalances.

The starting premise for this chapter is that institutions, especially institutions in the security sector, are gendered. We begin by highlighting the literatures that make this argument, relying mainly on sociological institutional theory and feminist scholarship. Building on this scholarship, we argue that gender power imbalances in security institutions, specifically PKOs, serve as root causes for the exclusion and discrimination of women in PKOs, the relegation of female personnel to safe spaces, and perpetual issues related to SEAHV. In turn, we develop a number of observable implications, which we test in later chapters and use to demonstrate the challenges that gender power imbalances pose to PKOs. The chapter concludes with an exploration of the two policy levers mentioned above.

Institutions are gendered, but not equally—imbalances in gender power relations exist within them. To understand this imbalance, we relate the concept of gender to institutions. Conventionally, "sex" refers to the biological differences between men and women, usually distinguished by the differences in reproductive capability.[2] In contrast, "gender" refers to the socially constructed and defined practices associated with a division of people into male and female types. Gender is often thought of as different, identifiable characteristics associated with men and women. For example, characteristics commonly associated with masculinity include strength, protection, rationality, aggression, public life, domination, and leadership, whereas femininity is thought to include characteristics such as weakness, vulnerability, emotion, passivity, privacy, submission, and care.[3] Gender is learned through socialization and shapes a person's position and authority in given contexts and spaces. Gender, unlike sex, is a dynamic concept; it changes based on context, time, and place and is constructed through narratives, texts, images, and actions.[4] As such, much of the feminist literature on sex and gender emphasizes the distinction between them in its analysis of social phenomena.[5]

The process of gender socialization begins at birth. For example, as gifts for newborns, many individuals often buy dolls for girls or wrap presents in pink and give cars to boys and wrap presents in blue, mimicking what society determines is appropriate for girls and boys. Society establishes norms, rules, and practices based on gender, and these norms outline the behavior by men and women and the relations between them that are considered appropriate. For instance, the norm that men should protect women translates to the expectation that men should be chivalrous (i.e., hold doors open for specifically women). When women and men behave discordantly with the gender norms, it may be considered unnatural or undesired by society.[6] Some norms establish a hierarchy for appropriate behavior. As an illustration, in many societies women's promiscuity is frowned on but male promiscuity is lauded, which means that the same behavior is privileged for one sex (male) over another (female), based on gendered norms of appropriate behavior. Similarly, women and girls are often mocked as "bossy" for assertive participation that is otherwise considered normal or even desirable for men.[7] As such, gender is vitally important when understanding women and men's experiences in different societal contexts and institutions, including peacekeeping.

As a dynamic social construction, gender norms play a crucial role in defining the relative power of men and women and what might be considered normal behavior in various contexts.[8] This is especially important when studying differences, within and across institutions, in the relative value of masculine and feminine characteristics and the socially constructed expectations for men and women. An institution is an established set of rules, practices, and/or customs and provides the primary structures for social order. Institutions often govern the behavior of a set of individuals in a given community or organization. Governments and international organizations may be thought of as formal institutions. We include PKOs, as well as national militaries and police organizations, as formal institutions in the security sector.

Institutions are social creations, which means that their rules, practices, and customs reflect the preferences and values of those who created them.[9] As such, there are power differentials between institutional actors that arise from differential access to resources. This access is tied to "rules and worldviews" (Olsen, 2009: 9). Dana Britton (2000: 419) explains how institutions may be gendered—that is, "institutions are defined, conceptualized, and structured in terms of a distinction between masculinity and femininity"—and are often male or female dominated. Institutions may be gendered when they "are symbolically and ideologically described and conceived in terms of a discourse that draws on defined masculinities and femininities" (420). Louise Chappell (2010: 183–189) explains that "gender is embedded in institutions through ongoing practices, values, and expectations of appropriate behavior and that institutional rules and norms privilege certain forms of behavior and certain actors over others."

In most cases men have historically created formal institutions.[10] As a result, particular types of masculinity—with masculinity defined as "a set of expectations that society deems appropriate for a male subject to exhibit" (Gates, 2006: 28)—often govern the institutional space. In such institutions, the gender power imbalance may displace and devalue femininities and less dominant forms of masculinity.

Some have suggested that an institutional "gender order" exists that entails historically constructed patterns of power relations between men and women and notions of femininities and masculinities (Connell, 1987: 99). Taking a sociological perspective, R. W. Connell goes further in *Gender and Power* (1987) and *Masculinities* (2005) in explaining how institutions are gendered. In the former, he argues that an institutional gender ordering is manifest through divisions of labor and structures of power. The sexual division of labor is the allocation of work based on whether a person is a man or a woman. Traditionally and historically, women have been relegated to jobs that involve nurturing and caring, whereas men have been relegated to jobs that involve rationality or authority. This segregation has persisted and has become the basis for new forms of constraints, such as skills development—men obtain certain skills while women do not, and this perpetuates the segregation in jobs.[11] Structures of power have privileged a connection between masculinity and authority, with the denial of authority to women and some other groups of men— particularly those who display more feminine characteristics.

In *Masculinities*, Connell makes the case that different forms of masculinities exist in institutions, and that some are hegemonic—a "configuration of gender practice which guarantees the dominant position of men and the subordination of women" (2005: 77). Many institutions are formed on the basis of such hierarchies. He provides the example of hegemonic masculinity organized around direct domination (i.e., corporate management and the military) and hegemonic masculinities organized around technical knowledge (i.e., professional and scientific institutions). These two co-exist as forms of hegemonic masculinities in many institutions, such as government, the military/police, academia, and business, to name a few.

If institutions are gendered and involve some sort of gender hierarchy or order, then there is an imbalance in power and authority in which some groups of people and certain practices are privileged. "Power" and "authority" here refer to the ability to influence the behavior of others and are often conceptualized as a zero-sum relationship—when one group/person has power in an institution, other groups do not. "Power" is relative in this context. When there is an imbalance in power relations, it means that within an institution certain masculinities have power while femininities and other masculinities do not. The structures, rules, practices, and customs of the institution are oriented around the leading masculinities, and other forms of masculinity and femininities are subordinate.

While a given institution may privilege some forms of masculinity, it is important to note that other masculinities (and femininities) may form to challenge this hierarchy or may play more dominant roles under different institutional configurations or contexts. This means that particular forms of masculinity do not always have to stay dominant. This point suggests possible approaches, discussed below, to challenge gender power imbalances.

GENDER POWER IMBALANCES IN MILITARY, POLICE, AND PEACEKEEPING INSTITUTIONS

Militaries and police organizations constitute institutions that are accorded the authority to use force. This authority comes from the relationships between the military and the state and between the police force and the state—the military's role is to protect the state from external threats, and the role of the police is to protect citizens from internal threats. They need to be able to use force in order to achieve these ends. This is the fundamental social contract between states and citizens—order in exchange for loyalty (Boix, 2015).

The development institutions mandated to protect the population has traditionally been accompanied by at least three processes that have entrenched gender power imbalances within the security sector: the idealization of a warrior identity, the emergence of a gendered protection norm, and the pursuit of militarized cohesion. Through these processes, the respective masculinities of warrior masculinity, protective masculinity, and militarized masculinity are valorized and privileged. These processes, which give rise to gender power imbalances, can vary in strength across military institutions and indeed might compete with one another, but the key is that femininities and other forms of masculinity are typically treated as subordinate in security institutions. For example, in contrast to the security-oriented roles men are expected to play, women in a conflict context typically fulfill the roles of peacemaker, victim to be protected, or object to be dominated.

Specific, observable barriers to gender equality in and through peacekeeping missions emerge from the privileging of the warrior identity, protection norm, and militarization processes in the security sector. Because peacekeeping missions are composed of military and police personnel,[12] the institutional gender hierarchies in domestic security institutions transfer to peacekeeping missions. We note three consequences in particular: the exclusion of and discrimination against women, the relegation of women to safe spaces, and violence against women.[13] The different processes behind the gender power imbalances contribute to all three of these observable implications in peacekeeping missions to different degrees, although we focus on how the warrior versus peacemaker dichotomy exacerbates exclusion and discrimination, how the gendered protection norm perpetuates the relegation of women to safe spaces, and how militarization contributes to violence against women. It is also important to note that we are not suggesting that gender power imbalances constitute a necessary or sufficient condition for these outcomes but rather that they are contributing factors to many of the challenges that affect PKOs. In what follows, we unpack the different sources of gender power imbalances and their consequences for peacekeeping missions.

The Warrior Identity

The first source of gender power imbalances in security sector institutions centers on conflating masculinity with idealized traits of the warrior. Historically, for many men, the ultimate test of manhood has been participation in combat. The warrior identity and the need to demonstrate manliness through combat has ancient origins (Duncanson, 2013; Goldstein, 2001). War-fighting is seen as a rite of passage, and battle turns "boys" into men (Enloe, 1983; Elshtain, 1987; Goldstein, 2001: 264–267). The security sector, where fighting is expected as part of normal activities, becomes in part a crucible in which men are able to prove their worth as men. The warrior identity has thus become an object of aspiration within security institutions, where fighting prowess is privileged above other characteristics.

The warrior identity's elevated position can also be understood using a biological understanding of male and female differences. According to Barbara Smuts (1992), male aggression among humans is a strategy to dominate women and their reproductive capability. In turn, men's physical abilities are honed, and men are biologically programmed to be more violent, to make them better suited to be warriors.[14] Francis Fukuyama (1998) and David Marlowe (1983: 190) have argued that biologically men are more closely associated with aggression, which makes them natural fighters.

The warrior identity can be seen in contrast with other legitimate masculinities such as the metrosexual, the stay-at-home dad, and the homosexual male (Duncanson, 2013: 78). Also in contrast, societies across the globe tend to associate women with an inherent peacefulness, if not fragility. The notions that men are violent and women are peaceful are reified through social interaction, and in stories such as Aristophanes's play *Lysistrata*, where Lysistrata organizes the Athenian and Spartan women to withhold sex from men until they stop the Peloponnesian War.[15] These stories and the many examples of women engaging in peace activism strengthen the association of peacefulness with the female sex. Scholars and policymakers like to point out that when women mobilize collectively, they do not use violence. In fact Lionel Tiger and Robin Fox (1998: 213) have suggested that "if all the menial and mighty military posts in the world were taken over by women, there would be no war." When warrior-oriented masculinity is idealized, a dichotomy emerges with men perceived as natural warriors and women perceived as natural peacemakers. In this sense, as "natural warriors," men in security institutions have a monopoly over the use of force, and women are considered subordinate because they are not expected to have the skills or demeanor to use force.

Feminist scholars argue that the gendered war-peace dichotomy has larger geopolitical consequences (Enloe, 1983, 1990, 2000, 2004, 2007, 2010), particularly that conflict and combat approaches to international relations are favored over political or economic solutions to insecurity (Cohn, 1987; Tickner, 2001). Claire Duncanson (2013: 137) argues that the dominance of warrior masculinity shapes policy priorities, privileging combat over other activities that may be better for those on the ground. For example, politicians are reluctant to cut military spending, and threats are often met with the most "manly" response, usually involving force. To opt to take a more cautious approach is not a part of the warrior culture and is seen as feminine (Duncanson, 2013).

Helena Carreiras (2006: 31–32) interprets the dichotomy as having some form of "explanatory power" regarding gendered patterns of behavior in security institutions, such as the gendered division of labor, organizational culture, and the interactions and identity formation of individuals in the organization. For example, she argues that there are structural divisions along gender lines, such as in recruitment and selection procedures that systematically deem those who provide a "caring" service not fit to be soldiers or police officers. This may lead to the exclusion of women in these institutions. Indeed, the evidence strongly points in that direction as traditionally women have been excluded from the military. It also leads to the exclusion of women in particular areas of these institutions, particularly combat. For example, only in 2015 did the United States lift the combat exclusion rule for women in the military, and many countries in the world continue to prevent women from engaging in combat.

Carreiras (2006) also argues that another byproduct of the gender dichotomies is rigid ideas about what attributes are valued in the security institutions. Masculine traits such as leadership, strength, ambition, and assertiveness—the characteristics associated with being a warrior—garner the most value. Promotions and other advances accrue for those who perform better on these attributes, with women typically overlooked, not because they are necessarily worse than men in performing tasks but because as women, they are not perceived to excel in these attributes. Moreover, feminine traits are less valued, so those that possess skills and attributes that are feminine do not get promoted.

The emergence of the warrior identity as emblematic of security personnel has also dictated behavioral norms within the security institutions. Men and women who deviate from the established dichotomies—men who behave in a feminine way and women who behave in a masculine way—may be maligned for their "divergent" behavior. Particularly, women who exhibit characteristics consistent with the warrior identity may be socially spurned for being "un-female-like." For example, according to Annica Kronsell (2012: 51–54), women constantly negotiate their identities in a military setting. They may adopt different identities, such as the "bimbo"—the very feminine, beautiful sex object—or, in contrast, the "feminist," who actively and "too eagerly" pursues gender equality and challenges the gender hierarchy. Kronsell also describes the "manly woman," who evokes an androgynous image of a woman—big, strong, hairy, and unattractive.[16] Rosabeth Kanter (1993) lists four identities or role entrapments that women face in male dominated institutions: mother, pet, seductress, and iron maiden.[17] Melissa Herbert (2010: 112) quotes one female officer: "one of the hardest parts of being a military woman is just the constant scrutiny and criticism," because if you "act 'too masculine' you're accused of being a dyke; act 'too feminine' and you're either accused of sleeping around, or you're not serious." This identity negotiation by women also occurs in policing (Rabe-Hemp, 2008).

Military institutions may even engage in overt practices to try to maintain strict gender dichotomies for men and women. For example, in a study of the United States Marine Corps, Christine Williams (1989) reports that the Marine Corps took direct action to maintain femininity among women. They commissioned several studies on the "defeminization" of women and "femininity tests." Women were required to wear makeup; had classes on makeup, hair care, poise, and etiquette; and were encouraged to use umbrellas, whereas men were not (Williams, 1989). In addition, the UNSCR 1325 Review states: "more often than not, military women tend to be subject to discrimination in their military careers, passed over for promotions and opportunities—including deployments in PKOs—or assigned to menial tasks that do not correspond with their training" (UN Women, 2015: 139). The 1325 Review also offers examples of gendered discrimination stemming from overt maintenance of gendered dichotomies: in 2015, the chief of the Indonesian armed forces reportedly defended the practice of virginity tests for all female recruits, and in Pakistan women compete for thirty-two spots in the Pakistan Military Academy each year, compared with the approximately two thousand spaces allotted to men (139).

Despite women having to negotiate their identities, Carreiras (2006) suggests that many men *and women* in military and police institutions do not necessarily recognize the dominant models of masculinity and femininity or the power asymmetry on which they are founded. Rather, they tend to share the normative assumptions of the models and reproduce them, because norms and beliefs about what constitutes an ideal soldier or police officer pervade society. For example, if women believe that, as women, they are not warriors, then this may contribute to the low numbers of women in militaries and police forces. Parallel work by Richard Fox and Jennifer Lawless (2005) finds that the gender gap in women running for political office is due to gender socialization processes among women, such that women do not have the same aspirations for public office and rule out their own potential to contribute as political leaders. In a similar vein, women might be less prone to consider themselves as suitable to enter into the military and police forces because they do not fit the dominant image. In this way, both men and women perpetuate and reinforce gender dichotomies.

The institutionalized entrenchment of strict gender dichotomies has contributed to practices of discrimination and exclusion that are often categorical, as when women as a whole are precluded from serving in various capacities, even when some women more closely embody the warrior ideal than many of the men chosen for service. To give an example, one of the critiques of the 2015 Marine Corps study on integrating women into combat positions[18]—in which women who passed the necessary requirements on average achieved lower scores than men—is that the report expressed concern about *overall* women's performance even though some women beat the scores of men.[19] In this case, women as a collective were perceived to perform less well than men as a collective, despite evidence that individual women achieved enviable marks.

Challenges from the Warrior Identity for Peacekeeping: Exclusion of and Discrimination against Female Peacekeepers

In considering the privilege that warrior masculinity has in security institutions, one challenge that arises for peacekeeping missions relates to Connell's (1987) conception of the gendered division of labor and Carreira's (2006) notion of structural labor divisions. Both stress the segregation of jobs and roles based on what is deemed gender-appropriate behavior. The sex segregation of those entering the military and police has been extreme, and the low participation of women in militaries and police forces affects the availability of women to serve in peacekeeping missions. Since the contributing countries have full discretion over both providing troops and the composition of their personnel, a reluctance to recruit women into the domestic forces directly translates into limitations on the number of women who are available to serve in peacekeeping missions.

Aside from mere availability, reluctance in willingness to include women in peacekeeping forces may emerge from strict conceptions of gender roles, particularly that men are conceived of as natural warriors. Both men and women may hold these views. Women who hold beliefs about particular roles and actions being appropriate for women may make decisions in accordance to those beliefs. As such, women may opt out of peacekeeping missions because they do not think they are qualified for them. Moreover, it is possible that women are systematically kept out of the missions because of the "women as peaceful" stereotypes that are held by men and others who are gatekeepers of force composition.

A second challenge for peacekeeping stems from the gendered division of labor once women join security institutions. That is, women may also face discrimination once in PKOs, particularly limiting the range of activities in which they participate. This may be due to a tendency for women, even though they have ascended into a sphere that is male dominated, to be typecast as peacemakers, nurturers, and caregivers. These stereotypes may confine women to certain jobs in the peacekeeping missions, particularly to roles that fit the stereotypes, such as nurses, administrative assistants, and other subordinate and noncombat roles in the PKOs. Just as many countries have combat-exclusion provisions for women in their national militaries, female peacekeepers may be prevented from participating in particular roles because of expectations that women are not natural warriors.

Furthermore, even when female peacekeepers make up units that have mandates to defend territory, they may not be perceived as capable of engaging in these roles, or they may not be lauded for their accomplishments in areas that are traditionally associated with conflict or combat. In this sense, promotion or the awarding of medals in peacekeeping missions may skip over women who have performed as well as men in carrying out the mission objectives because, as women, they do not fit the mold of being capable fighters or leaders. Moreover, the feminine characteristics ascribed to women, whether the individual servicewomen have them or not, are not well valued as assets to help the missions carry out their mandates.

Thus, specifically related to PKOs, we explore two observable implications from the expectation that the warrior identity tends to be idealized within security institutions and contributes to gender power imbalances. First, the extent to which decision-makers in troop and police contributing countries abide by a gender dichotomy that sees men as natural warriors could limit the number of women that these countries are *able* to contribute to peacekeeping missions and the number that they are *willing* to contribute. Second, we expect female peacekeepers will be excluded from some roles in the peacekeeping missions and will face discrimination in the promotion processes.

Our key point here: Expectations surrounding security institutions that men are natural warriors whereas women are natural peacemakers entrench exclusionary and discriminatory practices against women in peacekeeping missions, particularly in terms of limiting the number and full agency of female peacekeepers.

The Protection Norm

Another dichotomy that has given rise to gender power imbalances pervades military and police institutions: men are seen as natural protectors, and women are seen as natural victims. This dichotomy, like the one just discussed, stems from the cultivation of identities related to the provision of security and involves distinct notions of manhood and womanhood: the protector (male soldier) and those to be protected (women and children).[20] Jean Elshtain (1995) uses the concept of male "just warriors" and female "beautiful souls" to describe the historical dichotomy in national defense and the privileging of protection. The "just warrior" is chivalrous and finds purpose in protecting the "beautiful soul"—who is removed from war, being too weak to provide defense, while at the same time inspiring the soldier to fight and cheering him on.

In a critique of this dichotomy, Cynthia Enloe (1989: 12) asserts that in a world that is dangerous, men are expected to "become the protectors of this world" and to "suppress their own fears, brace themselves and step forward to defend the weak, women and children," while women are expected to "turn gratefully and expectantly to their fathers, husbands, real or surrogate." The soldier is supposed to fight for mothers, wives, and daughters and defend them from the horror of war.[21] The role of the masculine protector puts those protected, paradigmatically women and children, in a subordinate position of dependence and obedience;[22] as women are thought to be programmed for caring and nurturing roles and to be unable to summon the aggressive impulses necessary for effective security provision, which means that they must be the ones protected.[23] This dichotomy entails a gendered norm of protection, or the belief that men are the natural protectors of women and children.[24]

Ironically, the gendered protection norm is bolstered by the downstream consequences from well-intended efforts to address the widespread abuse of women in conflict zones. Charli Carpenter (2003, 2005, 2006a) demonstrates that the protection of civilians as an international issue has been framed, based on gender stereotypes, to characterize women and children (but not men) as innocent and vulnerable. As such, the term "civilian" serves as a proxy for women and children and excludes men, who are supposed to be the protectors. She argues that both international organizations such as the UN and transnational advocacy networks, or "civilian protection networks," reduce civilians to women and children in need of protection, because doing so resonates with international donors (2005). The civilian protection network—composed of citizens, journalists, protection organizations, and statespersons—entrenches a gendered protection norm by focusing only on women and children as the population in need of protection (2003). She finds that while this norm may indeed help protect women and children, among other issues, it has led to a greater likelihood for male noncombatants to be targeted in conflict (2003, 2006a, 2006b).

The complex nature of advocacy has entailed trade-offs such that advances in some dimensions of gender security and equality have impeded progress in other dimensions. UNSCR 1325 and subsequent resolutions regarding the state of WPS actually to some extent reify the protection norm. The resolutions explicitly state that war impacts women and children differentially from men and that special protection is needed for women and children during conflict. Indeed, some scholars have critically argued that UNSCR 1325 has helped institutionalize women's vulnerability and victimhood.[25] While UNSCR 1325 has made significant strides in promoting women's issues during conflict and in peace-building, it potentially has also entrenched ideas about women as a population that needs protection, mainly from men. Thus, there is opportunity for the UNSCR 1325 regime to address the needs of female victims of violence and inequality—undoubtedly an important priority—but there are also challenges in that this could entrench a norm of protection that ultimately institutionalizes other sources of gender inequality in PKOs.

The gender dichotomy surrounding norms of protection in security institutions privileges men in those institutions. In contrast to the "protector man," women are perceived as weak or as victims. Kronsell (2012: 51–54) highlights that women in the security forces are portrayed as weak and in need of defense and protection, despite their participation in the military or police force. The presence of "weak" females appeals to the kind of chivalry and heroism that has been historically associated with the male soldier. The soldiers treat a woman differently by carrying her backpack, offering her better accommodations, and other privileges. Indeed, one common justification for keeping women out of combat roles is the fear that men would feel the need to protect their female comrades and consequently jeopardize mission efficacy.[26] Thus, this privileged form of "chivalrous" or protective masculinity at the heart of the gendered protection norm circumscribes the roles that women can play in security institutions.

Challenge from the Protection Norm for Peacekeeping:
The Relegation of Female Peacekeepers to Safe Spaces

The gendered protection norm may be more prevalent in institutions with civilian protection as a more explicit goal. The typical peacekeeping mandate to protect vulnerable populations demands attention to who is protecting whom and whether at-risk populations are being secured or exploited. Peacekeeping missions tend to deploy to places with weak central governments and places that are at risk for humanitarian crisis.[27] In these cases, peacekeeping missions serve to bolster state capacity as a means to establish order and can even be conceived as surrogates for governments (Blair, 2015). Lisa Hultman, Jacob Kathman, and Megan Shannon (2013) have found that peacekeepers play a significant role in protecting civilians from violence, especially when missions are adequately composed of military troops and police in large numbers. In another study, Hultman (2013) finds that the likelihood of a UN peace operation is higher in conflicts with high levels of violence against civilians, but this effect is mainly visible after 1999, which was the year that the UN first issued an explicit mandate to protect civilians. Since then, conflicts with high levels of violence against civilians are also more likely to get operations with robust mandates.

In the context of missions where protection is such a priority, we argue that the gendered protection norm can relegate female peacekeepers to safe spaces and safe tasks. That is, an expectation for women to not have a comparative advantage in protection may contribute to *where* women deploy and *how* they participate in the missions. Safe spaces include assignments to countries or territories that have minimal danger associated with them. These are areas with little ongoing armed conflict, areas that are unlikely to see a return to violence, or areas with fewer peacekeeping deaths. Safe tasks include those that are done within the barracks or compound as opposed to in the field. Once peacekeepers leave the base, they may face heightened danger from host country civilians or nonstate armed actors.

Thus, one observable implication of the entrenchment of a gendered protection norm in peacekeeping missions builds off of our earlier work;[28] it expects that lower proportions of women are sent to the missions with the highest risk of harm to the deployed personnel. The protection norm works at the level of both the policy-makers and the general constituency of the contributing countries' "selectorates." Policy-makers who have a normative obligation to protect women, as well as policy-makers who are sensitive to political backlash for sending women into harm's way,[29] can directly reduce female contributions to peacekeeping forces in dangerous missions and/or less actively recruit women for such missions. In addition, women themselves may also buy in to the gendered protection norm and not believe that they are qualified to provide protection. They may simply opt out of dangerous missions.

As a second observable implication, the norm to protect women can limit the range of movement for female peacekeepers within the mission. For women who do deploy on peacekeeping missions, the protection norm can restrict the extent to which they are in harm's way, thereby limiting their ability to perform all the peacekeeping functions and reducing their opportunities for commendation and promotion. Female peacekeepers more likely are confined to operations on base or at headquarters. In particular, women may be withheld from more combat-oriented tasks that would require them to leave the base.[30] Compounding this tendency, female personnel that subscribe to the gendered protection norm may, if they can, opt out of tasks that could take them into the line of fire.

Our key point here: A gendered protection norm pervades many PKOs and thereby limits the movement of female peacekeepers to safe spaces, both in terms of the countries to which they deploy and within the mission.

The Militarization Process

A third source of gender power imbalance in security institutions relates to the process of militarization. Across the globe and historically, cultures develop concepts of masculinity that maximize the capability and willingness for men to fight. Staffing the military and to some extent the police requires convincing a large subset of the population—men—to sacrifice their lives for the nation. This process relies on the social construction and priviledging of a certain form of aggressive masculinity.

One facet of militarization involves the creation of an "in-group" and an "out-group." In order for the military to be effective in combat, it must be cohesive, and cohesiveness is achieved by strengthening the bonds of the men in the in-group. An integrative relationship in smaller groups, or unit cohesion, is essential for the military unit to carry out its tasks under duress.[31] James Griffith (2007: 138) has argued that "while there are many factors that motivate soldiers to fight, the nature of relationships within the small unit or group cohesiveness is one of the primary explanations in the military literature," and cultivating a shared masculinity is a key part in creating and sustaining the cohesion.

Often times, the creation of an out-group is associated with sexuality and gender.[32] According to David Marlowe (1983: 190), the soldier is evaluated based on stereotypical masculinity: "His language is profane; his professed sexuality rude; his maleness his armor, the measure of competence, capability and confidence in himself." In this way, anything that does not fit this archetypical mold of masculinity is considered ineffective and degraded, including femininity and women. Both military culture and society promote this kind of aggressive masculinity, or "militarized masculinity," which rejects all that is "feminine" in order to be a "real man," and "real men" prove themselves on the battlefield.[33] Militarized masculinity relies on the construction of the "other" as feminine.[34]

Critiquing militarization, Ann Tickner (1992, 2001) has argued that promoting a culture of militarism is done by devaluing femininity. Moreover, she posits that the association between masculinity and violence is dependent not on men's innate aggressiveness but rather on the creation of a gendered identity that heavily pressures soldiers to "prove themselves as men," which is often done by casting their sexual identity into question. Melissa Herbert (2001: 45) concurs: "the military continues to see femininity as something to be denied or, at the very least, controlled."

As such, militarized masculinity is one where soldiers demonstrate a willingness to use violence without emotion, thereby ridding one's self of femininity. The process sometimes means devaluing and degrading femininity and other, subordinate masculinities.[35]

Men are socialized to become militarized through carefully planned training regiments.[36] Joshua Goldstein (2003) has argued that soldiers require intense socialization and training to fight effectively. Providing a criticism of the militarization process, Sandra Whitworth (2007: 155) outlines the military indoctrination process and training, including hazing, that "breaks down the individual and replaces it with a commitment to and dependence on the institution of which [one is] now a part." She finds that tactics to socialize recruits into soldiers include rituals related to proving one's manhood, the suppression of emotions and identity, shaming when men behave like "women," and feminizing the enemy. Military academies also emphasize certain characteristics that are deemed to enhance military effectiveness, such as toughness; rationality; discipline; patriotism; courage; endurance; avoidance of fear, uncertainty, guilt and remorse; and heterosexuality (Whitworth, 2007; Woodward and Winter, 2007).

Societies, moreover, create institutions to restrain men from inciting violence, directing much of their aggressiveness toward outside enemies.[37] Thus, according to Whitworth (2007: 153), "soldiering becomes the natural activity of young males who are drawn into it by instinct and encouraged by older men who see it as a proper way to channel potentially violent and disruptive behavior into the defense of the community and nation." Whitworth concludes that the military is a strictly hierarchical organization with the purpose of creating men who will be warriors and who are prepared to kill and die for the nation.

One byproduct of militarization may be the systematic exclusion of women. While the institutionalization of the warrior identity contributes to the exclusion of and discrimination against women in the military, the militarization process may as well. Some have suggested that when women are allowed into the military and into combat roles, women's presence may become a problem for the bonding between men in the group.[38] Moreover, Valerie Hudson and her colleagues argue that the exclusion of groups in general, including women, is a means of creating a bond (Hudson et al., 2012). Other scholars have even found that the acceptance of women into military units decreases as the proportion of women in the group increases.[39] The historical exclusion of women (and African Americans and homosexuals in the American context) from the military has helped, according to this logic, to ensure the development of unit cohesion by way of creating a feeling of "us."[40] Such justifications have been used as the basis for excluding women both from the military as a whole and from particular units, such as combat units.

Moreover, the perceived importance of group bonding and unit cohesion for military effectiveness may also contribute to sexual violence, which has been used as a way to increase group cohesion in cases where there is little group bonding in the first place. According to Dara Cohen (2013, 2016), women and girls are sometimes raped during war as a way to encourage male bonding. She finds that gang rape is common among rebel groups with minimal social cohesion and among domestic militaries that use forced conscription. Rape and gang rape are also sometimes used by state sponsored militaries that are less cohesive (Cohen and Nordås, 2015). Not valuing women as equals and seeing them as objects to dominate make gang rape a plausible strategy to increase rebel group cohesion. Indeed, throughout history, males have excluded women from their own group from battle while also treating the women in conquered territory as "hunting trophies," exemplifying the link between combat and sexual identity. Participation in a group activity of sexual violence allows for each man to demonstrate a raw form of "manhood" while simultaneously reducing normative barriers because it is considered a group activity for the sake of bonding.

Domestic violence as well as rape and harassment of female military soldiers also have roots in militarization. Soldiers are socialized to behave in certain ways for combat and cannot necessarily "turn off" their learned behavior at home or in public;[41] as such, ideas about masculine dominance permeate other areas outside combat roles. Militarized masculinity thus has links to domestic violence and abuse at home.[42] This corroborates the literature suggesting that domestic violence and rape may increase after a war ends because soldiers come home unable to handle their battlefield experience.[43] There are also negative effects for the soldier when he fails to live up to being a "man"; some resort to physically hurting others.[44]

Militarized masculinity may also play a part in the sexual harassment and sexual abuse of women in the military.[45] Sexual assault and rape in the U.S military has received media attention in recent years, with reports of high incidence rates.[46] One study found that in the U.S. military, 30 percent of military women were raped while serving, 71 percent were sexually assaulted, and 90 percent were sexually harassed (Benedict, 2009). The 1325 Review states that "in 2013, a US Congressional Commission found that 23% of US military women had experienced unwanted sexual contact since enlistment, ranging from groping to rape" (UN Women, 2015: 139).

Individual female officers or recruits who challenge the masculine norms of the military organization by participating and by engaging in male-coded tasks such as handling a weapon may be subject to sexual harassment or abuse.[47] Carreiras (2006: 170) argues that the control of women's sexuality seems to be particularly amplified in the military environment, and women's sexual behavior is a matter of organizational anxiety. When women enter areas where men constitute a majority, men may use sexuality to maintain their dominant position—sexual language and sexual harassment can be a way for individual men to assert their positions of power.[48] James Gruber (1998: 314) argues that in organizations that are predominantly male, men may objectify women and women may be more likely to be harassed.

Before turning to the implications of militarized masculinity for peacekeeping missions, it is worth recognizing that there may be discordant tendencies across the three sources of gender power imbalances that we have emphasized. Warriors are valuable because of their ability to defend the homeland, and the chivalrous man is expected to protect women, but the militarization process employed to socialize men (and women) to become warriors and protectors often entails the abuse of women and other out groups. This abuse is in obvious tension with a vocation of protection. Militarization thus produces a paradoxical unintended consequence: those who are trained to protect may end up being more likely to use violence against innocent people.

Aside from the potential for unintended consequences, it should be noted that it is possible for these different masculinities—warrior masculinity, protective masculinity, and militarized masculinity—to compete for dominance in the gender hierarchy and to vary in strength from context to context.

Challenge from the Militarization Process for Peacekeeping: Sexual Exploitation, Abuse, Harassment, and Violence

Applied to PKOs, the militarization process may lead to SEAHV of both female peacekeepers and local women in the host country.[49] Allegations of peacekeeper sexual involvement with local women in particular—including rape, sexual exploitation, and human trafficking—are numerous.[50] As mentioned, SEAHV of women within the missions and outside them may be partly due to the socialization process of militarization that makes soldiers into aggressive humans, particularly such that they may pit their anger against out-groups, such as women. In this way, the unfortunate and somewhat ironic by-product of militarization may be violence against women, despite the fact that fundamentally the peacekeeper's job is to protect.

Scholars have argued that militarized masculinity is responsible for much of the SEAHV that occurs near military bases.[51] When soldiers are on a base and have nothing to do, they may be more likely to engage in such behavior. Historically, when military officers deploy abroad, transactional sex with locals is a common phenomenon.[52] It is possible, furthermore, that men who engage in transactional sex may be more prone to commit sexual exploitation and abuse of the local population.[53] Military and peacekeeping missions have shrugged off such behavior as unavoidable and to be expected. For example, in Cambodia in the early 1990s, the UN had no official policy on SEAHV, but UN Special Representative of the Secretary-General Yasushi Akashi responded to NGO concerns about sexual misconduct by UN peacekeepers by saying "boys will be boys."[54]

The constructive harnessing of militarized masculinity becomes particularly challenging for peacekeeping missions, which can be thought to have a dual mandate that poses somewhat of an identity crisis for military institutions and their personnel. On the one hand they must continue to keep their combat capacity robust to protect the population from national security threats. On the other hand participation in the peacekeeping missions requires that officers be flexible and effective state-builders. Dag Hammarskjöld, the second secretary-general of the UN, once said, "peacekeeping is too important to be undertaken by soldiers, but soldiers are the only ones who can do it." Implicit in this statement is this fundamental contradiction: soldiers are trained to fight wars, but peacekeeping requires that soldiers prioritize peace activities, not war activities. On this point, Whitworth (2007) argues that when peacekeeping troops are unable to fulfill their function as soldiers conditioned for combat, they may resort to sexual exploitation of the local population, violence against the local population, and sexual harassment of other members of the UN mission. Paul Higate and Marsha Henry (2009: 154) similarly argue that "masculinity matters" in the rampant level of SEAHV in peacekeeping missions. Foremost, the tension that many peacekeepers face in their dual roles as armed enforcers and promoters of peace can lead to a dangerous combination of militarized masculinity and a sense of emasculation, which could increase the extent to which the military personnel use sexual abuse as an outlet.[55]

Thus, we expect that some peacekeepers will engage in SEAHV against women and that this will be a problem both within missions and in interactions with local populations. Female peacekeepers, and not just local women, may be subject to SEAHV. In PKOs, because different countries are deployed together and because there is diversity and variation in the country deployments of women, it may mean that for some military personnel, it is the first time they are working with women. This could further open the door for some personnel to engage in SEAHV against their female colleagues.

Our key point here: SEAHV in and through peacekeeping missions—directed against peacekeeping personnel and against members of the local population—is a symptom of militarization and resulting gender power imbalances in security institutions and presents a crucial challenge to PKOs.

Gender Power Imbalances in Policing?

Most of the discussion thus far has focused on gender power imbalances in military forces. Similar to military indoctrination, some evidence suggests that law enforcement academies encourage aspects of gendered power imbalances among recruits. Anastasia Prokos and Irene Padavic (2002), for example, find that by watching and learning from instructors and each other, male students develop a form of masculinity that excludes women students and exaggerates differences between them and men; and that denigrates women in general. As such, they conclude that the masculinity that is characteristic of police forces and is partly responsible for women's low representation is not produced exclusively on the job but is taught in police academies as a subtext for professional socialization. Steve Herbert (2001) finds that a prevailing masculinity in policing favors an aggressive patrol style, emphasizes felony arrests, and belittles community policing because officers would rather chase "bad guys" than attend community meetings. The study suggests that in police departments, even though policing increasingly entails more "feminine" activities, such as community policing,[56] militarization is still privileged over community-oriented activities—the types most needed in peacekeeping police operations. This is especially true given the rise of militarized police units, such as SWAT.[57] Just as with the military, a culture of privileging warrior identities, protection, and militarization may prevail in policing as well.

Nevertheless, we expect a difference in degree between military and police personnel in peacekeeping missions. In PKOs, the military troops' role is to enforce peace agreements and protect the local population and international personnel, and the military observers' role is to record violations of peace treaties. The role of UNPOL includes supporting human rights; reporting on situations and incidents; and advising, training, and monitoring the performance of local law enforcement.[58] The objective of the FPU is to serve as backup if a situation escalates into a crisis. In this sense, the police have more contact with locals than the military, as their daily activities involve interacting with locals and responding to low-scale incidents. Importantly, police are not trained to fight in the same way that soldiers are conditioned to adopt militarized masculinity.[59] Moreover, the activities of UNPOL better mimic their jobs at home, and policing may embody more of the characteristics necessary for peacekeeping in that the personnel have more chances to empathize with locals.[60] It is thus possible that they do not suffer from the same frustrations that might arise for soldiers, who tend to experience a mismatch between their aggression-laden training and their peacekeeping missions. Thus, placing an emphasis on policing may help prevent some of the unintentional consequences of the prevalence of privileged masculinities in peacekeeping missions. Though still a concern worth addressing, we expect gender power imbalances to dominate police components of peacekeeping missions to a lesser degree than military ones.

OVERCOMING GENDER POWER IMBALANCES
IN PEACEKEEPING OPERATIONS

While the gender power imbalances have endured over time, they are by no means permanent. Duncanson (2013), for example, argues that soldiers, police officers, and peacekeeper identities are not fixed and that small steps such as soldiers empathizing with locals and "the other," among other mechanisms, could lead them to question the gender hierarchies that exist and may even result in challenges to gender power imbalances. Particular practices and changes may lead to gender power reordering.

We turn to two possible mechanisms that may help overcome the challenges mentioned in the preceding sections. The first, female ratio balancing, assumes that gender norms are fixed; the other, equal opportunity peacekeeping, focuses on transformation of the gender order. Female ratio balancing focuses on increasing the representation of women in peacekeeping forces, presuming that if the purpose of peacekeeping is peace and not war then women are better suited as peacekeepers or at least as an important counterbalance to the dominance of various masculinities. Equal opportunity peacekeeping, in contrast, focuses more on challenging the gender dichotomies through changes in practices and structures in military, police, and peacekeeping institutions.

In short, while increasing the proportion of women is important in its own right, the justification for it in terms of improving the success of peacekeeping missions falls back on stereotypes at the root of gender power imbalances. Instead, what is necessary is a reprioritization of gender so that the warrior, protection, and militarized masculinities are not hegemonic or privileged. A balancing of all forms of masculinities and femininities in PKOs is needed.

These two policy options are not mutually exclusive, as improving the representation of women can be part of broader reforms. We are using the focus on female ratio balancing as a foil—as a point of contrast to highlight the value of a more holistic approach. So much attention, in policy discussions, media coverage, academic discourse, and, we assume, the public consciousness has been given to the consequences of increasing the proportions of women in security institutions that it is natural to start there and then see if other approaches can do better.

Policy Lever 1: Female Ratio Balancing in Peacekeeping Operations

The purpose and function of peacekeeping missions, as noted, do not well align with those of national security institutions, especially militaries. In peacekeeping, soldiers of other countries (peacekeepers) are actively engaged in helping to rebuild domestic institutions; they are actively involved in creating peace, not war. As mentioned in chapter 2, PKOs now take on a more multidimensional role that includes peace- and state-building. As such, peacekeeping and peace-building missions do not require the constellations of skills, socialization processes, and preparation necessary for militaries to be effective in combat.

Kronsell (2012) has argued that peacekeeping and peace-building missions are a part of a new "post-national defense" and do not require the combat mentality and unit cohesion necessary to fight a war.[61] Sandra Whitworth (2007) even suggests that the traits and masculinity needed to win a war may be detrimental in the context of peacekeeping. The combat role is minimized, as the majority of the mission's duties and responsibilities require soldiers to observe, relate to the local population, mediate conflicts, and work with many different countries. In this sense, peacekeeping has a lesser "warrior purpose" than that to which national militaries have been socialized to perform.

That peacekeeping missions contradict some of what it means to be a soldier—a negation of the use of force—has provided a core justification for the inclusion of women in peacekeeping forces. If we accept that gender dichotomies are fixed—that women are instruments of peace and that men, especially those who have been militarized, are instruments of violence—then a key to successful peacekeeping would lie in increasing the proportion of women in peacekeeping missions. Increasing the number of women would theoretically enhance the number of "peacemakers" and would decrease the number of potential exploiters, abusers, and perpetrators of violence. That is, women fulfill the "peace" part of peacekeeping missions. Since protection is still a part of peacekeeping mandates, men, again assuming that gender dichotomies are fixed, may be equally needed to serve as protectors. Thus, in this sense, the most successful peacekeeping missions should be ones where there is relative parity in the representation of women and men. Indeed, one policy lever to promote gender equality in and through missions has been to balance the ratio of men and women—gender balancing, or, more precisely, female ratio balancing.

This policy lever relies on instrumental justifications, which treat gender identities as fixed. Kathleen Jennings (2011: 1) has noted that the dominant form of argumentation for including more women "is instrumentalist: deploying more women peacekeepers is seen as necessary to achieve a more successful mission and not as an end in itself." Instrumental claims argue that increasing women's representation in peacekeeping missions brings a broader range of experiences, skills, and perspectives to missions, which improves their ability to provide security and respond to potential threats. It is an argument based on difference—women's experiences are different from men's, which means that women provide certain skills, assets, characteristics, and knowledge distinct from men's that make them more effective in peacekeeping efforts.[62] These claims may be rooted in biological arguments that women inherently possess certain proclivities and sensibilities that are different from men, which make them better suited to make peace. They may also be rooted in sociological arguments that women and men have been socialized into particular gender roles, which makes them better suited for gendered tasks oriented around peace. Regardless of the biological or sociological claims about gender, these arguments that female peacekeepers provide an added benefit to the mission rest on categorical differences between men and women. They are instrumental arguments intended to exploit gendered comparative advantages as the basis for policy decisions.

To illustrate the use of an instrumental justification, we look at UN and NGO documents. We then highlight two dominant discourses or forms of instrumental justifications: (1) female peacekeepers improve trust with citizens of the host country, thereby legitimizing the mission in the eyes of civilians, and (2) female peacekeepers improve the mission environment, specifically ensuring that peacekeepers are less likely to engage in sexual transgressions. We then provide a critique of this policy lever, arguing that it will do little to mitigate the gender power imbalances in peacekeeping missions, followed by a short aside on the representation of women and operational effectiveness.

Instrumental Justifications for Increasing Women's Representation in Peacekeeping

Since UNSCR 1325, much of the international community's argument for female ratio balancing in peacekeeping missions has focused on claims that women bring an added benefit to peacekeeping missions. The UN specifically states that "women and men experience conflict differently and therefore understand peace differently."[63] Other language used in UN publications, for example, has argued that female peacekeepers act as role models in the local environment; that female peacekeepers inspire women and girls in male-dominated societies to push for their own rights and for participation in peace processes; and that the increased recruitment of women is critical for empowering women in the host community, helping to make the peacekeeping force approachable to women in the community and mentoring female cadets at police and military academies.[64] The UN consistently contends that the presence of female peacekeepers can also help to reduce conflict and confrontation; improve access and support for local women; provide role models for women in the community; provide a greater sense of security to local populations, including women and children; and broaden the skill set available within a peacekeeping mission.[65] Here is a sampling of some instrumentalist justifications the UN and NGOs have made regarding female ratio balancing in PKOs.

"Women peacekeepers also improve targeted outreach to women in host communities. This is crucial for various reasons, including capitalizing on women's familiarity with local protection strategies that affect women, and on their capacity to provide early warning" (UN Women, 2015: 141).

"Female military officers are in great demand for mixed staff protection teams and investigation teams looking into incidents involving female victims or witnesses. They drive strong civil-military coordination, and together with civilian and police counterparts, can more effectively reach out to and interact with civilians in the host country, as they appear less threatening and more accessible to affected populations" (141).

"Recent peacekeeping experience confirms that uniformed female personnel play a vital role in reaching out and gaining the trust of women and girls within local communities, understanding and detecting their unique protection needs and tailoring the responses of peace operations" (UN, 2015: 67).

"Inside the mission, the female presence can sometimes act as a brake against possible violations of the code of conduct. Where the presence of women in peacekeeping operations was higher, such as in the missions in Guatemala and South Africa, the missions were completed with enormous success and the mandates were completely fulfilled" (Bertolazzi, 2010: 18).

"The operational imperative of having a critical mass of female military peacekeepers is widely acknowledged, as it enables better access to women in post-conflict environments to support mandate implementation" (UN, 2010c: 13).

"Gender balance in peacekeeping can help the UN to 'lead by example' in relation to women's empowerment as both security providers and beneficiaries. Women may have a comparative operational advantage in sexual violence prevention, having greater proximity to groups at risk" (UN Women, 2010: 14).

"The presence of uniformed female peacekeepers has had a positive impact, challenging traditional ideas of gender roles and encouraging many women to enter the security sector" (UN, 2010a: 27).

"The fifth basic requirement is an increase in the percentage of female peacekeeping personnel. That would facilitate the mission's task of making meaningful contact with vulnerable groups and non-governmental organizations in the local community in its effort to eliminate sexual exploitation and abuse. Victims and their spokespersons tend to be female and the presence of female interlocutors, especially in senior positions, would facilitate efforts to encourage the reporting of abuse, which is the first step in eliminating it. Finally, the presence of more women in a mission, especially at senior levels, will help to promote an environment that discourages sexual exploitation and abuse, particularly of the local population" (UN, 2005, March 24: 18).

"Recognizing that an understanding of the impact of armed conflict on women and girls, effective institutional arrangements to guarantee their protection and full participation in the peace process can significantly contribute to the maintenance and promotion of international peace and security" (UNSCR 1325, adopted October 31, 2000).

"Women's presence [in peacekeeping missions] improves access and support for local women; it makes male peacekeepers more reflective and responsible; and it broadens the repertoire of skills and styles available within the mission, often with the effect of reducing conflict and confrontation" (UN DPKO, 2000: 4).

"A more equitable gender balance and the increased presence of female civilian, police and military peacekeepers can have a positive influence on Peace Support Operations and their relations with local populations. In the handful of UN peacekeeping and observer operations where women constituted significant proportions (30–50%) of the professional posts (e.g., MICIVIH in Haiti, MINUGUA in Guatemala and UNOMSA in South Africa) a gender-balance produced positive perceptions and interactions with the host population and contributed to the success of the operation" (International Alert, 2002: 23).

"Evidence suggests that the increased presence of women helps to create good relations with local communities, since the establishment of trust is an essential element in any peacekeeping operation" (UN, 1995: 8).

"It has also been contended that the presence of women contributes to differences in decision-making in terms of content, priorities, management style, organizational culture and group dynamics" (UN, 1995: 9).

While this list demonstrates a wide range of instrumental justifications for increasing women's representation in PKOs, we focus on two in particular. The first has to do with how female peacekeepers may improve the legitimacy of peacekeeping missions, and the second with how female peacekeepers improve the mission environment. Both arguments rely on an argument of difference—that women make the environment more "feminine" and less "masculine." The added "feminine touch" supposedly enhances the "peace" in "peacekeeping." As such, Gerard DeGroot (2001) observes that the feminine traits that once served as a justification to keep women out of the security sector and away from combat positions—because they were seen as disruptive to combat effectiveness—are now used as a justification to *include* women in the security sector, because they are seen as particularly important for peacekeeping missions.

Female Peacekeepers Improve Mission Legitimacy

The UN DPKO advocates that the presence of female peacekeepers may reduce conflict and confrontation and provide a greater sense of security to local populations, including women and children. According to Jennings (2011: 3), policy-makers and scholars have argued that integrating female peacekeepers will enhance protection, as "PKOs with more women peacekeepers are better able to protect citizens, especially women and children, because women peacekeepers bring a greater awareness of and sensitivity to their particular needs and challenges, and because women peacekeepers are less intimidating or provocative than men peacekeepers." Female peacekeepers will improve assistance to victims of sexual violence, as "women peacekeepers ensure a more compassionate or empathetic response to victimized women and children, especially those that have been sexually assaulted; it is often claimed that it is 'easier' for a raped woman to talk to another woman about her assault." And female peacekeepers will provide inspiration, as "women peacekeepers help contribute to more equitable gender relations within the local society by serving as role models or mentors for local women and girls" (3).[66]

In this line of thought, female peacekeepers have particular traits and skills that legitimize the mission in the eyes of the locals. Sahana Dharmapuri (2012) argues that the presence of female peacekeepers can increase local communities' acceptance of a UN force but urges caution in generalizing from such assumptions. The stereotype that women are softer, more peaceful, more nurturing, and more prone to cooperation enables female peacekeepers to gain trust among the host population. For example, Kari Karamé (2001) highlights how female soldiers from Norway in the UN Interim Force in Lebanon (UNIFIL) helped Lebanese women by being able to relate to them as women and such interactions built trust and allowed the peacekeepers to better carry out their duties. Similarly, Donna Bridges and Debbie Horsfall (2009) found that female Australian peacekeepers improved the reputation of the contingent in the UNIFIL mission and helped to normalize the presence of the peacekeepers.[67]

One area where voices at the UN have argued that female peacekeepers are particularly important for building local trust is in addressing SGBV suffered by women in the local community.[68] In a 2008 speech, Secretary-General Ban Ki-Moon called for more female peacekeepers to help counter "the abominable practice of sexual violence" resulting from armed conflicts.[69] Indeed, adding female peacekeepers has been thought to automatically increase gender mainstreaming, including policies to help prevent SGBV.[70] Leslie Pruitt (2013, 2016) also specifically calls for the inclusion of more female police officers in missions to address SGBV. The presence of female peacekeepers is supposed to help address the poor understanding and reception of victims of SGBV in the host country because women are thought to be better attuned to women's issues. In practice, this assumes that female peacekeepers are more attentive to SGBV in conducting their daily operations, local women are more willing to report cases of SGBV to female peacekeepers, and female peacekeepers are better able to question and offer assistance to survivors of SGBV.

Moreover, scholars have suggested that women can both "actively" and "passively" represent women through their actions or presence in the bureaucracy.[71] When there is active representation, women may promote issues related to the minority within the bureaucracy, and when there is passive representation, women may change the behavior or the public's perception of the institution by virtue of being women (or from the minority). For example, according to Kenneth Meier and Sean Nicholson-Crotty (2006), women may be more likely to report sexual abuse to female policy officers because they feel more comfortable talking to someone who "looks more like them" (i.e., is also female). It is also believed that women in the security sector may advocate for women's issues and their presence may thus shape public opinion and actions toward the security institution. Women may act as symbols of change for local women and maybe for the mission itself. Leslie Pruitt (2016: 10) writes that the all-female Indian FPU in Liberia "continues to inform and to give legitimacy to women's needs and concerns both as stakeholders in peace and security processes generally and as potential or actual peacekeepers."[72]

Using female ratio balancing to increase the legitimacy of peacekeeping missions often relies on a critical mass argument. If on average women possess these peace-building proclivities, then an increase in the number of women past a certain point will mean that the overall mission takes on the character of those proclivities.[73] Thus, based on the critical mass argument, many targets for women's representation in peacekeeping missions have been set at particular thresholds, such as 10 percent, 20 percent, 30 percent, and so on. When missions reach these target numbers, the idea is that they can better realize the benefits listed above.

Female Peacekeepers Improve Mission Environments

Female peacekeepers may also improve the mission environment, especially in regard to reducing peacekeeping-perpetrated SEAHV. Including more women has been considered as an important policy lever to address such misconduct. While critiquing the instrumental approach, Jennings (2011: 7) notes that some make an assumption that "women's presence makes for a more compassionate, empathetic and *better behaved* operation" (emphasis added). Olivera Simić (2013) also criticizes the argument made by some that an increase in the representation of women in PKOs will lead to a decrease in the number of HIV/AIDS cases directly or indirectly linked to PKOs, a decline in the number of brothels around peacekeeping bases, and a reduction in the number of babies fathered and abandoned by peacekeepers after their missions come to an end.

Again one suggested mechanism by which female peacekeepers can attenuate SEAHV is through attaining a critical mass. Increasing the proportion of women in peace operations is thought to decrease the number of perpetrators of misconduct as long as women are less prone to misconduct than men. For example, the Swedish government explicitly argues that one way to deal with sexual misconduct is to include more women because they are less likely to participate in the sexual exploitation of local people.[74] The more female peacekeepers replace male ones, the fewer men there are to engage in SEAHV. Sahana Dharmapuri (2011) notes that a 1995 study for the UN Division for the Advancement of Women found that the incidence of rape and use of prostitution fell significantly with even a token female presence and notes, and as yet, that there is no indication that female peacekeepers have engaged in SEAHV in a UN mission.

Aside from critical mass, another suggested mechanism by which female peacekeepers can attenuate sexual misconduct is through monitoring the behavior of their male colleagues and deterring unsanctioned behavior by security personnel.[75] Jennings (2011: 3) summarizes a typical claim that female peacekeepers will deter SEAHV: "by having a 'civilizing' effect on their male colleagues, women's presence ensures a better-behaved, less-corrupt and less-abusive PKO." The Zeid Report, for example, recommends that including more female peacekeepers, who might help introduce a different culture and bolster accountability, should be a crucial element in a "comprehensive strategy to eliminate future sexual exploitation and abuse in United Nations Peacekeeping operations" (UN, 2005).

The Limits on the Impact of Female Ratio Balancing

The discussion above presents a compelling case for the instrumental merits of female ratio balancing. Women and feminine traits have much to contribute to PKOs. Additional consideration, however, suggests that gender reforms in PKOs must not place all hope in the transformative potential of increasing the representation of women. Here, we note some of the limitations on what female ratio balancing can achieve and why an overemphasis on instrumental justifications for it might actually impede efforts to address gender power imbalances in PKOs.[76] In doing so, we do not question whether improvements in the representation of women in missions provide net positive benefits. Nor do we question whether female ratio balancing should be pursued as an end in itself and can serve as one metric of progress in institutional reform. Instead, we caution against overreliance on a single tool in the toolkit. We also recognize that attempts to improve the representation of women frequently occur in parallel with other reforms. We urge caution in, not abandonment of, the current initiatives to improve women's representation in peacekeeping.

A singular focus on female ratio balancing as the primary policy lever to counteract male dominance in PKOs might not realize the return on investment that instrumental justifications based on gender differences expect for at least four reasons: instrumentalist justifications tend to (1) overlook the real barriers posed by gender power imbalances, (2) reduce the contribution of women to feminine stereotypes, (3) presume that gender similarities will trump other cultural differences between locals and peacekeepers, and (4) displace an undue share of the burden for reforms onto the female personnel. We explain each of these in turn.

First, the pursuit of female ratio balancing alone may not be the most effective strategy to combat gender power imbalances precisely because the lack of female presence is one of the pernicious effects of gender power imbalances. That is, one of the consequences of privileging the warrior, protection, and militarized hegemonic masculinities is the restriction on female participation, particularly in key roles likely to shape the local perceptions of missions' legitimacy and opportunity for SEAHV. A solution that calls for an increase in female participation without a clear strategy of how to tackle the underlying problem is more of an aspirational hope than a constructive solution.

Second, a reduction of the value added by female peacekeepers to feminine stereotypes can entrench those stereotypes and will miss much of the variation in the tendencies of women. Jennings (2011: 7) has used the label of "affirmative gender essentialisms" to capture the perspective that "while the feminine traits associated with women may be generally positive, they nonetheless dismiss women's diverse capabilities, experiences and interests in favor of a particular ideal based on the 'essential' character of womanhood." Stereotypes about women being irrelevant to or a liability in providing physical protection become entrenched when female peacekeeping successes are highlighted based on their performance in engaging in feminine tasks. In light of the specific challenges from power imbalances delineated above, the reduction of female peacekeepers to feminine stereotypes has the potential to exacerbate the belief that women are not suitable for the role of warrior or protector.

At root here is the reliance of instrumental justifications on the fundamental assumption that gender norms are fixed. In actuality, gender stereotypes often mischaracterize the behavior of many female peacekeepers. Many women are not more peaceful, conciliatory, and collaborative than men, especially those women who are militarily trained. Women perpetrate, are accomplices to, and are complicit in acts of violence, both political and nonpolitical, challenging the notion that what it means to be a woman is to be peaceful, mothering, and caring.[77] While traditional gender roles have historically recognized men and women as "natural" warriors and homemakers, respectively, women's participation in violence is not a new phenomenon, even if the media have treated it as such, with increased coverage of female suicide bombers and other female rebels as deviant.[78] One study has found that women have been active in fighting forces in fifty-five different conflicts.[79] Gender is a social construction, and as such, women may be socialized, such as through the militarization process, to reproduce certain forms of masculinity. The pressure, sometimes self-imposed and sometimes externally incentivized, to conform causes women constantly to negotiate their femininity within masculine spaces.[80] As Liora Sion (2008: 580) argues, it is possible that female recruits will "estrange themselves from 'femininity' as it is portrayed by the army and mock other women who are viewed as stereotypical females." Furthermore, there is a selection effect surrounding women who join the military and police forces. In many countries, choosing to join the military or police entails a certain tolerance for violence. Women who self-select into the military and police thus may not possess the peaceful and cooperative traits women are presumed to have. As such, there is no guarantee that the presence of women means that the mission will be more "feminine."

These justifications also miss the point that even though women's representation may increase, their roles may not. Adding female bodies cannot solve the underlying barriers because, as V. S. Peterson and A. S. Runyan (2010) argue, the aggressive and militarized culture of militaries is particularly hostile to feminized identities and bodies, so that women and feminized men are not and arguably cannot be treated as equal, no matter how well-intended policies such as female ratio balancing may be. Peterson and Runyan state that merely increasing women's presence in militaries without also analyzing the power of gendered institutions will simply resex militaries to a certain degree without challenging the hegemonic masculinities of the war system.

Third, female peacekeepers may not be the best advocates for local women. Expecting women to focus their attention on helping other women because they share a demographic similarity may be unrealistic. Gender is not the only relevant axis of identity. Class, race, religion, education, language, ethnicity, locality, nationality, North/South, and so on all feature heavily in the intersection of peacekeepers and locals.[81] The category of "woman" is not a homogenous group that always shares common interests, which means it may be unrealistic to expect women across different countries to form alliances and advocate for the same issues. Beth Reingold (2000, 2008) suggests that women do not necessarily agree on a set of "women's interests" to advance. On a more global scale, while the adoption of female quotas,[82] in both parties and parliaments, has helped increase the number of women in politics,[83] political representation of women does not necessarily lead to better outcomes for women,[84] and gender quotas are often instituted not to promote gender equality but due to other national interests.[85] The same could be true for women in peacekeeping missions where female peacekeepers do not have a unified understanding of how to help local women.

In addition, while women's sensitive issues may be better handled by women—we consider below how in many cultural contexts, contact with men regarding sensitive issues is prevented—foreign women remain potentially limited in helping survivors of SGBV or in handling other gender-related issues. Cultural sensitivity is not likely to be undone by gender similarities. Female peacekeepers from outside the host country region may not be better equipped to judge whether cases involve SGBV, interview perpetrators, or attend to the needs of survivors than their male counterparts. In many countries, there are traditional and informal cultural practices for addressing issues of SGBV, of which peacekeepers potentially are not knowledgeable. In fact, peacekeepers may even do harm in advocating for external-centered remedies to SGBV, as such practices may run counter to traditional and more culturally appropriate responses. Foreign women rarely share the same experiences as local women, making the expectation of solidarity between women of different cultures, races, ethnicities, classes, religions, and countries illusive. In addition, Jennings (2011: 6) argues that the assertion that female peacekeepers' presence is comforting to female victims of sexual violence is extremely difficult to assess, because locals are as likely to "see the uniform" as they are to "see the gender."[86] We thus temper expectations that female peacekeepers can and will advocate for other women in the mission and for local women.

Fourth, an overemphasis on differences between women and men as the basis for gender reforms places the onus of the mission's success on the women, who are likely to remain the minority sex, and overlooks the potential role that all peacekeepers, including men, can play in carrying out reforms. The expectation that female personnel will be better suited to keeping their male counterparts in line displaces the responsibility of individual behavior of male peacekeepers onto female personnel, and that may be a burden the women choose not to carry. Instead of men holding themselves accountable for their behavior, women are expected to be a deterrent and have a "civilizing" effect on their male colleagues, as women's presence is supposed to ensure a better-behaved, less-corrupt, and less-abusive PKO. The resulting burden on women puts a woman in a bind, as the role of monitoring the behavior of her fellow friends, colleagues, and even superiors could disrupt her career advancement and increase undesirable interpersonal conflict. Much more, policy reforms that exclude much of a role for the male peacekeepers miss out on harnessing change in the largest demographic segment of the missions.

Related to this undue burden placed on the female personnel, instrumental justifications for female ratio balancing entail that women are evaluated as "female peacekeepers" and not as "peacekeepers." In this way, different standards apply to women and men in the same occupation. Men are assumed to be naturally competent at providing security and engaging in peacekeeping labor, whereas women's presence in the security sector has to be made intelligible through a discourse of effectiveness. If the justification for including women into peacekeeping is based on the assumption that women improve mission legitimacy and gender equality by adding a "feminine touch," then they are evaluated based not on the skills they have gained through training but on their ability to conform to specific ideas about femininity and their ability to transform the mission culture.

The notion that women are well suited to carry such burdens in the first place is flawed for other reasons. The expectations for female peacekeepers to hold their male counterparts accountable for committing sexual transgressions is problematic because women may be more loyal to their comrades than to local women. Simić (2010) has argued that the expectation that women can police the behavior of men is based on essential claims about female solidarity. There is little evidence that female peacekeepers have a "civilizing" effect on male peacekeepers, as women do not prefer to be "sex police." Therefore, integrating more women may not help reduce the prevalence of SEAHV in the mission area.[87] Jennings (2008) also has shown that female soldiers are not likely to report misconduct, even in cases of sexual abuse, by their male colleagues, because their national loyalty trumps gender solidarity. She contends that female informants exhibit no real differences from male informants in their willingness to report, in their decision-making process around reporting, or in the distinctions they make between the severity of different types of offenses. "Tattling" on male colleagues could create a hostile work environment or even cost them their jobs, as military organizations emphasize unit cohesion and group loyalty. Just like men, women do not want to interfere in their colleagues' private lives, and most women do not want to be seen as judgmental or disloyal. The assumption that women have an underlying loyalty to other women simply by virtue of some shared sisterhood is in tension with other loyalties that women might have, such as with their colleagues.

Female Peacekeepers and Operational Effectiveness

That some minimal representation of women is necessary for operational effectiveness provides another type of argument to include more women in peacekeeping that relies on the practical realities in the ways that societies differentiate between the sexes but avoids more universal and subjective claims about gender differences. Operational effectiveness encompasses the objective requirements for the military and police to carry out their work. It has more to do with practical considerations than with a grand strategy to leverage gender differences for maximal efficacy.

Fulfilling mission mandates entails carrying out everyday operations and tasks. The success of these everyday jobs depends on whether the mission includes capabilities to overcome certain obstacles. Such obstacles might include cultural barriers or the host society's gender norms. In light of these obstacles, including women in missions can open up points of engagement between the mission and the local communities and thus enhance operational effectiveness.

Including women provides a number of practical advantages: women are often needed in the dynamic context of PKOs to conduct security checks on women and girls, interview women, work in female prisons, address specific needs of female ex-combatants during the process of demobilizing and reintegration into civilian life, interview survivors of gender-based violence, and interact with women in societies where women are prohibited from speaking to men.[88] Men simply cannot do these tasks because of the gendered context; the cultural environment is often such that men are prohibited from doing these tasks. In this sense, the environment in which peacekeepers work is gendered, and the peacekeeping mission is tasked with responding to the gendered environment. Women are thus able to enhance the operational effectiveness of the mission by engaging in activities inappropriate for men.

While the argument still relies on women's differences from men, it does not rely on women or men possessing a set of inherent qualities that are ascribed, esteemed, or valued. That is, these differences cannot be exploited to shape gender power dynamics—there is symmetry in the sense that what makes women necessary for some tasks that involve communicating and interacting with local women also makes men necessary for some tasks that involve communicating and interacting with local men.

Operational effectiveness arguments have been quite potent in convincing military officials to take active measures to increase the number of women in security forces and change standards, such as combat exclusion. For example, according to Stephanie Erwin (2012), the Female Engagement Teams in Iraq and Afghanistan demonstrated that women are helpful to operations and contributed to the removal of combat exclusion in the U.S. military. These teams were able to speak to women in Afghanistan and Iraq, where sex segregation is a common practice, and gather intelligence from women, pat women down at checkpoints, and provide sensitive services to women—all tasks men could not do. Robert Egnell et al. (2014) suggest that using an "insider" strategy that ties gender perspectives to military tactical effectiveness has led to Sweden being a model for the world in terms of promoting gender equality in and through its military.

While women do enhance operational effectiveness, and recognition of this is not likely to have the same trade-offs as the essentialist claims we have discussed, the operational effectiveness angle is a thin basis by itself for major gender-based reforms to peacekeeping. The arguments that women are necessary for operational effectiveness in these ways only necessitate the inclusion of a small percentage of women. As such, these arguments may spur initial reforms away from full exclusion of women, but operational effectiveness may not provide a sufficient impetus for substantial increases in the proportions of female peacekeepers or other major gender-based reforms that are part of the WPS agenda. Moreover, solely using operational effectiveness arguments to increase the number of women may diminish women's roles to those tasks that only women can do. Again, this could have detrimental effects on gender power imbalances in missions; women would be confined to a finite set of roles and evaluated based on how well they perform these specific duties.

Our key point here: To counteract gender power imbalances, improving the representation of female peacekeepers may make a unique positive impact on peacekeeping missions by increasing their legitimacy and improving the mission environment, but the impact of a singular focus on female ratio balancing may be stymied because it ignores the underlying issues, reduces the contribution of women to feminine stereotypes, presumes that gender similarities trump other cultural differences, and displaces an undue share of the burden for reforms on female personnel.

Policy Lever 2: Equal Opportunity Peacekeeping

A more holistic and transformational approach that focuses on changing gender power structures is necessary to overcome the challenges mentioned in this chapter. Such an approach involves taking measures to change the gendered nature or culture of the missions through shifts in structures, practices, roles, priorities, and activities that treat genders equally—hence equal opportunity peacekeeping.

While gender equality is the end outcome of interest, we believe that a traditional understanding of gender equality is insufficient. Recent critiques by scholars have suggested that an approach to study women's empowerment using aggregate indicators that compare the participation of women to that of men fails to distinguish sources of power from actual empowerment. Zehra Arat (2015) makes an eloquent argument that the UN's model of pushing for women's empowerment includes lofty rhetoric about transformational change but in practice uses a liberal feminist approach, which includes aggregate indicators of gender equality to measure success.[89] She argues that this method falls short of empowering the majority of women because it ignores the "diversity of women and structural foundations of subordination, such as capitalism, race, and class systems and international power differentials" (2015: 675).[90]

Gender equality cannot be achieved through "inclusion" alone, and removing gendered power hierarchies must extend beyond "sex discrimination." Thus to achieve gender equality in a more holistic way, we opt for *equal opportunity peacekeeping*. This more comprehensive form of gender equality means that women and men enjoy the same rights and opportunities across all sectors of society, including economic participation, decision-making, and institutional space.[91]

This broader understanding of gender equality requires equality at different levels: gender identities, gendered characteristics, belief systems, and composition.[92] Equality among gender identities means ensuring that other masculinities and femininities, such as those related to "peace-builder" and "cosmopolitan" identities, are as valued as the warrior, protective, and militarized masculinities (Duncanson, 2013; Kronsell, 2012). Equality among gendered characteristics means taking steps to boost the value ascribed to other masculine and feminine characteristics, such as empathy, caring, and communication, among others. Parity in belief systems is specifically related to perceiving members of the opposite sex as equals. Parity in composition means continued increases in women's representation in these institutions such that there are more balanced ratios of men to women. These changes may be achieved through framing; leadership; recruitment and standards; promotion, demotion and discipline; training and professionalism; access and accountability; representation; and gender mainstreaming (broadly defined). We call the end product of these changes "equal opportunity" peacekeeping.

Equal opportunity peacekeeping, thus, requires a shift in the norms, culture, practices, and customs of an institution. Scholarship on institutions suggests that transformational change is possible, particularly in the literature that focuses on "feminist institutionalism."[93] Fiona Mackay, Meryl Kenny, and Louise Chappell (2010) argue that feminist institutionalism sees institutional change (and stability) as driven by gendered processes from within and considers actors in the institutions as having agency. Thus, the norms, practices, culture, and customs governing institutions, or what is considered "appropriate," can change over time. For Johan Olsen (2009: 9), understanding how this process of transformation works requires knowledge about "the internal success criteria, structures, procedures, rules, practices, career structures, socialization patterns, styles of thought and interpretive traditions, and resources of the entity." The change process is often driven by policy or norm entrepreneurs from both inside and outside the institutions, although some argue that change is more likely to be effective if coming from within (Egnell et al., 2014; Katzenstein, 1998; Olsen, 2009).[94]

Challenging dominant forms of masculine identities, characteristics, beliefs, and composition requires a shift in the hierarchy that privileges certain ways of being a man over other ways, and over ways to be a woman, to one of equality (Duncanson, 2013: 144). Duncanson (2013) argues that the goal should be to develop gender practices for men that shift gender relations in a democratic direction. Democratic gender relations are those that move toward equality, nonviolence, and mutual respect between people of different genders, sexualities, ethnicities, and generations. Connell (2000b: 29–30) states that "some of the qualities in 'traditional' definitions of masculinity (e.g., courage, steadfastness, ambitions) are certainly needed in the cause for peace . . . the task is not to abolish gender but to reshape it, to disconnect (for instance) courage from violence, steadfastness from prejudice, and ambition from exploitation." In a similar vein, Cynthia Cockburn and Meliha Hubic (2002) suggest a "regendering" of soldiers. They suggest that a regendered military would be one made up of men and women in equal numbers, enacting roles that are neither masculinized nor feminized. It would mean creating soldiers who are assertive, competent, courageous, responsive, and caring—soldiers who keep desirable masculine traits while throwing out some of the less desirable ones. Finally, it would entail creating a military culture that is respectful to women and also toward things usually associated with femininity, such as domestic life and the nurturing of relationships. Some countries have taken measures to reorient their militaries along these lines, such as Sweden (Kronsell, 2012; Egnell et al., 2014).[95]

Gender identities and hierarchies are not fixed, which means that hegemonic masculinities can be replaced with other forms of masculinities and femininities. Indeed, scholars have found that the warrior, protection, and militarized masculinities may be more fragile than anticipated. In her study of British soldiers, Duncanson (2013) finds that combat is often perceived negatively by soldiers. Through interviews, some soldiers expressed fear of combat and their distaste of it once they had experienced it (Duncanson, 2013). Aversion to combat by individual soldiers could open the door for other forms of masculinity and femininity to override combat pressures.

That institutions are malleable is a key insight and suggests that change is possible. In theory this makes sense, but in practice change might be difficult to realize. In our concluding chapter, we offer policy recommendations in a number of areas to demonstrate how such transformational change could be possible.

Our key point here: to counteract gender power imbalances, a holistic approach that privileges equality by valuing nondominant forms of masculinity and femininity, nondominant masculine and feminine characteristics, parity in belief systems about the opposite sex as equal, and parity in sex composition is needed. The end result is "equal opportunity" peacekeeping.

CONCLUSION

This chapter has provided the theoretical foundations for the rest of the book. We have highlighted specific challenges for PKOs that stem from gender power imbalances: exclusion of and discrimination against female peacekeepers, relegation of female peacekeepers to safe spaces, and SEAHV against female peacekeepers and local women. We have also suggested two policy levers that may mitigate these challenges. While improving the representation of women may be a common way to address gender inequalities, we opt for a more ambitious goal for peacekeeping missions, one that stresses equal opportunity.

Part II of the book analyzes the exclusion of and discrimination against female peacekeepers, the relegation of female peacekeepers to safe spaces, and SEAHV cross-nationally in peacekeeping missions from 2006 to 2013. Part III analyzes these challenges in a case study of UNMIL. At the cross-national level and in the case study, we also explore how well the two policy levers potentially perform to overcome the challenges. We find that the policy lever of equal opportunity peacekeeping better addresses the underlying challenges in peacekeeping missions. In theory, reforms that spur transformational and structural change are appealing, but in practice they are much more difficult to conceive and implement. We return to a detailed description of equal opportunity peacekeeping and its implementation challenges in the concluding chapter.

PART II

Discrimination, Protection, and SEAHV in UN Peacekeeping Missions (2006–2013)

Chapters 2 and 3 provided an overview of gender reforms that have been implemented in and through peacekeeping missions and the underlying theoretical foundations for addressing several challenges that peacekeeping missions face with regard to gender equality. These challenges stem from gendered power imbalances in PKOs, which perpetuate exclusion, discrimination, relegation of women to safe spaces, and SEAHV. In Chapters 4 and 5, we look into the empirical evidence for these challenges in peacekeeping missions from 2006 to 2013.

In chapters 4 and 5 we also examine the potential for two overlapping solutions to address these challenges: increasing the representation of women in peacekeeping missions and promoting equal opportunity peacekeeping. Solely relying on female ratio balancing may not be enough to sufficiently address the gender power imbalances that pervade peacekeeping missions. A more holistic approach, which involves taking measures to change the gendered nature or culture of the missions, is needed.

Before turning to chapter 4, we provide background here on the context of peacekeeping missions during the time frame 2006–2013. The UN Charter gives the Security Council the power and responsibility to authorize peacekeeping missions. In most cases, the PKOs are established and implemented by the UN, with member states contributing troops and police. In other cases, operations are led by regional organizations, such as the EU, NATO, African Union, or the Economic Community of West African States. We look at PKOs authorized by the UN Security Council and that fall under the jurisdiction of the UN DPKO or the UN Department of Political Affairs between 2006 and 2013.

When considering the roles peacekeepers play, it is important to consider how military and police personnel serve different functions in missions. Troop contingents are units from the same country that are sent to different parts of the host country to enforce or keep the peace. They are called out in emergency situations, provide security to key assets and people, and can sometimes enforce the peace if violence erupts. They can also play a number of other roles, including engaging in civil-military activities such as building roads and bridges, as well as community outreach. They have their own military compound and do not usually leave it unless called on. In addition to troop contingents, there are also military observers. These are individuals typically sent to help coordinate operations or to deploy to different parts of the country to report on the level of risk for violence to escalate and the scope of compliance with peace agreements. Many missions also include police, which might be sent as country contingents (FPUs) or as individuals. The FPUs protect key institutions, provide security to key individuals and assets, serve as backup in riot situations, and serve as backup during domestic law enforcement patrols. They also have their own compound and sometimes engage in community outreach. Individual UNPOL officers are sent in smaller numbers to monitor, advise, and train local law enforcement. They are not a part of contingents and do not respond to incidents. They are, however, perhaps the most visible to the local community and domestic security sector.

Between 2006 and 2013, there were twenty-two missions that either ended in this time period or are still ongoing. We chose this time period because cross-national data on peacekeepers that are disaggregated by sex and data on SEAHV only became available in 2006. The average number of years for missions that ended in this time period was nine. A brief overview of each mission follows. Table II.1 provides a summary of the missions' beginning and ending dates and host countries.

The UN Security Council established the UN Mission in Ethiopia and Eritrea (UNMEE) to monitor the cease-fire between Ethiopia and Eritrea and to help ensure compliance with the cease-fire's security commitments. The mandate included monitoring the cessation of hostilities, assisting in observing the fulfillment of security commitments, verifying redeployment of Ethiopian forces, monitoring the positions of Eritrean forces, monitoring the temporary security zone, and coordinating and providing technical assistance for humanitarian mine-action activities in that zone and areas adjacent to it. The Security Council terminated the mandate because of "crippling restrictions imposed by Eritrea on UNMEE, as well as the cutting off of fuel supplies—making it impossible for the operation to continue carrying out its mandated tasks, and putting at risk the safety and security of UN personnel."[1]

The Security Council established the UN Operation in Burundi (ONUB) in order to support and help implement lasting peace and bring about national reconciliation, as provided under the Arusha Agreement. This operation successfully completed its mandate by 2006 and was succeeded by the UN Integrated Office in Burundi (BINUB).

After the signing of the Lusaka Ceasefire Agreement in 1999, the Security Council authorized the UN Organization Mission in the Democratic Republic of the Congo (MONUC), which was originally meant to monitor and observe the peace. The mandate was later expanded and was renamed the UN Organization Stabilization Mission in the Democratic Republic of the Congo (MONUSCO) in 2010 to reflect the core multidimensional nature of the mission.

The Security Council authorized the UN Mission in the Central African Republic and Chad (MINURCAT) in response to the conflict in Darfur, Sudan. The mandate was to provide security and protection to civilians, ensure human rights and the rule of law, and support regional peace. It completed its mandate in 2010, and the UN Integrated Peacebuilding Office in the Central African Republic (BINUCA) has remained in the country.

Table II.1. UN PEACEKEEPING MISSIONS (1948–2013)

Mission	Start year	End year	Host country/countries
UN Truce Supervision Organization (UNTSO)	1948	Ongoing	Egypt, Israel, Jordan, Lebanon, Syria
UN Military Observer Group in India and Pakistan (UNMOGIP)	1949	Ongoing	Kashmir
UN Peacekeeping Force in Cyprus (UNFICYP)	1964	Ongoing	Cyprus
UN Disengagement Observer Force (UNDOF)	1974	Ongoing	Golan Heights
UN Interim Force in Lebanon (UNIFIL)	1978	Ongoing	Lebanon
UN Mission for the Referendum in Western Sahara (MINURSO)	1991	Ongoing	Western Sahara
UN Interim Administration Mission in Kosovo (UNMIK)	1999	Ongoing	Kosovo
UN Organization Mission in the Democratic Republic of the Congo (MONUC)	1999	2010	DRC
UN Mission in Ethiopia and Eritrea (UNMEE)	2000	2008	Eritrea and Ethiopia
UN Assistance Mission in Afghanistan (UNAMA)	2003	Ongoing	Afghanistan
UN Mission in Liberia (UNMIL)	2003	Ongoing	Liberia
UN Operation in Burundi (ONUB)	2004	2007	Burundi
UN Operation in Côte d'Ivoire (UNOCI)	2004	Ongoing	Côte d'Ivoire
UN Stabilization Mission in Haiti (MINUSTAH)	2004	Ongoing	Haiti
UN Mission in the Sudan (UNMIS)	2005	2011	Sudan
UN Integrated Mission in Timor-Leste (UNMIT)	2006	2012	East Timor
UN/African Union Mission in Darfur (UNAMID)	2007	Ongoing	Sudan
UN Mission in the Central African Republic and Chad (MINURCAT)	2007	2010	Chad, Central African Republic
UN Organization Stabilization Mission in the Democratic Republic of the Congo (MONUSCO)	2010	Ongoing	DRC
UN Interim Security Force for Abyei (UNISFA)	2011	Ongoing	Sudan
UN Mission in the Republic of South Sudan (UNMISS)	2011	Ongoing	South Sudan
UN Support Mission in Libya (UNSMIL)	2011	Ongoing	Libya
Multidimensional Integrated Stabilization Mission in Mali (MINUSMA)	2013	Ongoing	Mali

The UN Mission in Sudan (UNMIS) ended its operations on July 9, 2011, after monitoring the Sudan People's Liberation Movement following the Comprehensive Peace Agreement, signed in 2005. The mission ended its six years of mandated operations once South Sudan declared independence as part of a referendum, provided by the Comprehensive Peace Agreement, on January 9, 2011. A new mission was set up: the UN Mission in the Republic of South Sudan (UNMISS). In 2011, the Security Council responded to escalating violence in Sudan's Abyei region by establishing the UN Interim Security Force for Abyei (UNISFA). The mission is mandated to monitor the border between the North and South and to facilitate the delivery of humanitarian aid and is authorized to use force in protecting civilians and humanitarian workers in Abyei.

The Security Council authorized the UN Integrated Mission in Timor-Leste (UNMIT) in response to internal crisis in Timor-Leste in 2006. The mandate instituted a fully multidimensional mission, including "mandating UNMIT to provide interim law enforcement and public security until Timor-Leste's national police could be reconstituted and able to resume these roles."[2] The mission completed its mandate in 2012.

The Darfur Peace Agreement was signed on May 5, 2006. Shortly afterward, the Security Council replaced the African Union mission there with the UN-African Union Mission in Darfur (UNAMID). Its mandate includes protecting civilians, contributing to security for humanitarian assistance, monitoring and verifying implementation of agreements, assisting an inclusive political process, and contributing to the promotion of human rights and the rule of law.

The UN Support Mission in Libya (UNSMIL) is a special political mission and was authorized after the crisis in Libya in 2011 to help with democratic transition, rule of law, human rights, SSR, and international assistance coordination. The mission is overseen by the UN's Department of Political Affairs, which provides guidance and operational assistance.[3]

In 2013, the Security Council authorized the UN Multidimensional Integrated Stabilization Mission in Mali (MINUSMA) after violence escalated there. The mission mandate includes supporting the political process, carrying out a number of security-related stabilization tasks, protecting civilians and human rights, monitoring the peace, creating the conditions for the provision of humanitarian assistance and the return of displaced persons, and helping to prepare for elections.

After peace agreements were signed in 2003, the Security Council set up the UN Operation in Côte d'Ivoire (UNOCI). Following the 2010 presidential election and the ensuing political crisis, UNOCI has "remained on the ground to protect civilians; provide good offices; support the Ivorian Government in disarmament, demobilization and reintegration (DDR) of former combatants as well as on security sector reform; and monitor and promote human rights."[4]

After the Liberian civil war ended in 2003, the Security Council authorized UNMIL, deciding that the mission would be responsible for enabling the transition of full security responsibility to the Liberia National Police by strengthening its capabilities; promoting human rights; supporting national processes of reconciliation, constitutional reform, and decentralization; enhancing support for security sector and rule of law reform; supporting the participation of women in conflict prevention, conflict resolution, and peace-building; enhancing cooperation with UNOCI for the stabilization of the border area; and coordinating and collaborating with the Peacebuilding Commission on its engagement in Liberia.

The UN Mission for the Referendum in Western Sahara (MINURSO) was established by the Security Council in 1991 in accordance with settlement proposals accepted by Morocco and the Frente Popular para la Liberación de Saguia el-Hamra y de Río de Oro (POLISARIO Front). The mandate includes monitoring the cease-fire; verifying the reduction of Moroccan troops in contested territory; monitoring the confinement of Moroccan and POLISARIO troops to designated locations; taking steps with the parties to ensure the release of all Western Saharan political prisoners or detainees; overseeing the exchange of prisoners of war; implementing the repatriation program for refugees; identifying and registering qualified voters; and organizing and ensuring a free and fair referendum.

The only peacekeeping mission in the Americas, the UN Stabilization Mission in Haiti (MINUSTAH), was authorized by the Security Council in 2004 after President Bertrand Aristide departed Haiti into exile and after armed conflict spread to several cities across the country. This mission has a vast multidimensional mandate that includes everything from DDR of soldiers to carrying out free and fair municipal, parliamentary, and presidential elections. The overall force level was increased after the 2010 earthquake. Since the presidential elections in 2011, MINUSTAH has been working to fulfill its original mandate: to restore a secure and stable environment, promote the political process, strengthen Haiti's government institutions and rule-of-law-structures, and protect human rights.

In 1949, the UN authorized military observers to supervise the cease-fire between India and Pakistan in the State of Jammu and Kashmir. Following renewed hostilities in 1971, the UN Military Observer Group in India and Pakistan (UNMOGIP) has remained in the area to observe the 1971 cease-fire and report activity to the secretary-general.

The UN Assistance Mission in Afghanistan (UNAMA) is a political mission established by the Security Council in 2002. The goal of this mission is to continue leading and coordinating international civilian efforts in assisting Afghanistan with its democratic transition. The UN DPKO oversees the mission. It is an "integrated" mission, which means it has two main areas of activities: political affairs and development and humanitarian issues.

In 1948, the Security Council called for a cessation of hostilities in Palestine and decided that the truce should include military observers. The first group of military observers arrived in 1948 in what came to be known as the UN Truce Supervision Organization (UNTSO). They were tasked with monitoring the Armistice Agreements between Israel and its Arab neighbors. This mission's activities have been and still are spread over territory in Egypt, Israel, Jordan, Lebanon, and Syria.

In the aftermath of the October War in 1973, the UN Disengagement Observer Force (UNDOF) was established in 1974 by the Security Council following the agreed disengagement of the Israeli and Syrian forces in the Golan Heights. Since 1974,

"UNDOF has remained in the area to maintain the cease-fire between the Israeli and Syrian forces and to supervise the implementation of the disengagement agreement."[5]

In 1978, the Lebanese government submitted a formal protest to the Security Council against an Israeli invasion, which led to the Security Council establishing UNIFIL. The original mandate included confirming the withdrawal of Israeli forces from southern Lebanon, restoring international peace and security, and assisting the government of Lebanon in ensuring the return of its authority in the area. After the 2006 war, the mandate was expanded to include monitoring of hostilities; the accompaniment of the Lebanese armed forces as they deploy and as Israel withdraws its armed forces from Lebanon; providing humanitarian assistance; and assisting the government of Lebanon in securing its borders and entry points.

The Security Council set up UNFICYP in 1964 to prevent further violence between the Greek and Turkish Cypriot communities on the island. The mission's responsibilities expanded in 1974 after a coup d'état and military intervention. UNFICYP has "supervised the ceasefire lines, provided humanitarian assistance, and maintained a buffer zone between the Turkish and Turkish Cypriot forces in the north and the Greek Cypriot forces in the south."[6]

In 1999, the Security Council established UNMIK, which marked the end of the NATO intervention in Kosovo. NATO intervened due to the massive human rights violations by Serbian authorities in Kosovo and because of clashes between the Kosovo Liberation Army and the Yugoslav forces. The Security Council gave UNMIK authority over the territory and the people of Kosovo, including all legislative and executive powers and administration of the judiciary. The mission was asked "to perform basic civilian administrative functions; promote the establishment of substantial autonomy and self-government in Kosovo; facilitate a political process to determine Kosovo's future status; coordinate humanitarian and disaster relief of all international agencies; support the reconstruction of key infrastructure; maintain civil law and order; promote human rights; and assure the safe and unimpeded return of all refugees and displaced persons to their homes in Kosovo."[7]

CHAPTER 4

Discrimination and Protection Revisited

Female Participation in Peacekeeping Operations

In 2012, Major Lola Aduke Oyediran Ugbodaga was the most senior Nigerian female military peacekeeper in UNMIL. She participated in different military activities throughout her time in UNMIL, including being deployed as an observer to remote parts of Liberia and working under the civil-military relations department at UN Headquarters in Monrovia. In general, she has described her experience as a positive one but notes that she has faced hardship in all of her roles. Particularly, she describes feeling alone most of the time because she did not have many women with whom to relate. When deployed to remote areas, she noted the poor facilities, especially for women, where there was little privacy. And at UN Headquarters, she noted the rampant discrimination and even harassment she faced in her role there. In this chapter, we focus on her first complaint, the fact that too few women were deployed with her in Liberia.

The Nigerian contingents in Liberia actually have better representation of women than many others, although that is not saying much. During 2013, 111 Nigerian female troops were deployed to UNMIL (7.6 percent of 1,467 total troops) and 245 Nigerian female troops were deployed globally (5.1 percent of 4,780 total troops).[1] By way of contrast, another top contributor to UNMIL, Pakistan, deployed only 8 female troops to UNMIL (0.4 percent of 1991 total troops) and 18 globally (0.2 percent of 7,593) in 2013. A number of questions arise from this comparison. Why, even for the relatively diverse country contingents like those from Nigeria or, even better, Ghana (about 9.8 percent, or 70 of 709, of its troops contributed to UNMIL in 2013 were women), are the proportions of women still so meager? Why is there such variation across the contributing countries? Why is there such variation across the missions, as both Nigeria and Pakistan contributed higher proportions of women to the UNMIL mission than their global average?

In order to answer these questions, we analyze country motivations and deterrents for sending women to peacekeeping missions. Since the force-contributing countries have discretion over whether to contribute personnel, as well as the composition of the personnel, we focus on the factors that affect the proportions of women the countries send.[2] We argue that the dominance of the warrior identity and the gendered protection norm in security institutions, along with militarization processes that emphasize group cohesion, crucially shape the degree to which and where countries send female peacekeepers abroad.

We first focus on why many countries send low proportions of women to peacekeeping missions. Most straightforward, the availability of female security personnel in the contributing countries plays a role in the representation of women in the peacekeeping forces deployed. The exclusion of women from national militaries and police may be explained by perceptions of appropriate gender roles for women and men—mainly that men are fit to be warriors and that the inclusion of women would interfere with group cohesion. If both men and women view the military and police as institutions that are not appropriate for women, then women are less likely to join these institutions, which then limits the availability of women to deploy to peacekeeping missions.

In addition to exclusion, we also find evidence that contributing countries tend to be specific about *where* they send female peacekeepers. Female peacekeepers are often deployed to the safest peacekeeping missions, which we argue is a function of the gendered protection norm. This line of thought contends that women are not sent in large numbers to peacekeeping missions because peacekeeping missions entail risk of harm, and the norm is to keep women out of harm's way rather then send them to risk their own safety for the protection of others. Recognizing that some peacekeeping missions entail greater risk than others, we should expect that if a norm of protection does indeed suppress the participation of women, missions that operate in more dangerous security environments should contain lower proportions of women. Specifically, we find that high prior levels of violence, especially conflict-related sexual violence, in the host countries and low levels of development in the host countries well predict where female peacekeepers *do not* go. Moreover, we find that contributing countries that have experienced prior high levels of armed conflict, such that peacekeeping service abroad might not register as particularly risky relative to military service at home, tend to contribute relatively greater proportions of women to peacekeeping missions.

We also find that the practice of gender equality in force contributing countries may shape contributing-country outputs in positive ways but that the protection norm remains strong even among countries that have better records on gender equality.[3] Countries with better records of gender equality may contribute higher numbers of female peacekeepers, but such countries are still likely to send those female peacekeepers to safe missions. Most, if not all, contributing countries still have a way to go toward embracing equal opportunity peacekeeping.

FORCE-CONTRIBUTING COUNTRY INCENTIVES

To explain variations in the representation of women across missions, it is important to understand the locus of decision-making. Since the UN lacks both a standing army and executive authority to enforce standards in the composition of troop contingents, the force-contributing countries have sole discretion in determining whether to provide any troops or police to missions and the composition of their contributions. The UN Security Council frequently includes language in the authorization mandates that calls for states to contribute, and to consider the importance of female representation when doing so, but the language never provides any enforcement provisions, and we do not know of any cases where countries have been sanctioned for not providing women or rewarded for doing well in this regard. Moreover, the secretary-general's office actively recruits states to contribute, but this is primarily an exercise in coordination, not in inducing compliance.

Preferences and characteristics at the level of the UN, therefore, cannot well explain variations in mission composition. The focus must be on the incentives of the force-contributing countries. Decisions about whether to contribute to particular missions are driven by many factors,[4] and countries also decide where they send different types of personnel. For example, members of the Filipino contingent in UNMIL stated in interviews that their air force contributed to a different mission than their army and navy. Similarly, officials in contributing states make mission-by-mission decisions about where to deploy certain types of personnel, such as women.

In explaining variations in total personnel contributed, Vincenzo Bove and Leandro Elia (2011) develop a supply-side argument and find that since the compensation per head is fixed across all contributing countries, the most prolific contributors are those with large populations and low costs of living because these countries find the compensation profitable and also have an abundance of available personnel. Moreover, Alex Bellamy and Paul Williams (2013) suggest that decisions about peacekeeping contributions are shaped by political rationales, whereby regimes might participate in peacekeeping because it helps them fulfill domestic political goals; economic rationales, whereby states receive resources for participation; security rationales, whereby deployments pursue national security interests regionally or globally; institutional rationales, whereby participation stems from civil-military relations; and normative rationales, whereby countries may provide peacekeepers to improve their self-images by providing a public good to the international community. Jacob Kathman and Molly Melin (2014) find that contributions increase as states spend less per soldier on their militaries, that states embroiled in ongoing rivalries with other states in the international system contribute more personnel to ongoing missions, and that fear of coup attempts motivate deployment levels. Gary Uzony (2015) finds that countries are more likely to contribute when the mission has the possibility of attenuating costly refugee flows into the contributing countries. Hugh Ward and Han Dorussen (2016) use a network approach and conclude that a contributing country's network placement relative to other contributors strongly shapes its allocation of peacekeepers.

While these contributor-level explanations help us understand general contributions, they do not much help us understand the representation of women in the deployments. Kerry F. Crawford, James H. Lebovic, and Julia M. Macdonald (2015) analyzed data on contributions from 2010 and 2011 and found that the supply of female peacekeepers may be driven by the strength of democratic values and the regard for women's rights in member states. Their findings support the notion that variation at the level of the contributing country matters greatly in explaining variation in the composition of the peacekeeping missions. We further explore the potential for contributing countries to assess the mission environment when allocating their contributions. Thus, we explore the variation in the deployment of female peacekeepers based on contributing-country characteristics and mission-level characteristics.

THE EXCLUSION OF WOMEN FROM PARTICIPATION IN PEACEKEEPING MISSIONS

In 2009, in anticipation of the UNSCR 1325's ten-year anniversary, Secretary-General Ban Ki-moon launched a campaign to increase the share of female peacekeepers to 10 percent in military units and 20 percent in police units by 2014. The UN did not meet this deadline. The responsibility for not meeting this goal lies with contributing countries. Thus, we start by examining countries that have provided the most female peacekeepers and examining which countries have contributed few if any women in their contributions. Figures 4.1 and 4.2 plot the average female ratio balances from each of the force-contributing countries (military contributors and police contributors, respectively) by the logged average of total military and police contributions.[5] The point here is not to see if there is a relationship between total contributions and balance but simply to sort out the high overall contributors from the low contributors because the high overall contributors matter the most in shaping mission composition.

Noticeably, the upper right quadrant, where countries provide both many peacekeepers and a relatively high proportion of female peacekeepers is blank for military contributions (figure 4.1) and sparse for police contributions (figure 4.2). The contributing countries that send the highest proportions of women do not send many

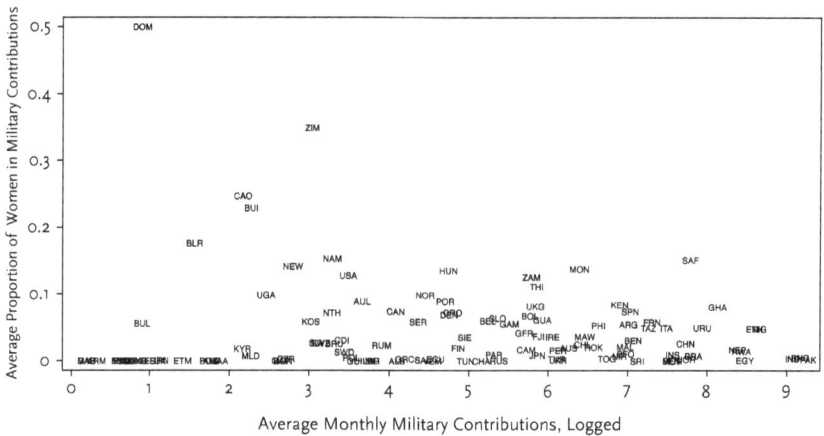

Figure 4.1. Contributor proportions of women in military contributions, by total military contributions.

Note: On a natural-log scale, a "5" represents about 148 personnel, and a "9" represents about 8,103. The country names that correspond to the abbreviations are provided in appendix 1.

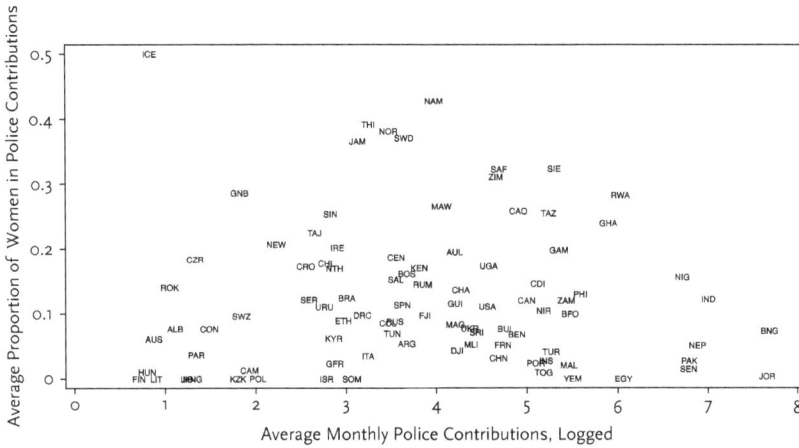

Figure 4.2. Contributor proportions of women in police contributions, by total police contributions.

Note: The country names that correspond to the abbreviations are provided in appendix 1.

peacekeepers, and vice versa. Figure 4.1 especially indicates that the countries that contribute the most military personnel are some of the worst performers in terms of the representation of women in their contributions. The cluster of countries in the lower right include India, Pakistan, and Bangladesh, which contribute the most troops but also include few women in their contributions.

The top five contributing countries in terms of proportions of women sent are the Dominican Republic, Zimbabwe, Cameroon, Burundi, and Belarus for military contributions and Iceland, Namibia, Thailand, Norway, and Sweden for police contributions. The top five contributing countries in terms of total women sent are South Africa, Nigeria, Ghana, Ethiopia, and Uruguay for military contributions and Bangladesh, India, Nigeria, Rwanda, and Ghana for police contributions. Most of these countries contributing the highest numbers and proportions of women to military and police roles are not the developed, liberal countries one might expect, in part because many developed countries do not much contribute any personnel to UN missions and instead conduct peacekeeping-type activities through other organizations (e.g., NATO, EU), through ad hoc coalitions, or through supplying the funds for PKOs.

One of the main limitations on contributing countries' ability to send more women to PKOs stems from a lack of availability of female personnel from their domestic security sectors.[6] The gender adviser in the Directorate of Operations Headquarters for the Swedish Armed Forces, Susanne Axmacher, notes that one major challenge to improving the representation of women in peacekeeping missions is recruiting women into the missions when there are hardly any women in the armed forces from which to draw.[7] About 11 percent of Swedish military personnel are women, which is relatively high by global standards yet still constrains the ability to send an abundance of female personnel.[8] Countries with few women in domestic forces simply have a depleted ability to contribute substantial proportions of women to peacekeeping missions.

As discussed in chapter 3, we contend that one of the main factors contributing to the low numbers of women in national militaries and police forces is the perceived gendered dichotomy of men as warriors and women as peacemakers. A related common justification to keep women out of certain military roles is that women would disrupt group cohesion. Recruitment efforts in national police and militaries thus may be less likely to target women, or women themselves might not be socialized to consider themselves good fits for such vocations. National militaries' and police institutions' low numbers of women, due to rigid gender norms that deem it appropriate for men to participate in security institutions but not necessarily women, thus have downstream effects on contributions to peacekeeping missions.

As a first cut at exploring the relationship between the representation of women in the national militaries and police forces and contributions to peacekeeping missions, figures 4.3 and 4.4 plot the average proportion of women in each country's contributions (military and police, respectively) against the average proportion of women in each country's domestic armed forces and police forces, respectively.[9] A positive relationship appears with regard to the military contributions. Those countries with higher proportions of women in their domestic armed forces, such as New Zealand, South Africa, Hungary, Namibia, and the United States, tend to send higher proportions of women in their military peacekeeping contributions. Again, there is a lot of variation among these countries, and they are not all rich, highly economically developed countries. In terms of police components, we do not see as much of a discernible positive relationship between the proportions of women in domestic forces and the proportions of women contributed. Slovakia and Iceland have sent the highest proportions of women in their contributions to police components, but, to be sure, both countries have contributed very few total personnel.

It is interesting that even for the military contributions, there is plenty of variation around the positive trend. This means that other factors besides the domestic

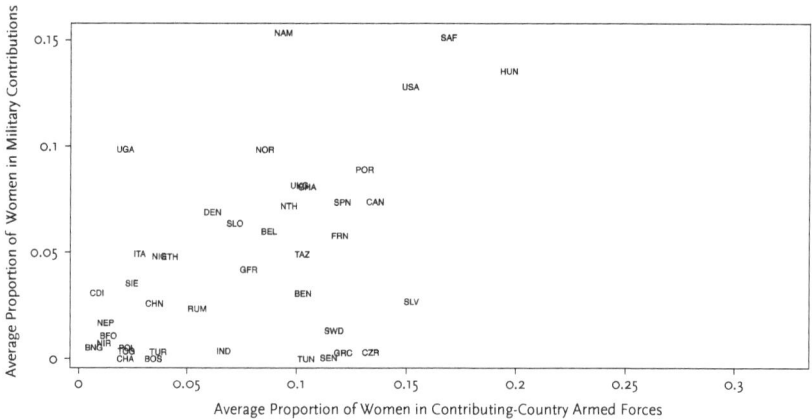

Figure 4.3. Contributor proportions of women in military contributions, by domestic proportions.
Note: The country names that correspond to the abbreviations are provided in appendix 1.

Equal Opportunity Peacekeeping

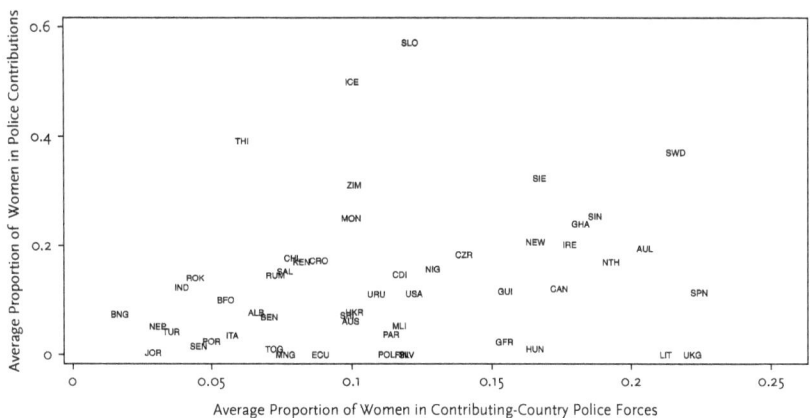

Figure 4.4. Contributor proportions of women in police contributions, by domestic proportions.
Note: The country names that correspond to the abbreviations are provided in appendix 1.

representation of women in the armed forces can be important predictors of the representation of women in peacekeeping contributions. Especially for police contributions, the composition of the forces sent does not simply mimic the composition of the domestic forces.

Thus far, the approach has only considered a bivariate relationship between domestic force sex demographics and those of the peacekeeping contributions. A regression framework can help control for confounding factors that, if ignored, would mislead our inferences regarding how the representation of women in force contributions varies with the domestic representation of women in military and police forces. Since a number of our variables only have annual variation, we use a dataset in which we have one observation for each force-contributing country for each mission to which forces were sent for each year (a contributor-mission-year unit of analysis). The dependent variable is the proportion of women in force contributions.[10] We estimate the association that variables have with this measure of female representation by using a mixed effects generalized linear model, with random intercepts estimated for each contributing country and each mission.[11] We provide a table of coefficients in appendix 1.

Figures 4.5 and 4.6 plot the predicted proportions of women in peacekeeping troop and police contributions for different levels of the domestic ratios in the armed forces and police forces, respectively.[12] Like the above scatterplots, the regression results suggest that the representation of women in the domestic military armed forces correlates positively with the representation of women in the contributed military forces. The relationship is statistically significant with regard to military contributions but not with regard to police contributions. In terms of effect magnitudes, it is important to remember that increases by one to two percentage points in the percentage of women on missions can be quite substantial, given typical current percentages. These results suggest that some of the culpability for failing to achieve greater female ratio balance in peacekeeping forces lies on the contributing countries for failing to attract and recruit more women into their national militaries. One important caveat

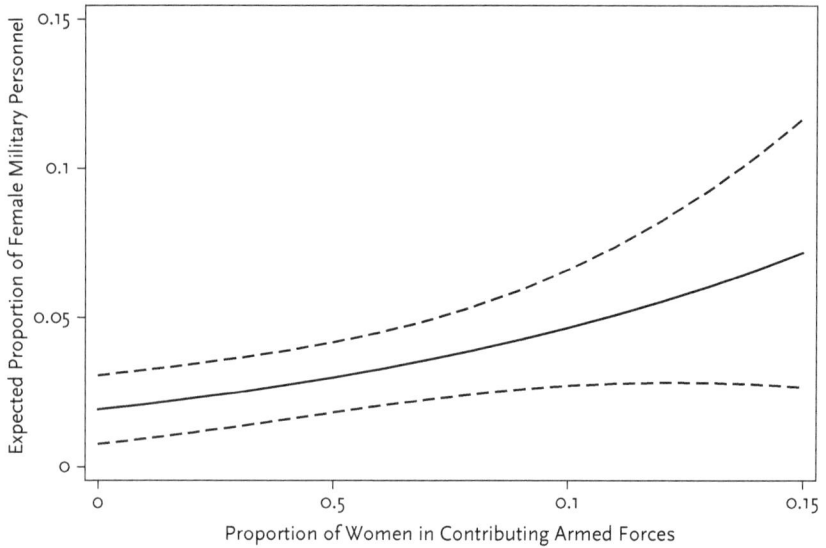

Note: p = 0.029 in a two-tailed test

Figure 4.5. Predicted proportion of women in military contributions, by domestic proportions.

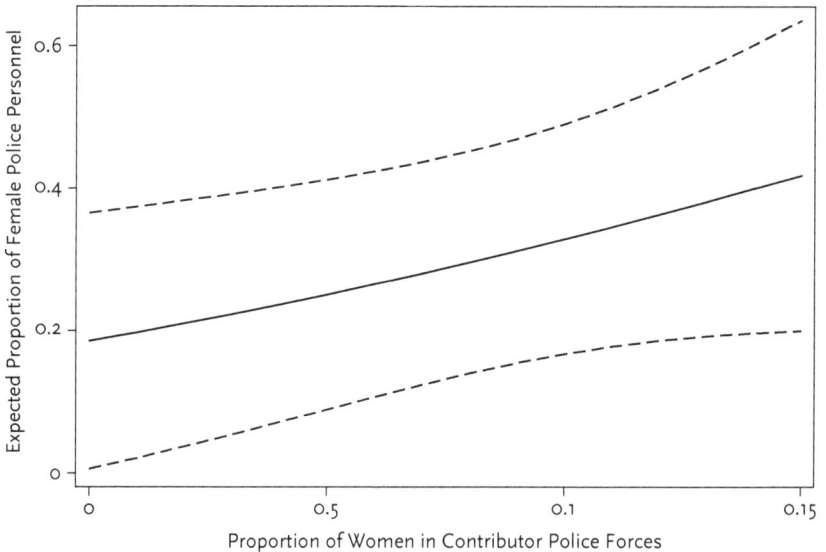

Note: p = 0.196 in a two-tailed test

Figure 4.6. Predicted proportion of women in police contributions, by domestic proportions.

to these findings is that, as discussed in appendix 1, many of the observations of the representation of women in domestic security forces are missing, and we urge caution in generalizing the findings beyond the set of countries that have reported the proportions of women in their national militaries and police forces.[13]

Are contributing countries also culpable in failing to recruit more women from their domestic forces to serve in peacekeeping missions? While at first it may not seem as if there are clear mechanisms to recruit women, contributing countries have direct influence on the process of including female personnel in their force contributions, which became apparent in interviews with peacekeepers on UNMIL.[14] It is important to first note that the recruitment process for military components is different from that for police components, which may explain why the correlation between the representation of women in the domestic forces and that in the peacekeeping contributions was weaker for police components.

When countries send military troops to peacekeeping missions, they usually send entire contingents and are not likely motivated to find women in other contingents to add to the contingent that is deploying. In other words, if women are already a part of the contingent, then they also deploy, but if they are not, then they do not deploy. If women only deploy if their unit deploys, then female deployment to peacekeeping missions depends crucially on the proportion of women in different units of the contributing country's military. This is also similar to the case of FPUs, where large contingents are sent based on the home structure of the police force. Many countries, however, do not have a national police force or police battalions. As a result, FPUs are sometimes formed for the specific function of deploying to missions and include a mix of different in-country units. That said, not all military contributions are contingents. Countries also send individual military officers in small groups as observers or to direct operations at UN mission headquarters. In this case, individuals are either recruited for positions or apply for positions, which means that there could be more intentionality in militaries for selecting female observers and senior officers.

For UNPOL, individuals are either recruited or apply positions. The representation of women in UNPOL units thus depends less on the pool of women in different units and more on the willingness of women to apply and the willingness of senior officers to accept applications from women for deployment. Recruiters or individual decision-makers are well positioned to exercise significant discretion over recruiting and selecting people for police contributions and maybe military observers (although there are sometimes prohibitions in place for women to be observers as we see below). For example, in Bangladesh, female peacekeepers suggested that there was a policy to include more women in peacekeeping, but it was not always followed. In contrast, in Zimbabwe, which is one of the top contributors of women police and military personnel, Zimbabwean female police officers said that the country commanders or province heads nominated individuals who applied for the job. These province heads ostensibly are doing relatively well in recruiting women to send abroad and thus may serve as role models for other countries. Thus, the proportions of women in the domestic police forces may matter less to the composition of UNPOL contributions than the rigidity of gender hierarchies in the domestic police forces.

DEPLOYING FEMALE PEACEKEEPERS TO SAFE MISSIONS

While the presence of female peacekeepers may be at least partially explained by the availability of female personnel from national militaries and police institutions, this is only part of the story. Contributing countries also make decisions about *where* to send female peacekeepers. We argue and find evidence that female peacekeepers tend to deploy to the safest missions. As a case in point, in August 2014 Major General Kristin Lund of Norway was appointed force commander of UNFICYP.[15] The UN hailed this as a major step toward gender parity in missions.[16] However, she was deployed to arguably the "safest" peacekeeping mission in the world. Moreover, in 2012, forty peacekeepers died as part of the UNAMID mission to Darfur. That year, the percentage of women in military contingents in the UNAMID mission was only 3.7 percent. In comparison, the UNFICYP mission to Cyprus experienced no peacekeeper fatalities and had 8.7 percent women as part of its military contingents. Does this cursory comparison reflect a general trend for women to deploy in greater proportions to the safest missions?

Figure 4.7 plots the missions in terms of their maximum military contingent (troops and military observers) size and average proportion of women from 2006 to 2013. From this plot, we can see that the missions that fare the best in terms of the representation of women tend to be rather small and in countries that are not involved in active conflicts. Those missions that are the largest and in the most challenging environments—for example, MONUC/MONUSCO (DRC), UNAMID (Darfur), UNMIS (Sudan) and MINUSTAH (Haiti)—tend to have lower ratios of women to men. Figure 4.8 provides the same type of information for police components (individual police and FPUs) of the peacekeeping missions. Again, we see that the missions with the highest proportions of women tend to be the smallest ones, while the missions that have the most police personnel and are in particularly challenging areas—for example, UNAMID (Darfur), MONUC/MONUSCO (DRC) and MINUSTAH (Haiti)—tend to have lower percentages of women.

While the UNAMA (Afghanistan) and UNISFA (Sudan) missions deployed to relatively precarious conflict zones and received the highest proportions of female police personnel, these missions' mandates are much more oriented toward political and observer responsibilities than toward the physical provision of security. This is an

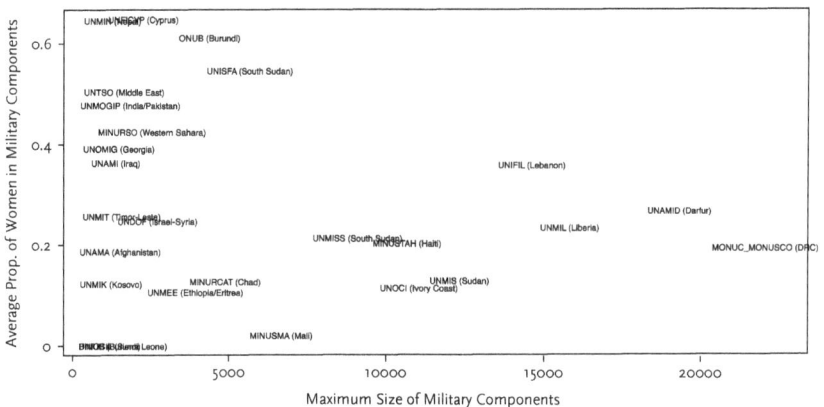

Figure 4.7. Proportions of women in military components of UN missions, by size.

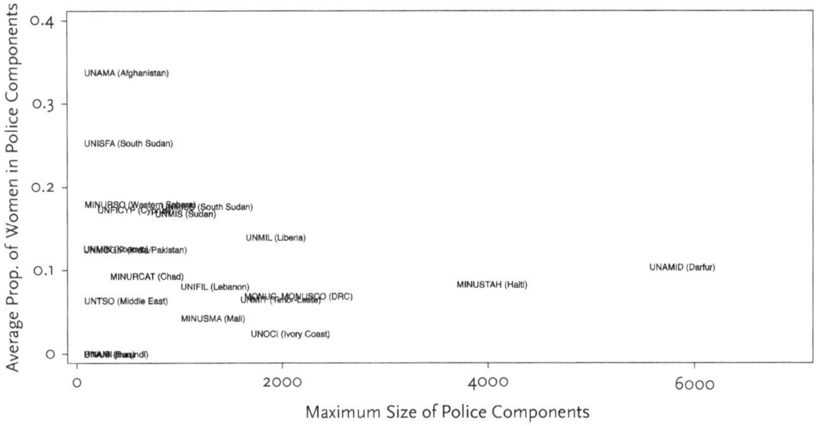

Figure 4.8. Proportions of women in police components of UN missions, by size.

important distinction because it highlights the fact that the function of peacekeepers is not the same in all missions. Larger missions and missions with more comprehensive mandates, such as multidimensional PKOs or peace enforcement missions (or what Bellamy, Williams, and Griffin [2010] call "peace enforcement, assisting transitions, transitional administration and peace support operations"), are arguably more dangerous because they entail security roles that may include combat and more interactions with locals. These missions often not only involve keeping the peace, enforcing peace agreements, and building institutions but also can involve the assumption of administrative authority over particular territory and can even make and enforce the law using military force (Bellamy, Williams, and Griffin, 2010). Such activities make peacekeepers more susceptible to not only violence but also disease and accidents (such as vehicle accidents). In contrast, observer missions (or what Bellamy and Williams [2013] call "traditional peacekeeping") may be less risky because they entail minimum use of force and are much less likely to encounter hostility in their interactions with members of the local community. In these missions, the typical job is to observe, fact-find, and create a political space for peace.

These plots speak to the question about whether the women who are deployed to peacekeeping missions tend to deploy to the "safest" ones. In chapter 3, we described the potential emergence of a gendered protection norm that privileges men's role as protectors while women are treated as a special category that warrants greater protection. It is plausible that this norm extends even to the women who are supposed to be the protectors—the women who serve on peacekeeping missions. To get a more thorough analysis of whether female peacekeepers are indeed deployed to the safest missions and to understand whether countries are influenced by the gendered protection norm, we must look closer at the data, specifically at force-contributing countries' incentives to send more female peacekeepers.

We consider how the norm of prioritizing the protection of women from harm can affect variation in the proportions of women that force-contributing countries send. Carpenter (2006a, 2006b, 2003) has argued that although the norm of protecting civilians is an important development in limiting the humanitarian consequences of armed conflict, the gendered element of focusing on women has placed male non-combatants at greater risk for abuse and death. We consider an additional adverse effect of the norm of protecting women, which is that it runs directly counter to initiatives to empower women in the security sector. If female peacekeepers are to be fully utilized and have maximal impact in promoting gender equality in their missions and in the local communities they serve, the women in the peacekeeping missions need to be seen not as "protectees" but as protectors.

We argue that a norm of protecting women from harm creates a tendency for women to be held back—or to hold themselves back—from some of the key missions where peacekeepers of any gender are needed. That is, peacekeepers potentially have maximum impact in the situations that are most insecure, so the ability for increases in the representation of women to transform the way peacekeeping is done and perceived is quite limited if the increases in representation are confined to relatively safe missions.

Moreover, we explore whether women are also less likely to deploy to the locations that have experienced high rates of sexual violence.[17] A history of sexual violence in an area indicates deep societal issues with gender power imbalances and a high potential for female peacekeepers to improve operational effectiveness by working with segments of the population who cannot be engaged by male peacekeepers as well, due to typical cultural norms. If women have less representation in missions to such locations, this represents a mismatch between the deployment of women and their potential for maximum impact. In line with the argument about the gendered protection norm, such locations, because they have a history of sexual violence, may be deemed unsafe particularly for women. Those in charge of deployments in contributing countries may be more reluctant to send female peacekeepers to places where they are at greater risk of sexual violence.

The gendered protection norm might constrain the representation of women in peacekeeping contributions to the riskiest conflict environments via two mechanisms. First, the withholding of female peacekeepers from the riskiest missions could reflect the concerns of policy-makers and elites in the contributing countries. Whether out of trying to avoid political blowback in case casualties to women deployed on the peacekeeping missions lead to widespread criticism from a public influenced by the gendered protection norm,[18] or out of their own sense that women should be protected, we expect political and military elites to be less likely to send women on missions with higher risks of casualties. For example, a group captain in the Bangladesh Air Force, Sade Uddin Ahmed Sohel, who has been responsible for deployments in the Bangladeshi armed forces, said in an interview:

> Although officially risk factors are not taken into consideration while selecting female officer in mission areas, but till today female officers are deployed with contingent only where other officers and soldiers resides in a secured camp area. They remain as a team. Female officers have not yet been deployed as military observer where they are generally unarmed and remain alone in a remote area just to observe and report the hostile activities if any. Definitely, safety, security and cultural factors

are taken into consideration while selecting female officers for mission areas. I have seen in two mission areas like East Timor and D R Congo, other countries are also taking risk factors in consideration. They also deploy female officer or female soldiers with contingent only.[19]

We note a few observations from this statement. First, he confirms that female officers are selected to serve in troop contingents and not as observers, which we suggested above was one reason for disparities between police and military female peacekeeping contributions. Second, he confirms that safety and security are taken into consideration in terms of deciding where female peacekeepers are deployed. It is important to note that it is not official policy in Bangladesh to do so but that in practice such considerations are still influential.

Decisions by elites can be at the point of determining deployments or at the point of recruiting volunteers to go to the missions. Countries differ on whether troop contributions consist of personnel who have volunteered or who have been assigned. In some instances, potential peacekeeping recruits apply for positions; in others, their superiors select them without their undergoing an application process. In both situations, the gendered protection norm can shape the composition of deployments. When applicants volunteer, it is plausible that recruitment efforts will be less likely to target women for the missions that entail the most risk to the personnel. When recruits are assigned, commanders or supervisors may be intentional in not sending women to particularly dangerous missions, as mentioned by Group Captain Sohel.

Second, the women themselves might not be socialized to consider themselves good fits for the riskiest missions or for the most vulnerable roles in them. Again, in some countries, female military and police personnel have considerable agency in volunteering for missions. When a norm of protection prevails, women might subconsciously be less likely to consider it appropriate for themselves to be part of missions that engage in combat or otherwise deal with dangerous environments.[20] Women are, at an early age, socialized to identify with roles that experience protection instead of identifying with vocations that protect (Goldstein, 2003). Women are also socialized to avoid danger (Harris and Miller, 2000). In addition, whether genetic or socialized, evidence has shown that women tend to be less risk-seeking in their psychological personality profiles than men (McDermott and Cowden, 2001; Byrnes, Miller, and Schafer, 1999).

To the extent that the foregoing logic holds and that a gendered norm of protection shapes the incentives of policy-makers to send female personnel into harm's way and/or the incentives of the female military personnel to step into high-risk environments, it can be an important barrier to greater improvements in the representation of women in many peacekeeping missions. The foregoing logic has the observable implication that the proportions of women in peacekeeping missions should be especially low in the conflict environments that pose the greatest security risks to peacekeepers.

A prima facie glance at figures 4.7 and 4.8 earlier suggested that some of the most challenging missions from a security perspective receive lower proportions of women. We now use the same regression models to assess the relationship between the mission environment and the proportions of women that contributing countries send to each mission. To begin, we use three measures of the conflict environment, in terms of the risk to the peacekeepers. The first is the fatality rate for peacekeepers. Using UN DPKO data for each year, we summed up the cumulative number of peacekeepers who have died on each mission and then divided by the number of years the mission has been active and the number of peacekeepers deployed. The resulting variable ranges from 0 (multiple missions) to 0.25 (UNMIK) fatalities per year per peacekeeper, with a median of 0.001.[21] The second measure is the maximum severity of conflict during the previous ten years. For this indicator, we used the estimated battle deaths for the worst year in the previous ten years, from the Uppsala Conflict Data Program (UCDP) Armed Conflict data.[22] The third measure is the per capita GDP of the destination country, from the World Bank, which captures other elements of risk—not just risks of violence but also health risks—related to deployments in the least developed countries with weak or failed-state governments.[23]

Using these measures of the conflict environment, we find that the observed data comport well with some of our expectations. For military deployments, the relationship between the proportions of women in the contributions and previous battle deaths is negative and statistically significant. Moreover, proportions of women in military contributions tend to be higher when the per capita GDP in the host country is greater, and this relationship is also statistically significant. Contrary to expectations, however, the observed relationship between proportions of women in military contributions and peacekeeper fatalities is close to zero and not statistically significant. The respective relationships involving the proportions of women in police contributions also do not reach statistical significance.

Figures 4.9 and 4.10 depict the relationships that the proportion of women in military components has with violence severity and with per capita GDP in the

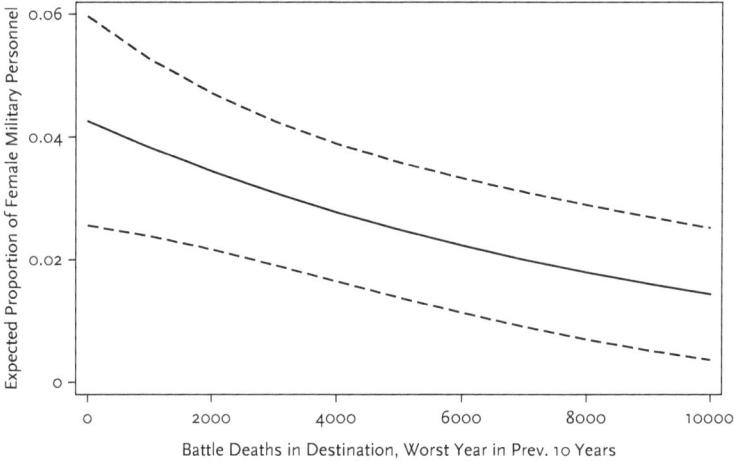

Note: p = 0.025 in a two-tailed test

Figure 4.9. Predicted proportion of women in military contributions, by severity of violence in destination.

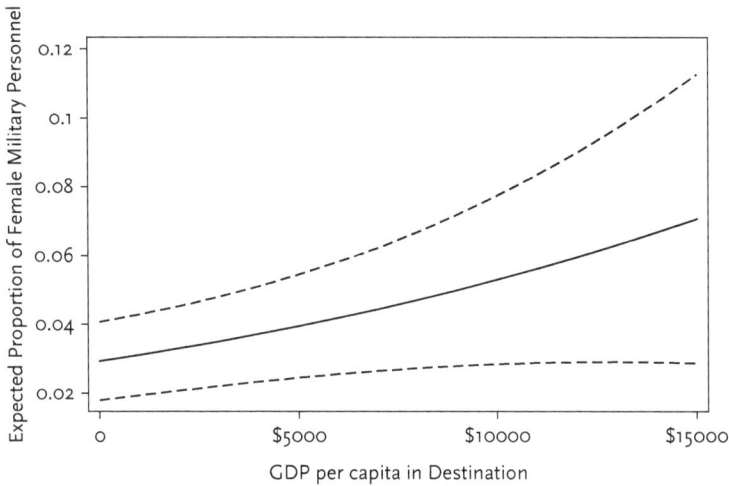

Figure 4.10. Predicted proportion of women in military contributions, by per capita GDP in destination.

destination countries.[24] Notably, the expected proportion of women in a contributor's military contributions drops by half when the number of battle deaths in the bloodiest year in the previous decade increases from 0 to 6,000 in the host country. Moreover, the expected proportion of women contributed about doubles when the per capita GDP of the host country increases from $5,000 to $15,000. The evidence is consistent with the argument that norms of protecting women are suppressing the representation of female peacekeepers in conflict environments that pose the greatest risks to the peacekeepers.[25]

In addition to the measures listed above, we also test whether prior levels of sexual violence in host countries may inhibit some contributing countries from sending female peacekeepers. Elites in contributing countries and women themselves may be more reluctant to go to places where gender violence has been higher because it may pose particular "gendered" danger for them. On the other hand such places are arguably where female peacekeepers may be most needed. If, as many suggest, female peacekeepers are better at helping survivors of SGBV, then their presence is most important in missions where there have been high levels of such violence.

Thus, we consider models that look at the history of sexual violence in a host country as a predictor of the representation of women in peacekeeping contributions. We use the Sexual Violence in Armed Conflict data created by Dara Cohen and Ragnhild Nordås (2014) to identify which host countries experienced widespread sexual violence in the most recent civil wars. Of course, a measure of whether sexual violence was high during a civil conflict may not capture the level of violence in the postconflict period, but some work has suggested that such violence continues well after armed violence has abated (Meintjes, Turshen, and Pillay, 2002). When this dichotomous variable is included in the models above, we see a strong negative association related to the deployment of women in military contingents. As shown in

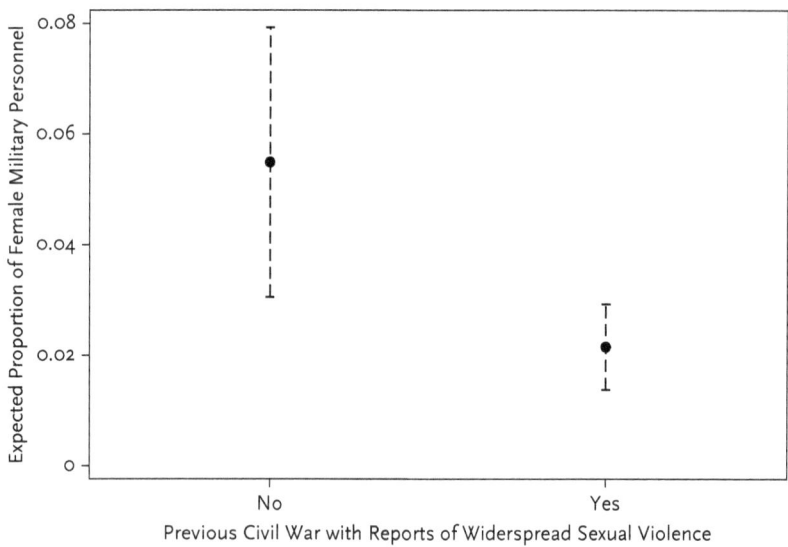

Figure 4.11. Predicted proportion of women in military contributions, by history of widespread sexual violence in destination.

figure 4.11, much lower proportions of women in peacekeeping military contingents are expected to deploy to countries that have a history of widespread sexual violence, and this relationship is statistically significant. Moreover, with the inclusion of this variable, the associations with battle-related fatalities and per capita GDP in the host countries no longer achieve statistical significance.[26] In other words, it appears that the representation of women in troop contributions is especially responsive to patterns of sexual violence in the destination countries. Contributing countries appear especially hesitant to send female peacekeepers to places where gendered violence may be higher.

This observed relationship only applies to military contingents, as we do not observe a statistically significant relationship related to police contingents. We can only surmise why the protection norm may be stronger for the military than for the police, but one reason may be due to differences in the selection criteria for military versus police personnel. For example, as mentioned, police personnel are more likely to apply individually for positions or to be selected individually. In particular, female police officers may be more likely to volunteer for missions with high levels of sexual violence because they feel that they are able to make more of a difference. Indeed, chapter 6 demonstrates that many female police officers volunteered for peacekeeping missions because they wanted to help local women. In addition, it is also possible that gender dichotomies may not be as strong in police forces as in the military. Decision-makers may be less reluctant to send female police officers to places with higher levels of sexual violence because addressing rape is an important function of police forces worldwide. Either way, the differences between contributing countries' female military and police personnel are noteworthy and a ripe area for more research.

If there is greater potential for female peacekeepers to have maximum impact when there has been widespread sexual violence—for reasons related to operational effectiveness or the fact that sexual violence is a symptom of deep problems related to gender power imbalances—then it is especially noteworthy that female peacekeepers are much less likely to deploy to such missions. As discussed in chapter 2, we find evidence that peacekeeping missions go to countries with higher levels of sexual violence, but it appears that even though peacekeeping missions may be deploying to address the protection needs of locals with respect to sexual violence, female peacekeepers are not the ones providing the protection.

Overall, the analysis in this section has provided evidence confirming that a protection norm exists among contributing countries. They appear to send women to the safest missions, especially with regard to military contributions. The implication is that women are not being sent to missions where the security situation is worse, despite the fact that peacekeeping has the potential to make the biggest difference to the security environment there, particularly, as some have noted, when it comes to addressing SGBV.

DEPLOYING FEMALE PEACEKEEPERS FROM UNSAFE CONTRIBUTING COUNTRIES

While we have considered how the dominance of the warrior identity and the militarization process contribute to excluding women from participating in the security sector, including PKOs, and how the gendered protection norm may contribute to the deployment of female peacekeepers to safe missions, these gender dichotomies may, in some instances, actually play a role in increasing the proportions of female peacekeepers sent by contributing countries. For some contributing countries, sending women to peacekeeping missions, rather than keeping them at home to serve in the nation's defense, can be more consistent with the prevailing gender dichotomies. The gender power imbalance in these countries may work in a counterintuitive way by actually serving to help increase the proportion of women sent beyond what would be expected from the representation of women in the security sectors of the contributing countries.

While one factor that influences whether countries send women to peacekeeping missions is the proportion of women in the national militaries and police forces, figures 4.3 and 4.4 show that some countries send higher proportions of women to peacekeeping missions than they have in their national militaries or police forces. Notably, Uganda, Namibia, Côte d'Ivoire, Italy, Norway, Nigeria, Sierra Leone, Denmark, Ethiopia, and Nepal lead the list in sending higher proportions of women in their peacekeeping military contributions than they have in their national militaries. If women are perceived as natural peacemakers, just as men are perceived as natural warriors, then two explanations might be at work here. First, the notion of a "postnational defense" (Kronsell, 2012)—the reorientation of armed forces toward a wider array of peaceful objectives abroad—might be emerging in some of these countries. Such an emergence would help explain the presence on the above list of some of the European countries, which are relatively peaceful and are increasingly finding uses of their militaries not for national defense but for improving human security abroad. In such countries the norms are changing, such that it is more natural to expect female personnel to be included in peacekeeping missions because military recruitment in the first place is based less on conceptions that the military's primary purpose is the protection of the homeland and more on conceptions that the primary purpose is to contribute to international peace.

Note, however, that the list of countries that tend to deploy higher proportions of women than the proportions in the domestic armed forces only includes a few relatively peaceful countries that have less need of their militaries for national defense. Rather, it is filled more with countries that have need of their militaries to confront significant threats to their security, such as Uganda, Côte d'Ivoire, Nigeria, Sierra Leone, Ethiopia, and Nepal. These countries have all recently experienced or continue to experience civil war. To explain the patterns of peacekeeping contributions from these conflict-prone countries, a second explanation expects that some countries reserve their male personnel for more combat-oriented activities at home. The protection norm discounts the role of women as protectors; therefore, countries that need their militaries for the protection of the state are perhaps more willing to send women on peacekeeping missions because they are seen as less useful at home. Relatedly, the degree to which peacekeepers are in harm's way also can be considered relative to the security situation in the contributing country. If peacekeeping missions are "peace-oriented," then service in the missions might actually be more peaceful and safe than in stateside service in some home countries. Countries that have a recent history of major civil strife and/or international war thus might not be so reluctant to send women on peacekeeping missions. Indeed, given that peacekeeping is often perceived to be too "feminine,"[27] for conflict-prone countries to send higher proportions of women instead of keeping them home to fight imminent security threats comports well with existing notions of appropriate roles for female security personnel.

These two explanations—that peaceful contributing countries tend to send higher proportions of women to peacekeeping missions as part of their post-national investments in international peace, or that conflict-prone countries tend to send higher proportions as part of their focus on imminent national security threats—share a common thread. From the gendered protection norm and association of women with peace activities, women are not perceived as valuable to the protection of the national defense. These explanations, however, differ in their expectation of the relationship between recent conflict history and the composition of peacekeeping contributions. To examine whether either of these competing expectations does better in explaining the sex composition of peacekeeping contributions, we include in the regression model used above a measure of recent conflict severity in the contributing country. This variable is coded like conflict severity in the destination country—we use the battle deaths from the deadliest year in the previous ten years, with the value of zero given to those contributing countries that have not participated in an armed conflict in the previous decade.

We find that, for both military and police contributions, higher recent conflict severity involving the contributing countries leads to higher proportions of women

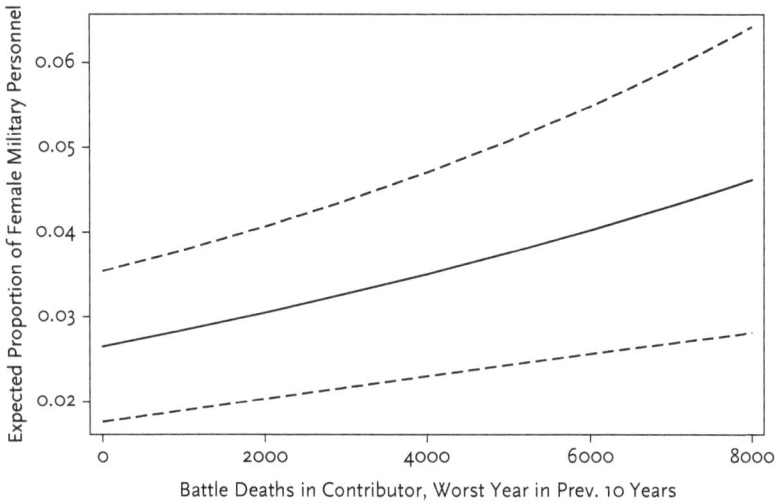

Figure 4.12. Predicted proportion of women in military contributions, by conflict severity in contributor.

sent to peacekeeping missions, and the effect is statistically significant at conventional levels for the military contributions and at a 90 percent confidence level for the police contributions. Figure 4.12 presents the substantive effects for the military contributions. The evidence supports the notion that countries that have recently had to fight to protect the national defense are more willing to send their female personnel abroad, perhaps because peacekeeping missions are perceived as relatively less risky for the women and/or perhaps the female personnel are less valued as protectors of national defense.

It appears that manifestations of gender power imbalances and associated gender roles—women as peacemakers and subjects of protection—can have counterintuitive effects of actually increasing the proportion of women sent to peacekeeping missions, precisely because peacekeeping may be perceived as "peace-oriented" (Whitworth, 2007; Kronsell, 2012). These effects must be understood in combination with the additional effect that women are on average being sent to safer missions. Gender dichotomies persist, and women are still perceived as peaceful and weak. True progress in addressing the exclusion of women from certain types of missions and roles requires a dismantling of the gendered power structures so that women can fully participate in all capacities in the military, police, and peacekeeping.

WILL CHANGES IN SOCIETAL GENDER EQUALITY AFFECT WOMEN'S PARTICIPATION IN PEACEKEEPING?

An expectation that gender power imbalances are at the root of the observed exclusion patterns of female peacekeepers yields an expectation that those exclusion patterns will attenuate with changes in the underlying societal gender norms. This is an observable implication of our underlying theory and would be consistent with our emphasis on equal opportunity peacekeeping as an end to which the international community should aspire. Other scholars have found that changes in gender equality in society have led to higher proportions of women joining the military. According to Segal (1995), increases in women's participation are likely when a country's social structure changes, military institutions reform, and a country's gender norms shift.[28] Similarly, Carreiras (2006) finds that changes in gender norms in society have led to increases in women's participation in the military. In the peacekeeping literature, Kerry F. Crawford, James H. Lebovic, and Julia M. Macdonald (2015) find that gender norms in society do affect the participation rates of military personnel and female peacekeepers. Notably, these scholars suggest that gender norms in society, such as strict dichotomies for the role of women and men, contribute to the gendered division of labor and thus exclusion of women from the security sector. By implication, countries that have opened up more roles for women in society, particularly ones in traditionally masculine spaces, should include more women in their militaries and police forces.

While the link between a country's gender norms and the representation of women in the security sector follows from existing work (Segal, 1995; Carreiras, 2006), we explore the direct link—separate from an indirect path from gender norms to representation in domestic security sectors to representation in PKOs—between the underlying gender norms and the representation of women in peacekeeping missions. That is, we explore whether countries with better records of gender equality are more inclined to send higher proportions of women in their peacekeeping contributions, even when accounting for the propensity for such countries to also have higher proportions of women in their domestic forces. For example, in our interview with the top-ranking female police officer in UNMIL in 2012, from Ghana, a country that does relatively well in contributing women to missions, she said that in Ghana there is little societal discrimination against women and there was no problem for her to participate in a PKO.[29]

At least two logics could support the potential for a direct link. First, women are an important constituency in countries with strong records of gender equality. We might expect that the intended beneficiaries of ongoing reforms to improve the representation of women in peacekeeping missions are transparently women, a potentially huge constituency. Political motivation to comply is a fundamental requirement for moving forward with reforms such as those regarding the UNSCR 1325 agenda, and such motivation grows when women's rights are championed in a particular society.[30] In other words, as the political opportunism model of social movements indicates,[31] when the conditions are such that gender norms have shifted in society, commitment to increasing women's representation may be stronger.[32] The easier it is for women to have a voice and shape policy, the more likely will be a strong effort to comply with international efforts that further improve the protection of women's rights.

This argument parallels the work of Xinyuan Dai (2005), who has argued that compliance with international agreements will be most likely when the groups that benefit most from compliance have an electoral advantage. Emily Hafner-Burton (2008), Oona Hathaway (2007), and Beth Simmons (2009) also contend that countries will participate in and strengthen human rights regimes only when it is politically expedient to do so. The electoral advantage that women can muster in those countries with strong women's rights and responsive electoral institutions would lead us to expect that such states are prime candidates for participation in the UNSCR 1325 regime.[33] Amitav Acharya (2004) posits a related theory: that states' ability to adopt norms promoted by international actors is contingent on local actors' ability to make those norms congruent with local identities. Having a preexisting tradition of protecting women's rights as a result of structural changes in society should require less effort to generate enthusiasm within countries to participate in the UNSCR 1325 regime. By implication, such countries should also be more likely to heed calls for sending peacekeeping contingents with stronger representations of women.

Second, it is possible that as women engage in more public roles, for example becoming more active in the formal labor force, then their roles slowly become less defined along gendered lines. In other words, if women are observed more in public, professional roles, then this may lead to a socialization process that attenuates gender power imbalances, allowing for the emergence of norms that establish women as being just as capable as men and that push back against the protection norm.[34] One example of such an "exposure" mechanism is the removal of the combat exclusion in the United States. Until 2013, the U.S. government banned women from participation in active combat in the military. However, women's roles in the wars in Iraq and Afghanistan often entailed engaging in combat situations, which demonstrated that women could participate in combat roles. As a result, the United States removed the combat exclusion provision. While this example is specific to the military, broader changes in perceptions of gender roles may have a similar effect on peacekeeping recruitment and deployment decisions. The expectation again is that countries with better records in their existing practices of gender equality are more likely to contribute higher proportions of female peacekeepers.

We explore whether the empirical data confirm this idea that countries with stronger records of gender equality will send higher proportions of women in their peacekeeping contributions. As one measure of gender equality in the contributing countries, we focus on the percentage of women participating in the labor force, using data from the World Bank.[35] This measure captures the extent to which societies are permissive of women taking on nontraditional roles and is an important gauge of the practice of gender equality in a society. Even though macro, country-level variables do not most accurately reflect gender norms in society, they can reveal information about the state of women's presence in public life.[36] Using such a proxy, we are then able to test whether countries that have less strict gender dichotomies, measured in terms of the participation of women in the labor force, have better participation rates of women in peacekeeping missions.

The results indicate a positive and statistically significant additive relationship between gender equality at home and the representation of women in peacekeeping military and police contributions. Figure 4.13 portrays the results for the military

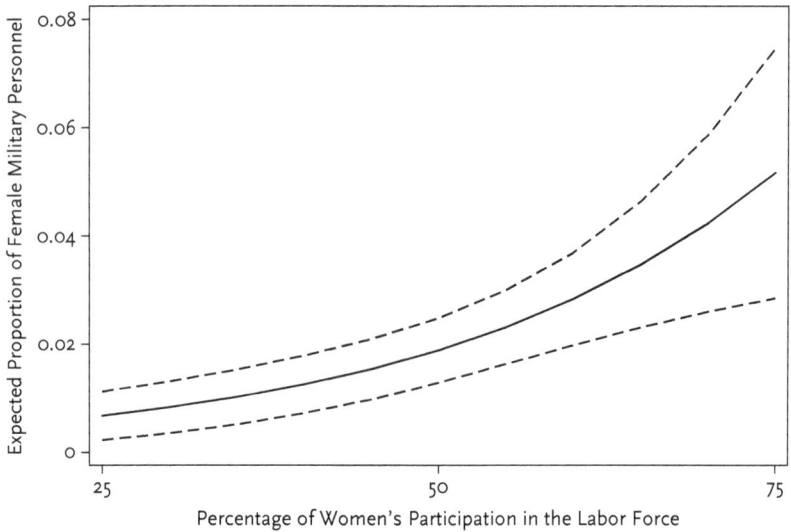

Figure 4.13. Predicted proportion of women in military contributions, by female participation in labor force.

contributions. Countries with more women in the labor force tend to contribute higher proportions of women to peacekeeping missions, even when accounting for higher proportions of women in the domestic armed forces.

The more gender equality is practiced in a society, the higher the probability that the country will send greater proportions of female peacekeepers to missions. The results corroborate findings by Segal (1995), Carreiras (2006), and Crawford, Lebovic, and Macdonald (2015) that gender norms in society affect the participation rates of women in the security sector. And all of this fits with the idea that dismantling gender hierarchies reduces women's exclusion from traditionally masculine environments. A broader implication thus emerges that as states' gender norms change, the more they are likely to send female military and police personnel to peacekeeping missions.

Thus far, we have explored the relationship between the participation of women in the labor force and the representation of women in peacekeeping contributions. We have not explored the relationship between the practice of gender equality in contributing countries and the propensity for women to actually deploy to missions with the greatest threats to security. We consider the potential for the protection norm to remain strong in the countries that have made substantial progress with regard to women's rights. Carpenter (2005, 2006a) has argued that transnational human rights advocacy networks have been especially important in diffusing the gendered protection norm. One implication might be to expect that force-contributing countries in which there is a lot of NGO activity related to human rights, and consequently advocacy of women and children's protection, should still be wary of sending women into the most dangerous environments.

To investigate, we constructed additional regression models (shown in appendix 1) to consider the potential for a conditional, or interactive, relationship in which the strength of gender equality at home affects the strength of the correlation between the indicators of host country riskiness and the representation of women in peace-keeping contributions. If the practice of gender equality at home affects the strength of the gendered norm of protection, then we would see countries respond to mission risk differently, depending on their records of gender equality. The results did not provide much evidence for an interactive effect related to either military or police contributions. The gendered protection norm appears strong even among contributing countries that have less rigid gender roles.

Our finding of an unmitigated gendered norm of protection even among countries with relatively strong records of gender equality must be understood along with the finding that the countries with the relatively strong records still significantly outperformed those countries with worse records in their willingness to contribute female peacekeeping personnel. The key implication is that domestic reforms that improve gender equality interpreted broadly,[37] especially in countries that contribute many peacekeepers, can produce downstream effects in increasing the representation of women in peacekeeping missions.[38] Removing gender power imbalances in society as a whole in contributing countries may help to increase the representation of women in *all* peacekeeping missions, albeit at different rates.

CONCLUSION

This chapter has examined variations in the representation of women in peacekeeping force contributions. We have considered the tendency for gender power imbalances in the security sector, arising from the privileging of warrior identities and the militarization process, to limit the available resource pool of women for peacekeeping forces, particularly for troops due to their deployment to peacekeeping missions through contingents. We have also examined how the gender protection norm affects where female peacekeepers deploy—mainly to the safest missions. Women are less likely to be sent to missions that have experienced high levels of conflict-related violence, particularly sexual violence, and are located in countries with low levels of development. While it is arguably in such countries that peacekeeping is most needed to improve the security environment, women are being systematically excluded from these important missions.

Yet we also uncovered a potentially "positive" result of these gender dichotomies. In some instances, the women-as-peacemaker identity may spur increases in female peacekeeping deployment because women are seen as less relevant for national defense and are more likely to be sent on peacekeeping missions when there are great needs for national defense at home and/or when the security sector is associated with postnational defense. While at a first glance this unintended consequence may appear to be positive, we urge caution in exploiting these mechanisms to increase women's representation in peacekeeping missions because they continue to rely on gender stereotypes and resulting gender power imbalances, reinforcing the gendered protection norm.

Finally, we found evidence that countries with better records of gender equality, particularly related to the labor force participation of women, tend to deploy higher proportions of women to both military and police components of peacekeeping missions. At the same time, however, we find that the gender protection norm and tendency to restrict women from the missions with the greatest security threats remains strong even among contributing countries with relatively strong records in the practice of gender equality.

The core findings in this chapter point to a paradox. The justification, used in many mission mandates and other Security Council resolutions, that female peacekeepers are needed for the protection of the female victims of violence is centered on a broader norm of protecting women that, when applied to female peacekeeping personnel, is a crucial impediment to being able to increase the representation of women in peacekeeping missions. If, as we find, women are much less likely to deploy to missions where there has been recent widespread sexual violence, this gendered norm of protection is especially debilitating for the effort to reach the desired ends of the WPS agenda. That is, a norm of protecting vulnerable women in devastated communities has both heightened the call for greater participation of women in peacekeeping forces to reach out to those women and limited the representation of women in the peacekeeping missions that serve the most devastated communities. It is thus conceivable that the norm that drives much of the demand for more female peacekeepers undermines the supply.

Based on this chapter's findings, we suggest that there should be much more focus on recruitment of female peacekeepers. Changing the structure and focus of recruitment for both domestic forces (recruitment into national militaries and police forces) and international peace operations may lead to changes in overall gender power structures that keep women from deploying to peacekeeping missions, especially to the missions where they could have maximum impact.

First, bolstering the representation of women in domestic military forces is an important ingredient in efforts to increase the representation in peacekeeping missions. In this sense, the UN and other advocates of gender equality in the security sector are right to emphasize domestic reforms worldwide and not just in conflict-prone locations. A key element in these efforts is the formation of NAPs as part of the UNSCR 1325 initiative, in which countries self-assess and develop plans to improve gender equality in the security sector. Yet this is not enough, as additional evidence suggests. In separate analyses, we do not find that countries that adopt NAPs are more likely to deploy female peacekeepers. Much more fundamentally, the recruitment of women into national militaries should center on the encouragement of women from an early age to join such institutions by suggesting the wide range of activities the institutions perform outside combat. Reforms also need to include setting up mentoring networks, training, and targeted recruitment. We return to these methods and other tactics to recruit more women into the military in more detail in the concluding chapter.

Second, many countries could stand to adjust their policies to more effectively recruit women to their peacekeeping mission contributions. In some countries such as Turkey and Bosnia, men and women are selectively screened for open peacekeeping positions. The screening usually entails some combination of physical, medical, mental, driving, and computer tests. The problem here is that some qualification requirements may exclude women. For example, if the qualification for joining peacekeeping missions is that the person must have been in the service for a certain number of years and reached a particular rank, women may be disadvantaged because they may have joined the service later and thus are behind in reaching rank. Recognizing this type of issue, Norway amended its qualifications and application process. According to the Norwegian UNPOL officers in Liberia, Norway used to require potential recruits for missions to have been officers for six years but has lowered the limit to three years to try to encourage more women. Such reforms may help explain why Norway has one of the higher proportions of women sent to military components of peacekeeping missions. Norway's decision to lower the years in service is a way to deal with gender gaps domestically whereby delays in women's entry and promotion have hindered their career progress. While making changes to recruitment processes may not cause more women to apply, it certainly enables more women to apply and is an important first step.

Countries might consider other means to improve the active recruitment of women to their force contributions. For example, a Bosnian female peacekeeper noted that after her involvement in peacekeeping, the government started using her success story as a way to motivate other women to apply for missions. In this way, states might facilitate potential recruitment cascades, as the experiences of women that have served encourage the participation of others, who then encourage still others. Modest efforts to improve the participation of women might build on each other and eventually precipitate a type of regime shift in how people imagine gender in the security sector.

In order to ensure that women are able to make use of their talents by deploying to all different types of missions and not just the safest ones, the international community would do well to address this gendered protection norm, as well as the privileging of the warrior identity and the militarization process. These norms and processes are much more rooted in sociology than in biology and thus are potentially responsive to the legal and institutional environments. This means that changes in policy, such as in standards and recruitment, could alter the degree to which gender power imbalances suffuse countries. Such reforms may include educational programs and classes, that promote "healthy masculinities."[39] Gender norms, however, take a long time to change throughout society as a whole.[40] Changes in the gender hierarchies of national militaries and police institutions may be a more realistic place to start if the goal is to increase women's representation in PKOs. We return to other possibilities in the conclusion of the book. If countries like Nigeria successfully implement reforms in their military and police institutions, then maybe the next time that Major Lola Aduke Oyediran Ugbodaga from Nigeria deploys to a peacekeeping mission abroad, she will be accompanied by more female peacekeepers.

CHAPTER 5

The Spoils of Peace

SEAHV in Peacekeeping Operations

On July 24, 2014, nineteen-year-old Cynthia gave birth to her first child.[1] The father of the child does not know that he has a Liberian son. In fact, he does not even know that he got Cynthia pregnant after forcing himself on her. The father is a Nigerian peacekeeper, who was stationed with the Nigerian peacekeeping contingent in Monrovia, Liberia, but he left months ago. Cynthia's father is also a Nigerian peacekeeper—she has never met him, and he also does not know that she exists. This story is somewhat common in Liberia, which has experienced the presence of UNMIL since 2003 and previously hosted a regional Economic Community of West African States Monitoring Group mission and the UN Observer Mission in Liberia in the 1990s.[2] The story highlights how SEAHV by peacekeepers has been a major problem for peacekeeping missions, not just in Liberia but in many countries. Peacekeepers have been involved in exploitative behavior ranging from the routine use of young girls and boys and adults for sex to manufacturing pornographic films and to the trafficking of girls.[3] Despite the UN's zero tolerance policy and explicit messaging against SEAHV, from 2006 to 2013 the UN reported a total of 595 allegations of SEAHV allegedly perpetrated by its peacekeeping personnel. Yet this number is likely to be a considerable underestimate, because most individuals do not report cases.[4]

The issue of SEAHV has drawn so much attention that the UN commissioned a report to study the problem. On May 15, 2015, the UN's Office of Internal Oversight Services (OIOS) released an evaluation of efforts to confront SEAHV in UN PKOs that made headlines worldwide.[5] After chronicling the severity of the problem, the OIOS report concluded that "the effectiveness of enforcement against sexual exploitation and abuse is hindered by a complex architecture, prolonged delays, unknown and varying outcomes and severely deficient victim assistance" (Office of Internal Oversight Services, 2015: 27).

From the example given about Cynthia and from the OIOS report, we can see that SEAHV is a real problem in many peacekeeping missions. Chapter 4 focused on how gender power imbalances, related to the privileging of the warrior identity, gendered protection norm, and militarization processes, affected the participation of women in peace operations; in this chapter we focus on how gender power imbalances affect patterns of SEAHV in peacekeeping missions. In chapter 3, we highlighted how militarization provides a foundation for the perpetuation of SEAHV against local populations, fellow service members, and civilians at home. In this chapter, we specifically examine the potential for peacekeepers to commit acts of SEAHV against members of the local community while deployed.

In addition to describing the state of SEAHV in peacekeeping missions, we also analyze some of the conditions that raise or lower the proclivity for such offenses.[6] We specifically test whether missions with higher proportions of female peacekeepers are less prone to SEAHV. This allows us to explore whether efforts to include more women in PKOs can, among other objectives, reduce the proclivity for SEAHV offenses. We also test whether peacekeeping missions that consist of more personnel from countries with a strong record of gender equality have lower rates of SEAHV accusations. In doing this, we test the conjecture that improving the value of gender equality among all peacekeeping personnel affects the gender power imbalances in missions and mitigates the pernicious problem of SEAHV. Such an approach is in line with "equal opportunity peacekeeping"—advancing more holistic gender-related reforms that seek to recruit and train peacekeepers of either sex to be more gender-aware and sensitive to the potential for SEAHV.

THE PROBLEM: SEAHV IN UN PEACEKEEPING MISSIONS

When peacekeepers engage in SEAHV in peacekeeping missions, it is a major problem for multiple reasons. First and foremost, when individuals experience SEAHV, they face physical and psychological trauma that has long-term consequences both for the individual and for the state. They are more likely to experience higher levels of anxiety, depression, health problems, and PTSD and are more susceptible to violence in the future.[7] Such experiences could have lasting consequences for the economic prosperity of the country, as widespread issues of health and psychological problems lead to labor shortages and market inefficiencies.[8]

In addition to the threats to the human security of the communities to which peacekeeping missions deploy, SEAHV creates an obvious source of mistrust between local populations and the peacekeeping missions. It undermines mission efficacy and legitimacy. The exploitation itself is antithetical to the goal of enhancing the quality of peace through bolstering human capital in war-torn societies, not draining it. Kate Grady (2010) suggests that when peacekeepers commit SEAHV, they breach the principle of impartiality. When locals view UN peacekeepers exploiting local women (and others), they form certain perceptions about peacekeepers, especially doubts that the peacekeepers are there to protect and not to abuse. As members of the local communities experience this abuse, they will find the peacekeeping mission less beneficial and therefore less legitimate.

SEAHV also poses a major health threat.[9] If peacekeepers have multiple partners and do not use proper precautions, whether they are engaging in transactional sex or sexual violence, they create a health risk that the local government may not be able to handle. The health system in postconflict countries is already dire, which means other health concerns such as sexually transmitted infections add stress to it. The introduction of cholera by UN peacekeepers in Haiti, killing some six thousand people, serves as a tragic reminder that peacekeepers can be agents of the spread of disease.[10] The prevalence of HIV/AIDS in Africa, the relatively large number of UN missions there, and the correlation between transactional sex and the spread of disease makes SEAHV a particularly important problem for missions.

Finally, SEAHV hampers the promotion of gender equality locally. If peacekeepers are supposed to promote gender equality, then SEAHV becomes particularly alarming. UNSCR 1325 and subsequent resolutions have formally recognized and institutionalized the differential and unique impacts of armed conflict on women and men and have observed that women and children together represent the majority of those adversely affected by conflict. As we highlighted in chapter 2, in many multidimensional missions a large component of the peace-building activities involve promoting gender equality through the UNSCR 1325 mandate, which means that if peacekeeping personnel are involved in activities that violate gender equality, locals will find it hard to take these programs seriously. Moreover, such behavior and activity perpetuates gender power imbalances in the host country. For example, there is anecdotal evidence that this behavior by peacekeepers fosters the growth of an illicit sex industry and its associated problems.[11] Kathleen Jennings (2010) has detailed the link between peacekeeping deployments and the growth of local sex economies, which cater to the tendency for male security personnel to sexually exploit local communities and may contribute to countries becoming sex tourism destinations once the missions leave. In order for the WPS agenda to gain traction, peacekeepers must lead the way by example.

Unfortunately, peacekeepers do not always do so, as is detailed by the OIOS report and is evident in every story of peacekeeper misconduct that emerges. In Liberia alone, allegations of SEAHV are numerous. Reports from Refugee International highlight the problem in Liberia: "This behavior would not be acceptable in the home country of these soldiers. Why are these soldiers playing around with our children?" A Liberian woman went further to say, "these girls that [UN peacekeeping soldiers] go off with are just children. They cannot reason for themselves. They are hungry and want money for school. The peacekeepers give them that. But the peacekeepers are adults. They should act responsibly" (Martin, 2005: 5). This statement resonates with a study Sabrina Karim completed with Bernd Beber, Michael Gilligan, and Jenny Guardado (Beber et al., 2017). Despite the UN's zero tolerance stance, the high level of transactional sex between peacekeepers and local women is still a problem. The study found that in a representative sample of Monrovia, half the women aged eighteen to thirty engaged in transactional sex and that of these about 75 percent had done so with UN personnel (around 58,000 women). In most cases sex was exchanged for money. The introduction of UNMIL in 2003 caused a substantial and statistically significant increase in the probability that a woman would engage in her first sex transaction. While transactional sex is not always within the purview of SEAHV (Kanetake, 2010; Simić, 2009), there are clear power dynamics associated with peacekeepers and local women. It is also very possible that men who engage in transactional sex may be prone to commit more insidious forms of SEAHV.[12] There is no doubt that the findings point to a widespread violation of the UN's zero tolerance policy against transactional sex by peacekeepers. This type of peacekeeper misconduct poses a prodigious threat to the nurturing of gender equality locally, as peacekeepers serve as models for relations between the security sector and the public in not only their constructive engagements with the local population but also their destructive engagements.

Do the experiences in Liberia parallel those in other missions? Figure 2.2, from chapter 2, shows an indicator of SEAHV over time, demonstrating that SEAHV is still a problem despite the UN's zero tolerance policy. The count of military SEAHV allegations increased by more than 50 percent from 2012 to 2013, with a mean of two allegations per mission in 2013. With many fewer deployed personnel, allegations against police personnel are lower than military allegations, with a mean of just under 0.5 allegations per mission in 2013.[13] Such counts of SEAHV allegations are almost certainly a gross undercount of actual SEAHV offenses because most victims do not feel comfortable reporting.[14]

It is important to note that UN civilian personnel, in addition to military and police personnel, are major contributors to SEAHV in missions. In fact, the 2015 OIOS report specifically stated that UN civilians may be the most likely perpetrators and the UN Conduct and Discipline website statistics show that, in absolute terms, civilians have the second highest level of allegations reported against them, after the military. As civilians make up fewer personnel in missions, the relative proportions of allegations of SEAHV by civilians are all the more alarming. More attention should be devoted to understanding the variation in civilian-perpetuated SEAHV, but such a study lies outside of the scope of our focus on security sector institutions and norms.

EXPLAINING PATTERNS OF SEAHV: MILITARIZATION AND OPPORTUNISM

In order to understand why peacekeepers might behave in such a manner, it is important to contextualize peacekeeping within the broader military and police environments. As we discussed in chapter 3, SEAHV may be a major symptom of a heightened sense of militarized masculinity, an aggressive form of masculinity needed for warrior culture to flourish.[15] It is pervasive in military institutions because of the belief that effective combat and group cohesion sometimes require the privileging of aggressive masculinity and the construction of "in" and "out" groups.[16] Often the out-group includes women and anything related to being feminine. As such, this perpetuates the idea that women are sexual objects to be conquered. Enloe (1990), for example, highlights the problems that militarism creates for male sexuality and misconduct and observes that sexual misconduct by security forces is common in areas with military bases or other large congregations of security sector officials. Because peacekeeping forces draw from military institutions, such a culture translates into PKOs as well.

Given the general link between militarized masculinity and SEAHV in the security sector writ large, there could also be a link between SEAHV and peacekeeping forces. With the evolution of more complex and multidimensional PKOs,[17] peacekeeping asks soldiers to do work that might normally be done by civilians—for example, promote human rights and organize elections. That soldiers are expected to do what some consider to be more mundane work might contribute to "identity crises" that are manifested in violence.[18] Whitworth (2007) argues that when soldiers are unable to fulfill their function as soldiers conditioned for combat, they may resort to sexual exploitation of the local population, violence against the local population, sexual harassment of other members of the UN mission, or participation in human trafficking rings.[19] Moreover, Higate and Henry (2004) have argued that sexual relationships in missions are central to men's identity in them and that men construct their identities in relation to local women. With sexual relationships so tied to male peacekeeper identities, Martin (2005) has suggested that a "hypermasculine" culture that encourages tolerance for extreme sexual behaviors has evolved in peacekeeping missions.

Alongside militarization, the deployment among "vulnerable" populations could increase the opportunity for SEAHV offenses. While militarization focuses on the "supply" side of the problem, exploitation by peacekeepers is enabled by local economic poverty that increases the incentives for locals to participate in sex trafficking and prostitution.[20] In this regard, Ragnhild Nordås and Siri Rustad (2013) find that SEAHV is more frequently reported the lower the levels of battle-related deaths, the larger the operation, the more recent the operation, and the less developed the country hosting the mission and in operations where the conflict involved high levels of sexual violence. According to this evidence, the opportunity for SEAHV, in terms of the vulnerability of the population and the lack of accountability in larger missions, is a strong factor driving variation in offenses.

In addition, Keith Allred (2006) has suggested that there are several problems that enable peacekeepers to engage in SEAHV. He notes that peacekeepers tend to perceive that they are immune from the prosecution of crimes. When contributing countries supply peacekeepers, they have a Memorandum of Understanding that the contributing country will take legal action for any offenses committed by their forces, which means that host countries lack jurisdiction over prosecution. This policy is compounded by the fact that contributing countries have little incentive to prosecute their soldiers and police officers. To save national and international embarrassment, contributing countries rarely prosecute offenders.[21] Keith Allred suggests that the UN can learn from the American and NATO experiences and ensure proper training programs, an enforced zero tolerance policy, increased recreational opportunities, hotlines, and heightened sensitivity to the relationship between SEAHV and human trafficking.

With multiple potential origins of SEAHV by peacekeepers, we examine separately the dynamics in military and police components.[22] On the one hand personnel in police components are less "militarized" than personnel in military components[23] and face less of a gap between their roles as UNPOL officers and their roles as police officers in their home countries. That is, military personnel face greater exposure to institutionalized hypermasculinity and a greater disconnect between their duties as soldiers and their duties as peacekeepers. On the other hand personnel in police operations have greater access to and engagement with local populations and, consequently, greater opportunities for SEAHV involving local communities. Patterns of SEAHV are thus likely to vary across the police and military components of PKOs.

OVERCOMING THE NEGATIVE EFFECTS OF MILITARIZATION

While a number of suggestions have been made to reduce levels of SEAHV, such as increasing recreational activity among peacekeepers, physically barring them from interacting with locals, and more drastic penalties for committing SEAHV,[24] we focus on how adjustments to the composition of peacekeeping forces can mitigate the potential for SEAHV. One mechanism, female ratio balancing, has been touted as a means to change the gender power imbalances and hypermasculine norms that may perpetuate SEAHV in peacekeeping missions, but following our critique in chapter 3, we posit a number of reasons why such expectations should be bounded. We suggest that a more holistic approach to dismantling gender power imbalances within and through peacekeeping missions can more substantially address the underlying causes of SEAHV. One implication for force composition is that we expect peacekeeping missions that are composed of more individuals from countries with strong records on gender equality to commit fewer SEAHV offenses. These countries may already have stronger records of breaking down gender power imbalances and may maintain a more credible threat to hold their personnel accountable for SEAHV offenses.

Solution 1: Female Ratio Balancing as a Policy Lever

UN officials have suggested that increasing the representation of women in peacekeeping missions may have an effect in reducing SEAHV.[25] A possible connection between female ratio balancing and SEAHV offenses might be expected from a number of different angles. Most straightforward is the expectation that men are the predominant SEAHV offenders, so increasing the proportion of female peacekeepers simply shrinks the pool of possible offenders.[26] This approach to attenuating SEAHV offenses concedes that reductions in SEAHV will be limited because, as we explored in chapter 4, the proportion of women in peacekeeping missions is unlikely to increase by a sufficient amount without drastic changes in the priorities of contributing countries and increases in the representation of women in military institutions.[27]

Less straightforward is the expectation that the type of militarization that fosters sexual misconduct can be mitigated by including more women. If SEAHV abuses are symptomatic of a culture of gender power imbalance in the missions, we then need a connection between female participation and changes in the mission culture. Part of this expectation stems from arguments that the women being included are both highly feminine and influential in counteracting the militarized masculinity with their femininity. For example, Comfort Lamptey, a gender adviser in the UN DPKO, has argued that "the presence of more women can actually help dilute a macho approach to peacekeeping."[28]

Another strand of argument connecting the inclusion of more women to reductions in SEAHV offenses could stem from an expectation that men will be less likely to engage in abusive actions, especially rule-breaking actions, when more woman are present to possibly report the infractions or more proactively confront the potential offenders with the moral argument for why abuse is wrong. In his report on SEAHV to the UN General Assembly, Prince Zeid argued that a higher number of female peacekeepers was required to facilitate an environment that discouraged sexual exploitation and abuse (UN, 2005). Donna Bridges and Debbie Horsfall (2009) have argued that the presence of women can have a deterrent effect. The argument is simply that women may police their male counterparts and deter such behavior when they are present. This explanation assumes a general solidarity between women across cultural contexts: that female peacekeepers will take actions to mitigate aggressive male masculinity because they believe it hurts local women and gender equality in the mission.

The latter claims can be critiqued, which chapter 3 has done at greater length, from the position that women entering the security sector might not in fact be well characterized as feminine and even those who are might not be able to much affect the culture of gender power imbalance because that culture is likely to curtail their influence.[29] An approach aimed at trying to reduce the pool of potential perpetrators also overlooks the potential for women to perpetrate SEAHV.[30] In addition, SEAHV might often be well hidden from female group members, so there might not be substantial opportunity for improvements in intragroup accountability.[31] And even if SEAHV abuses are observed, female group members might not be more likely than their male counterparts to report them. In this vein, Jennings (2008) has found that female peacekeepers may be more loyal to their country than to local women and thus may not report abuses. The expectation that women are much more likely to decry SEAHV offenses by their colleagues than men are might be a bridge too far in leaning on essential differences between women and men.

Moreover, women face pressures in the job and may feel too intimidated to report any misconduct. Just as it is assumed that many male personnel are hesitant to report SEAHV abuses for fear of upsetting group cohesion—indeed, the process of establishing group loyalty in military organizations could increase the incentives for group members to turn a blind eye to sexual exploitation and abuse[32]—female personnel are also likely to face the same dilemma, and even more so if women suspect that they must overcome gender biases to prove that they are team players.

Even more important, increasing the proportion of female peacekeepers as the primary vehicle to address SEAHV places the burden on the small numbers of women deployed and overlooks the potential for both women and men to value egalitarianism. Overinvestment in female ratio balancing places the entire burden on the women—the men are oddly taken out of the equation as if they are uniformly a problem against which balance must be brought.[33]

Solution 2: Gender Equality and Equal Opportunity Peacekeeping

As an alternative, we focus on the importance of all personnel, men and women, holding values and norms related to gender equality. As stated in chapter 4, by "gender equality" we mean the norms, values, customs, and practices that underlie institutions that treat all genders and sexes equally, fairly, and respectfully. No one sex or gender is privileged in behavior and practice. Those who hold norms and values that treat genders equally may be less prone to engage in SEAHV, and those who have values and norms contrary to gender equality may be more prone to commit SEAHV.

Indeed, previous work suggests that there is a link between stronger norms of gender equality and reduced levels of abuse against women (Hunnicutt, 2009; Aguayo et al., 2016). The argument is simply that men and women who believe women to be equals are more likely to treat women with respect. In its most obvious form, this means not engaging in SEAHV against women. When men believe that they can and even have the right to dominate women, it may make them more abusive toward women, and, tying into our theoretical framework, more prone to translate militarization into acts of SEAHV against women. Cohen, Hoover-Green, and Wood (2013) argue that patriarchy is a necessary, although insufficient, condition for sexual violence, especially as it relates to the security forces. So, on the flip side, movements away from patriarchy should translate into reductions in the potential for SEAHV.[34] We surmise that, on average, peacekeepers from more gender unequal countries are more prone to commit SEAHV, or at least less willing to denounce it.

Moreover, contributing countries that have a record of valuing gender equality are also potentially more likely to hold their peacekeepers accountable for misdeeds and likely to incentivize compliant behavior. Aspirations for gender equality likely accompany other desirable characteristic of security institutions. If security personnel and elites value gender equality, they likely also value democracy, representation, accountability, and other forms of good governance. Thus, we posit that those personnel who come from countries that perform better on gender equality may be less likely to commit acts of SEAHV, as they may be prone to hold more equal views about gender hierarchies and/or to be deterred from taking advantage of local communities by a heightened potential for accountability.

We thus examine whether peacekeepers who come from more gender unequal countries are more likely to be associated with SEAHV. As mentioned, how countries perform on particular indicators of gender equality, such as the participation of women in the labor force, provides a basis for comparison of the state of gender power imbalances in the societies. Recognizing the flaws in using aggregate measures,[35] we still opt to use such proxies as a way to empirically examine whether practices associated with gender inequality correlate with the pernicious effects of SEAHV and thereby demonstrate proof of concept.

To the extent that gender norms in the contributing countries do shape patterns of SEAHV, this means that men and women can share in the reform process—an especially important policy objective, because men will likely constitute the majority of peacekeeping personnel for the foreseeable future. Gender norms vary across male (and female) personnel, and gender equality can be enhanced among male (and female) peacekeepers. By focusing on mission composition, we not only explore the underlying foundations of SEAHV variation across missions but also gain traction on possible policy approaches to help reduce SEAHV.

The composition of forces can be tailored to include individuals who hold more gender equal beliefs. For example, Kronsell (2012) argues that Sweden has done well to intentionally develop, through training programs and regulations, a gender-aware postnational defense, despite not achieving substantial gains in gender balancing of the forces. A reliance on female ratio balancing as the key policy lever thus can miss valuable policy instruments related to gender mainstreaming, training, and recruitment when they do quite well, and perhaps even better than female ratio balancing, toward advancing gender equality. In addition, a more holistic approach that looks beyond female ratio balancing is also important to avoid an overcorrection such that men, and masculinity in general, are disparaged to the detriment of male engagement with mission goals and to the detriment of sanguine intergender relations.

RESEARCH DESIGN

We examine the variation in SEAHV activity across missions and across years, from 2009 to 2013.[36] As the outcome measure, the UN reports data on the number of allegations of SEAHV in each mission and separates whether the allegations pertain to the military, police, or civilian members of the mission.[37] We thus use the yearly counts of military and police SEAHV allegations in each mission as the dependent variable. We then model the effects of our explanatory variables on such allegations, using random effects event count models.[38]

In these data, two-thirds of the observations (mission-years) had no SEAHV allegations related to the military units, and three-quarters of the mission-years did not have any SEAHV allegations related to police units. The highest numbers of yearly military SEAHV allegations came from the MONUC/MONUSCO mission, which consistently led all missions and maxed out at forty in 2009. With regard to yearly police SEAHV allegations, MONUC/MONUSCO also had the highest number in a single year, with seven in 2007, but other missions, such as UNMIL, UNMIS, MINUSTAH, and UNMIT, also had yearly totals that were noticeably higher than those of other missions. Table 5.1 presents the missions with nonzero SEAHV allegations related to the military and police components and those with zero allegations in the period 2007–2013.

A standard process exists for collecting allegations in missions.[39] An allegation is an unproven report of alleged misconduct, which may not necessarily lead to a full-scale investigation. Each mission has a Conduct and Discipline Unit that is responsible for tracking allegations and reporting them to the Investigations Division of the OIOS within a ten-day window (Office of Internal Oversight Services, 2015). Missions have established a range of reporting mechanisms, including locked drop-boxes, private meeting rooms to allow reporting in a confidential setting, telephone hotlines, secure email addresses, regional focal points, local women's organizations, and the local UN-NGO network. OIOS provides

Table 5.1. MISSIONS AND SEAHV ALLEGATIONS, MILITARY
AND POLICE (2007–2013)

Nonzero SEAHV allegations	Zero SEAHV allegations
MINURCAT (Chad)	BINUB (Burundi)
MINURSO (Western Sahara)	UNAMA (Afghanistan)
MINUSTAH (Haiti)	UNDOF (Israel-Syria)
MONUC/MONUSCO (DRC)	UNIFIL (Lebanon)
UNAMID (Darfur)	UNIOSIL (Sierra Leone)
UNFICYP (Cyprus)	UNISFA (South Sudan)
UNMEE (Ethiopia/Eritrea)	UNMIK (Kosovo)
UNMIL (Liberia)	UNMIN (Nepal)
UNMIS (Sudan)	UNTSO (Middle East)
UNMISS (South Sudan)	
UNMIT (Timor-Leste)	
UNMOGIP (India/Pakistan)	
UNOCI (Côte d'Ivoire)	
UNOMIG (Georgia)	

the aggregate statistics on monthly SEAHV. Thus, the standard for the definition of SEAHV and for compliance with the zero tolerance policy is consistent across all missions, although it is possible for norms of reporting abuse to be inconsistent across missions.[40] Host country variables may also be a factor in reporting allegations. The local dependence on the peacekeepers is one of the key factors preventing more victims from reporting SEAHV.[41] Access to the peacekeeping mission may vary based on resource availability. Thus, we control for the level of income in the host countries, as noted below, to account for differences in economic dependence across missions.[42]

In order to test whether missions with a stronger representation of women tend to commit SEAHV at lower rates, the first explanatory variable is the proportion of women in the military (or police) contingents. The UN DPKO reports these for each mission on a monthly basis, and we choose the maximum monthly proportion as the yearly indicator.

We use country-level characteristics of the contributing countries to approximate the extent to which the societies from which the peacekeepers originate practice and value gender equality. Erik Melander (2005a, 2005b) and Valerie Hudson and colleagues (2012) similarly use country-level characteristics related to observable indicators of gender equality to measure societal gender norms and find that countries that do well on observable indicators of gender equality tend to have less propensity for violent conflict.[43] We focus on measuring three dimensions of the practice of gender equality in the contributing countries.[44]

First, as in chapter 4, the visible presence of women in non-traditional roles is an important factor because it both indicates sex-specific constraints on women and the extent to which men (and women) are able to observe that women are fully capable in many societal tasks. To measure the visibility of women in society, the percentage of women in the labor force helps indicate the value placed on women seeking gainful employment. As more women are present publicly in roles that were traditionally considered for men, egalitarian values may be more widespread in society.[45]

Second, the degree to which there are legal institutional protections for women is indicative of the state's commitment to protecting women's rights. Indeed, existing scholarship has used legal standards as a measure of violence against women.[46] To measure the institutional and legal protections for women, we use the WomenStats physical-security-of-women index that provides information on whether the legal and institutional infrastructures are oriented in such a way as to prevent SEAHV against women.[47] This indicator reflects the government's degree of acceptance of abuse and violence, which relates to the potential for contributing countries to hold their personnel accountable.

Third, we assess whether variation across contributing countries in compliance with the UNSCR 1325 agenda also helps explain variation in SEAHV in peacekeeping missions. Specifically, we examine whether successful National Action Plan adoption informs the types of peacekeepers who are deployed on peace operations. These NAPs offer a tool for governments to articulate priorities and coordinate the implementation of UNSCR 1325 at the national level. For example, in each NAP, countries indicate objectives and timelines to achieve them. Objectives may include goals such as increasing the number of women in peacekeeping forces, increasing the number of women in political participation, and enhancing the protection of women and girls in the country.[48] We expect that a commitment to domestic reforms will improve the egalitarian values of all types of personnel, regardless of gender, that a contributing country deploys on peace operations and will strengthen the contributing countries' willingness to hold perpetrators of SEAHV accountable. The potential dividends from such reforms in reducing peacekeeper misconduct, therefore, could be quite substantial. By 2015, forty-four countries had adopted NAPs that committed them to self-assessment and institutional reforms with the goal of improving gender equality in the public sector. Table 5.2 lists the NAP-adopting countries by year and shows that NAP adoption cuts across the developed and developing worlds.[49]

We aggregate these measures to the mission-year level, forming separate measures for the military and the police contingents. We take weighted averages of the respective contributing-country characteristics, where the weights are the proportions of total military or police personnel in the mission who were contributed by each country.[50] We recognize the ecological inference problem of ascribing group characteristics (practice of gender equality in contributing countries) to components of the groups (peacekeeping personnel from the countries). But it gives us an observable implication that can be tested, such that failure to confirm the expectation should lead us to call into question whether or not peacekeepers who come from countries with strong records on gender equality are actually more likely to hold gender equal values than peacekeepers who come from countries with weaker records. We should further emphasize that this assumption is not a statement about all peacekeepers

Table 5.2. NATIONAL ACTION PLAN ADOPTERS (2005–2015)

Year	Country
2005	Denmark
2006	UK, Sweden, Norway
2007	Switzerland, Spain, Netherlands, Côte d'Ivoire, Austria
2008	Uganda, Iceland, Finland
2009	Liberia, Portugal, Belgium, Guinea, Chile
2010	Sierra Leone, Rwanda, Philippines, Italy, France, Estonia, DRC, Canada, Bosnia and Herzegovina
2011	Nepal, Lithuania, Georgia, Guinea-Bissau, Ireland, Serbia, Burundi, Slovenia, Croatia, Senegal, USA
2012	Germany, Ghana, Australia
2013	Nigeria, Macedonia, Kyrgystan
2015	Afghanistan

from each country and does not preclude the likelihood that some peacekeepers from countries with poor records regarding gender equality can be quite egalitarian in their values or that some peacekeepers from countries with strong records of gender equality can be quite patriarchal in their values. In addition, we do not deny that individuals who are more prone to militarism and patriarchy self-select into the military or police professions, and thus that peacekeepers from countries with strong records on gender equality are still quite prone to exhibit behaviors and profess beliefs that are consistent with patriarchy and militarized masculinity. Our expectation is that, while gender hierarchies may tend to be stronger among peacekeepers than among others outside the security sector in their home countries, the peacekeepers from those countries with better records on gender equality will more highly value egalitarianism than peacekeepers from countries with poorer records. Our aggregate indicators are intended to capture this variation. Further details about the models, including information about control variables and robustness checks, can be found in appendix 2.

RESULTS

We find some support for "solution 1," the expectation that a greater representation of women in peacekeeping missions decreases the propensity for SEAHV allegations. Although the relationship is consistently negative in all of the models, for allegations against both the military and police personnel, it is not statistically significant across the various specifications.[51] It is possible that the increases in the proportion of women in missions have yet to reach a high enough threshold to produce a robust measurable treatment effect with such a small sample; at present we can only tentatively conclude that increasing the proportion of women in missions reduces levels of SEAHV in them.

The empirical results reveal a strong relationship between our measures of gender equality in the contributing countries and lower SEAHV allegations in military units. Contingents from countries with better records of gender equality—especially when defined in terms of visibility—experience lower levels of both military and police SEAHV allegations. When military and police contingents consist of more personnel from countries with high rates of female participation in the labor force, the expected counts of SEAHV allegations are substantially lower, and the relationships are statistically significant. We also see support for the expectation that SEAHV allegations are lower when the legal protections of the physical security of women are better (when the index approaches zero), although this relationship is only statistically significant in the models of SEAHV military allegations. Similarly, as the proportion of personnel from countries that have adopted NAPs increases, the expected instances of SEAHV allegations decrease. Figure 5.1 depicts the relationship between the weighted average of the labor force participation of women in the contributing countries and military SEAHV allegations. Figure 5.2 shows the relationship using the physical-security-of-women index (higher values indicate *less* security) weighted average, and figure 5.3 depicts the relationship using the NAP adoption weighted average.

Even while controlling for the proportion of women in missions, contingents that consist of military personnel predominantly from countries with strong records of gender equality are less prone to SEAHV allegations. While the expected absolute magnitudes of the decreases in SEAHV allegations may not seem like a major decrease in reports, it is important to remember that the counts of allegations are likely to be underreported, such that the substantive effects are likely to be scaled up if we had better information about the extent of abuse. In addition, most missions

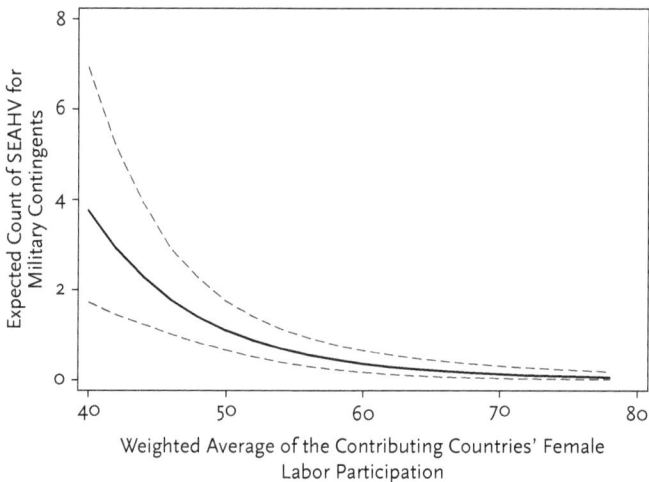

Note: p = 0.009 in a two-tailed test

Figure 5.1. Expected SEAHV allegations in military contingents, by female labor force participation rate in contributing countries.
Note: The plots reflect a military contingent of ten thousand personnel, and other variables held at their means.

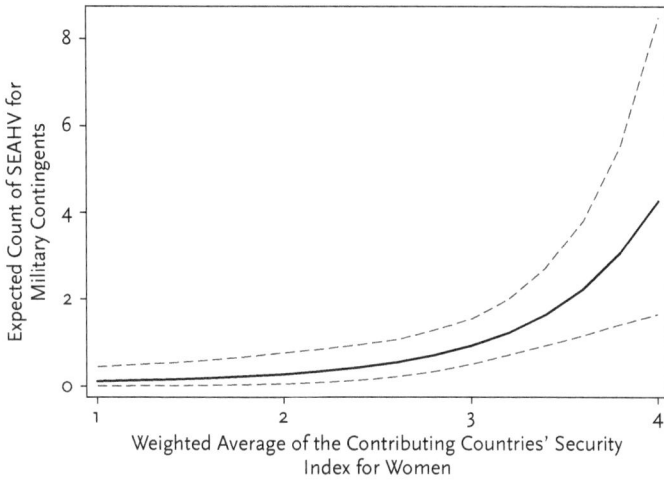

Figure 5.2. Expected SEAHV allegations in military contingents, by security index for women in contributing countries.
Note: The plots reflect a military contingent of ten thousand personnel, and other variables held at their means.

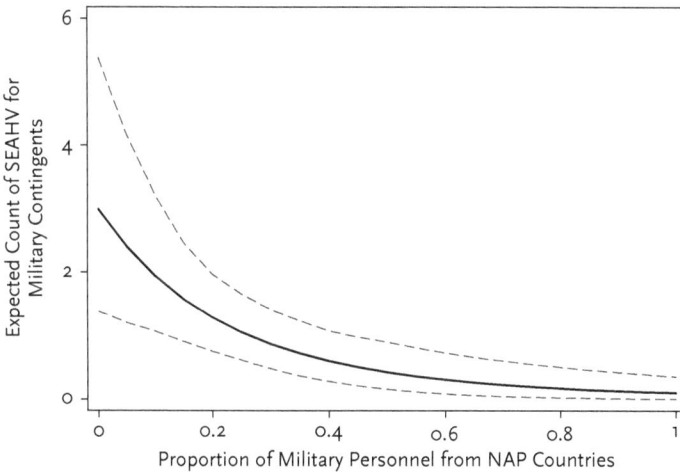

Figure 5.3. Expected SEAHV allegations in military contingents, by NAP adoption in contributing countries.
Note: The plots reflect a military contingent of ten thousand personnel, and other variables held at their means.

do not have high levels of reported SEAHV, which means that a drop in just a few allegations per year can be noteworthy.

With regard to police personnel, only the measure of the participation of women in the labor force well explains police contingent SEAHV allegations, and even that relationship is weaker than the respective one corresponding to military personnel. The smaller sample size could explain some of the inability to confirm our expectations for police contingents. It is also possible that unreformed military contingents, more than police contingents, particularly struggle with the type of gender power imbalance that would contribute to higher rates of SEAHV. Recall from chapter 3 that one of the mechanisms through which gender power imbalances lead to increases in SEAHV was that military peacekeepers may face an identity crisis in their dual roles as warriors and peace officers, which could create a sense of emasculation. This tension is likely mitigated among UN police personnel. The role of UNPOL includes supporting human rights, monitoring performance of the local law enforcement agencies, advising local police on effective law enforcement, reporting on situations and incidents, training local law enforcement, and responding to low-scale incidents.[52] The activities of UNPOL better mimic their jobs at home, and policing may embody more of the characteristics necessary for peacekeeping than typical military activity.[53] Similarly, police are not trained to be warriors in cohesive combat units in the same way that soldiers are conditioned to adopt militarized masculinity. If such militarized masculinity is not as strong in police contingents, then we should not observe the same effects of personnel composition as we do with the military contingents.

Two additional points are worth noting with regard to the relationship between NAP adoption in contributing countries and SEAHV peacekeeping allegations. First, these results do not necessarily indicate that NAPs are *causing* reductions in SEAHV allegations. Many, but certainly not all, of the NAP countries have had a lengthy history of reforms related to gender equality, and it is not clear whether the NAPs have been fully implemented and actually improved egalitarian values in the security sector in those countries or if the NAPs are merely symptoms of preexisting positive efforts on that front.[54] Even if NAPs are merely cosymptomatic, the relationship between NAP adoption and SEAHV allegations suggests that countries that are taking gender equality reforms seriously enough that they make the effort to

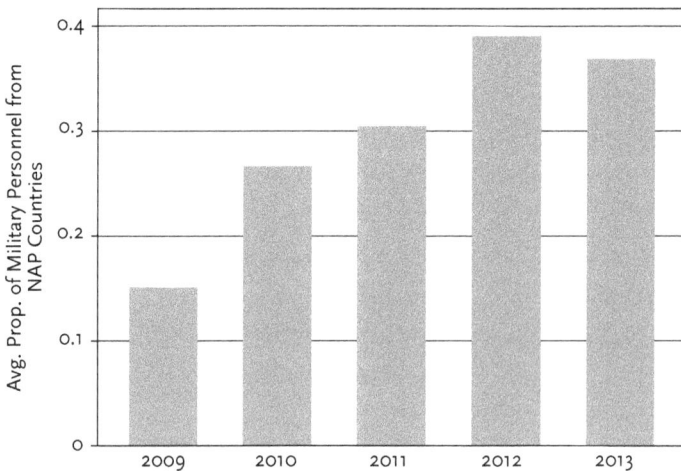

Figure 5.4. NAP countries' contributions to peacekeeping forces.

institutionalize UNSCR 1325 through the adoption of NAPs are better predisposed to send personnel who are not likely to commit SEAHV offenses.

Second, an additional reason for optimism can be seen in the fact that peacekeeping missions consist more and more of military personnel from NAP countries. Figure 5.4 depicts the average proportion of military personnel who originate from contributing countries that have adopted an NAP. In 2009, the average mission's portion of military personnel from NAP countries was about 15 percent, and that figure rose to about 40 percent by 2012, followed by a slight dip in 2013. Whether the NAPs are having an exogenous effect or not, this trend demonstrates that PKOs are increasingly receiving contributions from countries that have at least taken an initial first step in planning reforms related to gender equality in the security sector.

A CLOSER LOOK AT MONUC/MONUSCO AND AT SOUTH AFRICA AS A CONTRIBUTING COUNTRY

To better understand the link between variation in the practices of gender equality in contributing countries and reduced levels of SEAHV in peacekeeping missions, or between the representation of women in missions and reduced levels of SEAHV, we examine two cases: the MONUC/MONUSCO mission in the DRC and South Africa as a force-contributing country. The MONUC/MONUSCO mission is an outlier when it comes to SEAHV, as it has significantly higher rates than other missions (a total of 275 allegations from 2007 to 2012). Military soldiers perpetrated most of the allegations of SEAHV in MONUC/MONUSCO. India, Pakistan, Nepal, Morocco, Tunisia, South Africa, and Uruguay were allegedly reported to have been involved in SEAHV in the MONUC/MONUSCO mission.[55] Notably, these are all countries that contribute high numbers of troops to MONUC/MONUSCO. Among these, the UN has identified South Africa as the object of the highest number of allegations of any contributing country across all missions (Office of Internal Oversight Services, 2015).

Table 5.3 shows the top contributing countries to the MONUC/MONUSCO mission between 2007 and 2013,[56] along with the gender equality indicators used above, and shows whether any personnel from the troop-contributing country were accused of SEAHV allegations. With the exception of Nepal and Uruguay, table 5.3 shows that most of the countries that received allegations do not score very well on female labor force participation or physical security protection laws, relative to the countries that did not have any allegations lodged against them (with the exception of Jordan and Egypt).

In addition to the gender equality indicators, table 5.3 includes a measure of whether the military personnel of the troop-contributing country had experienced domestic allegations of its soldiers being involved in rape, based on media reports of rape allegations.[57] This gives an idea of the level of militarized masculinity within the institution. Again, those countries that were accused of SEAHV more often had media reports of their militaries being involved in rape at home than did countries that were not accused of SEAHV.

Table 5.3. TOP TROOP-CONTRIBUTING COUNTRIES AND SEAHV ALLEGATIONS IN MONUC/MONUSCO (2007–2013)

Top troop-contributing countries to MONUC/MONUSCO	Labor force participation	Physical security index	Allegations of rape committed by military in the media (outside missions)	Proportion of female peacekeepers (military)	SEAHV allegations in mission
India	29.3	4	Yes	0.002	Yes
Pakistan	22.4	4	Yes	0	Yes
Nepal	80.3	4	Yes	0.01	Yes
Morocco	26.0	4	Yes	0	Yes
Tunisia	25.3	3	No	0	Yes
South Africa	44.0	3	Yes	0.17	Yes
Uruguay	55.5	3	No	0.06	Yes
Bangladesh	57.0	4	No	0.004	No
Senegal	66.0	3	No	0	No
Benin	67.2	3	No	0.03	No
Ghana	66.8	4	Yes	0.12	No
Egypt	23.5	4	Yes	0	No
China	67.9	2	No	0.07	No
Jordan	15.4	4	No	0.007	No

Note: The average of the indicators is taken for all the years in the dataset.

Finally, table 5.3 includes the proportions of female peacekeepers that each country from the dataset contributed. Here, there does not seem to be much difference between countries with or without allegations based on the proportion of female peacekeepers contributed. For countries like South Africa or Uruguay, which both have higher-than-average proportions of women sent to the mission, the presence of female peacekeepers does not seem to affect the number of SEAHV allegations.

In fact, South Africa has the highest proportion of female peacekeepers in its contingents sent to the mission—and is one of the highest overall contributors of women to UN peacekeeping missions (averaging nearly 15 percent). However, South Africa has faced the highest number of allegations in all UN missions, including MONUC/MONUSCO. This may suggest that women in the South African contingents have not yet reshaped the contingent culture. While inconclusive, this evidence calls for further caution against strategies that solely focus on improvements in the representation of women in security forces as a vehicle to mitigate SEAHV allegations. Looking more closely at the MONUC/MONUSCO mission, the evidence indicates that personnel from contributing countries with better records of gender equality may not engage in SEAHV at the same level as those from troop-contributing countries with poorer records of gender equality.

CONCLUSION

We find that missions that consist of more military personnel from countries with better records of gender equality tend to experience fewer SEAHV allegations. These findings are consistent with the logic that gender equality is a value that both women and men can hold and that increases to the extent to which mission personnel hold it reduces some of the pernicious manifestations of gender power imbalances such as SEAHV.

We find limited evidence that increasing the proportion of female peacekeepers in missions much explains the counts of SEAHV allegations. This is consistent with some of the critiques that caution against relying too heavily on female ratio balancing as a salve for male misconduct. Female peacekeepers may not be able to observe SEAHV offenses and may not be more likely to report them even if they did. Female peacekeepers also may not be able to counteract militarized masculinity if they themselves—as products of selection into male-dominant institutions and participants in socialization that contributes to "masculinization"—are not particularly feminine and if the institutional structures are responsible for bolstering the power imbalances. Moreover, a policy that displaces the burden of solving a problem onto the shoulders of a minority group is likely to have limited efficacy. That being said, we cannot rule out the possibility, and indeed expect, that increasing the representation of women is at least a bellwether for gender power imbalances in peacekeeping missions and also can help mitigate power imbalances at the margins.

In focusing on the stronger findings that the gender equality performance of the contributing countries well explains variation in SEAHV allegations, we demonstrate the potential for positive dividends from more rigorous and institutionalized reforms that promote gender equality. These include gender sensitivity training and gender mainstreaming as part of participation in peace operations; they also include changes in recruitment methods and in mission culture, particularly in the way group binding is achieved. Chapter 3 highlighted some potential alternatives to the creation of in- and out-groups. For example, attention to task cohesion or the formation of solidarity through practices that include tolerance, appreciation of difference, and empathy may be more helpful for moving away from militarization while still creating the bonds necessary for group cohesion.

That the gender equality performance of the contributing country matters is consistent with the notion that a proclivity for SEAHV offenses is learned behavior and not essential to either men or military personnel. As learned behavior, such proclivities can be unlearned as well, and training programs should continue to be oriented toward such progress. Thus, values that dismantle gender power hierarchies can be learned and adopted as a part of the culture, thereby challenging the militarized masculinity in PKOs that may be contributing to SEAHV that currently occurs.

That being said, the findings should not be taken to suggest that SEAHV can be sufficiently attenuated by relying on more troops from countries with strong records of gender equality. Not only is it politically infeasible to drastically change the portfolio of countries that are most willing to contribute troops, but SEAHV remains a problem even among personnel from such countries with strong records. For example, French peacekeepers have been at the center of atrocious acts of SEAHV in MINUSCA.[58] All contributing countries have work to do toward reducing their peacekeepers' propensity to abuse local populations.

In considering the potential for reforms, it is important to note that suggestions have been made to reduce the levels of SEAHV, such as increasing recreational activity among peacekeepers, physically barring them from interacting with locals, and more drastic penalties for committing SEAHV.[59] These suggestions have in some cases been implemented, but they also leave much to be desired. The purpose of a UN mission is to keep the peace, but also to rebuild local institutions, which means fostering some sense of trust by locals. This necessitates and involves interaction with locals, so physically barring the peacekeepers from such interaction may be counterproductive and sends locals the wrong message. And, while it is also important to enhance the punishment of SEAHV perpetrators both to deter future offenses and to provide victims with a sense of justice, there is little the UN can do, because it is still up to the contributing countries to decide on appropriate repercussions, which usually entail sending the individual home. Little justice may be achieved for the victims of SEAHV under current practice, and addressing this deficit could be especially important in repairing the damage done to their sense of security and to the mission's legitimacy. In the concluding chapter, we consider potential reforms in greater depth.

PART III

Discrimination, Protection, and SEAHV in the UN Mission in Liberia

Chapter 3 highlighted how gender power imbalances perpetuate exclusion, discrimination, protection restrictions, and SEAHV through peacekeeping missions. Chapter 4 showed that the full participation of women has suffered as a result of gender dichotomies and militarization processes. As such, the expectation among policy-makers that improving the representation of women is a key policy lever to improve the nature of peacekeeping may be placing the cart before the horse, especially because the evidence points to the fact that the women who are deployed are not likely to go to the missions where they can have maximum impact. Moreover, the exploration of patterns of SEAHV through peacekeeping missions in chapter 5 demonstrated that variation in the representation of women does not well explain variation in the propensity for SEAHV, and we argued that this should not be surprising when one considers the theoretical roots of the problem. Nevertheless, we have found evidence that societal-level challenges to gender power imbalances, such as the promotion of gender equality, help to increase the participation of women in peacekeeping missions and to prevent SEAHV. Countries with better records of gender equality tend to contribute more female military personnel; moreover, fewer SEAHV allegations tend to occur against personnel in missions with higher proportions of military personnel from countries with relatively strong records on gender equality.

The analysis thus far has been in the aggregate, with little consideration of the experiences of individual peacekeepers or locals. To get a deeper understanding of how gender power imbalances affect exclusion, discrimination, protective restrictions, and SEAHV *within* missions, in chapter 6, we explore the perspectives of many female peacekeepers in UNMIL with regard to how these challenges limit their ability to fully and freely participate in that mission. To get a deeper understanding of how gender power imbalances operate *through* missions, chapter 7 explores the role of female peacekeepers and peacekeepers in Liberia in terms of how members of the local community and police force have responded to their interactions with UNMIL.

We choose to use UNMIL as a case study for a number of reasons. First, it has been heralded as a success in terms of gender reforms with its inclusion of the first all-female FPU.[1] It is also one of the first missions that had references to gender in its original mandate. The mandate stated the importance of "reaffirming the importance of a gender perspective in PKOs and post-conflict peace-building in accordance with Resolution 1325 (2000), recalls the need to address violence against women and girls as a tool of warfare, and encourages UNMIL as well as the Liberian parties to actively address these issues" (UNSC, 2003).[2] In later mandates, a zero tolerance policy for sexual exploitation and abuse was added. Thus, there might not be a better place to understand the relationship between peacekeeping efforts to promote gender-based reforms than in UNMIL, given its precedence in terms of gender reforms.

Second, UNMIL may be considered a mission that is dangerous. One of the key findings from chapter 3 is that female peacekeepers are less likely to go to dangerous missions. Thus, what happens to female peacekeepers who deploy to hazardous missions? UNMIL has experienced some of the highest rates of peacekeeper fatalities, with around twenty deaths per year. The average annual fatality rate per year among missions active from 2006 to 2012 is 5.6, and the maximum is 24. Thus, we are able to gain insight about the perspectives of female peacekeepers who have been deployed to a dangerous mission.

Third, the mission is in a state of drawdown, which means that reforms have already been implemented and evaluated, giving us a rich body of data with which to work. Moreover, our extensive fieldwork in Liberia provides us with rich data on which to draw with regard to UNMIL and local perceptions of it. While some may point to the uniqueness of the Liberian case, such as the fact that in 2006 Liberia elected Africa's first female president, which may have made gender a salient national issue, the gender reforms implemented in UNMIL are found in other missions as well. Moreover, the considerable attention to and relative success of the Liberian mission suggests that it is likely to serve as a model of missions to come.

Before turning to the chapters, we provide a little background on the context. Liberia's history is integrally tied to that of the United States. In the early nineteenth century, the American Colonization Society purchased land in West Africa in order to settle freed American slaves in that territory. This land eventually became the country of Liberia after it gained independence in 1847. A small group of elite Americo-Liberians governed the country and subjugated the indigenous population in a series of small wars. The group of Americo-Liberians, who were descendants of freed slaves, created an elitist system that included forced labor and excluded the indigenous population from governance and education (Ciment, 2013).

This system lasted from 1847 until 1980, when a small group of indigenous officers from the Armed Forces of Liberia (AFL), led by Master Sergeant Samuel Doe, stormed the presidential palace and killed President William R. Tolbert, Jr. At first the indigenous population welcomed the violent coup, but Samuel Doe led an authoritarian, corrupt government that mostly benefited his ethnic Krahn tribe. Many of his initial supporters were gradually eliminated or suppressed (Ciment, 2013). Widespread discontent with the Doe regime led to the onset of an insurgency led by Charles Taylor, who led the National Patriotic Front for Liberia into Liberia in December 1989. In response to Taylor's advances and the entry of a second rebel group—the Independent National Patriotic Front of Liberia, led by Prince

Johnson—the Nigerian-led Economic Community of West African States deployed a cease-fire monitoring group called the Economic Monitoring Group. However, during the 1990s fighting did not stop, even after Samuel Doe was captured and killed in 1990. Instead, different warring factions became involved in a power struggle. The warlords negotiated twelve separate peace settlements, but each one collapsed. In 1996, the Abuja agreement outlined a timeline for the disarmament, demobilization, and reintegration of soldiers and a timetable for democratic elections in 1997. Under the supervision of the Economic Monitoring Group and the UN Observer Mission in Liberia, thousands of soldiers disarmed and demobilized, and elections were held in 1997. Charles Taylor won 75 percent of the vote in the first round.

Within several months in office, Taylor began to suppress the activities of political opponents, and the regime slid back into authoritarianism. He rearranged the security sector by placing his most reliable fighters into the "Anti-terrorist Unit" and "Special Operations Division," both of which have been linked to human rights violations. By 2000, his regime had all but put an end to organized opposition to his government. By July 2000, a new armed opposition group, Liberians United for Reconciliation and Democracy, launched attacks on the government forces and advanced to a position near the capital. Taylor declared a state of national emergency in 2002. The situation deteriorated over the prevailing year, and Taylor, in the face of military defeat, resigned and fled Liberia in August 2003. One month later, UNMIL entered the country with around fifteen thousand international troops.

These civil wars claimed the lives of almost 150,000 people—mostly civilians—and led to a complete breakdown of law and order. The wars displaced many, both internally and beyond the Liberia's borders, resulting in some 850,000 refugees in the neighboring countries. Postwar Liberia lacked any effective rule of law. By the end of the war, Liberia had fifteen different security agencies with overlapping functions and mandates; many police stations had been abandoned, destroyed, or taken over by rebel forces; the state lacked basic equipment, vehicles, fuel, and communications systems; and many police officers and other government officials had fled the country (Friedman, 2011). It is in this context that UNMIL arrived in 2003 to monitor the peace and rebuild the domestic institutions, such as the security sector.

The mandate of UNMIL was a multidimensional PKO from the beginning. It included providing support for the implementation of the cease-fire agreement. Among other stipulations, it stated that the mission objectives included the following:

> to observe and monitor the implementation of the ceasefire agreement and investigate violations of the ceasefire; to establish and maintain continuous liaison with the field headquarters of all the parties' military forces; to assist in the development of cantonment sites and to provide security at these sites; to observe and monitor disengagement and cantonment of military forces of all the parties; to carry out voluntary disarmament and to collect and destroy weapons and ammunition as part of an organized DDRR [Disarmament, Demobilization, Reintegration, and Repatriation] program; to provide security at key government installations, in particular ports, airports, and other vital infrastructure; to contribute towards

international efforts to protect and promote human rights in Liberia, with particular attention to vulnerable groups including refugees, returning refugees and internally displaced persons, women, children, and demobilized child soldiers, within UNMIL's capabilities and under acceptable security conditions, in close cooperation with other United Nations agencies, related organizations, governmental organizations, and non-governmental organizations; to ensure an adequate human rights presence, capacity and expertise within UNMIL to carry out human rights promotion, protection, and monitoring; to assist the transitional government of Liberia in monitoring and restructuring the police force of Liberia, consistent with democratic policing, to develop a civilian police training programme, and to otherwise assist in the training of civilian police, in cooperation with ECOWAS [Economic Community of West African States], international organizations, and interested States; and to assist the transitional government in the formation of a new and restructured Liberian military in cooperation with ECOWAS, international organizations and interested States (UN Security Council, Security Council Resolution 1509, 2003).

In 2013, UNMIL began drawing down and transitioning into a smaller peace building mission. In response to incremental improvements in Liberia's security situation, UNMIL's military strength has been reduced from 15,000 at its peak to around 5,279 today, and many FPUs have replaced military contingents. Resolution 2066 of 2012 mandated UNMIL to decrease its military strength to 3,750 troops by June 2015 and includes an increase in police strength from seven to ten FPUs, raising the total authorized number of police officers to 1,795. However, the transition occurred in the context of an Ebola outbreak that greatly weakened the state, during the enforcement of large concession agreements, and during midterm elections. The security situation remains precarious, as numerous riots have broken out in response to the handling of the Ebola problem and also over land concessions since 2012. It is not clear whether UNMIL will need to revamp its personnel to ensure peace and security in Liberia going forward.

CHAPTER 6

Perspectives on Discrimination, Protection, and SEAHV in the UN Mission in Liberia

In 2012, Jane Rhodes was the only serving female police officer from the United Kingdom (UK) to work for a UN mission. While the UK had many women working in EU missions, particularly in Afghanistan, and in others around the world, there were no other women working specifically in the capacity of a UN police peacekeeper. Jane had wanted to work in Africa for a long time, and the UN ad for a lead position as UN police reform and restructuring coordinator for UNMIL circulated at a time when she was ready to make the move. However, the job required her to take unpaid special leave from the UK police, and in order to stay on the UK pension plan, she paid her own pension every month.

In December 2011, she moved to Liberia to start her new job managing seven different UNPOL teams in UNMIL, covering all different aspects of policing. She was the reform and restructure coordinator and then became the head of the administration and reform section. Before leaving in 2014, Jane was nominated for the International Female Police Peacekeeper Award for 2013—the second nominee from UNMIL in two years. The award is "a competitive award given to an outstanding female police peacekeeper serving in a UN peace operation."[1] During her two years in UNMIL, she was the cofounder of the Female Police Support Network; planned a launch of the network and a mentor/mentee scheme for the LNP and the Bureau of Immigration and Naturalization; organized a Regional Workshop for LNP female officers in Gbarnga; chaired a conference for sixty female UNPOL officers in UNMIL; and held the position of UNMIL's female focal point for women for two years.

She loves the challenge of working in a multicultural environment, the diverse nature of the work, and the sometimes complex relationships with counterparts and managing officers from all over the world with different cultures, behaviors, attitudes, and experiences. The environment, nevertheless, has also been difficult for her. In our interview with her, she said that being a woman in the mission had its distinct challenges. She has been the subject of sexual harassment and has had to deal with cultural attitudes toward women from male counterparts who sometimes have challenged her authority as a senior manager. She has also been mugged in broad daylight and burgled.

In May 2012, Jane volunteered to be appointed as a gender focal point for the UNMIL uniformed staff. Serving as the first and only woman in uniform in the gender focal-point team, she wanted to make a real difference for uniformed women in the mission. Despite having worked with the focal-point team to arrange meetings, organize conferences, complete surveys, and establish the Female Police Support Network for UNPOL, having worked on establishing the same network for officers of the LNP and the Bureau of Immigration and Naturalization, and having completed all the projects mentioned above, she still thinks she struggled to do what the UN has suggested female peacekeepers should do in missions: include a more gendered approach in all peacekeeping activities. To give an example, given that women in the military part of the mission and the police part of the mission rarely interact with one another, attempts were made to organize a task force of uniformed women from both the military contingents and UNPOL who would work together on a project assisting women in a local Liberian community. Despite the need, this project did not obtain sufficient support to progress.

This setback notwithstanding, in Jane's opinion female peacekeepers play a positive role in changing the mission environment. She thinks women play crucial roles in missions because they bring a different perspective to policing. Moreover, she thinks that there are some roles in which women particularly excel, such as dealing with rape survivors and serving as role models for local police—encouraging more women to join the local police and to take on roles that challenge stereotypes. She believes that policing is male dominated and that the attitudes and culture of a team are often influenced by the presence of female team members, particularly in the more male-dominated specializations, such as firearms. In general, she strongly believes that female peacekeepers make the peacekeeping mission more effective.

Jane represents one of the hundred or so female peacekeepers in UNMIL in 2012. Her story highlights not only the problems of gender power imbalances in missions but also the efforts female peacekeepers are making to overcome the barriers to make a real difference in missions. Women like Jane are on the frontline of reforms across the international community to address many of the overlooked issues related to gender, peace, and conflict. These reforms remain incomplete and are evolving. Jane continues to be an advocate for reform while also encountering the problems that the reforms aim to address.

In this chapter, we focus on the experiences of female peacekeepers like Jane. Using numerous interviews and focus group discussions conducted with female peacekeepers in UNMIL,[2] we gain further understanding about the experiences of women's lives within the mission. We are interested in understanding how much women's experiences in the mission are constrained by the mission environment—particularly the gender power imbalances mentioned in the previous chapters. In order to do this, we look at how women have defined their roles and whether they perceive adequate opportunities to fulfill them. Constraints on the female peacekeepers can be observed in both the scope of the roles that they perceive themselves to play and in their ability to play them. While the mission is not representative of all missions or all women,[3] it does give us insight into some general barriers women from many different countries face while deployed to a mission that is relatively dangerous.

At the end of the chapter, we also include a brief analysis of the impact female peacekeepers may have on the ground. In addition to the voices of female peacekeepers, we believe that the voices of locals are important (Pouligny, 2006). Using a representative survey of Monrovia, Liberia, we assess whether female peacekeepers are actually having the impact that the UN and many female peacekeepers themselves believe they are supposed to have. We find that female peacekeepers have had a positive impact in terms of perceptions, particularly on the perceptions of those local men who have had more contact with female peacekeepers. Nevertheless, the low rate of female peacekeeper contact corroborates some of the concerns mentioned by female peacekeepers themselves relating to the fact that the mission policies and culture seriously curtail their interactions with locals. Interviews of female peacekeepers and locals thus demonstrate that gendered barriers exist, preventing female peacekeepers from reaching their full potential.[4]

THE ROLE OF FEMALE PEACEKEEPERS ACCORDING TO FEMALE PEACEKEEPERS

We start by considering what female peacekeepers had to say about their roles as peacekeepers. Such a consideration is instructive in two ways. First, the perspectives women have about the roles of women in the security sector can tell us about the types of femininities and masculinities that are prevalent among female peacekeepers. Recall that Kronsell (2012) suggested that there are many different identities women may adopt to navigate the gender power hierarchies, such as the "bimbo"—the very feminine, beautiful, sex object—or, in contrast, the "feminist," who actively and "too eagerly" pursues gender equality and challenges the gender hierarchy. This suggests that women play different roles in missions and these roles are understood in relation to masculine roles. Institutions that privilege certain masculinities are also likely to privilege those women who are deferential to and complementary with the dominant masculinities. In support of this tendency, we observe many female peacekeepers who have expectations about their roles that appear to be curtailed by the realities of discrimination, a gendered protection norm, and the threat of SEAHV. They may be inhibited from full and free participation due to the consequences of these power imbalances in missions.

Second, these perspectives shed light on the extent to which there are common expectations across women on what they can bring to PKOs. Women may define their roles in political institutions distinctly, and there may not be a common understanding of women's roles in institutions, contrary to a widespread assumption. For example, in politics, there is considerable uncertainty about what constitutes "women's issues" among female politicians (Reingold, 2000, 2008). A lack of consensus on what "women's issues" are may be one reason why women do not consistently initiate policies "for women." In actuality, we do not observe much heterogeneity in beliefs about women's roles in missions. In our sample from UNMIL, there was commonality among women in different contingents (both police and military and among different countries) about the role of female peacekeepers. Nevertheless, we also observe, related to the problems of gender power imbalances that we have explored up to this point, that there are outstanding barriers related to discrimination, protection restrictions, and SEAHV that inhibit female peacekeepers from advocating for local women.

In order to gauge how female peacekeepers perceive their roles in the mission, we asked female peacekeepers in UNMIL to fill out a questionnaire. This survey was not a representative sample of female peacekeepers in all missions but rather a convenience sample from ninety-five female peacekeepers in UNMIL in 2012. As such, the observations should be treated as anecdotal and uncertain as to whether they generalize to typical female peacekeepers.

In our sample of survey respondents, female peacekeepers strongly believed that their presence, as women, made a difference. They believed that their presence inspired local women, improved gender equality in the host country, and improved the overall mission environment. According to the survey experiment in the questionnaire,[5] female peacekeepers were more likely to think that women are more important than men in promoting peace in the community, improving locals' quality of life, and improving the security of women in local communities.

Interestingly, figure 6.1 demonstrates that the longer individuals had served in the military or police, the more likely they were to think that female peacekeepers were better at promoting peace, improving locals' quality of life, and providing security for women.[6] We believe that gender power imbalances may have less influence over women who have been in the institution for a longer period of time. Higher ranking and more tenured women perhaps have experience navigating the gendered hierarchies. In other words, when women first begin working in the military or police, the pressure may be greater for them to conform to gender roles and expectations in the mission. However, as women spend more time in the institution, it is possible that they begin to see gender power imbalances as a problem and also feel more comfortable speaking out about it. By this time, women also may be in higher ranking positions, where they do not feel that they will be sanctioned for holding views about gender inequalities. This is supported by some of our observations when speaking to female peacekeepers in the field. The highest ranking female officers were much more up front about their experiences and offered a number of solutions to improve mission life for women. In contrast, some of the women who were lower ranked often deferred to higher ranking officers to answer questions and participated less.

In addition to statistical evidence that women see themselves as playing a valuable role in the mission, comments from interviews and focus groups strongly suggest that women think they make a unique difference in the mission. A Bosnian female UNPOL officer, for example, said that when it came to interacting with the community, female police officers are better suited for the job:

> The community police concept is actually favorable for females more than males. Females are more soft and open; they can get things done smoothly. They understand better, and they are better at getting along with the community members, they are more open.

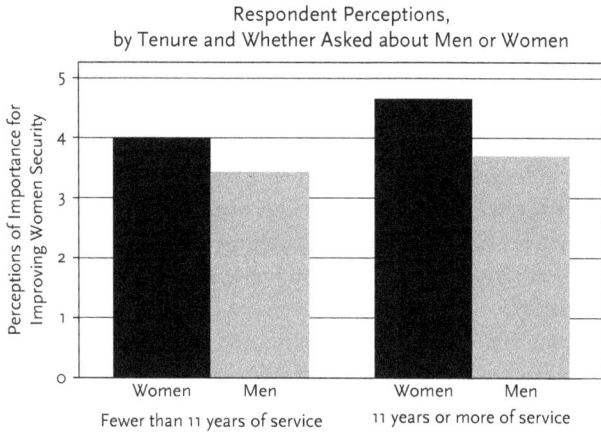

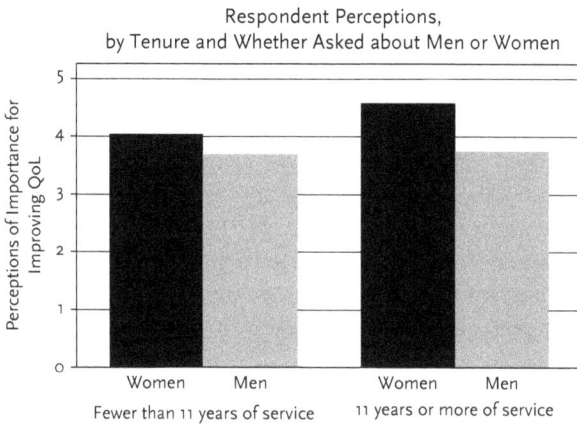

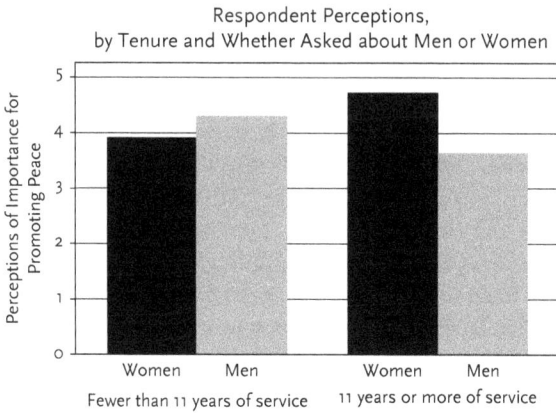

Figure 6.1. Mean survey responses of ninety-five women in UNMIL, by time in service.

Almost unanimously, a favorite part of the job for the female respondents was interacting with other female peacekeepers and with local women. For example, a Jordanian woman said that her favorite part was "when we make contact with Liberian females and all the UN females. Because, when we make contact with all the females, US, Bosnia, Romania, British, we learn a lot from other cultures and traditions from other missions." A Norwegian UNPOL officer similarly remarked, "I like the leeward [rural areas] because I came in contact with so many Liberian people and see how they live." One female UNPOL officer from Zimbabwe said, "I like the patrols, because I am interacting with many people, it is just exciting, mixing and mingling with the LNP counterparts, sometimes they feel so open, sometimes we talk, you get to know more about them; they are so open to me."

Related to their interactions with Liberian women, most women respondents felt that their presence helped inspire and encourage local women. This was especially true for the all-female Indian FPU. The female FPU commander proclaimed that her contingent had had the most effect in influencing Liberian women:

> In case of any problems, we are the ones they [Liberians] approach first, instead of police, the local population approach us first, the girls come first here, even they [Liberian girls] want to join the police force. Five years ago, out of twenty police-women, one was female, the application has tripled because of the female FPU presence. So, the next generation of Liberians, they have a feeling that females can do the jobs that men can do, so you will see more females standing on the street with uniforms; they are controlling the traffic, they are getting training in the academy, and the percentage has increased in five years.

These views were not limited to the all-female FPU. Views about the important influence female peacekeepers have on the local population also came from women in military contingents. One Nigerian woman said:

> We encourage Liberian women; that they see one of us with a rifle, then they also feel the courage, and we encourage them to join the army too. [The mission] gives other countries the knowledge that Nigerian women can do what they can do. [We] show other countries that Nigerian women can do what men can do.

Women in UNPOL also thought that they positively influence local women due to their presence. One Ghanaian officer said, "I don't know the culture here yet much, but I think women in uniform generally serve as role models to other women. I don't think it is different in Liberia." A Turkish woman concurred: "when they see us, they [Liberian women] feel that they can be the same." Female officers from Zimbabwe also said that their presence in Liberia encourages local female LNP officers who are concerned about leaving family and children for work:

> We can give them [Liberian women] moral support, like 'no no you must keep working for your country.' They have to be patient, one day things will be in their favor. Keep on encouraging them. I think that we have left an effect on them, we have

come here and explain to them and let them understand us; they appreciate this. We show them that I am a lady like you, I have children, I have a husband, some of them even ask, so when you talk, they get know your status, they see she was able to leave her husband and children.

Norwegian female officers indicated that it was important to have more women present because they influence the local population, but they thought it was especially important to have more African women in missions, because Liberian women are more likely to be influenced by them:

> For Liberian women, there should be more African females. For the Liberians, for respect and cooperation, if they see that females are coming from African countries it is more important from underdeveloped countries, some countries similar to Liberia.

This sense that female security personnel are important in reaching out to civilian women also resonates with what the peacekeepers perceived in their home countries. A Zimbabwean female peacekeeper, for example, said that the presence of women police officers in her home country has made the public trust police more: "just seeing male officer they [the public] are scared, now they interact with female police officers."

Aside from encouraging and inspiring local women, the women in our sample also thought that female peacekeepers played an active role in improving the physical security of women in the local population. One anecdote from a Ugandan female UNPOL officer illustrates this point about how the presence of women may enhance law enforcement responsiveness to SGBV at the community level. When she was participating in a joint patrol with UNPOL and the LNP, the patrol stopped at one of the police stations, where a Liberian female civilian wanted to make a statement about the fact that she had been raped. The male LNP officer refused to take the complaint because, he said, the rape case was outdated. The Ugandan female UNPOL officer was able to calm the complainant down, compel the LNP officer to take her case, and make sure that the case was documented. Later, she explained:

> They [LNP male officer] didn't want to enter the case. [They asked] why didn't she come at the time she was supposed to? So I tried to advise them to enter the case and I advised the lady to go for treatment. I did follow up on the case. They did arrest the man. It was sent to WCPU [Women and Children Protection Unit], I went there the following morning, I went to the WCPU, to ask them. I asked the person in charge of WCPU to go to the person that entered the report so that they could locate the woman and they got enough information about the lady.

In this case, the Ugandan officer's presence as a woman appears to have mattered in two ways. First, the Liberian woman trusted her enough to tell her what had happened. She wanted to speak to a woman, not another man (a male UNPOL officer was also on the patrol). Second, the female peacekeeper followed up on the case the next day and a week later. While it is the job of any police officer to follow up on cases, the female UNPOL officer said that she checked up on the case because "women are suffering this way, the sexual harassment, maybe I could help." This means that she considered one of her roles, as a woman, to be directly helping other women in the community, especially when it comes to SGBV.

This example well demonstrates the means by which women can improve the operational effectiveness of peacekeeping missions. Women are serving functions that men simply cannot. In this vein, a Swedish UNPOL officer specifically stated that female peacekeepers play a unique role in advising on issues related to women and children:

> I would like to see more police officers work with women and children. Give more advice about gender equality and children. If they can get more female officers in these things, it will be better. The role model issue is very important. We women are role models and it is doing a lot for the LNP.

Many male peacekeepers also thought that women played an important, unique role in improving the operational effectiveness of peacekeeping missions. A man from the Ghanaian military contingent said:

> When we are visiting the orphanages, we have many kids. If you look at their age range, it's six months to eighteen years. So, those who fall under eight years, there are many. You see, naturally, mothers are caring. So, when you are going to orphanage, it's better to have some kind of refreshment with them so we go with many of our female officers. When they go, they give them that kind of motherly touch because, you know, they are orphans. When we are also going to prisons, you know, we have also female prisoners. And when we go, we do counseling. We give them items but also counsel them. We respect the sensitivities of women by having women go. If you go as man, there are certain things the women hide. We even learned that when you are searching a woman, a woman should do that. It's good that a woman does that when it comes to a woman. It's very gender sensitive. It's part of our training, as far as security is concerned.

Such insight is corroborated by actual instances when female peacekeepers have taken steps to promote gender equality in the local population. For example, at the institutional level, an American female peacekeeper in UNPOL was responsible for helping to create the Gender Unit in the LNP, and female peacekeepers were instrumental in creating the Women and Children's Protection Unit in the LNP and pushing for the female quotas in the LNP. At the community level, when patrolling, female peacekeepers help ensure that the LNP hear cases of SGBV, which might otherwise go unnoticed.

The above comments suggest that female peacekeepers do see their role as unique in the mission. These statements parallel much of the language from the WPS agenda on how female peacekeepers contribute to missions. The same sentiments of the UN, policy-makers, and scholars that were noted in chapter 3 about the importance of women for building local trust, addressing SGBV, and providing inspiration for women and girls are echoed here by the female peacekeepers. In general, they feel that they provide inspiration to the local population and can motivate local women to challenge gender norms. Female peacekeepers may also advocate for awareness about SGBV and provide practical assistance, as during community visits such as those described by the male peacekeeper. The implication is that many women like interacting with local women, and want to do more of those types of activities.

The perceptions among peacekeepers that women can serve unique positions to inspire and advocate for local women, and can interact with them in ways that men cannot because of gender privacy and sensitivity constraints, blend into instrumentalist claims about female peacekeepers, often in ways that are consistent with a gendered protection norm. That is, we find that many of the women in our sample defined their own roles in instrumental terms and perceived the women in the local communities as a special class of people in need of greater protection.

For example, women in our study described the characteristics of women that make the mission better. A member of the Indian all-female FPU stated that "females are more dedicated, loyal, and sincere." The Bangladeshi women in a military unit also stated that they thought the incorporation of women into UN missions was important because there are women and children in the local population who need help, and they also thought that women possess certain attributes that men do not. One of these women remarked:

> In war, the women and children are more damaged; if more women come then we can serve the women and children. Women are sincere and honest. They work harder. Ladies are more honest than men.

A Danish military officer also suggested that women help build confidence among local communities because of the empathy they bring to the situation and their ability to relate to local women and children:

> We have to have females in all missions, even Afghanistan, because what peacekeeping is about is about confidence building and information gathering and you will only get into half the population if you have men, you have to have mixed groups and one particular field where we have a lot of women is CIMIC [Civil-Military Cooperation] branch, civil military, relations. The UN Charter says we have to put extra attention to women and children, it is obvious that it is a good field for women to go into, there are a lot of things for women to do and it takes a lot of empathy.

This quote demonstrates two interesting points. First, the Danish officer is highly aware of the role of gender in military operations. She states that the "UN Charter" places emphasis on women and children, which means that she has clearly been trained on gender mainstreaming and gender perspectives. Second, she states that women should go to all missions "even in Afghanistan" implying that perhaps Afghanistan is a dangerous mission and not one normally suitable for women. This corroborates the gender protection norm from chapter 4.

The women in the Indian FPU also thought that their role is less focused on security provision and more on humanitarian peace-building, for which they perceive women to be well fit. One officer said:

> We should merge with the general population more, the aim of bringing FPU is over. Initially for three or four years it was a disturbed country, but now we should bring a more humanitarian touch to the civilians.

Related to another common instrumentalist claim, one Bosnian woman suggested that the overall mission would be improved with more women because of their demeanor in group decision-making.

> I think if we would have enough females, then the mission will be improved. Because the working atmosphere will be more relaxed and focused on problems and concentrated. It will be more smooth. I think everywhere has to have females and males. Especially for females to talk, because it's different when a male is giving his experience. For sure, when females go leeward [rural areas], it is more difficult for females than males because of circumstances, but if you had a leeward female talk about her experience, it is different.

She also thought that including more women in peacekeeping missions would do well to hold males accountable for SEAHV.

> For sexual exploitation by peacekeepers, it will be good if everywhere we have females and males. When you take special part in leeward and just males and no females. I think the atmosphere is, I don't know . . . But if you have females, it will be different. When you have a female, females will see how male colleagues are behaving according to sexual exploitation, they will say something, I think females will complain if behavior is bad.

That such views are common among those who might be limited by some of these same entrenched gender stereotypes speaks to the complex origins of gender-related norms and values. These are powerful accounts of the value that these women see in their efforts, and it would be a mistake on a number of levels to suggest some form of normative judgment. An instrumentalist perspective about the value of women serving on peacekeeping missions will undoubtedly remain part of the conversation for considering how to improve gender equality within and through peacekeeping. Our analysis throughout this book merely suggests that it should not be the only perspective in the conversation.

These views expressed by female peacekeepers—that women play unique roles—confirm that women widely place a high value on their own participation. The roles and identities that they believe themselves to play and hold parallel the notions that the UN, policy-makers, and scholars have of them. They also parallel notions about how peacekeeping missions *should* be done. That is, these roles and identities conform to a "peace-building" identity for security personnel, or ideals of a postnational defense, that is oriented around a vocation of peace and stability and not war and combat. The roles and identities that female peacekeepers both enjoy and embrace, for example, as producers of community trust, as attenders to SGBV, and as inspiration, fit well with the goals of PKOs. In this sense, in the eyes of female peacekeepers, increasing the representation of women in peacekeeping missions might lead to more efficacious PKOs.

It is also important to recognize that some male peacekeepers expressed views similar to those of their female counterparts, but their perceptions of their own roles were much more diverse—they included building trust with locals and protection and mentoring, but also combat. In addition, their motivation for joining peacekeeping missions tended to mostly stem from an interest in monetary compensation and adventure rather than wanting to help the local population, which female peacekeepers tended to suggest was the main motivating factor for their joining the mission.

It is unclear where these ideas about roles and identities come from, as the focus group and interview questions did not address the origins of the participants' ideas. It is possible that these female peacekeepers were mirroring the views of policymakers in order to demonstrate that they were indeed effective in peacekeeping in the ways they are expected to be. They might simply have been echoing the dominant discourse around them that centered on how the inclusion of female-specific characteristics made the peacekeeping mission more effective. However, based on the interviews and focus groups, we think these women actually had considerable agency in forming beliefs about and articulating their roles. Their tone and actions demonstrated that these areas in which they believed they excelled provide a great sense of pride and that they actively tried to make a difference in the mission in the aforementioned ways. They never explicitly compared their beliefs to what policymakers say about them.

Yet, in order for these women to fully maximize their potential contribution in the ways the UN, policy-makers, and they themselves want, they need to have considerable leeway to participate in a vast array of roles in the mission, to engage local civilians and members of the local armed forces, and to be uninhibited by risks of SEAHV. We find, however, that women face specific barriers, some of them related to discrimination, the gendered protection norm, and SEAHV, that limit their ability to fully carry out basic peacekeeping duties, not to mention these additional roles that they perceive as unique to women. Somewhat ironically, widespread instrumentalist perceptions that "women's work" is separate from "men's work," and that the actual provision of security is part of the latter but not the former, provide some of the strongest limitations on the female peacekeepers' ability to make full use of their talents.

DISCRIMINATION MANIFESTED IN "WOMEN'S WORK"

An observable implication from the gender dichotomy of the warrior identity, as well as the militarization process, is that women should be systematically excluded from various roles in the security sector. This expectation is similar to Connell's (1987) demonstration of the gendered division of labor and Carreira's (2008) notion of structural labor divisions. Both stress the segregation of jobs and roles based on what is deemed gender-appropriate behavior. Applied to peacekeeping missions, gender power imbalances and expectations about gender directly inhibit the full participation of female peacekeepers.[7]

While many of the women we studied suggested that they played a unique role in the mission by inspiring local women, promoting gender equality, and legitimizing institutions, most women in our sample did gendered work in the mission. In the military, most women were nurses or doctors or worked in administration. The police were more diversified, but many women worked in "gendered" divisions, for example advising special units for sexual and gender-based crime or crimes against children. According to the questionnaire filled out by ninety-five women, a plurality served in administration (43 percent), and 18 percent said they served in medical areas (the second highest category). To a much lesser degree, women served in more masculine roles, such as providing security (11 percent). Instead, they more typically were given roles that are traditionally considered feminine.

Discrimination is also pervasive in the all-female FPU. While the mandate of this unit is to serve as backup in case of riot situations and to provide protection, they have also engaged in a number of community-related activities, such as teaching classes at a local school on topics such as dancing and cooking. They also opened their medical clinic to Liberians. Interestingly, the media and UN have played up the all-female FPU's community work and not its role in security provision.[8] The implication is that community-oriented projects are widely regarded as great fits for women, who are celebrated for doing "women's work" when in the mission. Personnel in the all-female FPU, which is mandated to provide protection, are not actually evaluated or commended for the job of providing protection. The warrior–peacemaker dichotomy in this case dictates the "appropriate" roles for women in the mission: to engage in peaceful and feminine roles even if the mandate of the unit is oriented around protection.

The female commander of the Indian FPU recognized that gender power imbalance can manifest in the form of discrimination. She noted that the mandate of the FPU was to provide security, but the unit was only judged based on how well the women were upholding their end of the gendered division of labor in the mission. She noted that women provided security and work operations just as men did:

> The focus of success for the Indian FPU has been on their community initiatives, not the actual work, but the main point is that we play the role in reverse, we are the ones who provide security and the logistics are done by men, it's an example that this can work—that women can partake in operations.

In addition, the notion of "women's work" means that male or mixed peacekeeping groups who do "female-oriented" activities, such as community outreach, are not recognized. Female peacekeepers are not unique in their community involvement, but they are unique in the way they get recognized for conducting such initiatives. All contingents (including military ones and FPUs) engage with the community, usually through civil-military coordination (CIMIC) activities. To the extent that such important activities are considered gendered, they will not receive the full weight of attention from all peacekeepers and instead will be relegated to the purview of a small minority of them.

In addition to gender roles in peacekeeping missions, women have to constantly negotiate and renegotiate their identities to conform to what is expected. One European female officer said that one day an African female officer came to her and said that she had learned and adapted her behavior in the mission from watching the European officer and had learned that she should not have long nails, paint them red, or do her hair because she wanted to be treated professionally like the European officer. She changed her appearance and behavior as a result of observing other female officers, but in a way that suited the masculine environment. In this case, the African female peacekeeper thought that if she changed her appearance to something better resembling the "manly woman," she might gain more respect. The gender power imbalance induced her to change her appearance, not to try to change the men's behavior toward her. In the end, this did not change the nature of her interactions with her superior. She still felt disrespected by her male superior and was eventually demoted.[9]

Another barrier mentioned in conversations related to discrimination was the fact that men often have the ability to make informal ties and form relationships in masculine institutions that help them advance in their careers, whereas it is more difficult for women to do so in a male-dominated field. The structures and culture are set up in such a way that it is easy for men to cultivate relationships with mission leaders in a social setting—whether it is going to a bar or restaurant—whereas for women participating in a social setting with men may not be appropriate without questions being raised about their sexual modesty. The Danish officer suggested that these informal networks especially matter at the command level:

> Sometimes in the command level, you might consider [gender balancing], to have a rule saying you have to have both men and women apply, that is because when you are 5 percent of the total, you do not have the same informal networks as the males and coming to a certain level where it is not based primarily on your qualifications, but your networks, about getting a job or task or not is very difficult for women.

Turning to another challenge related to gender-based discrimination and exclusion from missions, many women self-exclude from foreign deployments. In their answers to the questionnaire, many women said that leaving their families and homes was the most difficult part of their job. One Ghanaian woman stated that the hardest part about the mission was "being away from family especially if you have children that are growing." Another Bosnian officer said, "I know it's difficult for those who have children, especially females, to leave family and go elsewhere." Another Kenyan officer said, "Women are not interested [in going on UN missions], people don't want to leave their husbands and children." The latter point was reflected in the demographic composition of women who participated in the UNMIL mission. In the majority of interviews and focus groups, the women were either single and had no children or had adult children. Cultural and religious traditions also made it difficult for women to leave their families and join missions. One officer said, "Our ladies in Bangladesh, in family matters, this is the first job, our prime duty is with family." In Bangladesh, ostensibly, family roles come first.

At a first glance, the problem of missing family may not seem associated with discrimination. However, the problem is symptomatic of institutionalized gender power imbalances that discount women's needs in a mission. Making missions family friendly may be a way to increase the number of women in them, especially police officers. Some countries, such as Norway, provide benefits for their officers that reduce the burden on the women (and men) who do have families. A Norwegian officer explained her government's policy:

> In Norway, we have good pay, and they pay us for six trips home paid. We have the best appointment; we have the best package for coming. They pay for the partner to come halfway for the kids to meet halfway. Norwegian government pays that. Since it is so many trips back home, I have family, two kids, it wasn't difficult to say yes [to deploying].

The female Indian FPU commander also noted the potential importance of specific benefits to women so that they could go home to visit their families: the contributing country should "arrange good accommodations for them, increase monetary benefits, [give them a] free leave pass back home, so [they] can frequently go back. Otherwise you have to spend so much from your pocket." Currently, the rules and norms are such that they privilege traditional masculine roles, and this does not include valuing childcare. Thus the playing field is not equal, and this has consequences for women's full participation in PKOs.

THE GENDERED PROTECTION NORM AS A BARRIER TO FEMALE PEACEKEEPERS' MOVEMENT

The women in our sample voiced a number of issues that prevented them from achieving maximum impact as peacekeepers in roles they did occupy. According to our questionnaire, the top five problems women faced were that they missed their families and friends back home, they endured sexual harassment, the rules of the UN were too strict, women are not treated as equals to men, and the facilities are not adequate for women. (Table 6.1) shows the results for the questionnaire and the coded responses from the interviews and focus groups.[10]

Some of the challenges women faced indicate that a gendered norm of protection inhibited their ability to interact with local Liberians. In chapter 4, we saw that female peacekeepers were relegated to safe missions. Within missions, they may also be relegated to safe spaces. In both the questionnaire and the interviews and focus groups, one major problem the women experienced across the board, but especially in the military contingents, was not having an opportunity to leave their base and interact with women in other contingents or with local Liberians. Accessing local communities was particularly important to the roles that the female peacekeepers

Table 6.1. FREQUENCY OF BARRIER REFERENCES

Barrier	Questionnaire total	Focus group and interview references
Miss family/friends home	22 (23%)	6
Sexual harassment	16 (17%)	7
Women are not treated as equals to men	9 (9%)	8
Inadequate facilities for women	8 (8%)	6
Too many rules and regulations	8 (8%)	18

Note: The numbers in the second column count for how many times each issue came up as the worst problem, out of ninety-five total respondents. The numbers in the third column count in how many focus groups or interviews the issue was referenced, out of twenty-nine different focus groups or interviews.

expected to excel at (discussed above), because inspiring local women, promoting gender equality, and helping to legitimize institutions required that local Liberians see and interact with female peacekeepers. If female peacekeepers were not allowed outside their compound, they were unable to have an effect on the local population in the ways envisioned.

Restrictions and rules appear to be stronger among those in the military contingents than among UNPOL officers. The restrictions for military women included not being able to leave the base, not having a vehicle, and being required to travel with men. Some women reported that they left the base once or twice during their six-month or one-year deployment, and this was when the contingent participated in community outreach programs. Many women wanted to interact more with the local population but did not have the opportunity to do so because of the restrictions. One Filipino woman said, "We meet very few women peacekeepers and we never get to leave." Another woman from the Jordanian contingent expressed her frustration:

The biggest problem is the restriction on women. We don't see anything here because we cannot leave [the base]. [We want] just an exchange in culture, and thought. We came here to know people from other countries, not just about us.

One Bangladeshi woman said:

If authority permits, then we can do things for women. [Permission must come] from the UN, then governments must agree, then it will come to us. Who decides the CIMIC activities is from force headquarters. There are so many things to do for women, but we cannot do anything.

A woman from the Nigerian contingent when asked about extending her stay in the mission even said she felt trapped: "We want to go home now, [we have] no freedom, we are in the cage. We don't make friends."

Some restrictions on leaving the base do apply to both men and women. None of the male peacekeepers we interviewed, however, voiced concern about the restrictions as a key impediment to their ability to serve as peacekeepers. Moreover, comments by the women suggest that restrictions for women may be unequally restraining and that this is especially true for contingents from countries where gender equality may be less valued and gendered protection norms are stronger. The Jordanian women were not allowed to leave the base at all (even with male escorts), and the women in the Bangladeshi contingent were only allowed to leave the compound with the escort of a man. A woman from the Bangladeshi contingent summarized the sentiment that restrictions applied more strictly to women:

> The disliking thing about our service is the restriction as lady officers, the various restrictions we have. We cannot leave the base, we cannot go anywhere alone. We cannot do this, or that. We could not go to Monrovia alone. We need men [to accompany us]. So many restrictions. We have gender equality, but we do not follow in practice.

One observation from these statements is that female military officers from Bangladesh, Jordan, Nigeria, and the Philippines, all countries that may, at face value, appear to have rigid gender norms at home, are allowed to go on missions. But they may be allowed to go precisely because the rigid gender norms at home can carry through to the mission. Decision-makers in the country know that because women are in the contingent, they can still be "protected" by the formal and informal rules that limit the ability of the women on the mission to be in harm's way. Indeed this is corroborated by the quote from Group Captain Sohel in Chapter 4 when he said that "Female officers [from Bangladesh] have not yet been deployed as military observer where they are generally unarmed and remain alone in a remote area just to observe and report the hostile activities if any." The female officers are allowed to go to missions in contingents because they are better protected.

We observed frustrations over the limitations on leaving base in both military and nonmilitary units. The Indian all-female FPU has similar restrictive rules as a military contingent, as they do not have vehicles at their disposal. They complained about being too restricted to the compound and not interacting enough with other women. Interestingly, the rules apply despite the fact that the Indian FPU has taken initiatives to work with local Liberians. The FPU women complained that they did not have interaction with UNPOL or with the Liberian LNP and that there was too much separation and not enough interaction between the contingents. One Indian contingent member said that she would love to work with other medical officers from other contingents but this is not possible unless authorized by higher command. And the commander that we interviewed said that the UN places the restrictions. There seems to be abundant ambiguity about the rules for leaving the base and interacting with the locals and other women. Contingents may be cautious about adhering to UN rules, so they err on the side of more restrictions, especially for women.

UNPOL women are more mobile and have more freedom than women in the military or FPU because they are not beholden to country-specific contingents. They do not face the same oversight by contingent commanders and often have access to vehicles. Nevertheless, many of the UNPOL women in our sample still felt restricted in their ability to take initiatives and be innovative in their jobs. For example, the UN obstructed an initiative by a European female UNPOL officer and a female Nigerian military peacekeeper to bring the uniformed women (military and police) together and work on a project to build a women's rights center in one of the poorest communities in Monrovia.[11] Such projects must go through a proper vetting and chain-of-command process. In this case, the officers wanted to submit a proposal for a Quick Impact Project, which means that vetting would have occurred through the application process. However, the vetting processes are frequently perceived as not clearly written and subject to arbitrary judgment. Ironically, in this case, two female peacekeepers (from Switzerland and the United States) who had not been informed of the plans to submit a project proposal put a halt to it, arguing that appropriate UN protocol had not been followed. They stated that the project had not gone through the proper chain of command, which included the two of them. Thus, in some cases, the UN's own bureaucracy and arbitrary restrictions obstruct the very ideas and innovations that women are supposed to bring to missions.

In the previous example, women obstructed other women's initiatives, demonstrating that solidarity among women and sisterhood are not to be taken for granted. Enloe (1999, 2000) argues that political and social elites have been remarkably successful in keeping women's experiences distinct and therefore preventing alliances among women based on their subordinate gender status. The above example may be a case where institutional rules and practices (such as competitiveness) prevented alliances from forming among the women in the mission.

SEAHV AS A BARRIER FOR FEMALE PEACEKEEPERS

Thus far we have focused on the extent to which discrimination and protection norms impede the ability of female peacekeepers to fully serve their roles. Besides the rules and restrictions, other barriers to female peacekeepers reaching their full potential stem directly from persistent gender power imbalances. In chapter 5, we considered the way strong gender equality values among all members of a mission, male or female, can have important effects on the propensity for SEAHV targeting the local population. Here, we consider how a lack of gender equality or a belief in privileging militarized masculinity within missions can negatively impact the performance and security of the female personnel.

Foremost, the problem of sexual harassment is particularly alarming. If women face a hostile work environment, individual and group efficacy becomes untenable. The women in a mission cannot fully serve the mission's objectives if they must watch out for their own security and cannot trust their colleagues. Moreover, recruiting more women to serve as peacekeepers is likely to prove challenging with high rates of harassment.

While the topic came up less during the focus groups and interviews, it certainly came up in the questionnaires. Over 17 percent of the women who took the survey listed sexual harassment as their biggest impediment to their service as peacekeepers. And the problem was not confined to women in lower ranks. Even some high-level female military officers and UNPOL officers experienced sexual harassment by their colleagues. One high-ranking European military officer stated: "I was considering filing a complaint about sexual harassment, but I didn't. It's because he feels inferior to me, threatened by my constant quest for decisions, I give him too much work."

Turning to harassment more generally, many women in the survey stated that they did not feel as though men treated them as equals and that they felt as if they were in an "out-group." Some stated that when there are many countries with different standards as to how women are treated, sometimes it makes it difficult for women to be taken seriously or treated with respect. In one example, the highest ranking Nigerian female officer in the mission, Major Lola Aduke Oyediran Ugbodaga—mentioned in chapter 4—was promoted to the position of the deputy in the CIMIC office. Her male American supervisor and the rest of the male team constantly put her down publicly and talked about her behind her back. She was sometimes asked to do tasks for which she was not trained and then publicly humiliated when she was unable to fulfill them. Eventually she was removed from her position.

When women experience this type of behavior, it can be hard for them to speak up. Some women speak up, but it takes them a while to confront their male counterparts, and some women remain quiet and acquiesce to the power imbalance. In the case of UNMIL, both the highest ranking female military officer and highest ranking female police officer experienced discrimination in their jobs. They complained that in meetings, often their authority was not respected and that lower ranking men did not obey their commands. They both complained that men would demean them publicly during meetings. One chose to confront the situation by directly addressing the individual(s) involved; the other one did not do anything and internalized the discrimination. One day, the female military officer simply yelled back at the individual(s) involved. She said that the behavior of the men involved improved after that altercation. But it took her nearly halfway into her time in the mission to confront them. The female police officer did not confront the situation and had a much more negative view about the mission than the woman who confronted her challenger(s).

Not only was sexual harassment and discrimination a problem in the mission, but it was also a problem as women worked in the host country. Women said that sometimes they had a hard time with adapting to and communicating with locals. In some cases, language was a barrier, but in other cases, gender stereotypes about women made it difficult for them to be taken seriously by local men. Women reported that many Liberian men approached them saying they wanted to marry them, even men whom the women were supposed to advise or work with as counterparts. A Norwegian female officer said:

> If I say something, I don't think they [LNP] will take me seriously, a lot of them ask me to marry them, and to bring them home and just to be their girlfriend. That's because I am a female.

The barriers mentioned in these sections are, in part, manifestations of gender power imbalances. The barriers make it difficult for women to carry out basic peacekeeping duties, in addition to performing the tasks and activities at which they, as well as many advocates in the UN, tend to expect women to shine. If women are discriminated against, relegated to certain safe spaces, and sexually harassed, how can they focus on improving the condition of locals? The restrictions and rules placed on women (and men) especially affect their ability to have a maximum impact on the local community. If women cannot leave their bases and visit communities, how can they inspire local women? If they are not allowed to be innovative and come up with projects to help communities, how can they help promote gender equality in the host country? In the absence of such barriers, women could contribute wholly and fully to a range of UN peacekeeping activities. Right now, this does not seem to be a reality.

MISSION BENEFITS TO FEMALE PEACEKEEPERS

The responses from our interviews and focus groups were not all negative. Many of the female peacekeepers in our sample maintained that their experience in UNMIL was, overall, positive. Both military and police female peacekeepers felt empowered in their roles. A Ghanaian officer said, "it is an opportunity to interact with other female colleagues from all over the world. It also broadens one's horizon about policing." Another Turkish female UNPOL officer concurred:

> I met colleagues or other people from different countries and I realized that they are not so different than me or my country. It is so nice to meet with different people. I learned all about myself and I learned a lot about the world I am living in. About how I can manage things. What are the weak points in me. That's the reason I am here for a long time.

In some cases, women reported that the experience made them better able to cope emotionally with rather difficult environments and experiences. In addressing the potential for women to get emotionally overwhelmed by the hardships they see, one woman said, "we are all females and we have more emotions than male colleagues and we are sorry, we feel sorry. Now I am much stronger, I improved myself." Another officer stated that the experience of working with a UN mission helps women grow professionally:

> You come to the mission with certain knowledge about yourself and then you realize that no, it is different. It also helps you to grow professionally. It has helped me to grow professionally. Even when I go back home, I will know how to relate to my children better.

Another female UNPOL officer stated that she feels a sense of purpose in the mission:

> I love it here, and it is good work and I feel that I am helpful to the mission, and I think the mission thinks that I am helpful a little bit, because if they don't think I am helpful, they wouldn't extend me.

If many of the female peacekeepers with whom we had a chance to engage felt positive about their experiences, even in the face of unequal restrictions, sexual harassment, unequal treatment, and greater burdens than men in serving away from their home countries, we might expect even greater opportunities for women to thrive as gender power imbalances in the missions are dismantled.

THE IMPACT OF UNMIL FEMALE PEACEKEEPERS IN LIBERIA

The views and experiences of female peacekeepers are important gauges for assessing what impact they believe they are having, given the gender power imbalances in peacekeeping missions. But whether and how they are uniquely serving local communities remains an empirical question. Given that there are significant barriers for female peacekeepers, how much does this affect their work on the ground, with locals? In chapter 3, we noted that the UN has suggested that female peacekeepers may help legitimize or improve the image of the peacekeeping mission. The female peacekeepers in our sample alluded to this, but they were much more focused on their impact on local women. We thus turn to gauging local perceptions of female peacekeepers and whether contact with them improves perceptions of the peacekeeping mission in Monrovia, both as a whole and in certain ex-combatant communities.

In order to assess different perceptions of Liberians based on their contact with female peacekeepers, we use data from a representative survey Sabrina Karim conducted in 2012, along with other coauthors.[12] The representative survey was administered to 1,381 respondents to gauge the level of transactional sex in Monrovia and asked whether individuals had social interactions with peacekeepers (and the sex of the peacekeeper with whom they had the interaction),[13] and it asked one question related to perceptions of how well UNMIL has provided security.[14] When individuals had social interactions with only female peacekeepers, as opposed to only male peacekeepers, they were about 16% more likely to answer that the presence of UNMIL had increased their personal security.[15] This difference is statistically significant, which suggests that there are positive dividends from including more women in peacekeeping missions. This survey's results indicate that social interactions with female peacekeepers, as opposed to those with male peacekeepers, enhanced peoples' perceptions of the security situation in Liberia.

These results are also corroborated in a separate study that was conducted in two-excombatant communities in Monrovia.[16] In this study, holding all else equal, contact with a female peacekeeper nearly doubled the likelihood of an individual answering that they believed female peacekeepers to be better than male peacekeepers, from a 14 percent likelihood to a 27 percent likelihood to agree.[17] These positive results could perhaps be scaled up if more women were added to peacekeeping missions.

Despite the positive indication from the studies, we still note the sparseness of local interactions with female peacekeepers. In the representative sample of Monrovia, 4 percent (57 individuals) reported having contact with female peacekeepers only, whereas 23 percent (318 individuals) of the sample reported having interactions with male peacekeepers only.[18] The overall contact rate for the Monrovia sample was 27 percent. Thus, the data confirm the aforementioned complaints by the female peacekeepers that they rarely got to interact with locals.

While the study by Sabrina Karim (2016b) of the ex-combatant communities in Monrovia found that contact with female peacekeepers, as opposed to male peacekeepers, leads to perceptions that women are more effective than men, none of the female respondents who had contact with female peacekeepers thought that female peacekeepers are better than male peacekeepers. In other words, the positive perceptions of security after meeting with female peacekeepers was mostly driven by local men who have contact with female peacekeepers. This is further corroboration of the quotes from female peacekeepers suggesting that there are real access barriers when it comes to interacting with locals, particularly women.

Moreover, the ex-combatant community study did not find that contact with female peacekeepers leads to perceptions that the security situation with regards to sexual violence has much improved. When locals in these two communities were asked "who do you think can best protect you from being raped?" only 4 percent of the sample thought that female peacekeepers could protect them from rape and only 6 percent of the sample thought that male peacekeepers could protect them from rape (Karim, 2016b). Instead, it appears that locals prefer domestic law enforcement to protect them from rape (figure 6.2).

Finally, the study found a positive and statistically significant relationship between those who had contact with female peacekeepers and beliefs about women joining the military (Karim, 2016b). At the same time, however, there was a negative relationship between contact with female peacekeepers and the belief that women should join the police. Among female respondents only, the relationship between contact with female peacekeepers and women's participation in the military and police was negative (Karim, 2016b), suggesting that contact with female

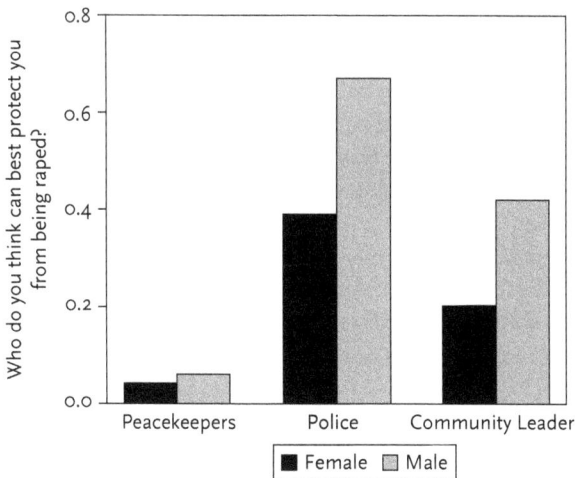

Figure 6.2. Perceptions of Protection from Rape Provided by Different Actors

peacekeepers reduced the likelihood of holding the opinion that women should join the military and police force.[19] The survey also asked individuals about if they would like to join the military and police and, if they said yes, they were also asked why they would like to join. Only eight respondents (3 percent) directly said they were inspired by female peacekeepers (Karim, 2016b).[20] These results from the ex-combatant survey do not support the prevailing hope expressed in many of the quotes by female peacekeepers suggesting that they are role models for women to join the domestic security forces. Again, female peacekeepers are hardly visible in local communities, and they do not much interact with the local population. Thus, if they are not visible to local women, they are unlikely to inspire them to join the security forces.

Overall the results from the surveys suggest that although contact with female peacekeepers is associated with enhanced perceptions of general security by the local population, much of the instrumental rhetoric surrounding female peacekeeper integration may be overstated. At this time, we cannot conclude from the evidence that contact with female peacekeepers much improves how locals perceive their abilities to address the security challenges in the country.

CONCLUSION

The evidence from women's experiences in this chapter corroborates the findings from chapters 4 and 5. Related to chapter 4, we found additional ways discrimination and the gendered protection norm curtail the ability of women to serve as peacekeepers. Discrimination is first manifested in the types of roles and jobs women occupy, which tend to be gendered. Women may not be perceived as capable of handling security roles and receive less commendation for participating in them. We saw evidence of the protection norm, as female peacekeepers said they often faced a number of protective rules and regulations that prevented them from interacting with locals and other peacekeepers. They appear to be relegated to safe spaces. Given that such interaction and collaboration are necessary to inspire local women, promote gender equality, and legitimize institutions, if women are unable to forge these relationships, they may not realize well the objectives they have for themselves. The ability for men to fully serve as effective peacekeepers is also constrained to the extent that they are not commended for doing the types of important activities traditionally associated with femininity.

Related to chapter 5, which focused on SEAHV perpetrated against local populations, we also find evidence of harassment perpetrated against fellow peacekeepers. Such behavior toward female colleagues is yet another symptom of gender power imbalances that can render missions dysfunctional and hostile to gender diversity. The level of sexual harassment reported in our survey sample is especially troubling, given that the response bias on such a sensitive topic is likely to be starkly downward.

Despite these constraints, many female peacekeepers still view their experiences positively and their roles as fundamental to the success of the mission. While this is good news for now, we presume that the female peacekeepers will tend to be even more content as gender equality improves in the wake of reforms related to the WPS agenda worldwide. In other words, if women were not discriminated against, if they were able to go to a diverse range of spaces and did not suffer from sexual harassment, they could more fully and freely realize their potential, as they and policymakers have so eloquently stated.

The restrictions that keep female peacekeepers from many local spaces perhaps help explain why the study by Sabrina Karim (2016b) found that they did not much contribute to addressing sexual violence and did not inspire local women to join the domestic security sector—adequate presence is required for such effects. Nevertheless, the finding that contact with female peacekeepers, especially by men, did improve perceptions of the overall security situation provides reason for hope. We contend that if we detect effects with such small numbers of women interacting with locals, such effects could be drastically magnified with less restricted participation by female peacekeepers. Allowing female peacekeepers to have a more ubiquitous presence could go a long way in improving the mission environment and security situation in the host country.

CHAPTER 7

On the Ground

Local Legacies of Gender Reforms in

the UN Mission in Liberia

SABRINA KARIM, KYLE BEARDSLEY, ROBERT BLAIR, AND MICHAEL GILLIGAN

Margaret joined the LNP in 2010 because she was inspired by women in the Police Support Unit (PSU), an elite arm of the police force responsible for responding to emergency situations. Specifically, the PSU is in charge of areas where UNMIL is drawing down. The women in the unit carrying arms and driving inspired Margaret, as she aspired to have similar responsibilities. Three years later, she was at the top of her PSU class and was a rising star in the LNP. Margaret's favorite part about training was the fact that she got to be trained by American UNPOL officers in firearms. As she speaks about the firearms instruction she received, she starts glowing and speaking excitedly: "I would love to instruct firearms at the Academy." Along with other officers, she contends that without the UN's presence and leadership on gender issues, the LNP would not have focused on improving the representation of women in the LNP. For that reason, she is thankful for the UN's influence. Yet, despite her success in the LNP and excitement about working for the PSU, she still notes that gender power imbalances are a problem in the LNP. Specifically, she notes, "there are not enough women in leadership positions in the LNP." Gender-based reforms in the LNP remain insufficient, with a dearth of women promoted to higher ranking positions, even when they are well qualified. Margaret strongly believes that women make an important contribution to policing and that it is important to have women in every unit, but she points out that while the LNP has made vast improvements since during the war, the state of gender equality in the LNP is still far from satisfactory. She hopes to one day climb the ranks of the LNP and maybe even become its inspector general.

Margaret is representative of a fundamental shift in not only Liberia's security sector but also SSR worldwide. Her ability to participate in the security sector, by joining the LNP and the PSU, is a direct result of the gender reforms instituted by peacekeeping missions and the government. As peacekeepers are increasingly involved in building the local institutions necessary for consolidated democracy and economic development, this has entailed, inter alia, assistance in the design and training of the police forces, judicial systems, and other elements of the security sector. UN peace operations have especially emphasized SSR as an integral step toward self-enforcing peace.[1] Through PKOs, SSR has played crucial roles in advancing gender reforms in host country institutions. As we saw in chapter 2, peacekeeping missions deploy to countries with higher levels of sexual violence, and they increase the probability that host countries will adopt gender reforms in the security sector and that they will adopt UNSCR 1325 NAPs.

It is also possible that peacekeeping missions impede the ability of the benefits of such reforms to be realized. We have already found that gender power imbalances in peacekeeping missions present a major challenge for the full and free participation of female peacekeepers. Do the norms and structures that perpetuate gender power imbalances transfer between the operations and local security forces? If PKOs are heavily influenced by exclusion, discrimination, protection, and SEAHV, we might expect greater involvement by peacekeeping missions in SSR to leave behind the same imprints on the local security sectors. To investigate these tendencies, we assess the local legacies of PKOs.

We begin by analyzing how gender reforms fostered by UNMIL may have shaped the local security sector with respect to discrimination, the gendered protection norm, and SEAHV. We do this using data from a lab-in-the-field experiment conducted with the LNP, in which we analyzed the extent and forms of male dominance in the institution.[2] We also use survey evidence from Liberian communities to analyze whether the public is still fearful of SEAHV by local law enforcement. In this way, we analyze the extent to which the peacekeeping mission and female peacekeepers have made an impact on local women's lives such as Margaret's, the extent to which Margaret and other women have been able to fully participate in the LNP, and the extent to which Margaret and other women affect Liberians' willingness to trust the LNP.

Moving forward, we want to make it clear that we are not suggesting that peacekeeping missions are the sole or even main drivers of gender equality in host country institutions.[3] Analyses by Helen Basini and Caitlin Ryan (2016) show the extent to which domestic actors have played a major role in many gender reforms.[4] Pamela Scully (2010) has also highlighted how women's organizations have been involved in the peace-building process in Liberia. Moreover, the fact that Leymah Gbowee won the Nobel Peace Prize in 2011 (along with President Ellen Johnson Sirleaf) for her work uniting women's groups during the civil war highlights the extent to which local groups have been active in peace-building.[5] Thus, our assessment of the extent to which peacekeeping missions are vehicles to promote gender equality should not diminish the work of these groups or be taken to suggest that peacekeepers are the only vehicles for promoting gender equality. Our goal is to isolate peacekeeping's contributions on mitigating gender power imbalances in host countries, knowing that women's organizations and other state and civil society actors are predominant in promoting reforms.

INTERNATIONAL INFLUENCES ON SECURITY SECTOR REFORMS IN LIBERIA

Increasingly, peace operations have entailed assistance in the design and training of the police forces, judicial systems, and other elements of the host country security sectors. Roland Paris (2004) has argued that the rebuilding of these institutions should precede democratic governance; otherwise peace becomes elusive. In the field, the UN and other international actors support national authorities to facilitate national SSR dialogues; develop national security and defense policies, strategies and plans; strengthen oversight, management, and coordination capacities; articulate security sector legislation; mobilize resources for SSR-related projects; harmonize international support to SSR education, training, and institution building; and monitor and evaluate programs and results.[6]

In Liberia, there has been no shortage of SSRs designed and implemented by UNMIL. The 2003 peace agreement designated UNMIL as the lead body to rebuild the LNP. The DPKO has given greater support to UNMIL than any other mission.[7] The parties agreed to dissolve security units that during the interim government in the 1990s had developed reputations for corruption and indiscriminate violence, such as Charles Taylor's infamous "Anti-Terrorist Unit," the "Special Operations Division," and the "Black Berets" (Friedman, 2011). They decided to initially create a professional police force that would be vetted and trained through the establishment of a national academy. The goal was to develop highly skilled officers and specialized units to combat specific threats, and this included the refurbishment of the National Police Training Academy and a comprehensive vetting strategy.[8] The initial, immediate reforms included removal of military rank (which helped to demilitarize the police), targeted recruitment of 3,500 officers, quick impact projects to rebuild police stations, implementation of new standards for recruits,[9] and new training based on scenarios (Friedman, 2011).[10] As of March 2014 there were 4,570 police officers in the LNP. Thus, for a country of more than four million people, there are 114 officers per 100,000 people. In the last ten years, the LNP has established a presence in all of the country's regions, created guidelines for recruitment and promotion, demilitarized the police, and maintained the National Police Training Academy.

In addition to these basic reforms, a number of special units have also been created. The US State Department has largely funded the training, armament, and equipment of the Emergency Response Unit (ERU) and the PSU of the LNP (the paramilitary braches of the LNP). These two units are mobile, combat-capable units designed to help regular police meet heightened dangers, confront armed groups formed in defiance of the state's authority, and cooperate with the AFL in countering major internal or external threats (Friedman, 2011). Both units were trained and vetted alongside the AFL by the US State Department. More recently, UNMIL and other LNP donors have called for specialists on terrorism, human trafficking, and transnational crime, currently issues of high priority, to come and assist the force.

Many LNP officers have also been able to travel abroad to undergo international training. According to LNP officers, beginning in 2013 and continuing into 2014, top LNP officers have been going to the Ghana Institute of Public Administration for further training and professional development. In 2011, the Bureau of International Narcotics and Law Enforcement Affairs, a bureau of the US State Department, funded officers to receive training in the United States. The training emphasized community policing and included instruction in the classroom, in practical exercises, and in on-the-job experience, in the hope that the newly trained officers would educate their peers on returning to Liberia. Other training has occurred in China, Nigeria, France, Turkey, Egypt, Niger, Ethiopia, Sierra Leone, Sweden, and Botswana. The hope is that this international training, in addition to UNMIL's lead in rebuilding and reforming the police, has led to the creation of a professional police force capable of handling the security situation in Liberia.

UNMIL'S INFLUENCES ON SECURITY SECTOR GENDER REFORMS IN LIBERIA

With respect to gender and state-building, chapter 2 highlighted how UN resolutions have propelled the WPS agenda to the forefront of international politics and inspired gender reforms in local countries. As such, UN peace operations have begun to participate more in peace-building and institution-building programs, and they have especially emphasized SSR with a gender focus as an integral step toward self-enforcing peace.

UNMIL is a prime example of how the international community has infused the SSR process with gender concerns.[11] The text of the original mandate in 2003 stated that the Security Council reaffirmed the "importance of a gender perspective in peacekeeping operations and post-conflict peace-building in accordance with Resolution 1325 (2000)" and that the mandate "recalls the need to address violence against women and girls as a tool of warfare, and encourages UNMIL as well as the Liberian parties to actively address these issues."[12] At the time, such language was relatively new for the UN. UNMIL strived to implement this part of the mandate and helped implement a number of reforms related to gender equality, particularly in the security sector. UNMIL specifically was integral in helping the Liberian government, through its Ministry of Gender and Social Welfare, to draft and pass its NAP.[13] UNMIL's influence in drafting the NAP is apparent because the NAP mentions UNMIL's own gender reforms:

> Liberia also has the only serving female Special Representative of the UN Secretary-General (SRSG) and the first All Female Formed Police Unit deployed by India. The United Nations Mission in Liberia (UNMIL) is one of the largest peace keeping missions with a clearly defined mandate to implement Resolution 1325 and the Office

of the Gender Adviser (UNMIL OGA) is very active in ensuring that this mandate is met. In addition to implementing Resolution 1325, UNMIL, in recognition of the high incidence of sexual and gender-based violence (SGBV) in Liberia, is also taking steps to implement Resolution 1820. Initiatives include supporting National Anti-Rape and other campaigns to raise awareness and eliminate violence against women and girls and a National Plan of Action on GBV. UNMIL also has a strong focus on ensuring zero tolerance to sexual abuse and exploitation (SEA) of nationals by peacekeepers and has supported government initiatives to prevent such abuse.[14]

That UNMIL served a crucial role in drafting the NAP illustrates the potential for peacekeeping missions to promote gender reforms in host countries. According to UNMIL's *Gender Mainstreaming in Peacekeeping Operations Liberia 2003–2009 Best Practices, Report*, UNMIL was instrumental in taking a gendered approach to the DDR process related to female combatants (UNMIL, 2010).[15] In fact, UNMIL has been heralded as the first mission that included women in the process (Basini, 2013). According to this report, UNMIL also ensured the widespread participation of women in the national elections and in mobilizing the participation of women in the local communities through strategic advocacy networks such as the Women's NGO Secretariat of Liberia.

The report also mentions that one of UNMIL's main focuses was SGBV.[16] With respect to SGBV, the Office of the Gender Adviser in UNMIL helped create the National Gender Based Violence Taskforce in 2006, helped create a National Action Plan for Gender Based Violence, helped create the four-year UN/Government Joint program on SGBV in 2008, and has ensured that the zero tolerance policy on SEA was enforced by creating the conduct and discipline team in UNMIL. The National Gender-Based Violence Plan of Action is constructed on four pillars: protection of women and children from sexualized and gender-based violence; prevention of sexual and gender-based violence; promotion of women's human rights; and participation of women in peace processes. The Office of the Gender Adviser in UNMIL was also instrumental in creating special Criminal Court E in 2009 for prosecuting sexual offenses, to help reduce the backlog of SGBV crimes. It helped launch the National Campaign on Violence Against Women in 2005, a campaign to raise awareness about SEAHV in 2006, and an antirape campaign in 2007. It has also helped to review and simplify laws that promote women's rights, for example passing a comprehensive antirape law and an equal rights in customary marriage law, and to establish a bureau of SGBV in the Ministry of Justice.

Finally, UNMIL has directly influenced gender reforms in the SSR process. UNMIL has played an integral role in Liberia's police reforms: Resolutions have called for increases in UNPOL to provide expertise in specialized fields, to provide operational support, and to serve as advisers to the LNP (Karim and Gorman, 2016). One of the first tasks of the UNMIL peacekeeping mission was to develop the Gender Policy for the LNP in 2005, which served as the primary document to motivate female ratio balancing in the LNP and was the first such policy in any UN mission (Bacon, 2012).[17] In 2008, the UN helped the LNP introduce a 15 percent quota in an attempt to increase the influence of women in the institution and to improve the LNP's capacity to respond to gender-based violence. UNPOL worked with the LNP on its Gender Advisory Work Plan, which increased the quota to 20 percent.[18] The UN owns much of the responsibility for institutionalizing these initial quotas, but in 2012 President Sirleaf, along with UN Women and UNMIL,[19] pushed an initiative that increased the quota to 30 percent. The LNP is close to meeting the 20 percent quota but far from reaching the 30 percent one. By January 2016, the LNP had 19 percent female officers (compared with 2 percent in 2005) (Bacon 2012).

One of the initial and major problems in recruiting women has been finding women who are qualified. In order to overcome this problem, the Committee for National Recruitment of Women, which included representatives from UNPOL (in UNMIL) and the Liberian government, developed the Educational Support program—a three-month condensed program that women could complete as a prerequisite for entering the police force. This helped increase the pool of qualified women for recruitment into the LNP (Bacon, 2012). In addition, a new recruitment campaign, sponsored by the UN, Australia, and the UK, to hire women from rural Liberia was under way in 2014 and 2015. Such initiatives help ensure that improvements in the representation of women in the LNP continues.

Aside from the recruitment of more women into the LNP, UNMIL has played a major role in ensuring that the LNP includes other gender reforms. In 2005, the Norwegian and Danish governments partnered with UNICEF, UNDP, and UNMIL to create the Women and Children Protection Unit in the LNP.[20] It was established to handle cases of crimes committed against women and children, such as sexual violence, domestic abuse, child abuse and abandonment, sexual assault, corruption of minors, and other such criminal offenses. The LNP also has the special Gender Unit, which is responsible for promoting gender equality within the LNP (see appendix 4). This unit administers gender-training programs that rotate among different zones and depots and monitors gender equality within the LNP. The unit was started by an American female officer in 2008 and has recently undergone a transformation funded by UN Women.

Despite the obstacles that discrimination, the gendered protection norm, and SEAHV can pose for female peacekeepers, female peacekeepers were still active in promoting and implementing gender reforms in UNMIL. As mentioned, an American female UNPOL officer pushed forward the formation of the Gender Unit in the LNP. In 2012, a Swiss female peacekeeper worked with the unit to get a sexual harassment policy implemented in the LNP. The formation of the Women and Children's Protection Unit was also the culmination of efforts by various actors, including female peacekeepers. More recently, the push for the new LNP recruitment campaign from rural areas came from Jane Rhodes (introduced in chapter 5), who has also worked to build a network of female law enforcement officers to encourage professional development in the LNP. The evidence from UNMIL thus shows that female peacekeepers have been instrumental in ensuring that gender reforms are carried out.

One item to clarify is that there is a distinction between UMMIL's Office of the Gender Adviser and female peacekeepers. The Office of the Gender Adviser consists strictly of civilian personnel. Female peacekeepers are police and military personnel from contributing countries. The Office of the Gender Adviser is responsible for larger gender reforms in missions, but much of the implementation of policies in the domestic security forces is done by peacekeepers. In many cases, female peacekeepers have taken their own initiatives without supervision or direction from the Office of the Gender Adviser, such as with the female recruitment campaign and sexual harassment policy. However, as we noted in chapter 5, female peacekeepers are prevented from reaching their full potential—and thus many female peacekeepers do not or cannot undertake their own initiatives even if they want to—and some initiatives are thwarted.[21]

While the foregoing discussion indicates that UNMIL has been quite active in promoting gender reforms, it would be nice to have a sense of whether the Liberian government would have implemented such reforms without UNMIL. This counterfactual is difficult to assess, given that we only observe a situation where UNMIL was present and did initiate reforms. Nevertheless, it is highly unlikely that the aforementioned reforms would have occurred without UNMIL. Compared to a case similar to Liberia, Guinea—used as a matched pair in the analysis by Michael Gilligan and Ernest Sergenti (2008)—has not had a peacekeeping mission and has not reformed its security sector to include gender reforms to the same extent as Liberia. It is thus plausible that gender reforms would not have achieved such momentum without the mission.[22] In addition, the resources necessary to recruit women, and to build and equip two new units from scratch, required initiative from the UN and donor countries.

With UNMIL's contribution to the reforms established, we now ask, have these reforms contributed to breaking down gender power imbalances in the Liberian security sector and among Liberians more generally? Or do gender power imbalances prevail, especially because manifestations of gender power imbalances are still such a major problem in UNMIL itself? The next sections are aimed at answering these questions.

THE PERSISTENCE OF GENDER POWER IMBALANCES IN THE LIBERIAN NATIONAL POLICE

Earlier chapters have highlighted how gender power imbalances are a major problem in PKOs. Recall that manifestations of the gender power imbalances, such as exclusion, discrimination, and the gendered protection norm, prevent female peacekeepers from participating in missions, particularly ones that are more dangerous, and from fully participating in all mission roles and activities. Moreover, SEAHV is a problem both within and through missions. It is possible that both these negative manifestations could carry over to local security institutions and further entrench preexisting domestic gender power imbalances. In order to assess peacekeeping's influences on male dominance in the Liberian security sector, we start with an assessment of some of the gender-related challenges that currently plague the LNP and then move on to whether we see any evidence of a value for gender equality, hence potential for equal opportunity, strengthening within and through the LNP as a result of the gender reforms supported by international actors.

We assess gender power imbalances within the LNP using evidence from a lab-in-the-field experiment involving 612 LNP officers in Monrovia in January 2013.[23]

We randomly selected these officers from their different departments in the LNP and randomly assigned them to groups of six. The groups contained differing numbers of women: no women, two women, four women, or all women. In total, we had thirty-three groups containing all men, twenty-nine groups containing two women, twenty-one groups containing four women, and nineteen groups containing all women. Officers were randomly assigned to one of each of these four types of groups. Teams of trained, Liberian enumerators were then randomly assigned to the groups to implement activities and record interactions among participants. In addition to the activities, we also administered background and exit questionnaires, including a survey experiment designed to assess gender discrimination in training. A full account of the experiment can be found in appendix 4.

Discrimination and the Protection Norm in the Liberian National Police

As one measure of latent discrimination against women in the LNP, we used a survey experiment as part of the postconflict questionnaire for these 612 participants in our lab-in-the-field experiment. For the survey experiment, we offered each officer two short profiles describing a potential firearms instructor. The qualifications of the instructors were very similar. One of the profiles always had the name "Abraham," while the other was named either "John" or "Patience" randomly. Aside from the randomly assigned names, the descriptions of this second instructor's qualifications were identical. This allowed us to determine whether the profile that was associated with a woman was less likely to be accepted than the identical profile associated with a man. In addition to this experiment, we asked the participants to vote for which member of the group they thought should serve as leader in the future. We also conducted a survey of our subjects on their opinions about women in the LNP.

We found evidence of discrimination in the LNP. When given identical backgrounds, individuals chose Patience as the firearms instructor 38 percent of the time when the alternative choice was Abraham, whereas officers chose John 46 percent of the time when the alternative choice was Abraham. There is a statistically significant difference between the two groups.[24] This means that in comparing the same biographies of firearms instructors, when choosing between John and Patience, individuals were more likely to choose John.

Moreover, and unsurprisingly, the difference was driven by gender bias among the male participants. Using a regression analysis described in appendix 4, figure 7.1 displays the predicted probability of choosing Abraham over the alternative, by sex and by whether the alternative was John or Patience. The points are the expected probabilities of choosing Abraham, and we also plot the 90 percent confidence intervals. On the left side of the graph, we see that men were significantly more likely to choose Abraham when the alternative was Patience than when the alternative was John. In contrast, there was no statistically significant difference in the propensity to choose Abraham when the alternative was John or Patience for the female participants.

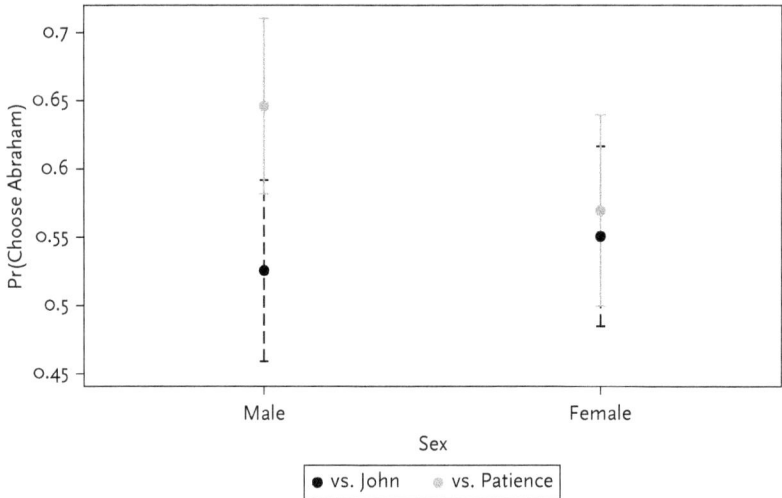

Figure 7.1. Probability of choosing Abraham, conditional on the alternative.

Firearms instruction may be considered a masculine activity, one that entails adherence to a warrior identity. As mentioned, security personnel may be socialized to think that men are better warriors and protectors. The evidence from the LNP illustrates that this may still be the case. The implication is that if men are the main decision-makers about promotions and deployments based on security provision, they may not be likely to choose women for promotion based on firearms aptitude, or for deployment in areas that require firearms, because they do not think that women will be as good at firearms instruction as men. For Margaret, who wants to be a firearms instructor, this could be bad news.

In 2012, like Margaret, Hazel, an officer in the ERU—the "national Liberian SWAT team"—believed women were just as good as men at policing. She stated that even though there were only three women in the ERU because it was a masculine-dominated unit, "I don't think that women should think that way, we have a female president so what the men can do, females can do it too." Such sentiment is reflected in our survey of the LNP in Monrovia: 95 percent of women thought that women were just as good as men in terms of policing, but only 76 percent of men thought so. Moreover, among the women, 97 percent thought that female LNP officers made good unit leaders, and among the men, 75 percent thought so. Again, this is problematic if promotion or other decision-making about sending individuals on operations is based on these types of perceptions about women.

Discrimination based on gender roles was also evident in the officers' opinions about whom they thought were better responders when called into certain types of situations. Table 7.1 looks at which sex LNP officers believed the public trusted more based on different job functions. The evidence suggests that the sex of the officers is associated with preconceived notions about the gendered division of labor.[25] Both male and female participants were unlikely to choose men as best suited to handle cases of rape, but the male participants were more likely than their female colleagues

Table 7.1. EXIT SURVEY RESULTS

Question	Female responders			Male responders		
	Women	Men	Both	Women	Men	Both
Who is better at handling cases of rape and domestic violence?	60%	2%	37%	38%	8%	53%
Who is better at handling cases of political violence and riot?	9%	42%	49%	1%	57%	42%
Who do you think the public trusts more with community issues?	35%	5%	60%	14%	19%	67%

to think that men and women were equally suited to handle rape cases. This means that women, and men to a lesser extent, tended to believe that responding to rape was gendered—that women were better at handling it. Moreover, while both male and female participants were more likely to choose men instead of women as best suited to handle cases of political violence, the gap was especially stark for the male participants, who almost never chose women as best suited. That is, both men and women tended to believe that responding to political violence was gendered—that men were better suited for it. This perhaps suggests that the discrimination and the protection norms are strong in the institution, as men, but also women, fail to see women as warriors and protectors. In terms of the perception of whom the public trusts with community issues,[26] the female respondents were more likely to perceive the work as gendered and believe that community work was best suited for women. Gender bias was thus quite evident among the LNP participants in our study, and it cut in interesting ways, depending on the issue and the sex of the respondent. Most prominently, the surveys captured widespread perceptions among both men and women that violence mitigation in the political arena was associated with men's work and violence mitigation in the domestic arena was associated with women's work.

We also looked at whether LNP officers voted for a female team leader after all the activities were completed. In total, 39 percent of the officers voted for a female leader, but there was a large discrepancy here between men and women in believing that women should be team leaders. Figure 7.2 shows the predicted probabilities of respondents in mixed groups (groups with both men and women) voting for a female team leader. In these mixed groups, the likelihood for women of voting for a female colleague as team leader was almost 60 percent, while the likelihood for men of doing so was less than 30 percent. These results comport well with answers to other exit survey questions, in which women were much more likely than men to think that women were as good police officers as men. Again, if promotion or leadership position assignments are based on preexisting perceptions, then women are disadvantaged in getting promoted or being assigned leadership positions.

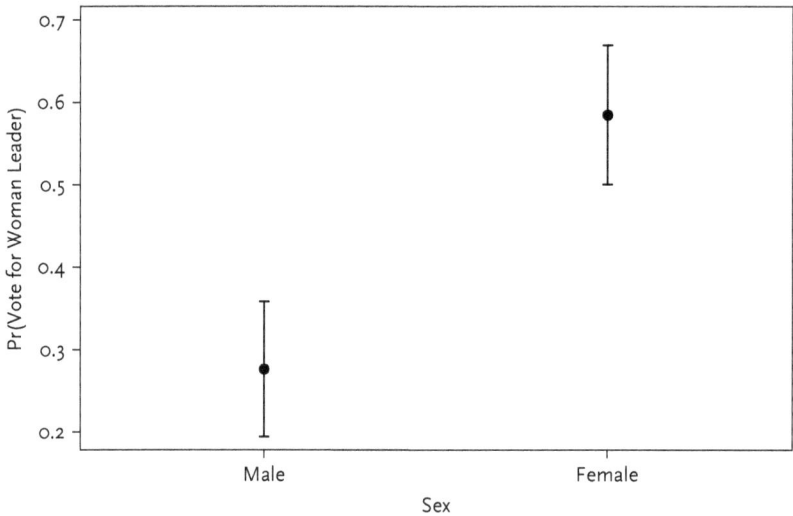

Figure 7.2. Probability of voting for a female leader in mixed groups.

The findings are consistent with other accounts from officers in the LNP. In a survey, female PSU officers voiced frustration about having distinct roles from men and therefore limited participation (Andersen, 2014). The challenge most commonly mentioned was that women had fewer opportunities in the unit than the men, and the majority of the women felt that their male colleagues, especially the senior officers, thought of them as second-rate officers. Much of this sort of sentiment may stem from gender power imbalances that perpetuate norms of appropriate roles for men and women based on gender. The warrior identity and the gendered protection norm instill the perception that the male officers are stronger and braver than the female officers and therefore more capable of controlling a unit oriented toward protection. According to one of the female peacekeepers assigned to help train the PSU, Hanne Andersen (2014), in the PSU no women carried firearms, even though several women had the certificate to do so; the PSU had no female drivers, even though several women had driver's licenses and had asked several times to be allowed to drive; the PSU had no women in leadership positions; no women were being tasked as leaders during operations; there were only four women with ranks above sergeant; and men were favored in service training, training abroad, special assignments, and extra pay and benefits. More broadly within the LNP, there has been one female deputy inspector general, and the LNP has had a female inspector general, but these are appointed positions and not based on promotion. Women's promotion from the lower ranks is the larger problem (see table 7.2).

There is also a large discrepancy in the representation of women across types of personnel that suggests the gendered protection norm may be prevalent. For example, in 2014 the ERU only had three women, or 1 percent women, while the Women and Children's Protection Unit had 39 percent (see table 7.3). Operations, which is the more masculine-dominated security arena, only had 17 percent women, whereas

Table 7.2. LIBERIAN NATIONAL POLICE PERSONNEL BY SEX AND RANK (2013)

Rank	Male	Female	Percent female
Inspector general	1	0	0
Deputy inspector general	1	1	50
Commissioner	4	0	0
Deputy commissioner	28	3	10
Assistant commissioner	38	5	12
Chief superintendent	59	6	9
Superintendent	77	9	10
Chief inspector	123	8	6
Inspector	139	18	11
Sergeant	260	45	15
Corporal	137	25	15
Patrol officer	2849	688	24
Total	*3716*	*808*	*18*

administration, which is associated with more feminine work (secretarial), had the largest percentage of women, 27 percent. These numbers provide additional evidence that gendered protection norms continue to impede local progress, as women are not equally dispersed among the sections and are especially absent in areas that are more security oriented, such as the ERU and the PSU.

SEAHV and the Liberian National Police

During and since the war, SGBV was and has been a major problem in Liberia. Many of the gender reforms instituted in the LNP have been targeted at addressing SGBV; however, whether these reforms have improved the condition in Liberia is up for debate. After UNMIL has worked closely with the LNP to institute reforms, do members of the community perceive the LNP as a partner in addressing the threat of SGBV and in helping the survivors pursue justice? Following an overview of the pervasiveness of SGBV in Liberia, we then use household surveys as a means to assess community trust in the LNP to address SGBV.

With the breakdown of infrastructure and social norms, Liberia experienced a dramatic increase in SGBV. During the war, women were abducted, gang-raped, forced to use sex as a means of survival ("survival sex"), and trafficked as sex slaves. Mats Utas (2005: 421) notes that women had to "provide sexual favors just to pass checkpoints, thus severely restricting their ability to travel." According to a 2011 report, some women intentionally engaged in sexual relations with combatants to acquire food and protection due to insecurity, minimal resources, and men's restricted ability to work during the war (Swedish International Development Cooperation, 2011).[27] As the Geneva Centre for the Control of Armed Forces reported in 2007, "acts of sexual violence were committed mainly against women and girls and included

Table 7.3. LIBERIAN NATIONAL POLICE PERSONNEL BY SEX
AND SECTION (2014)

Section	Male	Female	Percent female
Administration	*181*	*67*	*27*
Audit	2	0	0
Band Unit	2	0	0
Chaplaincy	9	3	25
Communications	22	19	46
Community Services	8	8	50
Court Liaison	8	4	33
Facility Management	4	0	0
Finance	7	1	13
Fleet Management	4	0	0
Gender	2	4	67
Legal Section	2	0	0
Library	0	1	100
Logistics	9	1	10
Mobile Unit	8	2	20
Motor Pool	3	0	0
Personnel	28	13	32
Planning and Research	11	2	15
Police Clinic	6	3	33
Press and Public Affairs	5	0	0
Protocol	4	0	0
Professional Standards Division	24	2	8
Sport	2	0	0
U-100 Office	6	1	17
U-101 Office	2	1	33
U-103 Office	3	0	0
U-111 Office	2	0	100
Crime Services Department	*354*	*84*	*19*
Anti-burglary	6	0	0
Anti narcotics	9	2	18
Anti-terrorism	1	1	50
Anti-theft	4	0	0
Auto Theft Boosting Squad	4	0	0
Crime against Person	9	1	10
Crime Services Department Administration	8	1	11
Crime Services Department Leeward	2	0	0
Forensics Laboratory	12	2	14
General Crime Services	148	3	2
Organized Crime	14	0	0
Property Crime Unit	1	1	50

Table 7.3. CONTINUED

Section	Male	Female	Percent female
Range	6	0	0
Records and Identification	4	3	43
Special Investigation Unit	6	1	14
Trans-national Crime	8	1	11
U-105 Office	5	1	20
Women and Children's Protection	107	67	39
Intelligence	81	16	16
Interpol	11	1	8
Operations	*3020*	*615*	*17*
Emergency Response Unit	291	3	1
Highway Patrol	31	9	23
Inspectorate Division	20	3	13
Internal Security Section	12	7	37
Motor Vehicle	18	11	38
Night Duty	3	0	0
Patrol	1523	418	22
PSU	819	114	12
Small Arms	2	0	0
Traffic Division	274	32	10
U-102 Office	2	1	33
U-104 Office	2	2	50
U-141 Office	4	0	0
U-142 Office	5	1	20
UTVTS	13	14	52
Vice Squad	1	0	0
Training and Development	65	23	26

rape—sometimes in front of family or community members."[28] The report notes that "rape, abduction for sexual slavery, forced marriage of women and girls to combatants, forced stripping, and insertion of foreign objects into victims' cavities" were common during Liberia's war.[29]

The extent of SGBV in Liberia is documented by several studies.[30] A 1998 study published in the *Journal of the American Medical Association* found that 15 percent of women reported rape, attempted rape, or sexual coercion (including "survival sex") (Swiss et al., 1998). Another survey conducted ten years later by the *Journal of the American Medical Association* found that both men and women in Liberia reported experiencing sexualized violence at high rates, although ex-combatants of either sex faced a much higher risk than noncombatants of either sex (Johnson and Asher, 2008). Of the female ex-combatants, 42 percent said they had experienced sexualized violence at some point. This is in comparison to 9 percent of female noncombatants who experienced sexualized violence. Of the male ex-combatant respondents, 33 percent reported experiencing sexualized violence, compared to 7 percent of male noncombatants. The study conducted and analyzed large samples after both wars. In a 2009 report, the Liberian Truth and Reconciliation Commission collected, coded, and analyzed more than seventeen thousand victim and witness statements containing information on more than ninety thousand victims and over 160,000 separate acts of violence.[31] A 2008 Demographic and Health Survey for Liberia (conducted by the Liberia Institute of Statistics and Geo-Information Services) found that 18 percent of Liberian women had experienced some form of sexualized violence in their lifetime.[32] Such violence included "being physically forced to have sexual intercourse or perform any other acts against one's will." For the majority of those who reported sexualized violence, the victims identified the perpetrators as a current or former partner. Eight percent reported that the perpetrators were soldiers or police. The survey also found that 33 percent of women who were married or cohabitating reported having experienced at least one incident of violence at the hands of their husbands or partners. Another recent survey of 1,666 Liberian men revealed that 33 percent of male combatants (118 of 367 combatant respondents) experienced sexualized violence, while 17 percent (57 of 360 combatant respondents) were forced to become sexual servants.[33]

In some cases, the LNP and other government security forces were implicated in this violence. Before and during the civil wars, the LNP were known for using excessive force, as many LNP officers took sides and used violence against political opponents and civilians. According to reports, groups such as Charles Taylor's infamous Anti-Terrorist Units and Special Operations Division were accused of being rapists and murderers (Bacon, 2012). Moreover, before the war, legal, health, and security services for survivors of sexualized violence were practically nonexistent outside the capital, Monrovia, and survivors had little redress to the formal system (Bacon, 2012). The LNP were known for their abysmal handling of cases related to SGBV. According to Jonathan Friedman (2011) and Laura Bacon (2012), the police did not know how to handle SGBV and often blamed the victims of domestic abuse and rape. The officers at the time did not have the will or the technical skills to deal with gender-based crimes and sometimes were perpetrators themselves. This suggests that the domestic security forces, including the LNP, were complicit and sometimes even implicated in the widespread SGBV that occurred before, during, and even after the war.

The first question, then, is whether Liberians continue to view the security sector, specifically the LNP, as perpetrators of this type of violence. We can assess this using three types of survey data: data from a study by Sabrina Karim from Grand Kru County, survey data from a study conducted by the Center for Action, Research and Training (CART) in Liberia commissioned by the Swedish Police, and data from a survey of the two-excombatant communities mentioned in chapter 6.

Using data collected from Grand Kru County,[34] which included 1,273 men and women aged eighteen and above from fifteen villages in the county,[35] about 7 percent said that the LNP treat women unfairly and discriminate against women, 8 percent of the survey respondents stated that the police engage in raping community members,

18 percent said that they cause problems in the community, and 31 percent said that the police behave like criminals. This can be compared to a more urban survey by CART of 2,516 individuals aged eighteen and over from six communities in Monrovia near police stations (Center for Action Research and Training, 2016).[36] About 33 percent thought women are treated unfairly, 22 percent thought that the police are active in their communities in a negative way, and of the female respondents, only 37 percent felt comfortable traveling alone to a police station to report a crime. There appears to be a divide between rural and urban respondents in terms of perceiving whether the police are abusive and discriminatory. In general, those in Grand Kru County had a more favorable opinion about the police. This could be due to the fact that there are very few police officers there in the first place.[37] In contrast, police are much more present in communities in Monrovia, which means that they have more of a chance to misbehave. We note that it is not possible to say whether the LNP has improved with regards to engaging in abusive behavior toward the public, because we do not have baseline data from before or during the war. We can only state that it appears that the LNP still has more work to do to improve its public image.

We also assessed the degree to which the LNP might perpetrate SGBV by asking whether people felt comfortable having the LNP handle cases of rape. While this is not the same as asking whether LNP officers routinely commit SGBV, it does give us an indication about how much trust communities have in the LNP to address such issues. If they continue to be fearful of the LNP handling cases of SGBV, it could be an indicator that they still fear the LNP or at the least continue to view them as incapable of handling SGBV.

In order to assess Liberian preferences about trusting the LNP to handle rape, we used a household survey of two of Monrovia's ex-combatant squatter communities: West Point and Peace Island.[38] The study surveyed 1,280 respondents.[39] In addition to assessing perceptions on the general population as mentioned above, we also chose to look at perceptions in ex-combatant communities because respondents in these communities are unlikely to have much trust in the government, and perhaps more likely to have experienced some negative and possibly violent interaction with government security forces. Thus, we expected their baseline level of trust in the LNP and the government to be low. The goal of the survey was to understand how people's interactions with the police affected their preferences over the organizations that might respond to different security threats and how contact might be conditioned by previous victimization, particularly during the war. Thus, survey questions asked people which security organizations they preferred as responders to rape. Ten options were offered.[40] In total, about 72 percent of the population preferred the LNP as responders to rape.[41] We also asked how much contact individuals had had with the LNP. By "contact," we mean that the community member in West Point and Peace Island had spoken to a police officer about an issue occurring in the community. Between 2014 and 2015, about 42 percent had had none, 26 percent had had contact once, 21 percent between two and four times, and 11 percent five times or more. Finally, we asked about previous exposure to violence during the war. About 41 percent had had such exposure.[42]

Figure 7.3 demonstrates that for those who experienced violence during the war, the more contact they had with the security sector, the less likely they were to prefer

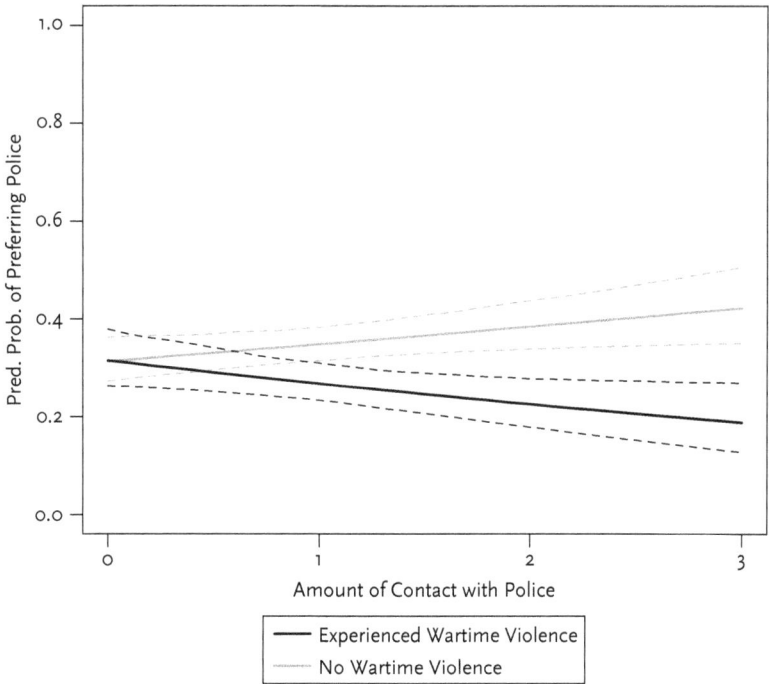

Figure 7.3. Predicted probability of preferring the LNP to respond to rape based on amount of contact with the LNP and victimization (95 percent Confidence Interval). On the x-axis, a "0" refers to no contact with the police. A "1" refers to interactions with police officers one time, a "2" refers to interactions with police officers 2–4 times, and a "3" refers to interactions with police five times or more. This figure presents the predicted probabilities for the bivariate relationship. However, the interactive relationships are significant even when controls are added; see appendix 4.

the LNP as responders to incidents of rape. However, for those who did not experience violence during the war, contact with police seemed to lead to favorable outcomes. These people were more likely to prefer the police as responders to rape. The results indicate that those who experienced violence during the war were still fearful of the security sector, which suggests that more should be done to alleviate the concerns of war survivors.

The results for preferring the police to respond to rape stand in contrast to preferences for the police to respond to other security needs. We assessed whether the amount of contact with the LNP affected the likelihood that people preferred the LNP as responders to other issues, such as security concerns, riots, and armed violence. For none of these issues did wartime victimization condition the effects of contact with the police on the preferences for the LNP as responders. In these models, previous victimization did make individuals less likely to prefer the police as responders to riots, abuse, and armed violence, but the amount of contact with the LNP did not have an effect on people's preferences for the police as handlers of such security concerns.

EQUAL OPPORTUNITY EMERGENCE IN AND THROUGH THE LIBERIAN NATIONAL POLICE

In this chapter, we have already shown that UNMIL, and especially female peace-keepers in UNMIL, has championed gender reforms in the LNP. We have especially focused on reforms related to the female quota in the LNP, on addressing SGBV, and on the general professionalization of the LNP. But the question remains whether, despite these reforms, the gender power imbalances still overshadow any improvements that might have developed since the end of the war. In this section, we evaluate the extent to which gender reforms in the LNP might be strengthening a value for gender equality—a crucial step toward equal opportunity—as a counterweight to some of the gender power imbalances that still exist. Or rather, we test how well gender reforms have affected beliefs about the role of women and men and opportunities for them in policing, both by the police officers themselves and by locals. Without a baseline sample, our results cannot tell us the overall effect of reforms that have been implemented. But they can help us identify the dimensions along which we see relative strength in the practice of equal opportunity and thereby suggest some of the mechanisms by which further reforms can bear more fruit. We conclude that the gender reforms—especially recruitment and training practices that enhance sensitivity to SGBV and gender issues, as well as improving the general competence of the personnel—can make significant headway in promoting gender equality in and through the LNP.

Practices of Equal Opportunity in the Liberian National Police

Turning back to our lab-in-the-field experiments with the LNP, we focus on two dimensions that indicate the value for gender equality. First, we assess whether individual behavior and group dynamics have changed as a result of increases in women's representation in the LNP. Second, we analyze how gender dynamics have changed depending on levels of competency, which is an important product of recruitment and training practices. We pay particular attention to cooperation between the sexes as a way to assess variation in the propensity for discrimination as well as variation in whether the gendered protection norm is prevalent. The extent to which male participants consider the input of their female colleagues can tell us how much they value women as police officers. We also pay attention to the participants' awareness of issues related to SGBV as a way to assess variation in norms and values surrounding SEAHV. The extent to which the participants are aware of the potential for SGBV to be committed can indicate their sense that SEAHV is widespread and a priority.

Starting with attention to gender-based crimes, as a part of one activity, we asked the groups to assess three crime scene photos that had hints that a sexual and gender-based crime had occurred (see appendix 4). The officers had to identify the crime(s) they thought had occurred, identify evidence to match the crime, and suggest what they should do on arrival of the crime scene. In total, 44 percent of the officers suggested that rape or domestic violence had occurred. Many more officers were likely to see the crime as rape than as domestic violence, with just three suggesting domestic violence as the possible crime. As mentioned, UNMIL has conducted numerous campaigns to raise awareness about rape, including helping to pass the antirape law, helping to establish the special Criminal Court E for prosecution of rape, and helping to create specialized units in the LNP and the Ministry of Justice to address rape. These campaigns' focus on rape may have increased the propensity for officers to pay attention to it. In contrast, little attention has been placed on domestic violence. There is no domestic violence law—one has been written but has not come up for a vote in the legislature—and there have been no nationwide campaigns to address the problem. That the LNP participants in our study rarely listed domestic violence as possibly contributing to what they saw in the crime scene photos likely stems from the lack of attention to this type of violence and from the absence of a law that establishes its criminality.

Based on traditional ideas about gender dichotomies, one might expect female officers to be more attuned to crimes related to SGBV. However, revealing the fallacy of such dichotomies, the sex of the respondents does not well predict whether they found the crime to be gender related. Similarly, we find that group composition did not affect whether individuals identified gendered crimes.

Figure 7.4 depicts the proportions of men and women in different groups choosing a gendered crime as their guess for what crime occurred. Women were *not* on average significantly more likely to see the crime as gendered, and men were not

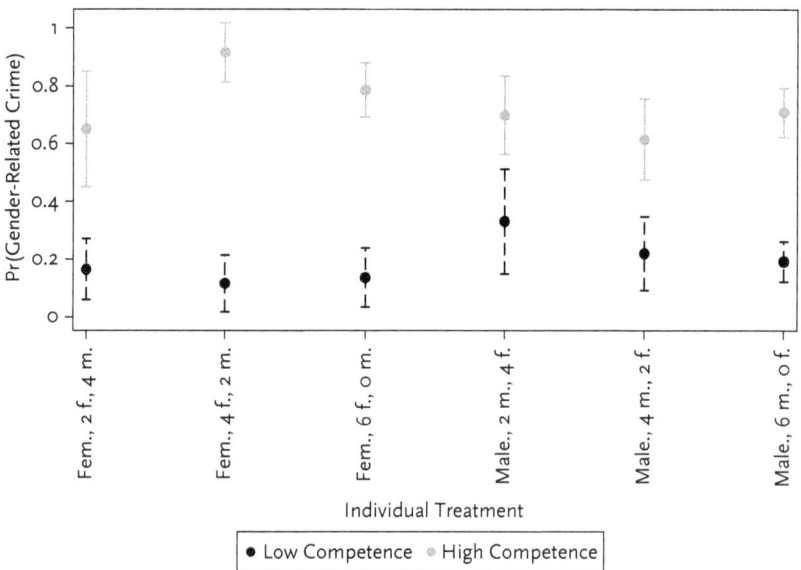

Figure 7.4. Probability of observing a gender-related crime, by competence differential.
Note: Low and high competence are defined based on the competence differential, which is the difference between each individual's latent competency score and the group's median value. We have chosen to plot the points one standard deviation below the differential median (0) and one standard deviation above.

more likely to see the crime as gendered when there were more women in the group. This lack of a systematic relationship across the individuals in the different treatment arms is perhaps a positive indication that recruitment and training is bearing fruit—reducing ignorance about the prevalence of SGBV and perceptions of the issue as just a "women's" issue.

While we do not observe that the sex of the respondents or the number of women in the groups affected sensitivity to SGBV crimes, we find that factors related to competence had more discernible effects. To measure competence, we used a latent-variable index generated using a Bayesian scaling model, based on individual responses to a set of cognitive questions, a set of questions assessing individuals' ability to recall details about the crime scene photo, and the validity of their crime scene answers.[43] The scale weights individual responses by the difficulty of the questions and gives a numerical output. This type of scale is often used in standardized testing, where students are given scores based on how well they did on answering different levels of questions (easy or hard). The indicators were used based on the training they were supposed to have received in their academy. High-competence individuals performed well in their knowledge about policing and in their cognitive ability. Results using the competence measure as an explanatory variable speak to the relative payoffs of recruitment and training reforms that emphasize gains in competence and professionalization as means to enhance values for gender equality.

Returning to figure 7.4, we observe strong effects of competency. High-competence individuals were much more likely to see the crime as gendered than low-competence individuals. The connection between competence and sensitivity to SGBV is perhaps also a positive indication that reforms in the LNP can pay dividends. For one, it indicates that recruitment and training programs that can increase the competence of the officers can have spillover effects that also increase their gender sensitivity. For another, it is likely that the high-competence individuals are most responsive to special training programs, and so one plausible implication of these findings is that the sensitivity training programs in place are indeed enhancing awareness and perceived importance of SGBV among those with the greatest uptake of the material.

Our study also looked at variation in the participation and contribution of participants within groups of different proportions of women. Most strikingly, the participation levels of the men changed with the composition of the groups. When outnumbered by women, men were more assertive and aggressive: both more talkative and more argumentative than the men and the women in the other groups. Figure 7.5 displays the results related to how talkative the individuals were, and figure 7.6 displays the results related to how much the participants argued with their group members during the cooperative games. The men in the four-women groups stand out as the most talkative and argumentative. Group composition did not much shape the propensity for women to talk or argue, aside from the low-competence women in the four-women group being rather restrained in their talking. This resonates with the survey findings, discussed earlier, that male participants tended to discount the merits of their female colleagues. The additional insight here, however, is that latent competence can condition the extent to which women exercise their

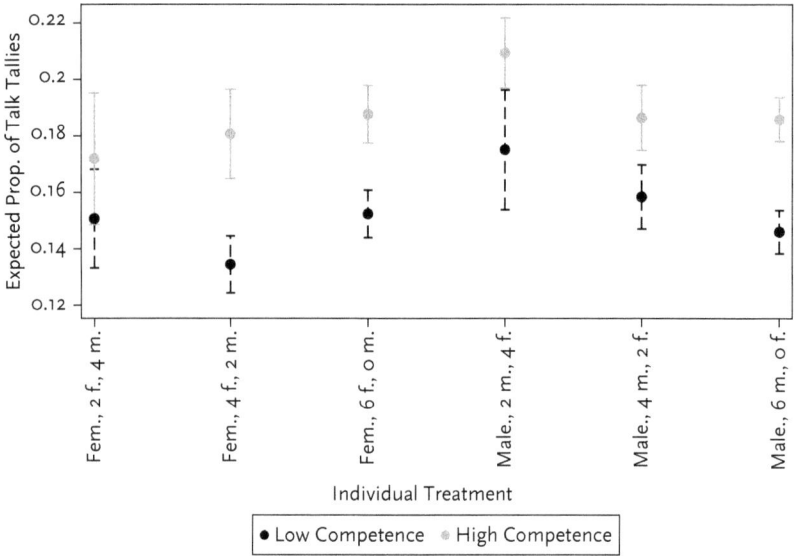

Figure 7.5. Talk Tally Proportions, by competence differential.

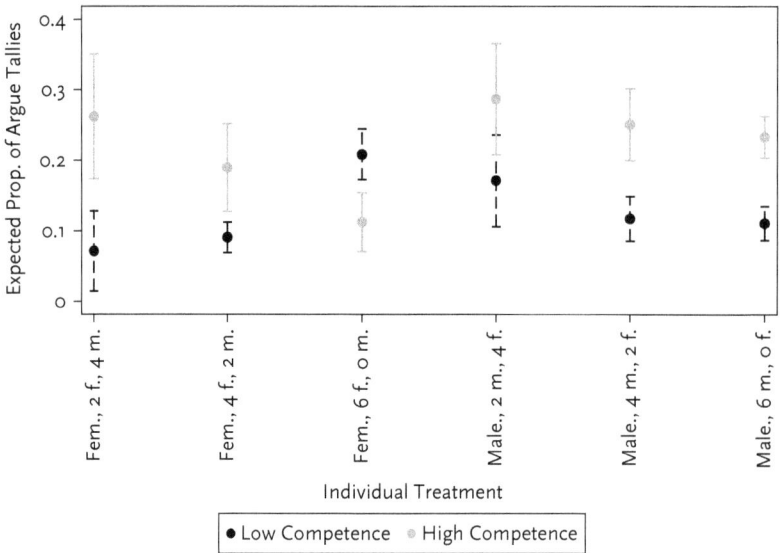

Figure 7.6. Argue Tally Proportions, by competence differential.

voice, especially in those situations where the men are most prone to try to drown them out.

Competence appeared to affect individuals' levels of participation. High-competence men were significantly more assertive than low-competence men, in terms of propensities to both talk and argue. The observed effects of competence were mixed for women. We also observe that the high-competence women, like the men, were much more talkative than the low-competence women. Importantly, the gap between the high-competence and low-competence women was starkest in the four-woman groups, where the men showed a tendency to be much more assertive. Competence appears to be essential for women to be able to contribute to group discussions, especially when the men are prone to attempt to dominate the conversation. Also of interest, the frequency of arguing is monotonically increasing in the number of women in the group for the low-competence women but decreasing for the high-competence women. That is, the willingness of low-competence women to argue in the groups drops substantially as the number of men in the group increases, and the low-competence women are quite argumentative in the all-women group. The opposite holds for high-competence women, who are more argumentative as the number of men increases. To the extent that arguing conveys an individual's desire that her views not be overruled by other views, competency appears to be crucial for women in majority-male groups to have voices that are heard.

Turning to the influence that individuals have in groups, we can look at the degree to which a participant's individual determination of what crime was committed matched that of the group. Specifically, we use the proportion of each individual's guesses about what crime occurred that matched the group's guesses. A low value indicates that the person did not much influence the group deliberation. Figure 7.7 shows how individuals varied in their levels of potential influence across the treatment groups and by competence level.

We do not see strong evidence that the men or the women were either more or less influential in the groups depending on the composition of the groups. That is,

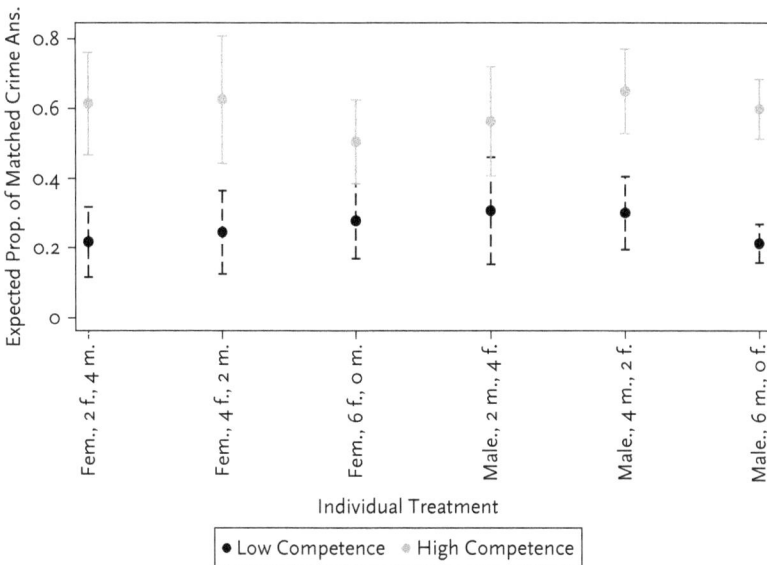

Figure 7.7. Proportion of matched crime answers, by competence differential.

even though the men in the four-women groups were much more assertive, their voices did not appear to drown out the influence of their female counterparts. Again, this suggests that gender-related reforms in the LNP might be bearing fruit in preventing the marginalization of women. The results more clearly show that high-competence individuals of either sex are much more influential than low-competence individuals, such that high-competence women are more influential than low-competence men or women and that high-competence men are more influential than low-competence men or women. Competence was a better predictor of individual influence than sex, and this result was consistent across other group decisions we measured in the study.

What can we conclude about the state of equal opportunity in the LNP following the UNMIL-led reforms? Our results suggest that even though men tended to overlook the contributions of women in the surveys, the men exhibited attentiveness to SGBV similar to that of the women, and the women in the mixed groups appeared to maintain their levels of participation and influence when compared to all-women groups. Again, without a baseline, we do not know what these dynamics would have looked like without the reforms, but the results are at least promising in suggesting that UNMIL is not leaving a substantial legacy of male dominance. In other words, the reforms may have helped ensure that all officers, especially competent ones, are more gender aware and inclusive in groups. More strongly, our findings show that improvements in the competence of LNP officers, of either sex, can enhance their sensitivity to SGBV, their levels of participation, and their influence. Reforms, such as professionalizing the police by mandating basic academy training and rigorous vetting of the recruits, potentially have had profound effects on both the participation of women in groups and sensitivity to SGBV. Earlier we mentioned some of the types of gender-neutral reform that UNMIL has instituted. We return to these in the concluding chapter as possible mechanisms to increase competency and therefore the practice of equal opportunity in police institutions.

Practices of Equal Opportunity through the Liberian National Police

Turning back to the household survey in West Point and Peace Island, we can analyze the extent to which the gender reforms in the LNP have helped to promote an appreciation of equal opportunity by assessing whether contact with specifically female police officers affected civilian preferences for security response. Recall that one of the major gender reforms initiated by UNMIL was increasing the number of women in the LNP—currently, efforts are under way to meet a 30 percent quota. More so than female peacekeepers, the presence of female LNP officers is highly visible. As noted, female peacekeepers rarely engage with local Liberians, whereas female LNP officers are present in many zones and depots throughout the country. So does their presence affect civilians' attitudes toward the police?

We find that the officer's sex does matter in improving perceptions of the LNP. In our survey, we asked respondents whether they had had contact with police and

Table 7.4. PREDICTED PROBABILITY OF CONTACT WITH MALE OR FEMALE
POLICE AND PREFERENCES IN SECURITY PROVIDERS

Security issue	Contact with only male police officers	Contact with only female police officer	Percent change
Prefer police as responders to armed violence	33%	38%	+ 5
Prefer police as responders to rape	31%	37%	+ 6
Prefer police as responders to riot	49%	58%	+ 9
Prefer police as responders to beating	36%	47%	+ 11

whether this contact had been with only a male or only a female police officer. The survey then asked the respondents whom they preferred as responders to rape, as responders to armed violence, as responders to riots, and as responders to a beating. Their options included religious leaders, Liberian NGOs, international NGOs, women's groups, community elders, police, judges, traditional leaders, peacekeepers, and the AFL. We assessed whether contact with only a female police officer, as opposed to only a male officer, affected the likelihood that they then preferred only the police to handle the security situation. Table 7.4 provides the predicted probabilities, holding all other control variables at their means, of preferring the police as responders based on previous contact with a female police officer.[44] The table provides evidence that contact with female officers may improve the image of the police in terms of community members preferring the police as responders over other security sector providers.

It is possible that these results are unique to the ex-combatant communities of West Point and Peace Island. We find, however, that the results are robust in comparison to those from other communities in various regions in Liberia. The Norwegian Refugee Council in Liberia shared their data with us and allowed us to add several questions to a survey they implemented in four Liberian counties. The thirty-two communities were selected purposively as part of an end-line assessment of an NGO program implemented jointly by the Norwegian Refugee Council, the Danish Refugee Council, and the Food and Agriculture Organization of the UN.[45] The total sample included 595 individuals in thirty-two villages from Nimba, Lofa, Grand Gedeh, and Maryland counties.[46] In the survey, we asked respondents if they had had contact with the LNP and with women in the LNP. In contrast to West Point and Peace Island, where we found that 70 percent of the population had had contact with the LNP, in these rural counties, only 23 percent had. In West Point and Peace Island, 36 percent of individuals had had contact with a female LNP officer, but in the rural counties, 11 percent had.

In the survey we included the following question: "If there is a hala hala [fight] between two tribes or religions in your community, who would you most like to resolve the situation?" We offered the following choices: the LNP, the AFL, UNMIL, community leaders, the community watch team, or traditional leaders. We then assessed the probability that individuals chose the LNP based on whether they had had contact with female LNP officers only. The results suggested that when individuals had had contact solely with female LNP officers in rural areas, regardless of the county, they were more likely to prefer the LNP for resolving a fight than when they had had contact solely with male LNP officers.[47] Among individuals who had had contact with a male LNP officer only, 19 percent responded that they preferred the LNP as responders to a hala hala, whereas 42 percent of the respondents who had had contact with a female LNP officer only preferred the LNP as responders.

A field experiment in Grand Kru County (Karim, 2016a),[48] where community members were randomly exposed to community policing by female-only police officers and male-only police officers, further has found that contact with female police officers improved community perception of the LNP. In particular, community members who were exposed to female officers were less likely to perceive the police as corrupt, were more likely to prefer female police to respond to threats (particularly rape), and were more hospitable to female officers than male officers (Karim, 2016a).

The evidence here comports well with the notion that contact with female officers has a positive side benefit of enhancing the image of the LNP in both urban and rural settings. More broadly, exposure to women in traditionally masculine positions may lead to positive perceptions of those institutions. The gender reforms in the LNP, which have included increases in the representation of women, appear to have been a positive step toward increasing the potential for the LNP to help advance equal opportunity in society.

Also related to the analysis of the data from West Point and Peace Island, we explore whether respondents' perceptions of gender equality are associated with their preferences over domestic security sector responses. In other words, we consider whether people who already have positive views about women's rights and empowerment are more accepting of state involvement in their affairs. The idea is similar to Ismene Gizelis's (2009, 2011) findings that societies where women enjoy a greater influence have greater prospects for successful peace-building. To measure perceptions of gender equality, we used questions about the respondents' perceptions of women's rights and empowerment in the survey from West Point and Peace Island. The questions asked:

- Do you think that women should be community leaders? Yes or No
- Do you think that beating/domestic violence is a problem in Liberia? Yes or No
- Do you think that women should join the LNP? Yes or No
- Do you think that women should join the military? Yes or No
- Do you think that rape is a problem in Liberia? Yes or No
- Do you think that female peacekeepers are better than male peacekeepers? Yes or No
- Can a woman do anything a man can do? Yes or No
- According to Liberian formal law, can it be a crime to beat one's wife? Yes or No

- According to Liberian formal law, can a husband be found guilty for raping his wife? Yes or No
- According to Liberian formal law, can a woman rape a man? Yes or No

Together, these questions ask about knowledge of women's rights and about people's opinions on women's rights and empowerment. Knowledge about women's rights is an unobtrusive way to gauge respondents' concern for gender power imbalances. We expect that the extent to which individuals, say, are unaware that it is against the law to rape one's wife or beat her provides an indication of the concern they have for gender equality. We aggregated the answers to create a composite score. On average, individuals scored 7, and the median score was 8 (with a minimum of 0 and a maximum of 10).

We also consider the possibility that prior beliefs and knowledge about women's rights affect the degree to which gender reforms affect confidence in the domestic security sector. In order to test whether beliefs about gender equality condition the effect of gender reforms on perceptions of the state, we explore the presence of an interactive relationship between contact with female LNP officers and the composite index of knowledge of women's rights when it comes to their joint impact on preferences for the police as responders to rape and providers of security.

We find evidence that gender norms, as they relate to these questions, condition how contact with female LNP officers affects perceptions of the LNP. In figures 7.8

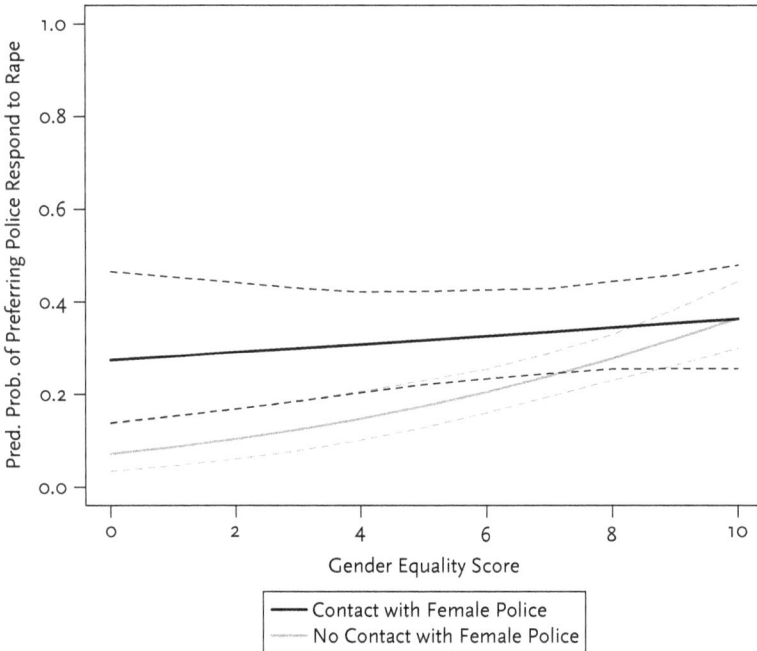

Figure 7.8. Probability of preferring the LNP as responders to rape, by knowledge of women's rights and empowerment.

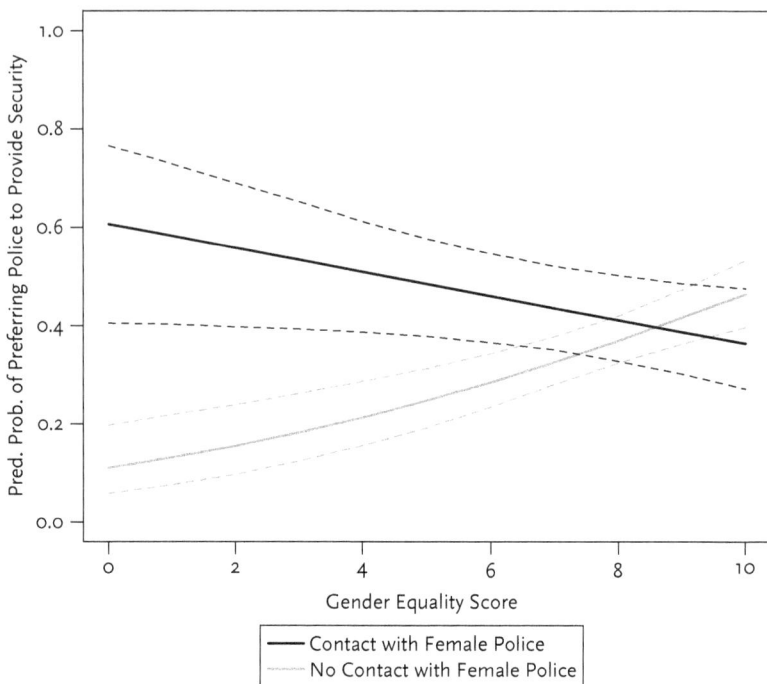

Figure 7.9. Probability of preferring the LNP as providers of security, by knowledge of women's rights and empowerment.

and 7.9, we see that contact with LNP women increases the preference for the LNP as responders to rape and providers of security, particularly when the respondent had a lower composite score.[49]

In finding that contact with the LNP has especially strong effects among individuals with less of an inclination for gender equality, we stress two key implications. First, it appears that respondents' contact with female LNP officers may have shaped their perceptions of police response, particularly for those who did not have much concern for gender equality. This is particularly interesting in that it demonstrates that gender reforms may have a positive effect on those who are least likely to be accepting of them. Gender reforms, therefore, have the potential for tremendous value added in sowing the seeds for even greater societal acceptance of a security sector that better embodies equal opportunity.

Second, contact with women does not appear to much affect those who already have egalitarian beliefs. In other words, individuals who value gender equality are already prone to prefer the police as responders to rape and providers of security irrespective of whether they have had contact with a female police officer. That there is a relationship between preferences for gender equality and preferences for state-supplied security is an important finding because it once again demonstrates that beliefs about equal opportunity—not necessarily descriptive representation of women—affect positive change in the legitimacy of security organizations.

CONCLUSION

This chapter has analyzed the extent to which peacekeeping missions leave local legacies by helping to initiate SSRs, many of which are gender related. With UNMIL as a case study, we have highlighted the enormous effort the peacekeeping mission has made to reform Liberia's security sector, especially the LNP. UNMIL not only helped to rebuild the LNP through implementing targeted recruitment and professionalization but also helped to implement numerous gender reforms, such as the quota for women, the Women and Children Protection Unit, and the Gender Unit. Female peacekeepers especially were instrumental in many of these gender reforms. However, while UNMIL played a major role in designing and implementing these reforms, we considered whether promoting a value for gender equality in and through the LNP might be disrupted by the problems related to gender power imbalances in peacekeeping missions—particularly in the form of discrimination, the gendered protection norm, and SEAHV.

We found that discrimination and the protection norm are still prevalent in the LNP, despite increases in the representation of women. Male officers are less likely to trust female firearms instructors, choose female leaders, and listen to women when they are outnumbered. Expectations about the role of officers are still gendered, whereby officers believe that women are better suited for addressing gender crimes and there are few women in units that serve more operational functions. We also found some evidence that Liberians still perceive the LNP as abusive, and that Liberians are reluctant to have the LNP be involved in SGBV, particularly when they have experienced wartime violence. This means that fears of sexual misconduct by domestic security forces, or at least perceptions that the domestic security forces cannot help fight SEAHV, may still be a problem.

However, we found more reason to be hopeful than discouraged. We found evidence that the gender reforms may have contributed to promoting a value for gender equality—a prerequisite for the practice of equal opportunity—in and through the LNP. Within the LNP, we found that gender-neutral SSRs, such as professionalization of the police, that can increase competence levels actually can improve concern for gender power imbalances and the ability of women to participate and have influence. When officers were competent, they were much more likely to be sensitive to SGBV, participate in groups, and have their views considered by the group regardless of sex and regardless of group composition. This means that one of the best ways to prevent discrimination, mitigate the protection norm, and prevent SEAHV is to include more competent police officers in the force. Targeted recruitment, screening, and training are important mechanisms to ensure quality officers.

We also found evidence that improvements in the representation and visibility of women can have an effect in legitimizing the overall institution. As individuals interacted with female LNP officers (as opposed to just male LNP officers), they were more likely to prefer the LNP as providers of security, responders to riots, responders to rape, and responders to a community dispute (hala hala) among other improved outcomes. Finally, we found that existing beliefs and knowledge about gender equality condition perceptions of the security sector. When respondents had *less* concern for and knowledge of women's rights and empowerment, the presence of female police officers mattered more in legitimizing the institution. In general, this suggests that gender reforms may be a key tool for state-building, particularly in terms of enhancing the perceptions of state institutions.

In this chapter, both professionalism (competency) and gender equality have been used as foundations for equal opportunity. It is worth pausing to note that the two concepts are not the same, but that there are possible relationships between the two. That is, as we have seen through the lab-in-the-field experiments, competency can enhance gender equality. It is also possible that when individuals have more gender equal beliefs, they are more competent, because they are better able to address the needs of both men and women in their work. Both can be achieved through changes in institutional practices such as more training, better recruitment standards, and other actions. The last chapter of the manuscript is devoted to developing ways to further such practices of equal opportunity.

Finally, the fact that there are signs of "equal opportunity" policing in the LNP, in spite of gender power imbalances in UNMIL and in society at large, gives reason for hope. No society transforms overnight, and all countries suffer from gender power imbalances. Nevertheless, peacekeeping missions do appear to be one mechanism through which the power imbalances may be mitigated in host countries. The hope is that the UNMIL legacy will be one of widespread Liberian ownership of the equal opportunity that has allowed women like Margaret, mentioned at the beginning of this chapter, to pursue her dreams in the LNP.

CHAPTER 8

A Call for Equal Opportunity
Peacekeeping

R ecent trends in international politics have opened space for an expanded conversation on the importance of gender equality globally. The feminist foreign policy in Sweden and the "Hillary Doctrine" have paved the way for gender equality to be at the forefront of global politics. Yet the UN, especially the UN DPKO, has been promoting gender equality in its peacekeeping and peace-building efforts for the past several years, at least since 2000, when UNSCR 1325 was adopted. This book has explored the motivations for and impacts of reforms that relate to gender equality in peacekeeping missions.

We find that the UN's historic initiatives on issues related to gender equality have led to mixed results. Peacekeeping operations have been vehicles for promoting gender equality in postconflict states, but they also continue to harbor many inequalities that ultimately threaten progress going forward. We contend that military and police institutions, of which peacekeeping missions are composed, are gendered institutions in that they project and replicate structures of power that privilege men and certain forms of masculinity. The imbalance between the sexes and genders creates and perpetuates particular "gendered" problems in PKOs. When the rules, regulations, activities, practices, and norms of institutions privilege certain forms of masculinity over other masculinities and femininities, adverse consequences result. We stated from the onset that gender power imbalances in PKOs have led to at least three challenges in and through peacekeeping missions: discrimination, a gendered protection norm, and SEAHV.

Throughout the book we have presented evidence of these challenges. Starting with the first problem, we found that discrimination is pervasive in all areas of peacekeeping missions. Related to the deployment phase, we found that countries with few women in domestic forces simply have a depleted ability to contribute substantial proportions of women to peacekeeping missions. In these countries, rigid gender dichotomies may play a major role in keeping women out of national militaries. Conversely, those countries with higher proportions of women in their domestic armed forces contribute higher proportions of women to peacekeeping military contingents.

While women in national militaries often deploy with their contingents, women from police forces often get selected or apply individually to join PKOs. The different recruitment method may explain why the composition of police contributions is less dependent on the proportions of women in forces at home.

Within peacekeeping missions, we also find strong evidence of discrimination. While many female peacekeepers in UNMIL suggested that they played a unique role in their mission by inspiring local women, promoting gender equality, and legitimizing institutions, most women do gendered work in the mission. Women tend to serve in roles such as nurses, doctors or administrators or serve as advisers for traditionally gendered units such as women and children's protection. Very few women serve in leadership roles. Moreover, women tend to only be lauded for doing well with respect to "women's work"—not for doing a good job in carrying out their mandate to provide security and protection—as seen in the attention given to the all-female FPUs. Finally, women constantly have to negotiate their identity in the mission to "fit in." In some cases, this has meant changing one's appearance to be less feminine; in other cases, it has meant attempting to break into "all-boys' networks." The evidence points to multiple layers of discrimination that female peacekeepers face within missions.

The second challenge—a gendered protection norm that pervades many PKOs—also limits the full agency of female peacekeepers. We demonstrated that gender-typing men as protectors and women as objects of protection manifests in an unwillingness on the part of contributing countries to put their female personnel into harm's way and in greater restrictions on the activities of those women who do serve as peacekeepers. Women are less likely to deploy to missions that are located in countries that have low levels of development and that have experienced higher levels of violence, especially SGBV. Peacekeeping is most needed in countries with high levels of SGBV to improve the security environment. Unfortunately, women are being systematically excluded from these missions. In addition, when there is a conflict in the contributing country it is *more* likely to send female peacekeepers, perhaps because those who decide prefer to keep men in-country to fight insurgents and because peacekeeping deployments appear safer when compared to the home environment.

In peacekeeping missions, such as UNMIL, women are being excluded from engaging in a wide variety of roles and from being able to leave the base and interact with other women and with locals. These symptoms of the gendered protection norm preclude female peacekeepers from being proactive in missions and fully contributing to the mission's goals.

Finally, SEAHV continues to pose a major problem in peacekeeping missions, despite the UN's zero tolerance policies. Reports of SEAHV committed by peacekeepers against locals are far too common in many missions. In Monrovia, over one-fourth of women aged eighteen to thirty have engaged in transactional sex with a peacekeeper. Moreover, SEAHV is a problem not only between peacekeepers and locals but also within the mission. In UNMIL, over 17 percent of the women who took the questionnaires listed sexual harassment as their biggest impediment to their service as peacekeepers.

These challenges affect not only peacekeeping missions but also the domestic security sectors of the host countries. Gender power imbalances in peacekeeping missions could be a part of their local legacies. We considered the potential for UNMIL to share some of the responsibility for the gender norms currently exhibited in local Liberian institutions. In doing so, we found that discrimination and the protection norm are still prevalent in the LNP. Male officers are less likely to trust female arms instructors, choose female leaders, and listen to women when they are outnumbered by female officers. Expectations about the role of officers are still gendered, in that officers believe that women are better suited for addressing gender crimes and there are few women in units that are more oriented toward operations. We also find some evidence that individuals still perceive the LNP as abusive and that individuals who had more contact with the LNP and were victimized during the war were less likely to prefer the LNP to respond to rape. This suggests that fears of domestic security forces perpetrating SEAHV and other human rights violations is still a problem.

A book simply about problems is not useful for an audience hoping for solutions. Thus, we also analyzed two potential solutions to these problems. One policy lever—female ratio balancing—relies on notions of fixed gender dichotomies. That is, if men exhibit certain masculinities and women femininities, then in order to gain some much-needed "feminine" qualities in peacekeeping missions, more female peacekeepers are necessary. The approach endeavors for female peacekeepers to make a unique positive impact on peacekeeping missions by increasing trust in the local population and improving the mission environment.

We argue that a singular focus on female ratio balancing ignores the real barriers posed by gender power imbalances, reduces the contribution of women to feminine stereotypes, presumes that gender similarities trump other cultural differences, and displaces an undue share of the burden for reforms on female personnel. Thus, solely relying on female peacekeepers to solve the gendered challenges in PKOs may not be realistic. A focus on increasing women's representation might not sufficiently shape the dysfunctional organizational cultures at the root of the problems.

Without ignoring the potential contributions of women in missions or ignoring that female ratio balancing should be pursued as an end in itself, we consider a second policy lever, equal opportunity peacekeeping. As a first step toward considering the potential for equal opportunity to matter, we examined whether variation in the practices of gender equality in the contributing countries explain participation and protection challenges. We found that contributing countries with relatively strong records of gender equality tended to deploy higher proportions of female peacekeepers to both military and police peacekeeping components. In addition, we found that missions that consisted of more military personnel from countries with better records of gender equality tended to experience fewer counts of SEAHV allegations. Thus, focusing on improving domestic practices of gender equality in the security sector has the prospect to return substantial dividends toward increasing the participation of women in peacekeeping missions and preventing SEAHV.

Successful reforms in the implementation of peacekeeping potentially have downstream benefits for an equal-opportunity agenda, as some of our findings point to peacekeeping missions leaving local legacies that help promote gender equality. Peacekeeping missions play a major role in the advancement of reforms, especially gender reforms, in the domestic security sectors of the host countries. They help introduce reforms such as professionalization, adoption of UNSCR 1325 NAPs, quotas to increase women's participation in the security sector, and the formation of new units to address SGBV.

Within the LNP, we found indirect evidence for gender-neutral SSRs, such as professionalization of the police, to heighten the sense of gender equality. When officers in our study had high competence, they were much more likely to be sensitive to SGBV, participate in groups, and have their views considered by the group, regardless of their sex and regardless of group composition. We also found evidence that increasing the proportion of women in the LNP had an effect in legitimizing the overall institution. As individuals interacted with female (as opposed to male) LNP officers, they were more likely to prefer the LNP as responders to a variety of security concerns. Finally, we found that existing beliefs about gender equality helped shape perceptions of the legitimacy of the security sector, again suggesting that domestic improvements to increase values related to gender equality can have lasting impacts on the functionality of security institutions. Nevertheless, for peacekeeping missions to continue to leave local legacies of equal opportunity in the domestic institutions of host countries, peacekeeping missions must, themselves, practice equal opportunity peacekeeping.

One common thread appears to be that stronger values for gender equality can attenuate the main threats posed by gendered power imbalances. The good news is that gender equality can be learned. Through changes in practices, rules, policies, and behaviors, it is possible that the norms and structures that perpetuate inequality will change to become more egalitarian. In this sense, it is important to not only include more women in these institutions but, even more so, to make efforts to change the institutional culture so all genders are equally valued. An improvement in the participation of female peacekeepers can and should occur along with these broader changes and be pursued as an end in itself, but such an improvement is only scratching the surface of the broader reforms needed. Thus, we next focus our attention on how to achieve gender equality in institutions through equal opportunity peacekeeping.

IMPLEMENTING EQUAL OPPORTUNITY PEACEKEEPING

To understand how to implement equal opportunity peacekeeping, we recall, as chapter 3 explained, that institutional culture is malleable. Similarly, according to Enloe (2000: 3), militarization is "a step-by step process by which a person or a thing gradually comes to be controlled by the military or comes to depend for its well-being on militaristic ideas." She argues that this step-by-step process is a result of "deliberate policy memos" and is not purely cultural. In this sense, even small policies, such as physical training standards, can have an effect on the perception that women are not as capable as men. Through changes in national policies, it is possible that norms and the structures that perpetuate the norms will change to become more egalitarian. Our recommendations are similarly premised on the belief that policy changes are greatly needed to erode the gender hierarchies in peacekeeping missions. Toward that end, this section considers possible methods for dismantling existing gender power imbalances in peacekeeping missions.

At least four areas of change are needed in order for equal opportunity peacekeeping to become a reality: parity in gender identities, gendered characteristics, belief systems, and composition. First, other peacekeeping identities that are more attuned to the needs of peacekeeping missions must be valued as highly as the warrior, protective, and militarized masculinities. Such identities include the "peace builder identity" and the "cosmopolitan identity," among others. Duncanson (2013) posits that the peace-building masculinity challenges the gender order because the orientation is around peace, winning support from locals, and winning "hearts and minds." The use of offensive force is not a part of the identity. In this way, the peacebuilder masculinity would be a greater asset to peacekeeping missions than the hegemonic masculinities discussed. Those who take on this identity might be less likely to be involved in unchecked aggression against civilians and SEAHV. They might be better able to ensure security without resorting to the use of force, opting for less violent means of achieving stability.

Kronsell (2012) highlights "cosmopolitanism" as another type of identity that has the potential to thrive in military institutions and thereby further deconstruct the extant hegemonic masculinities. Cosmopolitanism refers to the "common values and bonds among humans regardless of borders and territories" (Kronsell, 2012: 70). The task for cosmopolitan-oriented militaries is to defend "the other" rather than to "defend against the other."[1] She argues that Sweden has adopted such a cosmopolitan military, as have Canada, the Netherlands, and Finland. In addition to peace-building masculinity and cosmopolitanism, other forms of masculinities and femininities may emerge that challenge gender power imbalances.[2] These should be acknowledged, prioritized, and rewarded.

Parity in terms of characteristics is also an important aspect of equal opportunity peacekeeping. This means that characteristics that are associated with dominant forms of masculinity, such as strength, protection, rationality, aggression, public life, domination, and leadership, are valued as highly as supposedly feminine characteristics and less dominant forms of masculinity, such as emotion, passivity, privacy, empathy, caring, communication, and patience, among others. For example, Duncanson (2013) suggests that empathy is key for institutional transformation. Empathy is the willingness to enter into the feelings or spirit of something and appreciate it fully; to hear others' stories and be transformed by their experiences.[3] She contends that empathy played a key role in British involvement in Afghanistan: when soldiers began to empathize with locals, they started to dismantle dominant forms of masculinity within themselves such as the warrior masculinity.

Parity in terms of belief systems is also important for mitigating gender power imbalances. Fundamentally, this means respect for the opposite sex and believing that members of one sex can be just as capable of particular actions as the other sex. While this seems strikingly obvious, in practice it is difficult to achieve, due to the gender stereotypes that exist in all societies. As individuals' beliefs about men and women in society change to become more equitable, they may be more likely to also change their actions as well. This idea is the driving force behind much of the work by the international organization Promundo. Promundo engages in research, programs, and advocacy efforts to promote healthy masculinity (or positive notions of "what it means to be a man") and femininity (or "what it means to be a woman") and has research showing that such programming improves men's own lives, and the lives of women and girls.[4] These programs focus their efforts on changing gender norms and expectations as a way to mitigate violence against women (Aguayo et al., 2016). The effects of such programs are generally positive (Aguayo et al., 2016). This means that respect for the opposite sex can be learned, as can beliefs about equality. Militaries and police organizations could stand to benefit from some of this programming as well.

Finally, despite the critique of female ratio balancing policies as a policy lever in isolation, increasing women's representation toward parity in composition is part of equal opportunity peacekeeping. Increasing women's representation is a part of the transformational process to deconstruct gender power imbalances. Female bodies need to be involved in masculine spaces in order to begin the process of destabilizing the associations between those spaces and certain masculinities.[5] The appearance of women in such spaces is crucial in order to reorient what counts as masculine and feminine and to ultimately dismantle the hierarchical gender dichotomies.[6] Although a participation cascade has yet to materialize in PKOs and female peacekeepers have yet to unsettle the gender power imbalances, increasing the proportions of women in PKOs is part of the solution to the problem of how to challenge gendered power relations in peacekeeping missions.

Having identified four areas where change is needed, we next turn to providing some concrete recommendations about how this transformation may be achieved. We specifically focus on framing; leadership; recruitment and standards; promotion, demotion, and discipline; training and professionalism; access and accountability; women's representation; and gender mainstreaming (broadly defined). Before concluding, we also consider concurrent independent reform efforts from policy documents such as the High-Level Report (UN, 2015) and the 1325 Review (UN Women, 2015), as well as future research and evaluation.

Framing

One of the main ways to get sufficient "buy-in" from leaders and norm entrepreneurs who wield significant power in creating change is to first take an "insider-approach." Robert Egnell and colleagues (2014), for example, highlight the importance of framing changes in terms of operational effectiveness. This has meant tying a gender perspective to clear and achievable political aims, civil-military cooperation, building trust and support among the local population (winning hearts and minds), and having a cultural understanding of the local context (25). When the link is made, gender transformation may be seen as a legitimate way for militaries to achieve their goals and objectives.

Another way to frame change is by using the discourse of gender. While some identities like that of "peace-builder" may not be firmly "masculine," they can be portrayed as such. According to Duncanson (2013), the key is to make actions that are associated with peace-building—including moderation, control, intelligence, and decency—seem "manly." In Afghanistan, peace-building as a masculine identity was perceived by military leadership as "challenging" and "important" and was linked to heroism, courage, and bravery, which are a part of the traditional understanding of masculinity needed for warriors (90). For example, the World Bank has used this tactic in its "Real Men" campaign.[7] While this approach may be promising, one important drawback is that it still assumes gender dichotomies—that men are only men if they exhibit such-and-such an identity and characteristics. A fundamental change in power structures would be in tension with such a framing scheme. Therefore, such framing should be thought of as more of a short-term tactic, not a long-term transformational one.

Egnell and colleagues (2014: 126) also advocate for reframing at the strategic level, stating that missions should "expand the implementation of a gender perspective from an issue of traditional operational effectiveness to one that increasingly embraces the transformative nature of UNSCR 1325—challenging the way we conceive of security from a national to international issue to one of Human Security." This statement suggests that by broadening our understanding of what security means, we can also change which identities, characteristics, and beliefs are deemed important for PKOs. Thus, a reframing of the larger security objectives may be a better, and longer term solution to ensure transformation.

Specific recommendations:

- In the short run, frame gender issues in military and police institutions in terms of operational effectiveness.
- In the short run, use gendered language to demonstrate the importance of non-dominant forms of masculinities and femininities.
- In the long run, reframe the objectives of peacekeeping missions and other military/police endeavors around human security.

Leadership

Having institutional leadership prioritize new directions in peacekeeping is important in legitimizing certain less dominant masculinities and femininities. Hierarchy pervades security institutions, with lower ranked soldiers expected to take orders and respect higher ranked soldiers. This means that any structural or normative changes that occur must start at the top, with leadership. If senior ranked officers take gendered perspectives seriously, then the norm is likely to have trickle-down effects.

Higher ranked officials also have leeway in making structural changes without hurting their images. In her study of British soldiers, Duncanson (2013) found that the older, senior, and more experienced soldiers pressed most vehemently for peace-building identities. She argues that this was because "those with experience have already proved their masculine prowess in earlier operations and so have the license to articulate and enact alternative masculinities" (91). Lynne Segal (1997: 103) similarly writes that the senior commanders already "have reputations for being committed to the success of the institution, given their elite position and military record, allowing them to take on feminized traits without fear." Thus, institutional changes must start at the top, with leadership taking active stances on issues related to gender inequality in the institution.

In peacekeeping operations, mission leadership is based on the special representatives of the secretary-general (SRSGs), the force commander, and the police commissioner. These leaders serve as models for their subordinates and have substantial influence over the direction of the mission. When choosing individuals for these positions, it is important to ensure that they hold egalitarian values when it comes to gender and that they are aware of gender issues. For example, the selection process could include questions about gender equality as well as about other characteristics that are important for peacekeeping such as how well they perform on communication, empathy, and caring, among others. The High-Level Report recommends that heads of mission be evaluated for how well they have helped promote human rights and advance gender equality and that their performance in these tasks should affect their future assignments (UN, 2015: 84).

There may be challenges to ensuring that mission leadership understands and prioritizes legitimizing other less dominant forms of masculinities and femininities. First, the process of selecting leadership may be highly politicized. Selection for leadership positions is usually done by the UN Secretariat. Thus, as some have pointed out, there has always been and will continue to be a natural tension between the secretary-general's authority to select and appoint senior staff and the desire of Member States to ensure that their nationals are placed in such positions.[8] That the positions are highly political means that some potentially qualified individuals may not be appointed. Nevertheless, appointed candidates can be and should be screened on their values for egalitarianism in identities, characteristics, and beliefs. The secretary-general and other Secretariat leadership, who constantly advocate for the UNSCR 1325 agenda, must summon the political will to act and prioritize screening, lest the proclaimed support for gender equality be revealed as cheap talk.

In addition, mission leadership may not find it important to prioritize gender issues in peacekeeping missions. Thus, in order to ensure that mission leadership take the changes seriously, they should be specified in UN mandates. While there is gender language in almost all recent peacekeeping mandates, the language could be more specific in stating that it is the role of mission leadership to ensure that gendered barriers are dismantled. Current language in mandates includes vague phrases about gender mainstreaming, and it is up to the discretion of mission leadership to outline specific goals to achieve the mandate. Instead, the mandate could be specific about objectives to be achieved by mission leadership, for example: "the SRSG must suspend the activities of any peacekeeper found to be engaging in SEAHV." More specificity about how peacekeepers and particularly mission leadership can change the gendered culture of the mission would make it easier for mission leadership to carry out the mandate.

Specific recommendations:

- Select mission leadership based on their qualifications in gender equality and their ability to prioritize nondominant forms of masculinities and femininities.
- Incentivize mission leadership to prioritize changes in the culture of the mission.
- Reward mission leaders who have made gender equality in missions a priority and have prioritized nondominant forms of masculinities and femininities.
- Make mission mandates more specific with respect to achieving gender equality in and through the mission.
- Base evaluation of mission leadership on how well they perform on tasks related to gender equality and on their ability to prioritize nondominant forms of masculinities and femininities.

Recruitment and Standards

One of the main areas through which to challenge gender power imbalances may be changes in recruitment criteria and standards in security institutions. As it stands, standards of what constitutes appropriate skills and character are based on hegemonic masculine traits that were developed by men. However, other identities and characteristics are also important for successful militaries, police organizations, and PKOs. A thorough reevaluation of mission standards in security institutions is needed, such that gender considerations and qualities from other masculinities and femininities are also deemed valuable and included in the recruitment process.

Most obviously, standards that are based on biology should be reevaluated. Currently, standards are often based on male physiological advantages such as strength and not on areas where women have a physiological advantage such as agility. Changing standards for recruitment to reflect the needs and objectives of PKOs as a whole, as well as specialized units, will improve mission efficacy beyond the arbitrary and archaic status quo biological standards. In this way, improving standards to be more egalitarian also ensures that women are given an opportunity to succeed.

In addition, contributing countries can also change standards to be more accommodating to groups historically prevented from joining the military and police. For example, some countries require five years of service before officers can apply for PKOs, but this qualification can be reduced to three years, which would allow more women to participate in missions, given that they are likely to have joined the institution much later than men.

In terms of recruitment, security institutions could stand to broaden the characterizations of their ideal personnel. If one looks at the recruitment videos for the United States Marine Corps or other branches of the military, while they (now) include women and members of various racial groups, they speak to bravery, heroism, and adventure. Individuals who may not exhibit these characteristics or find them appealing are unlikely to join. Indeed, absent from the videos are displays of caring, nurturing, and empathy, which are qualities that should be recognized as valuable to the performance of many functions in security institutions. Arguably, such changes in recruitment may be particularly important for police institutions. Given that police are more likely to interact with citizens on a daily basis, recruitment should be based on their ability to communicate well and empathize.[9]

In addition, values for gender equality are important to screen for during recruitment into institutions that are trying to turn the corner against problems of gender power imbalance. Adding recruitment criteria related to egalitarian values is important to change the underlying power structures. Currently, the UN requires that peacekeeper candidates pass written tests and undergo interviews. It also requires that they drive manual cars and be able to use computers. As a part of the candidacy vetting process, it is possible to administer tests that assess individual beliefs about conflict resolution and gender equality. For example, questions about gender equality and awareness can be included in written tests or during the interview phase, allowing the UN to assess the quality of applicants on a gender awareness dimension. Questions can also be asked about the potential recruit's views about caring activities, empathy, communication, and other characteristics important for peacekeeping. This kind of targeted recruitment and screening means making equality a value desired in all potential recruits.

It is also important for peace-building activities to push for targeted recruitment in the domestic security sector of the host countries. The same vetting, screening, and recruitment processes used to recruit peacekeepers can also be used in the domestic security sectors. Peacekeeping success in promoting gender equality requires local ownership of the issue and thus personnel who can continue the pursuit of greater gender equality at home, even after the peacekeepers leave, by adopting the same types of standards as the peacekeeping mission itself.

In chapter 7, we found that competent security officials tend to be more gender conscious and open to women's participation. This means that recruitment for peacekeeping missions and the domestic security sector should be based not only on specific criteria related to equality in beliefs but also on broader criteria related to professionalism. In a study conducted by Sabrina Karim and Ryan Gorman (2016), professional (related to the objective of the job), social (prosocial behavior), contextual (awareness of surroundings), and individual (related to leadership qualities) attributes positively affected the likelihood of officers adopting gender equal beliefs. Recruitment tests should incorporate modules on these different competencies. When vetting officers, these criteria can serve as important tools for choosing officers in the security sector such that quality is privileged over quantity. Hiring quality officers of both sexes can help dismantle gender power imbalances. Indeed, having more personnel may not be as effective as having smaller numbers of qualified personnel.

One concern may be that prioritizing these nondominant identities and characteristics as new standards or as new criteria for recruitment could weaken the military and police's effectiveness. As new standards are adopted, they may dilute the existing ones, which are necessary for effective combat and protection. We contend, however, that the inclusion of different standards need not, indeed must not, eliminate existing standards but should merely add to them and ensure that other standards are appropriately valued. The new standards should not in any way diminish the value of, say, weapons skills, and they may actually make militaries, police, and peacekeeping institutions *more* effective, not less effective, with a deeper toolkit to achieve a wider array of objectives.

Specific recommendations:

- Change standards to include skills, identities, characteristics, and beliefs other than the dominants ones.
- Change standards to meet the demands of units and groups rather than developing standards based on biology.
- Reevaluate standards for fitness and equipment so as to include advantages for both sexes.
- Amend requirements for joining missions so as to account for historically underrepresented groups in PKOs.
- Change recruitment campaigns, including videos, to more accurately reflect the skills needed in the field (i.e., not just advertising about combat).
- In recruitment for missions and domestic security sectors, include screening for these two criteria: beliefs about egalitarianism and ability to prioritize nondominant forms of masculinities and femininities.
- Focus recruitment in peacekeeping missions and the domestic security sector on recruiting professional, quality, and competent officers.
- Take into account that the quality of officers in domestic security institutions may be more important than the quantity of officers.

Promotion, Demotion, and Discipline

Another area where the preeminence of certain masculinities may be cemented is through the awarding of promotion and through discipline. Promotion and demotion within the mission can be directly linked to gender issues and the (in)ability to value nontraditional identities, characteristics, and beliefs. Contributing countries have discretion over promotions and rank that are given with respect to performance in the peacekeeping mission (e.g., whether such service makes soldiers and police officers eligible for promotion), as well as normal standards for promotion. A part of the promotion considerations should focus on how well the candidate adheres to the principle of gender equality and whether or not he or she displays and values nondominant forms of masculinities and femininities not just in the context of peacekeeping but also within service in national police and military institutions.

Moreover, the UN heads of mission (SRSGs) have leverage over personnel matters. They control the distribution of positions in the missions. For example, individuals can request positions in missions, and such requests could be prioritized for individuals who have performed well, including adhering to egalitarian principles. In addition, leadership positions in missions (promotions within the mission) are also at the discretion of heads of mission. Awarding of such lucrative positions can also be based on adhering to beliefs about gender equality and valuing nondominant forms of masculinities and femininities.

As another example that relates to awards, there are several prestigious combat-related medals in the U.S. military, such as the Medal of Honor, the Distinguished Service Cross, the Silver Star, the Bronze Star, and the Purple Heart. While such medals of valor are important for bestowing honor on those who have been willing to sacrifice much for national defense, security institutions could stand to be more creative and intentional in awarding medals for distinguishable and/or sacrificial actions while on active duty that have promoted peace, helped avoid the escalation of a combat situation, or in some way exemplified admirable traits associated with femininities or less privileged masculinities.

Contributing countries and the UN could especially emphasize the awarding of such medals for peacekeeping personnel. During medal parades and other ceremonies, special medals can be given for individuals who have helped mainstream gender, paid particular attention to gender issues, or helped address concerns related to SEAHV.[10] Awards can also be given out to peacekeepers who consistently exhibit exemplary virtues consistent with a "peace-builder" or "cosmopolitan" identity or who perform notable acts of empathy and caring. If this kind of reward became highly valued in military and police institutions, it could have an important impact in terms of sending a message about the types of identities, actions, and characteristics that are valued in the institution. It could change existing ideas of heroism, such as executing rescue operations, to include (not replace) other forms of heroism, such as empathizing with the needs of locals and responding accordingly.

While UNPOL has taken measures to recognize women and give them awards, as in the case of the International Female Police Peacekeeper award, these recognitions are for women only and not for peacekeepers who display important characteristics associated with gender equality. Thus, we urge that both types of award should institutionalize a culture of equality.

Along with promotion and awards, demotion in the mission, and at home in contributing countries, should be directly linked to performance related to gender issues, as disciplining soldiers and peacekeepers for degrading women and other groups is also important for cultural transformation. In peacekeeping missions, while individual contributing countries have the most discretion over their personnel's demotion, mission leadership has some ability to punish individuals for not conducting themselves in a manner consistent with principles of egalitarianism. One way to do so is to base permission for mission extension on individual behavior. Individuals who have personal conduct records that do not reflect a value for egalitarianism should not be assigned to their desired positions, have their service extended, or be eligible for any awards and medals. In addition, leaders simply need to correct soldiers when they use gendered language, such as "stop behaving like a girl," as well as to fully discipline them for larger infractions, such as SEAHV.

Related to this last point, violations of SEAHV must be taken seriously and transgressors punished. Currently, sending countries have the sole discretion over sanctioning violators of the UN's zero tolerance policy. Most often, they are sent home as punishment and never prosecuted. The sending countries could stand to take violations more seriously by consistently prosecuting transgressors, thereby setting an example for the rest of the contingent or unit. The UN can also be more active in punishment by naming and shaming country contingents that have contributed soldiers and police officers (and civilians) who have engaged in such activity. The UN can give incentives to contributing countries by rewarding countries that prosecute offenders of SEAHV. In this vein, the UN should also motivate peacekeepers to help individuals report SEAHV by establishing clearer and more lucrative whistleblower protections. The 1325 Review suggests additional ways the UN leadership could punish SEAHV violators: by "withholding service medals, payments of premiums and subsistence allowances, and suspending the corresponding reimbursement payments for the military personnel involved in an investigation" (UN Women, 2015: 148). The 1325 Review also advocates for the creation of hybrid courts to prosecute transgressors. Thus, even though the UN does not have the authority to punish transgressors, it can take active measures to ensure less impunity.

Despite the importance of creating new standards for promotion and demotion related to gender equality and valuing nondominant forms of masculinities and femininities, there are challenges in implementation. Individual extensions in peacekeeping missions and placements are often highly political—based on ensuring that different countries get represented—again, sometimes preventing placement based on merit. We contend that including these new standards, however, can open up the pool of personnel with merit. Peacekeepers from underrepresented countries can then be allocated coveted positions without compromising skill—they may not necessarily embody the dominant attributes, but they do embody other necessary qualities. As an illustration, we can learn from the experience of Major Lola Aduke Oyediran Ugbodaga (chapter 4). Many of her colleagues thought that her placement as the deputy in the civil-military affairs division was solely due to the fact that she was a woman and Nigerian. (Some thought that African countries received many leadership positions because there was an effort to make UNMIL more "African-led.") Nevertheless, she was demoted on the basis of her inability to perform well in her job due to her computer skills. However, as a part of her role in the Civil Military Affairs division in UNMIL, her talents could have been used in a different, more efficacious way. For example, she was denied the opportunity to spend time getting to know local Liberians, which could have provided information for the types of quick impact projects that would have been most beneficial to locals. If the characteristics of communication and empathy were valued as highly as computing skills,[11] then she might have excelled at her job and not been demoted.

Specific recommendations:

- Base criteria for promotion in the missions (whether receiving a medal or mission placement or extension) on performance related to egalitarianism.
- Sanction behavior contrary to egalitarianism (whether by taking away medals or placing individuals in undesired positions).

- For offenses that violate the zero tolerance SEAHV policy, the UN should encourage contributing countries to take consistent measures to sanction the offenders, with criminal proceedings as appropriate, and reward them for doing so.
- The UN should name and shame contributing countries with frequent SEAHV violators.
- The UN should create a hybrid court to prosecute transgressors of SEAHV.
- The mission should reward peacekeepers who help report SEAHV.

Training and Professionalism

Conducting training on gender equality is also particularly important for institutional transformation. Currently, gender training is a part of predeployment training and is included in the orientation activities in missions. But this one-off training may not be enough to change perceptions and behavior that have been historically entrenched in national militaries and police institutions. In addition, observations and anecdotal evidence from peacekeepers suggest that many of them dismiss this type of training, which they perceive as too academic, not sufficiently practical, and not worth taking seriously.

There are several changes that can be made to ensure that training in peacekeeping missions on gender equality and egalitarianism are taken seriously.[12] Gender training should be integrated into all other training and should be conducted not only by gender focal points but also by the leadership in the units so as to demonstrate the importance of the topic. Both men and women should participate in providing training about egalitarianism. The training should be practical and not theoretical and should include role-playing and personal examples. Training in peacekeeping could benefit from curriculums developed by groups such as Promundo and other NGOs that have been working on "healthy masculinities." And instead of calling the training sessions "gender training," which may turn off certain populations who have yet to be convinced that gender dynamics matter, such training should be reframed as training to improve mission efficacy and legitimacy.

In addition, training individuals in senior positions is particularly important. For example, the 1325 Review suggests that the "SRSGs and Force Commanders [and police commissioner] should also get a week-long mandatory training week at headquarters on the prevention of sexual violence and abuse and other protection issues" (UN Women, 2015: 149). Missions should also invest in developing gender training tailored for senior managers to help them integrate a gender perspective into their work. At first, gender focal points, gender units, and/or the gender advisers can conduct gender training for senior officials. Then, "train the trainer" methods can be employed to ensure that all members of the mission are taking ownership of a gender approach. The gender focal points, gender units, and/or gender advisers can train key leaders of contingents or units in civilian, police, and military fields and then observe these leaders training the others in their units. Using a "train the trainers" approach ensures that the training is fully institutionalized and not just compartmentalized as a matter for the gender focal points, gender units, and/or the gender advisers.

Training is particularly important at the domestic level as well. The process of militarization often starts in training academies, which means that such locations should be focal points for changing the practices that cultivate the dominance of certain masculinities. In part, the reforms need to continue to help educate and remind personnel about the value that different masculinities and femininities bring and of the pernicious consequences of gender power imbalances, including discrimination, exclusion, and SEAHV. Examples in Sweden show that reconceptualizing training can shift gender power imbalances in the military. Kronsell (2012) and Egnell and colleagues (2014) have argued that, although the ratios of women to men in Swedish peacekeeping contingents remain low, levels of gender awareness are high due to rigorous training protocols that have transformed the culture of the defense forces. For example, Swedish military training now emphasizes respect for laws against discrimination and tolerance of difference through "new values for defense" (Kronsell, 2012: 83).

Other training reforms might target particular hazing rituals that denigrate women and other "out-groups." Much of the militarized masculinity literature suggests that it helps define the "in-groups," which may be crucial for unit cohesion and military effectiveness. However, recent scholarship challenges the notion that "out-groups" have to be created for military effectiveness. Robert MacCoun, Elizabeth Kier, and Aaron Belkin (2006) find that task cohesion (a sense of shared commitment to the unit's mission) rather than social cohesion (the strength of interpersonal bonds among members) may be more important for military effectiveness.[13] Through task cohesion, soldiers maintain close professional ties that are the result of a common goal, and these ties lack any kind of emotion or sentimental bonding.[14] In other words, professionalization of groups and focusing on task competency may be more important for military effectiveness than perpetuating practices such as hazing or defaming "out-groups" as a way to create bonds among soldiers.

Relatedly, David Segal and Meyer Kastenbaum (2002: 454) state that units may improve operational effectiveness when they adopt a sense of "imagined community." They write: "tolerance and appreciation of difference, furthermore, form a useful foundation for the creation of another kind of social cohesion in the military, often and inappropriately overlooked in discussion of the armed forces. . . . This sense of imagined community is precisely what may seem to distinguish the armed forces from the rest of society and simultaneously to bind members together." In this way, it is not the small-group unit cohesion that matters but a sense of overall purpose of the entire military (or peacekeeping mission). It is the "spirit" of the military (mission) that propels them to perform. Training that emphasizes professionalization can generate important dividends toward cultivating an "imagined community" of peacekeepers, whereby they feel loyal to the mission of peace. Thus, instead of focusing on differences with others, advancing activities that perpetuate solidarity may be more useful and more benign for breaking down power imbalances. Importantly, particularly in relation to women, it is imperative that any group solidarity activity that is performed include women such that "good old boys' networks" do not form.

Another area of training should focus on building the capacities of women (and men) who are new to peacekeeping or likely to become peacekeepers. This training should focus on building some of the healthy and useful skills and characteristics that are dominant. According to many of the women in UNMIL, women have less training than men, which makes them less competitive for promotions and also less likely to participate in peacekeeping missions in the first place. For example, one of the biggest impediments for female peacekeeping personnel is that they are often behind in driving, computer, and language skills. As such, peacekeeping missions can provide training to peacekeepers in driving, computing, foreign languages, and other technical areas. This can be done at the contributing country level or in the form of in-service training in missions. As an example of the former, the Ghanaian police have benefited from a Norwegian program where the Norwegians have helped train female Ghanaian officers in driving and computer skills. Scholarships for women from different parts of the world can be provided so that they can participate in such training. Scholarships should especially be provided for women who are identified as potential leaders. As another example, UN Women has recently begun conducting two-week courses exclusively for female military officers, as part of a professional development opportunity (UN Women, 2015).

In the form of in-service training, UN missions should offer different classes and make sure that women have better access to them. Professionalization opportunities should be accessible to all members of the mission, which means that contingent leaders should allow female peacekeepers and others to leave the base to attend these trainings. For the domestic security sector, it is important to ensure that women are always represented during any in-service training or training provided by the UN. This is an opportunity to improve women's capacity and provides a stepping-stone toward creating female leaders in domestic institutions.

Gender training for men (and women) could also be held in other parts of the world or at UN peacekeeping training centers. This makes the training more prestigious, and male officers may take it more seriously. For these trainings, it may be best to target not the most qualified individuals who already display characteristics of equal opportunity peacekeeping, but those individuals in militaries and police institutions who exhibit the least understanding of the importance of egalitarianism.

One of the difficulties of using training as a transformational tool is that it is unclear how much training is necessary to make a difference in the culture of the institution. Training provides knowledge, but does it actually change practice and behavior? To answer that question, we would need to conduct a randomized controlled trial where randomly chosen officers receive sustained training while others do not and then assess the outcomes. Barring such an evaluation, we can only suggest that comprehensive, sustainable training that is encompassing not just of gender training but also of professionalism and other characteristics, skills, identities, and beliefs that are important for breaking down gendered power imbalances is just as important as other forms of skills training that tend to be more valued.

Specific recommendations:

• Gender focal points and gender advisers should train those in leadership positions.

- A "train the trainers" approach should be used to ensure that gender training has wider ownership across the mission.
- Gender training should focus on practical aspects of gender issues.
- Curriculum for training should include elements of "healthy masculinities" programs such as those developed by Promundo.
- Gender training should be reframed and relabeled as training to enhance mission efficacy and legitimacy.
- Both men and women should be involved in training and leading trainings.
- Leadership should be involved in conducting gender training.
- Gender training should not be just one or two hours during predeployment or orientation but rather sustained training throughout the duration of the mission.
- Professionalization and skills training should be offered and accessible to all members of the peacekeeping mission.
- The UN should help train women in domestic military and police forces so that they meet the requirements for peacekeeping deployment. This can take the form of scholarships for female military and police personnel to attend peacekeeping training centers or training centers in other countries (e.g., the Folke Bernadotte Academy in Sweden or the Kofi Annan Institute in Ghana).
- Male personnel should be sent to gender training sessions at UN peacekeeping training centers or to those in other countries, such as the Nordic Centre for Gender in Military Operations. Scholarships should be provided for them.
- Contributing countries should ensure that women are present during in-service trainings.
- Military and police academies should find different ways to train their officers that do not rely on "out-group" denigration or hazing.
- Operational effectiveness should be enhanced through task cohesion and professionalism.
- Solidarity in military and police academies (and PKOs) should be achieved through outlining and promoting a common purpose instead of through the cultivation of differences between in-groups and out-groups.

Access and Accountability

In order to break down gender power imbalances in peacekeeping missions, it is important to focus on not only the individual personnel of the missions but also institutional rules and procedures. At present, the UN has a checkered record in terms of accountability and accessibility. For example, until 2016 the UN abnegated responsibility for the 2009 cholera epidemic in Haiti, which was started by the Nepalese contingent stationed there. Despite calls by international human rights lawyers, the UN had refused to compensate the victims of the epidemic. Such actions do little to strengthen confidence in the UN that it will hold its own people accountable for their actions. Thus, one of the first steps to demonstrate that the UN is committed to human rights and gender equality is for the UN itself to take responsibility for its own actions.

In addition, it is important to recognize that accountability for SEAHV offenses cannot occur if locals find the reporting process too difficult. Reporting instances of peacekeeper-perpetrated SEAHV requires filing a complaint at mission headquarters, which takes resources and time—something many people in postconflict countries do not have. And individuals may feel that they do not have support in the institutions for making such claims. They may fear reprisals from the community or even from personnel from the missions. As such, it is important to make sure that people know how to report and to make the process easier. Making the process easier could include having the UN conduct community forums and outreach to take reports of peacekeeper violations. Such outreach might partner with NGOs who are motivated more by addressing the issues than by preserving the legitimacy of the mission. Relatedly, the UN should establish relationships with local leaders so that they feel comfortable approaching the mission when complaints arise in the community.

Institutional inertia may be a factor that has prevented the UN from taking responsibility and making it easier for locals to make complaints against it. The UN is an institution that is interested in self-preservation and hence has an incentive to downplay allegations against it. To prevent such interests from infringing on the UN's actual objective of protection, watchdog groups, such as Human Rights Watch and others, should scrutinize the UN as much as they scrutinize countries that violate human rights. Policy research groups, such as the Stimson Center, that focus on peacekeeping should also play a part in monitoring the human rights records of peacekeeping missions.

Specific recommendations:

- The UN should take responsibility and offer redress for actions committed in peacekeeping missions.
- UN missions should conduct outreach to local communities, including partnering with NGOs, to make the missions more accessible and SEAHV reporting easier for locals.
- Outside watchdog groups should evaluate UN actions.

Women's Representation

In several chapters we have highlighted numerous barriers to women's full participation in peacekeeping missions. In this section, we address these barriers directly. We emphasize an institutional approach to resolving many of the barriers that were mentioned by the female peacekeepers we interviewed and surveyed. Currently, the institutional environment constrains women's ability to make the best use of their skills and talents, and we consider a number of ways to help transform the institutional environment into one that dismantles the barriers preventing women from serving, and serving fully, in PKOs.

Related to recruitment, female peacekeepers themselves have been successful in the recruitment of more female peacekeepers. Veteran female peacekeepers can travel to different countries—and within their home countries—to talk about their experiences and encourage women to participate in missions. Men in higher ranks can also advocate for including more women in subsequent deployments from their country. The UN can set up a way to incentivize such action. This would not take too many resources on the part of the UN, as it would only require selecting officers of both sexes to serve as liaison officers for recruitment. Moreover, the UN should tap into existing women's networks, such as the International Association of Women Police, to recruit women.

Improving the representation of women in peacekeeping missions incrementally could have a cascade effect on female participation. If female soldiers and police officers learn that there are female peacekeepers in missions, they may be more likely to join missions. In addition, as there are more veteran female peacekeepers who return to their home countries and talk about their experiences, more women from those countries may be inspired to join the security sector with the hope of eventual service as peacekeepers. The recruitment of individuals into national militaries and police starts in high school, and young women and men should understand the potential roles they can play as peacekeepers. In this sense, participation could beget more participation and precipitate a regime change in the gender balance of peacekeeping missions.

As for recruitment of more women into national militaries, Carreiras (2006) has identified a number of ways that NATO member countries have increased the proportions of women in their national militaries. She argues and finds that militaries that rely more heavily on volunteer recruits tend to have higher proportions of women and that women need to hold power in society in order for more structural changes (such as women in the labor force) to occur so as to increase the participation of women in the armed forces. Again, promoting beliefs about gender equality in an institution (and society) is an important means of transformation.

The 1325 Review also offers some guidance on how to increase women's representation in national militaries and police forces. It highlights the importance of "targeted recruitment campaigns; removing barriers and exclusion of women from certain categories of military personnel; improving and diversifying employment pathways; using images of female military officers in promotional and communications campaigns; conducting surveys and studies on recruitment and retention of women in the armed forces; tracking accurate data on women's representation and experiences in the military; changes in family policy; reforms addressing sexual harassment and abuse within the force; and changes to facilities, uniforms, and equipment" as ways to improve women's representation (UN Women, 2015: 137).

Institutional environments should also be transformed to reduce the uneven adjustments that women have to make to "fit" into this male-dominant occupation. Female peacekeepers have noted that one reason why few women apply to peacekeeping missions is that the structure of the institutions does not work in their favor. Women are reluctant to leave their children and families. As such, the UN can incentivize women by providing generous family visitation policies. Countries such as Norway, for example, subsidize some of the costs of family visitation. The UN could provide one round-trip ticket for all peacekeepers so they can visit their families at least once during deployment. And if it is not possible for the UN to subsidize such tickets for all their personnel due to resource constraints, the UN could have an application system for such benefits. If the UN DPKO opened a "family fund," similar to some of the benefits that civilian UN workers receive, then this might alleviate some of the burdens women face.[15]

Another problem highlighted by many female peacekeepers in UNMIL is the lack of facilities for women in the mission, especially when they deploy to the leeward or rural areas. Often, according to female peacekeepers, there is little privacy. Some facilities do not have women's bathrooms. This should be a consideration when building housing facilities in the host country. In addition, according to the 1325 Review, peacekeeping budgets should allocate sufficient funds to better accommodate greater numbers of women through necessary changes in mission facilities and life. This could include "special family or leave arrangements for women, adequate and appropriate mission facilities for women—from accommodation quarters and sanitary facilities to welfare and recreational spaces and activities, special medical and gynecological care, gender-specific uniforms or body armor; and investments in the internal safety of the compound, among others" (UN Women, 2015: 142).

Turning to the incentives of the contributing countries to facilitate better representation of women, the UN could provide additional resources to countries that send more women and that send women to dangerous locations. The UN should reward countries for sending female peacekeepers to different peacekeeping missions equally through what UN Women has called a "gender balance premium" (UN Women, 2015: 156). They urge a premium for contributing countries that send balanced forces; we also urge a premium for countries that send women to diverse settings.

Setting aside questions related to how to increase the number of women in peacekeeping, we now address issues related to barriers in the roles women play in missions. Efforts should be made to ensure that qualified women serve in a wide array of capacities. Gender-based reforms should not focus too much on the total numbers of women in the security forces; it is more important to be intentional about the work women do. If women are solely placed in traditional gender roles, such as nursing, office work, cooking, and cleaning, then this does little to challenge the gendered protection norm or to more broadly cultivate egalitarianism. Women must be placed in diverse roles, including driving vehicles and carrying firearms, in order to chip away at the participation gap. Relatedly, women should deploy to rural areas, which are currently underserved by women in peacekeeping missions.

The role of mission leadership is important to ensure that female peacekeepers are participating fully in missions. The female peacekeepers in our survey noted the importance of the force commander and police commissioner (and perhaps SRSG) in addressing female personnel without male leaders present and asking them about whether they are participating the same way as the men in the contingent. This ensures that women are able to speak freely to mission leadership without fear of reprisal from contingent leadership. It also allows information gathering at the leadership level so that appropriate changes can take place.

Moreover, the institutional environment should be reformed to improve the access women have to professional and social networks. We noted that women are prevented from collaborating in missions: female peacekeepers rarely interact with one another, especially across different mission components (police, military, and civilian). Peacekeeping missions should provide opportunities for women to collaborate on projects and to socialize with other members of the peacekeeping mission. Such collaboration is likely to provide momentum for important new initiatives and enable women to build networks of influence.

Related to networks of influence, participation of and promotion in the peacekeeping missions can still maintain a flavor of an "old boys' networks," which means that women have a disadvantage if they are less welcomed into the types of informal and social interactions that foster such networks. As a counterweight, the peacekeeping mission should help provide social and professional networking that women can better access through formal mentoring programs, or at least workshops where women can talk to one another about problems they are facing in the mission or, during predeployment training, about the realities they will face there. Women and men in leadership positions should take initiative in ensuring that female peacekeepers have equal access to these networking opportunities. One hopeful example is the Office of Military Affairs, which has initiated the establishment of the Female Military Peacekeepers Network to create a space of mutual support, mentoring, training, and advocacy for UN female military staff (UN Women, 2015). Another example is the work UNPOL has been doing. It has provided regular mentoring, networking, and training activities around the world on strategies to increase women in UNPOL and national police forces, and it has collaborated on projects aimed at strengthening specific skills that female police need to pass for the UN Selection Assistance Test (UN Women, 2015).

Ensuring professionalism across all personnel may also help address participation restrictions. In chapter 7, we found that more competent police officers are more likely to vote for female leaders and listen to women. We expect that individuals, both men and women, who excel in professionalism and leadership qualities are more likely to demonstrate prosocial behavior, have contextual awareness, and ultimately hold gender equal beliefs.[16] The more professionalism can be nurtured, the more women will feel empowered as contributors to peacekeeping missions.

Unfortunately, sexual harassment remains a major barrier to the full participation of women in peacekeeping missions. The female peacekeepers in our study mentioned harassment from both their fellow colleagues and the local population. Currently, there is no standard procedure for handling sexual harassment by locals against peacekeepers. The UN should develop procedures for this and conduct the appropriate training during the missions and during predeployment training. There should also be a clear zero tolerance policy of sexual harassment among mission personnel that is consistently enforced. Female peacekeepers often complained of such behavior, but they do not have the appropriate means to address the issues, for fear of demotion. Instead, the incentives should be such that the perpetrators fear demotion.

Another logistical challenge noted by Egnell and colleagues (2014) is the lack of female interpreters.[17] Even if female peacekeepers (or any peacekeepers) are able to go into the field, often they lack the language skills and cultural context, so they need local guides and local interpreters. These guides and interpreters, moreover, are often men, which means that the ability of the female peacekeepers to communicate with local women is still hampered. Egnell and colleagues (138) suggest that "more effort should be put into recruiting and training female military interpreters" so that women can more fully participate in all mission roles. This may also have the side effect of reducing sexual harassment of female peacekeepers by local men.

Reforms at the level of the contributing countries can also prove crucial to enhancing the full participation of women in peacekeeping missions. Archaic gender-based policies and practices in national militaries and police should be reformed. Countries should also eliminate policies that prevent women from engaging in combat. As mentioned, the United States removed its combat exclusion in 2015, which was in place since 1994, because many women had served in combat roles in Afghanistan and Iraq, demonstrating the impractical nature of the restriction. Other countries, such as New Zealand, removed exclusion policies in 2001, and in 1985 Norway became the first country to allow women to serve on submarines. In addition to removing restrictions and rules that prevent women from filling these positions, domestic reforms should take measures to ensure that women will be successful in new roles. For example, much of the equipment used for training and combat is physiologically designed for men, which makes using the equipment difficult for women.[18] This limits women's ability to perform well. Removing restrictions and ensuring that women can be successful helps demonstrate to societies, across the sexes, and especially to members of the security sector that women can provide protection.

Finally, it is worth noting that equal representation may not be culturally appropriate for some women from countries where it is still considered socially and culturally inappropriate for women to participate in the ways mentioned. Thus, many of the suggestions here may be applicable to some countries but not others. Nevertheless, it is important to respect such cultures but still find avenues for women's participation. One suggestion has been to create more all-female units. All-female units may provide an alternative or additional option for women wishing to pursue roles as peacekeepers yet not wishing to take on the many burdens that women in male-majority units have reportedly faced. Particularly, in order to avoid the potential for SEAHV within missions, all-female units may be a useful alternative. We note, however, that all-female units should not serve as a substitution for women's integration and representation in missions, because "separate representation" is likely to perpetuate an "unequal status of representation." Moreover, male peacekeepers still have an obligation to not sexually harass, exploit, or abuse their female colleagues who are not serving in all-female units. Thus integration can take different forms, and we urge all forms of representation while also cautioning against singular approaches to women's participation.

Specific recommendations:

- To improve women's representation, individuals should be recruited who display beliefs about gender equality and professionalism.
- To improve women's representation in national militaries and police institutions, recruitment should start early in high school. Female officers should go to high schools to recruit women.

- To increase the recruitment of female peacekeepers, male and female liaison officers should travel to different countries (and within their home countries) to encourage the recruitment of more female peacekeepers.
- Female peacekeepers should serve as recruitment officers after their deployments have finished.
- Missions should allow women to collaborate on projects and with local women.
- The UN should start formal mentoring programs, or at least workshops for women to discuss problems and expectations about the job, during the mission and during predeployment.
- The UN should ensure that proper facilities for women are built, especially in rural areas. This includes welfare and recreational spaces and activities; special medical and gynecological care; gender-specific uniforms or body armor; and investments in the internal safety of the compound.
- The UN should establish and enforce policies of sexual harassment, both in the mission and between peacekeepers and locals.
- The UN should help provide funds for family visitation during deployment. This could be on a rolling application basis.
- The force commander and police commissioner (and SRSG) should address female peacekeepers without male contingent leaders present.
- Missions should help organize women's professional networks within the mission.
- Contributing countries should send female peacekeepers to a diverse range of missions.
- The UN should reward countries for sending female peacekeepers to different peacekeeping missions equally. They could provide premiums both to contributing countries that provide female peacekeepers and to ones that send them to diverse settings.
- Countries should remove combat exclusions for women in national militaries.
- Women should be placed in diverse roles and not just traditional gendered roles.
- Peacekeeping missions should deploy women to rural areas.
- All-female units may serve as an alternative for women who come from cultures and backgrounds where it is not considered appropriate for women and men to be integrated in the same unit.

Gender Mainstreaming

One of the main ways the UN and the international community have sought to promote cultural transformation is through gender mainstreaming: the constant assessments of how policies affect women and men.[19] Related to peacekeeping, gender mainstreaming is achieved when mission leadership and personnel make conscious efforts to assess how the policies and decisions in the mission impact women and men and adjust policies accordingly when the impact may have negative gender-related ramifications.

According to the Office of the Special Adviser on Gender Issues at the UN, in order to gender mainstream at all decision-making levels, the first step is to develop a strategy, which requires an assessment of the connections between gender equality and the relevant issue, sector, or strategy.[20] After understanding how gender equality affects larger strategies and policies, opportunities for introducing gender perspectives need to be identified in the work tasks undertaken for each strategic area. These opportunities or entry points can be achieved through the creation of taskforces, research and analysis, policy development, use of statistics, training events and workshops/conferences, as well as in the planning and implementation of projects and programs. Finally, an approach has to be identified for successfully incorporating gender perspectives into these work tasks that facilitate influencing goals, strategies, resource allocation, and outcomes on a larger scale.

As discussed in chapter 2, gender focal points, gender units, and gender advisers have served as important facilitators for implementing gender mainstreaming in PKOs. According to the DPKO's Department of Field Support, the gender focal points, units, and advisers "can provide ongoing advice to contingent commanders on how a gender perspective can enhance the efficiency and effectiveness of the contingent's operational tasks" (UN, 2010c: 14). These gender focal points offer targeted in-service gender training to members of the contingent and serve as principal points of liaison between the contingent and the peacekeeping mission's Office of the Gender Adviser. These positions should be included in peacekeeping mandates to ensure that they are funded and that resources are available for them to do their job.[21] The gender focal points, gender units, and/or gender advisers should ensure that the objectives of gender mainstreaming are fully implemented and ensure that the gender resource package for PKOs is distributed in the mission.

In practice, however, these gender focal points, units, and advisers have the potential to represent an "add women and stir" approach. Most often the positions are held by women, and the gender units are composed mainly of women. We argue that gender mainstreaming may be an important tool for dismantling gender power imbalances but that the approach must be much more than adding female bodies to different parts of the mission in the form of technical advisers.

Thus, including gender focal points, gender units, and/or gender advisers is important but only if certain criteria are met. First, to ensure that their work is perceived as relevant to much more than "women's issues" and to increase their legitimacy from the perspective of both women and men, it is important to incorporate both men and women into these positions. Second, such positions must be given adequate resources to fulfill their functions. Third, the gender focal points and advisers should be integrated at all levels, especially in mission leadership. As an example of this, in the Swedish military, the organizational placement of the senior gender adviser was directly under the chief of joint operations as a way to maximize credibility and centrality (Egnell et al., 2014: 7). The alternative would have been to place the position in policy planning or human resources, which would have had the effect of sidelining gender and diminishing the importance of it (Egnell et al., 2014). As another example, the Office of Military Affairs of the UN has appointed a full-time military gender adviser with the rank of colonel, based at headquarters (UN Women, 2015). Egnell et al. (2014) further argue that gender advisers should include senior staff who are housed in the headquarters, as well as in satellite offices and offices that are associated with intelligence gathering, and gender focal points should be in all standing military units, the tactical command, and all schools and training centers (129). They also suggest that the units should have "positive, social, and diplomatic personalities," have experience either in the military or police, or have prior experience working with such institutions, have the rank of Major or higher, and should be older (135).

In principle, gender mainstreaming is much more comprehensive than just including gender focal points, units, and advisers. It includes broader operationalization, such as expanding women's participation in all levels of decision-making, collecting sex-disaggregated statistics, collaborating with local community and women's organizations on information gathering on all issues, and incorporating gender into all mission activities. For example, to give a concrete example of the latter: when writing a report on security, it is important, instead of creating a separate section on gender, to document how gender affects the security issues already included in the report. For instance, in DDR efforts, what happens to female ex-combatants who do not have weapons? Such concerns should be addressed in the DDR section and not in a separate section on gender. Gender should be integrated throughout the report rather than highlighting it as a separate area of concern.

It is also important to engage with the local community to ensure that gender mainstreaming occurs at the local level. Engaging and consulting with the local population about different policies and programs that pertain to security and development issues is paramount for gender mainstreaming. Local men and women must be involved in the implementation, monitoring, and evaluation phases. For instance, when a peacekeeping mission considers building some sort of infrastructure in a community, male community members may have different suggestions from female community members. If the mission only consults men, then women's development needs are ignored. Community consultation with both women and men makes certain that the policy impact is judged not on the basis of indicators formed irrespective of local context but rather on the basis of measures that consider the impact in terms of baseline cultural norms and practices.

It is important to note that gender mainstreaming does not only mean focusing particular attention on women. By turning "gender mainstreaming" into something like "female mainstreaming," two negative ramifications become possible. First, men may not mainstream gender into their activities because they see it is as the duty of women in the mission to do so. The men might miss that a large part of gender mainstreaming actually focuses on men, ensuring that local men and male peacekeepers understand gender inequality issues. Second, the needs of vulnerable populations such as men and women who do not conform to traditional gender norms related to masculinity and femininity (e.g., gay men or lesbian women) may be overlooked. As a result, it is important to ensure that gender mainstreaming includes all members of a mission and to pay particular attention to the gender implications of policies and not isolate gender issues as "women's issues."

One of the main challenges in implementing "gender mainstreaming" is that it has become a catchall phrase for promoting gender equality. Gender mainstreaming and gender balancing (female ratio balancing) are often conflated in terms of implementation, and anything related to gender is often equated with mainstreaming. Gender mainstreaming can be a vague concept with very little guidance on how to actually implement it. While there are handbooks, such as *DPKO/DFS Guidelines Integrating a Gender Perspective into the Work of the United Nations Military in Peacekeeping Operations*,[22] they tend to include anything that is related to gender, most often related to women. The guidelines call for everything from integrating gender into planning to force generation (gender balancing) to monitoring and reporting. There is literally a list of check marks at the strategic, operational, and tactical level for peacekeeping missions to tick off.[23] While this is a useful start, many of the items still contain vague language—for example, "include in all military guidance and military policy priorities provisions to enhance the protection of women and girls in areas of military deployment, in line with mandated tasks." When implementing such a provision, it is unclear what the "protection of women and girls" actually means in this context. In addition, most of the checklist items are related to reports to headquarters; there are simply too many check boxes for leadership to ensure that all items have been implemented, and often there is not enough political will or resources to implement many of the items. Even the 1325 Review notes that the current state of gender mainstreaming takes "a tick-box" approach and represents an "obligation, rather than a concrete tool to enhance the operational effectiveness of UN peacekeeping" (UN Women, 2015: 145). Thus, peacekeeping missions rarely fulfill the guidelines for these reasons.

Even if peacekeeping missions were successful in implementing gender mainstreaming, mainstreaming is only one part of a transformational process that ensures gender equality and equal opportunity peacekeeping as the end goal. Thus we urge the UN DPKO to revise its implementation guidelines to be more manageable and feasible, while also considering changes that are more transformational, such as the ones suggested in this book.

Specific recommendations:

- Consider the gendered impact on all policy issues (this includes all vulnerable populations, not just women).
- Include gender focal points or gender experts at all decision-making levels, but make sure they have resources and power in the institution.
- Gender focal points and experts should be men and women, should draw from senior staff, and should have experience with military/police personnel.
- Gender advisers and focal points should be integrated at the highest level of leadership.
- Collect sex-disaggregated statistics.
- Ensure that both men and women are involved in gender mainstreaming.
- Collaborate with local community and women's organizations in information gathering on all issues.

INDEPENDENT REFORM EFFORTS

We should note that many of the recommendations here are echoed in recent UN evaluations of PKOs and of UNSCR 1325. Recent UN reports also provide more guidance in how to implement gender mainstreaming. The High-Level Report on peacekeeping recommends that the Secretariat and missions maintain a gender-sensitive lens throughout the analysis, planning, implementation, review, evaluation, and drawdown processes of the mission, as well as integrating gender expertise within all functional components requiring gender knowledge and experience. This means that the mission's senior gender adviser should be located in the Office of the SRSG, reporting directly to the special representative and advising him or her and senior mission leadership at the strategic level on integrating a gender perspective into mission activities. The report also recommends that missions have full access to policy, substantive, and technical support from UN Women on the implementation of UNSCR 1325 (2000) and successive resolutions, together with support currently received from the Department of Political Affairs and the DPKO, and suggests that the Secretariat should ensure that compacts between the secretary-general and heads of mission specify performance indicators relating to gender (UN, 2015).

The 1325 Review suggests numerous recommendations as well. At the Member State level, the review proposes setting specific targets for the improved recruitment, retention, and promotion of women in the contributing countries' armed forces and the leadership of security institutions; ensuring that all soldiers deployed are thoroughly vetted, trained, and held accountable for their actions, including when they abuse or exploit women and girls; committing to doctrines and planning that take into account the impact on women and girls of every military deployment and operation and that consider the use of unarmed military protection as a preferable or complementary protection method, where appropriate (UN Women, 2015: 156). At the level of the UN DPKO, the review calls for it to encourage force contributing countries to deploy more female military officers to UN peacekeeping missions by adopting financial incentives, such as a gender balance premium; to conduct gender-responsive budgeting and financial tracking of investments on gender equality in missions by requesting peacekeeping budget experts and planning officers, along with gender-responsive budget experts, to review mission budgets and make recommendations on methodology and capacity needed; and to ensure that all UN peacekeepers are given scenario-based training on issues related to gender equality—from gender mainstreaming in peace operations to preventing and responding to conflict-related sexual violence (UN Women, 2015: 156).

Specifically related to SEAHV, the review suggests that

> countries that repeatedly fail to live up to their written assurances to investigate and prosecute their soldiers should not be allowed to contribute troops to peacekeeping missions; if the United Nations has obtained prima facie evidence of misconduct, the home country of the alleged perpetrator should be under the obligation to prosecute, and if they don't, they should be obligated to provide a detailed

explanation of their findings; the United Nations should empower an independent commission of inquiry to conduct a broad-based investigation on sexual exploitation and abuse and the handling of allegations by both member states and the UN itself, including the failure to systematically apply many of the powers that it already has to hold individuals accountable for their actions; consider engaging with States in support of establishing an international tribunal with jurisdiction to try UN staff and all categories of peacekeepers that have allegedly committed serious crimes, including sexual abuse; and make concrete proposals on the ground about how to fund Victims Assistance Mechanisms and render them operational, including from pooled funds in each country or from the operating budget of the entities that employ the accused. (UN Women, 2015: 156–157)[24]

Finally, the 1325 Review urges the UN DPKO to take steps to improve regulation and oversight of all private contractors hired by the UN with regard to sexual exploitation and abuse. The UN should revise and fully implement guidelines to regulate these companies, including through permanent or temporary debarment of companies from further contracts and keeping a centralized register of companies whose staff have repeatedly been linked to allegations of SEAHV. The UN should promote women's empowerment and nonviolent means of protection, and take into account the whole range of women's protection issues and the interventions to address them—including women's leadership and women's empowerment—in mission planning, implementation, and reporting, as well as in policy discussions on the protection of civilians in the context of peace operations. Furthermore, the review recommends that the UN scales up support to unarmed civilian protection in conflict-affected countries, including working alongside peace operations (UN Women, 2015: 157).

Both the High-Level Report and the 1325 Review highlight important recommendations that parallel some of our own. Much of what we advocate for is eminently achievable, and processes are already under way at the highest levels to implement these important steps that can help realize equal opportunity peacekeeping.

FUTURE RESEARCH AND EVALUATION

Despite the stakes, there is not much research on the effectiveness of policies related to promoting gender equality in peacekeeping missions. Indeed, as gender mainstreaming has been touted as a successful vehicle for promoting gender equality, it is unclear whether such policy changes would indeed help change the culture of missions. As such, much more research is needed to understand exactly which types of policies mentioned here actually help change the culture of the missions to be more in line with equal opportunity peacekeeping. This research could include conducting randomized controlled trials about the effectiveness of different gender training schemes. Survey experiments could assess the extent to which changing standards for promotion and punishment affect the creation of an equal opportunity culture. And studies could assess the extent to which targeted recruitment affects equal opportunity culture by comparing baseline surveys to surveys conducted after recruitment programs.

The larger recommendation is for researchers to partner with peacekeeping missions in assessing these types of changes. A collaborative relationship between researchers and peacekeeping missions would ensure that policies are evaluated appropriately. Input from researchers is needed to make use of state-of-the-art social science methodology in the context of program evaluation. Input from peacekeeping practitioners is needed to make sure that the right goals and mechanisms are evaluated.

Finally, researchers and peacekeepers can collaborate on finding the best policies for promoting gender equality in host countries. For example, our work in Liberia suggests that there are ways to examine the extent to which certain policy changes related to SSR in the host countries actually lead to the desired results. Thus, we advocate for a data-driven approach to peace-building and state-building.

Specific recommendations:

- Conduct randomized controlled trials to assess the impact of different policy changes to increase egalitarianism (especially for gender training).
- Peacekeeping missions should collaborate with researchers to ensure that policies are evaluated accurately.
- Peacekeepers and researchers should collaborate on evaluating the implementation of domestic security sector reforms.

ADDITIONAL CONSIDERATIONS AND CONCLUDING REMARKS

Reading this book, some may say that we are holding the military, police, and peacekeeping institutions to too high of a standard. After all, most (nonsecurity) institutions have not even reached the level of parity we describe here. In society as a whole, among other grievances, women still suffer from pay discrimination; are perceived to know less than men; and are still the main targets of SGBV more broadly. Thus, why should we hold peacekeepers to higher standards than civilians? The short answer is that many aspects of this book apply to many other institutions and can be applied accordingly. Nevertheless, when it comes to PKOs, the stakes are also quite high. Peacekeepers are sometimes the first responders to crisis and conflict, which means that their presence can have a profound impact on conflict-ridden countries. What they do on the ground has lasting, long-term consequence. In addition, given the link between gender equality and conflict, promoting gender equality in and through missions takes on particular urgency. Hence, equal opportunity peacekeeping is essential for ensuring that peacekeeping missions start off on the right foot and are models for how gender equality in institutions can function.

Others may argue that upsetting gender hierarchies in military and police forces, such that masculinities are no longer dominant, will make these institutions less effective in fulfilling their intended purpose: protection and combat.[25] The pursuit of gender equality, however, need not, indeed must not, eliminate masculine traits from the security sector. Instead, we suggest that the relationship among the genders does not need to be hierarchical but rather can be equal, such that both sexes and manifestations of them through masculinity and femininity receive similar value and opportunity to be valorized. Such equal opportunity has the potential to prevent the negative effects of gender power imbalances from materializing while still valuing and valorizing traditional masculine characteristics. There are some examples of militaries and police institutions that have proceeded down this path toward egalitarianism with positive results. For example, both Sweden and Norway have taken steps to be more equal, ostensibly without losing ground on effectiveness.[26] As such, it is important to establish that the changes suggested here and in other parts of the book will not detract from military and police effectiveness. In fact, we posit that these changes may actually improve military and police effectiveness because both men and women will be able to make full use of their talents without the headwinds of discrimination and SEAHV. In addition, new skills will be brought to the art of protection that were previously discounted.

There are no easy fixes to achieve equal opportunity peacekeeping. In reality, gender power imbalances have been historically embedded in military and police institutions, not to mention in society as a whole. Challenges include a lack of political will, a lack of resources, politicization of appointments and placements, a lack of information (especially about the effects of training), institutional inertia, cultural taboos, and vague language. Achieving transformation requires not just simple policy changes but rather the will to change such policies. Unless all parties fully buy into the importance of tackling power imbalances, change will not come quickly. Changing the mission culture requires commitment and resources from all relevant parties in the mission, from the UNSCR to the UN General Assembly to the secretary-general to the Secretariat to the UN DPKO to contributing countries to mission leadership to mission personnel. Moreover, not all countries are able to engage in transformation due to cultural factors. In addition, current attempts to mainstream gender or to fix the problems mentioned have been focused mainly on female representation, and language on gender mainstreaming is often too vague for implementing agencies to understand. Finally, more information is needed to understand which types of change are more effective in creating transformation. These are real challenges that may impede progress on achieving equal opportunity peacekeeping.

Nevertheless, as we have argued above in each section, we do not think that the challenges are insurmountable. We hope that practitioners, policy-makers, and scholars alike help to implement the requisite changes in how peacekeeping is done. We also hope that not only will policy-makers and scholars work together to promote gender equality in peacekeeping missions but also future work on international institutions will incorporate an "equal opportunity framework" as well.

Moving forward, there is reason for much hope for gender equality to be achieved in and through missions. While gender power imbalances are still entrenched in military and police institutions, more individuals are aware of the problems than ever before. This trend need not attenuate, and we anticipate a time when equal opportunity peacekeeping becomes synonymous with PKOs.

APPENDIX 1

Chapter 4 Appendix

COUNTRY ABBREVIATIONS

Table A1.1 presents the country abbreviations used in the chapter figures.

MEASURES OF THE REPRESENTATION OF WOMEN IN DOMESTIC FORCES

For the models of female military contributions, the domestic gender balance variable pertains to the ratio of women personnel to total personnel who are noncivilian and in the armed forces; for the models of female police contributions, this variable pertains to the ratio of women police to total police. With regard to the police, most of the information came from the *United Nations Surveys of Crime Trends and Operations of Criminal Justice Systems Series, Waves 1–10, 1970–2006*. This report had gender breakdowns for many countries from 2003 to 2006. We also augmented this data with some other sources. Since the time coverage varies, we took the average proportions of women for each country to form the measures for each contributor country.

No single source contains consistent and comprehensive data on the gender balance of military forces worldwide. As a result, we compiled information from national reports (2004–2012) of the NATO Committee on Gender Perspectives; a report from the Geneva Centre for the Democratic Control of Armed Forces titled *Security Sector and Gender in West Africa: The Military Balance;* a US Africa Command Study of Women in African Militaries; the 2012 UK armed forces annual personnel report; the active duty military personnel statistics of the US Department of Defense; reported numbers on a Nepalese government website; and reported numbers about Sweden's forces from a Bloomberg news article. Note that the time periods of each of these reports varies—although all this material is post-2000—so we averaged the yearly data that were reported to provide the measures for each contributor country. Moreover, the sources were inconsistent as to whether they reported the proportions of women in the armed forces including civilians, excluding civilians, pertaining only to troops, pertaining to specific branches of the military, or pertaining just to commissioned officers. Sometimes multiples of these indicators were provided and sometimes only one. To address this problem, we did some basic interpolation. We started with the proportion of women in the armed forces, excluding civilians, and then calculated the mean ratios of this proportion and the proportion that pertained to the entire armed services including civilians, the proportion that pertained to only troops, the proportion that pertained to only the army or ground forces, and the proportion that pertained to commissioned officers. With these ratios, we then calculated some of the missing expected proportions of women in the non-civilian armed forces from these other proportions if available, with the priority going from army to total armed forces including civilians to troops to officers. That is, if data were available on the proportions in the army, these would be used in the interpolations over any other of the proportions available.

Even with these efforts, we lack information about the representation of women in the security forces of many of the contributing countries. The results presented in tables A1.2 and A1.3 simply drop the contributing countries for which we have missing values. This has the potential for biased estimates, and so we verified the robustness of the key findings using multiple imputation. To estimate the missing values of the representation of women in the military and police institutions, we used as covariates per capita GDP (World Bank, 2014), the participation of women in the labor force (World Bank, 2014), the ratio of girls to boys in primary school education (World Bank, 2014), and three multivariate scales from Mary Caprioli's WomanStats database (Caprioli et al., 2009) the physical security index, the discrepancy between law and practice index, and the family law inequity index. The expected values and associated uncertainty of the missing entries are then used in the same regression models used above. We find that all of the key findings discussed in the main text are robust to the multiple imputation, with one exception. The estimated coefficient on the proportion of women in the domestic militaries did not achieve statistical significance, which is not surprising because it is that variable that was imputed for so many observations.

CONTROL VARIABLES

In each of the estimated models, we control for the total size of each contributor's military or police contributions and the total size of each mission's military and police deployments. In this way, the models capture key sources of heterogeneity in the missions and the contributors, which might also covary with our key explanatory and outcome variables. The models thus can hold constant whether the contributions are from a large contributor or a marginal contributor, and whether the contributions are to a large mission or small mission. The mixed effects estimation, with random intercepts at both the contributor and mission levels, allows the models to capture additional sources of heterogeneity.

ESTIMATION RESULTS

Table A1.2 presents the estimated coefficients for the models explaining the proportions of women in military components of the PKOs. Table A1.3 presents the estimated coefficients of the models explaining the proportions of women in the police components.

Table A1.1. COUNTRY ABBREVIATIONS

ID	Country name	ID	Country name	ID	Country name
AFG	Afghanistan	GAB	Gabon	NIR	Niger
ALB	Albania	GAM	Gambia	NOR	Norway
ALG	Algeria	GFR	German Federal Republic	NTH	Netherlands
ANG	Angola	GHA	Ghana	OMA	Oman
ARG	Argentina	GNB	Guinea-Bissau	PAK	Pakistan
ARM	Armenia	GRC	Greece	PAN	Panama
AUL	Australia	GRG	Georgia	PAR	Paraguay
AUS	Austria	GUA	Guatemala	PER	Peru
AZE	Azerbaijan	GUI	Guinea	PHI	Philippines
BAH	Bahrain	GUY	Guyana	PNG	Papua New Guinea
BAR	Barbados	HAI	Haiti	POL	Poland
BEL	Belgium	HON	Honduras	POR	Portugal
BEN	Benin	HUN	Hungary	PRK	Korea, People's Republic of
BFO	Burkina Faso (Upper Volta)	ICE	Iceland	QAT	Qatar
BHM	Bahamas	IND	India	ROK	Korea, Republic of
BHU	Bhutan	INS	Indonesia	RUM	Rumania
BLR	Belarus (Byelorussia)	IRE	Ireland	RUS	Russia (Soviet Union)
BLZ	Belize	IRN	Iran (Persia)	RWA	Rwanda
BNG	Bangladesh	IRQ	Iraq	SAF	South Africa
BOL	Bolivia	ISR	Israel	SAL	El Salvador
BOS	Bosnia-Herzegovina	ITA	Italy/Sardinia	SAU	Saudi Arabia
BOT	Botswana	JAM	Jamaica	SEN	Senegal
BRA	Brazil	JOR	Jordan	SER	Serbia
BRU	Brunei	JPN	Japan	SIE	Sierra Leone
BUI	Burundi	KEN	Kenya	SIN	Singapore
BUL	Bulgaria	KOS	Kosovo	SLO	Slovakia
CAM	Cambodia (Kampuchea)	KUW	Kuwait	SLV	Slovenia
CAN	Canada	KYR	Kyrgyz Republic	SOL	Solomon Islands

(continued)

ID	Country name	ID	Country name	ID	Country name
CAO	Cameroon	KZK	Kazakhstan	SOM	Somalia
CAP	Cape Verde	LAO	Laos	SPN	Spain
CDI	Côte d'Ivoire	LAT	Latvia	SRI	Sri Lanka (Ceylon)
CEN	Central African Republic	LBR	Liberia	SSD	South Sudan
CHA	Chad	LEB	Lebanon	SUD	Sudan
CHL	Chile	LES	Lesotho	SUR	Surinam
CHN	China	LIB	Libya	SWA	Swaziland
COL	Colombia	LIT	Lithuania	SWD	Sweden
COM	Comoros	LUX	Luxembourg	SWZ	Switzerland
CON	Congo	MAA	Mauritania	SYR	Syria
COS	Costa Rica	MAC	Macedonia (Former Yugoslav Republic of)	TAJ	Tajikistan
CRO	Croatia	MAD	Maldives	TAW	Taiwan
CUB	Cuba	MAG	Madagascar	TAZ	Tanzania/ Tanganyika
CYP	Cyprus	MAL	Malaysia	THI	Thailand
CZR	Czech Republic	MAS	Mauritius	TKM	Turkmenistan
DEN	Denmark	MAW	Malawi	TOG	Togo
DJI	Djibouti	MEX	Mexico	TRI	Trinidad and Tobago
DOM	Dominican Republic	MLD	Moldova	TUN	Tunisia
DRC	Congo, Democratic Republic of (Zaire)	MLI	Mali	TUR	Turkey (Ottoman Empire)
DRV	Vietnam, Democratic Republic of	MLT	Malta	UAE	United Arab Emirates
ECU	Ecuador	MNG	Montenegro	UGA	Uganda
EGY	Egypt	MON	Mongolia	UKG	United Kingdom
EQG	Equatorial Guinea	MOR	Morocco	UKR	Ukraine
ERI	Eritrea	MYA	Myanmar (Burma)	URU	Uruguay
EST	Estonia	MZM	Mozambique	USA	United States of America
ETH	Ethiopia	NAM	Namibia	UZB	Uzbekistan
ETM	East Timor	NEP	Nepal	VEN	Venezuela
FIN	Finland	NEW	New Zealand	YEM	Yemen (Arab Republic of Yemen)
FJI	Fiji	NIC	Nicaragua	ZAM	Zambia
FRN	France	NIG	Nigeria	ZIM	Zimbabwe (Rhodesia)

Table A1.2. MIXED EFFECTS REGRESSION OF THE PROPORTION OF WOMEN IN MILITARY CONTRIBUTIONS (LOGIT-TRANSFORMED)

	Model 1	Model 2	Model 3	Model 4
Domestic gender balance	9.182**	8.948**	10.81***	10.86***
of military	(4.216)	(4.257)	(3.760)	(3.743)
Conflict severity in	7.06e-05***	7.19e-05***	7.10e-05***	7.13e-05***
contributors	(1.98e-05)	(1.98e-05)	(1.92e-05)	(1.92e-05)
Per capita GDP in	1.08e-05	9.91e-06	1.16e-05	1.17e-05
contributors	(9.23e-06)	(9.30e-06)	(8.18e-06)	(8.14e-06)
Total military	0.000137	0.000138	0.000161**	0.000162**
contributions	(8.36e-05)	(8.43e-05)	(7.46e-05)	(7.42e-05)
PKO fatalities per annum	0.629	1.793	2.024	1.814
per capita	(2.857)	(2.497)	(2.459)	(2.461)
Conflict severity in	−0.000111**	−5.56e-05	−5.46e-05	−5.65e-05
destinations	(4.98e-05)	(4.37e-05)	(4.28e-05)	(4.27e-05)
Per capita GDP in	6.17e-05**	2.86e-05	3.02e-05	3.21e-05
destinations	(2.53e-05)	(2.27e-05)	(2.23e-05)	(2.23e-05)
Total military personnel	8.56e-05***	8.44e-05***	8.48e-05***	8.48e-05***
in mission	(2.07e-05)	(1.60e-05)	(1.56e-05)	(1.56e-05)
Widespread sexual		−0.971***	−0.986***	−0.129
violence in destinations		(0.273)	(0.266)	(0.726)
Women labor force			0.0417***	0.0517***
participation in			(0.0117)	(0.0141)
contributors				
Labor participation				−0.0150
(contributor) x sexual				(0.0118)
violence (destination)				
Constant	−6.819***	−6.136***	−8.672***	−9.244***
	(0.466)	(0.473)	(0.830)	(0.942)
Observations	886	886	886	886

Note: Values are estimated coefficients, with standard errors in parentheses.

*$p < .1$; **$p < .05$; ***$p < .01$ in a two-tailed test.

Table A1.3. MIXED EFFECTS REGRESSION OF THE PROPORTION OF WOMEN IN POLICE CONTRIBUTIONS (LOGIT-TRANSFORMED)

	Model 5	Model 6	Model 7	Model 8
Domestic gender	7.639	7.614	5.495	5.487
balance of police	(5.909)	(5.898)	(5.705)	(5.706)
Conflict severity in	0.000107*	0.000106*	9.97e-05*	9.98e-05*
contributors	(5.57e-05)	(5.57e-05)	(5.49e-05)	(5.50e-05)
Per capita GDP in	−3.96e-06	−4.17e-06	1.06e-07	1.03e-07
contributors	(1.63e-05)	(1.62e-05)	(1.57e-05)	(1.57e-05)
Total police	−4.46e-05	−6.59e-05	0.000129	0.000130
contributions	(0.000471)	(0.000470)	(0.000461)	(0.000462)
PKO fatalities per	−0.954	0.243	0.188	0.179
annum per capita	(4.804)	(4.732)	(4.744)	(4.751)
Conflict severity in	0.000122	0.000154	0.000160	0.000161
destinations	(0.000113)	(0.000112)	(0.000113)	(0.000113)
Per capita GDP in	6.03e-05	1.31e-05	1.49e-05	1.52e-05
destinations	(5.22e-05)	(5.72e-05)	(5.78e-05)	(5.80e-05)
Total police personnel	0.000339	0.000364*	0.000341*	0.000341*
in mission	(0.000209)	(0.000202)	(0.000204)	(0.000204)
Widespread sexual		−1.475	−1.469	−1.393
violence in		(0.966)	(0.974)	(1.313)
destinations				
Women labor force			0.0508***	0.0522**
participation in			(0.0193)	(0.0250)
contributors				
Labor participation				−0.00159
(contributor)				(0.0178)
x sexual violence				
(destination)				
Constant	−5.348***	−4.154***	−6.817***	−6.888***
	(0.830)	(1.106)	(1.489)	(1.678)
Observations	679	679	679	679

Note: Values are estimated coefficients, with standard errors in parentheses.
*$p < .1$; **$p < .05$; ***$p < .01$ in a two-tailed test.

Chapter 5 Appendix

MODEL SPECIFICATION

In estimating the regression models, we use random effects at the level of each mission because of the heterogeneity in baseline propensities for SEA across each mission. We also control for the size of the mission because larger missions have more opportunities for personnel misconduct and possibly also have different types of contributing countries involved than smaller missions. In addition, we control for the per capita GDP in the host country in order to account for variation in the local levels of human-security vulnerability and institutional infrastructure to hold peacekeepers accountable, and also because local per capita GDP is also plausibly related to composition of the peacekeeping forces. We considered controlling for the population size of the host country but did not find it to be a relevant variable, and the results remained robust with its inclusion. GDP data come from the World Bank (The World Bank, 2014). Finally, we control for the level of sexual violence in the preceding war, by using an indicator from Cohen and Nordås (2014) about whether there was "widespread" sexual violence in the most recent civil war. This variable captures the vulnerability of the population to sexual violence. Peacekeeping compositions might be structured to more intentionally address issues of sexual abuse and exploitation when there have been high rates of egregious abuses in the recent past.

In additional robustness checks, we control for the weighted average of the per capita GDP (in constant US dollars, from the World Bank) in the contributing countries and the weighted average of the Polity combined twenty-one-point index (Marshall, Gurr, and Jaggers, 2016). These results are not shown but can be found in Karim and Beardsley (2016a). The former allows us to parse out the levels of economic development in the contributing countries as distinct from other contributing-country characteristics related to the practice of gender equality. The latter allows us to parse out the levels of political liberalization in the contributing countries. The key results are robust to these additional variables.

ESTIMATION RESULTS

Table A2.1 presents the estimated coefficients for the model of SEAHV accusations in the military components of the PKOs. Table A2.2 presents the estimated coefficients for the model of accusations in the police components.

Table A2.1. SEAHV ACCUSATIONS IN MILITARY CONTINGENTS, RANDOM EFFECTS NEGATIVE BINOMIAL REGRESSION

	Model 1	Model 2	Model 3
Proportion of women in PKO mission	−11.51	−16.65	−6.176
	(18.17)	(17.08)	(16.03)
Average contributor women labor force participation	−0.141***		
	(0.0541)		
Average contributor physical protection of women index		1.512**	
		(0.750)	
Average contributor NAP adoption			−3.746**
			(1.546)
Size of military contingent in PKO	0.000200*	6.71e-05	0.000145***
	(0.000110)	(6.35e-05)	(5.13e-05)
Per capita GDP in host country	−8.94e-06	2.31e-05	−1.32e-05
	(7.43e-05)	(7.70e-05)	(7.25e-05)
Widespread sexual violence	0.275	−0.0151	−0.164
	(0.842)	(0.875)	(0.831)
Constant	6.995**	−4.148	0.873
	(2.745)	(2.655)	(1.058)
ln(r)	1.483	0.850	1.169*
	(0.927)	(0.564)	(0.637)
ln(s)	−0.0547	−0.250	−0.0829
	(0.739)	(0.632)	(0.640)
Observations	85	85	85

Note: Values are estimated coefficients with standard errors in parentheses.

*p < .1; **p < .05; ***p < .01.

Table A2.2. SEAHV ACCUSATIONS IN POLICE CONTINGENTS, RANDOM EFFECTS NEGATIVE BINOMIAL REGRESSION

	Model 4	Model 5	Model 6
Proportion of women in PKO mission	−0.714	−0.605	1.359
	(1.750)	(2.320)	(2.907)
Average contributor women labor	−0.134***		
force participation	(0.0357)		
Average contributor physical		−0.578	
protection of women index		(0.925)	
Average contributor NAP adoption			−1.786
			(1.385)
Size of police contingent in PKO	0.000433***	0.000568**	0.000586**
	(0.000110)	(0.000229)	(0.000260)
Per capita GDP in host country	−0.00187***	−0.00206**	-0.00165*
	(0.000388)	(0.000910)	(0.000888)
Widespread sexual violence		−1.665	−0.919
		(1.292)	(1.298)
Constant	7.179***	4.023	1.154
	(1.750)	(4.104)	(1.760)
ln(alpha)	−15.36	−0.394	−0.124
	(1,174)	(0.822)	(0.719)
Observations	64	64	64

Note: Values are estimated coefficients with standard errors in parentheses.
*p < .1; **p < .05; ***p < .01.

Chapter 6 Appendix

INTERVIEW AND FOCUS GROUP DESCRIPTION

We conducted interviews, focus groups, and a survey with the female contingents and peacekeepers in Monrovia, Buchanan, and Gbarnga (where the Ghanaian and Bangladeshi contingents were stationed) between May 2012 and June 2012. We also conducted a questionnaire of women in the mission, with ninety-five respondents. The authorities in UNMIL determined whether or not we conducted a focus group or interview. In some cases the UN organized focus groups, and in some cases they organized interviews. Focus groups included as few as four participants or as many as twenty. The breakdowns of the focus groups and interviews are presented in tables A3.1 and A3.2, respectively. We explicitly asked for access to female peacekeepers, but on many occasions we had the opportunity to speak with men as well, both formally and informally. Discussions with them (both formal and informal) are included in the tables.

In addition, we provide the list of focus group and interview questions we used as a guideline for the discussions with the peacekeepers, as well as the questionnaire that was used.

Focus Group and Interview Questions

1. How long have you worked in Liberia?
2. Why did you become a part of the armed forces in your home country? Why did you decide to become a peacekeeper?
3. How many women are in the armed forces/police in your home country?
4. How did you get selected to become a peacekeeper? How are women selected to become peacekeepers?
5. What do you do in your job? What is the favorite part of your job? What is your least favorite part of the job? What do you hope to be doing here?
6. On average, how many Liberian women do you interact with on a weekly basis?

7. Do you think you are able to help Liberians? Liberian women? If so, how do you help them?
8. Are you able to complete your job description? Have you done anything outside of your job description? Started any new programs etc.?
9. Do you feel respected by Liberians? By civilians? Do Liberian women change their behavior around you?
10. Do you think that contact with Liberians women changes their perception about security?
11. What do your friends and family think about your job?
12. Why do you think your country sent peacekeepers to Liberia?
13. What does your country do to recruit more women in the military? In peacekeeping?
14. What are the biggest problems in the UNMIL mission? How can UNMIL and future peacekeeping missions be better?

Female Peacekeeper Questionnaire

What country are you from? _____

Please circle: Military (UNMIL) Police (UNPOL)

What is your age? _____

What is your marital status (circle): married   single divorced/separated   widow

Table A3.1. FOCUS GROUP COMPOSITION

Country of origin	Number of people/sex	Type of peacekeeper
Jordan	4 women	UNMIL Military
Nigeria	30 women (2 focus groups)	UNMIL Military
Philippines	9 women	UNMIL Military
Bangladesh	6 women, 6 men	UNMIL Military
India	13 women	UNMIL FPU
Ghana	1 woman (mix focus group)	UNPOL
Kenya	2 women (mix focus group)	UNPOL
Pakistan	1 woman (mixed focus group)	UNPOL
Sweden	12 women	UNPOL
Turkey	1 woman (mixed focus group)	UNPOL
Zimbabwe	4 women	UNPOL

Table A3.2. INTERVIEW POOL COMPOSITION

Country of origin	Number of people/sex	Type of peacekeeper
Denmark	1 woman	UNMIL Military
Nigeria	1 woman, 1 man	UNMIL Military
Ghana	6 women and 6 men	UNMIL Military
Bosnia	1 woman	UNPOL
Nepal	1 woman	UNMIL FPU
Norway	2 women	UNPOL
Switzerland	1 woman	UNPOL
Uganda	1 woman	UNPOL
India	2 women	UNMIL FPU
United States	1 woman, 4 men	UNPOL, UNMIL Military
Gambia	1 man	UNMIL Military
Peru	2 men	UNMIL Military

What is your rank? _____

How long have you served in the military/police? _____

Do you have family in the military/police?   Yes   No

How long have you served in the mission to Liberia? _____

How many other UN missions have you served in? _____

If so, which other UN missions? _____

What role do you play in your job? Check all that apply

_____Administration

_____Provide security

_____Training local Liberians

_____Supervisor to other peacekeepers

_____Conduct projects with the local community

_____Observer

_____Medical

_____Patrol neighborhoods

_____Other _____

Why did you join the military in your home country? (please rank top 5, 1 highest, 5 lowest)

_____My family is in the military

_____Personal sacrifice to my country

_____For the pay

_____It is a stable career

_____To promote gender equality in my country

_____It was my dream to be in the military since I was a child

_____To help people

_____It is exciting work

_____To feel powerful and empowered as a woman

_____To gain respect

_____I did not have any other options for my job

_____Other _____

Why did you decide to join the UN mission? (please rank top 5, 1 highest, 5 lowest)

_____To travel the world

_____To help people

_____I am loyal to military/police

_____My country sent me on this mission/I did not have a choice

_____It is a personal sacrifice

_____To receive better pay

_____To get a promotion

_____To be a part of peacekeeping mission/I believe in the UN mission

_____To end conflict

_____To promote gender equality

_____Other _____

What are the biggest problems in the UNMIL/UNPOL? (please rank top 5, 1 highest, 5 lowest)

_____No promotion

_____No contact with the community

_____Sexual harassment

_____The rules are too strict

_____I do not get to interact with other peacekeeping units

_____I do not like my job that I do in the mission

_____I do not get to leave the base/headquarters

_____I miss my family/friends back home

_____The deployment is too long

_____It is hard to get anything done in the UN

_____Women are not treated as equals to men

_____The workday/work week is too long

_____There are not enough facilities for women

_____Corruption in the UN

_____Bad behavior among peacekeepers

_____No respect among Liberians

_____Other _____

What percentage of women serve in the military/police in your country?
_____

How often do you interact with local Liberians? (check mark)

_____Never

_____Once every 6 months or less

_____Once every month

_____Once a week

_____Daily

How long did you train before deployment? _____

Do you think the training was adequate for deployment?
Yes   No

On a scale of 1–5 (with 5 being most important) how important do you think male/female peacekeepers are to promoting peace in the local community? _____

On a scale of 1–5 (with 5 being most important), how important do you think male/female peacekeepers are to improving the quality of life in the local community? _____
On a scale of 1–5 (with 5 being most important), how important do you think male/female peacekeepers are to improving the security of women in the local community? _____

ESTIMATION RESULTS FOR SURVEY DATA

The survey included 1,381 randomly selected households throughout greater Monrovia. A comprehensive explanation of the survey data can be found in Beber et al. (2017), which describes the level of transactional sex by peacekeepers in Monrovia.

Table A3.3. PERCEPTIONS OF SECURITY AND CONTACT WITH PEACEKEEPERS

	Model 1	Model 2	Model 3
Contact with Female Peacekeeper	1.32** (0.62)		2.08*** (0.61)
Contact with Male Peacekeeper		−1.33** (0.63)	0.75*** (0.18)
No contact with peacekeeper	−0.75*** (0.18)	−2.08*** (0.61)	
Age	0.01 (0.01)	0.01 (0.01)	0.01 (0.01)
Savings	−0.74*** (0.15)	−0.74*** (0.15)	−0.74*** (0.15)
Female	−0.21 (0.16)	−0.21 (0.16)	−0.21 (0.16)
War Trauma	−0.52*** (0.17)	−0.52*** (0.17)	−0.52*** (0.17)
Muslim	0.40 (0.30)	0.40 (0.30)	0.40 (0.30)
High Cognitive Ability	−0.08 (0.17)	−0.08 (0.14)	−0.08 (0.14)
Constant	1.85*** (0.52)	3.17*** (0.79)	1.10 (0.51)
Observations	1,333	1,333	1,333

Note: The dependent variable is an affirmative response to the following question: "Has the presence of UNMIL increased OWN personal security?" Values are estimated coefficients with standard errors in parentheses. Model includes community-level fixed effects with 38 communities. *p < 0.1; **p < 0.05; ***p < 0.01.

Chapter 7 Appendix

DESCRIPTION OF BEHAVIORAL GAMES WITH LNP

The lab-in-the-field experiment consisted of a set of behavioral games designed to assess unit cohesion, stereotyping, and sensitivity to gendered clues in crime scene investigations, among other outcomes. The games were designed in collaboration with a police trainer from UNMIL to ensure as much correspondence as possible between the stylized, artifactual scenarios in the games and the real-world challenges of policing. Officers were randomly selected from available personnel in Montserrado County (Monrovia). At first, we used the LNP roster to randomly select people from the roster, and the LNP called them to participate. However, the roster was not up-to-date, and officers needed permission from their direct supervisors. As a result, we ended up calling every section in the LNP every day and having them randomly select people to show up for the games for the next session. We switched from using the roster to the second method after the first day of implementation. We did not reach the full number of people to participate on the first day using the roster sampling method, so we randomly selected people in the building on the first day of implementation. The sample is also biased in favor of officers who did not hold a high rank because they were often too busy to participate (such as the inspector general of the LNP). We should also note that our sample did not include officers who fell under "absence without leave"—LNP officers who had neglected to show up to work.

We oversampled women to compensate for the smaller number of women in the LNP overall. The sample included 356 men and 256 women. At the time of the study, in 2012, the LNP had 768 women and 3,607 men. In Montserrado County (Monrovia), there were 598 women and 2,735 men. Thus, we randomly sampled 13 percent of LNP men and 43 percent of LNP women in Monrovia.

The games were conducted in groups of six, with the treatment being the sex composition of the group: groups contained zero, two, four, or six women. We had thirty-three all-male groups, twenty-nine groups of two women, twenty-one groups of four women, and nineteen groups of all women. Officers were randomly assigned to one of each of these four types of group. Teams of trained, Liberian enumerators were then randomly assigned to the groups to implement the games and record interactions among participants. In addition to the games, we also administered background and exit questionnaires, including a survey experiment designed to assess gender discrimination in training.

We conducted two cooperative games in which each group was instructed to pursue a common goal. The first cooperative game required that each group build a free-standing tower using a single sheet of newsprint and a meter of masking tape. The group that built the largest tower would receive a payout of 600 LD, to be split evenly among the members of the group. This is approximately US$7.62. We scaled the pay-offs based on the daily pay for the LNP.

In the second cooperative game, officers were given a photograph of a hypothetical crime scene and instructed to memorize as many details about the scene as they could. They then answered a set of questions about the photo and were awarded 10 LD for each correct answer. After answering the questions individually, the group reconvened to reach consensus answers to the same questions. The group was awarded 60 LD to be split evenly among them for each correct answer.

In both of these games, we were most concerned with whether women were included in the decision-making processes and the extent to which they participated. During the group deliberations, three enumerators recorded who spoke, who argued, how aggressive people were, and in the case of the tower game who physically touched the materials in an attempt to build the tower. While there was certainly the potential for conflict in these games, that potential arose from differences of opinion about how best to achieve the group goal rather than fundamentally different primitives in subjects' preferences. In addition to the cooperative games, participants also played games that required them to make collective decisions despite conflicting individual preferences. We do not include the results from these games because they do not represent the types of deliberative processes LNP officers face in the job and instead captured more basic choices related to risk taking, reciprocity, and altruism.

The photograph used in the first cooperative game contained a number of ambiguous clues suggestive of several possible crimes: burglary, physical assault, murder, domestic violence, or rape. We asked subjects a series of questions about what crime(s) they thought the photo depicted, what evidence led them to that conclusion, and what they would do on arrival at the crime scene. We first asked the officers to answer these questions privately in a questionnaire, and then we asked them to conduct a group discussion to come up with a consensus "crime report" based on the evidence in the photo. Again, the enumerators recorded who spoke, who argued, and how aggressive participants were in the deliberation process.

Finally we also used an exit questionnaire to establish the severity of gender biases in the LNP and to assess whether participation in the group activities might alleviate those biases. The first was a survey experiment in which we offered each officer two short profiles of potential firearms instructors and then asked which of the two

Figure A4.1. Crime scene photos.

they would prefer. The qualifications of the instructors were very similar. One of the profiles always had the name Abraham; the other was assigned either "John" or "Patience" at random. Aside from the randomly assigned names, the descriptions of this second instructor's qualifications were identical. This allowed us to test whether participants tended to prefer the male candidate over the female candidate, despite their identical qualifications. In addition, we asked the participants to vote on which member of the group they thought should serve as leader in the future, among other questions.

MODEL SPECIFICATION FOR LNP GAMES

Depending on the hypothesis being tested, the variables are measured at either the individual or the group level. Some of the dependent variables are proportions, in which case we run generalized linear models with logit links. When the dependent variables are dichotomous, we run logit regressions. When the dependent variables are counts, we use negative binomial regressions. With the unit as the individual, the treatment can be considered as the number of participants from the opposite sex in the individual's group: women in groups with two, four or six women, and men in groups with two, four, or six men. With the unit as the group, there are four possible treatments, based on the number of women in the group (zero, two, four, or six).

Although we randomly assigned the individuals to their groups, we of course did not randomly assign gender and consequently still include control variables, to ensure that we are picking up the effects of gender and perceptions about gender rather than other individual attributes that are likely to vary systematically between the women and the men in the study and to control for any residual imbalance. Note that most of our analyses compare women to each other, across groups with different counts of men, and men to each other, across groups with different counts of women. Since we are not generally comparing women to men, concerns about confounding differences between women and men do not apply. The randomization procedure allows us to assume, say, that a woman in a group with two men is similar on average to a woman in a group with zero or four men in all other respects. We include the control variables to ensure consistency in the treatment—to maximize confidence that the treatment actually pertains to gender differences in the groups and not to differences in things like rank and age—and not to address concerns about differences across the characteristics of the subjects that are addressed in the randomization procedure.

Specifically, we control for the following covariates:

- *Age range.* Some respondents could only approximate their ages or were otherwise unwilling to give an exact value, so we used a categorical variable that indicates self-reported age range (18–24, 24–30, 31–40, 41–50, 51–60, 61 or above). For the group level, the mean age range was used.

- *Education*. A seven-point categorical variable of the respondents' self-reported level of education. For two respondents with missing education information, we used the lowest level. For the group level, we used the mean score.
- *Tenure*. The number of months from the start of the subject's LNP training until January 2013. When a month start date was not reported, we used June. For one respondent for whom the start information was not provided, we used the average tenure of the other LNP officers of the same rank. For the group level, we used the mean tenure of the group.
- *Rank*. A ten-point categorical variable for the subject's rank in the LNP. The lowest value is for probation officers. The highest level, category 10, corresponds to a rank of commissioner. For the group level, we use the maximum rank to capture the likelihood that participants would defer to rank in group interactions.
- *Number of friends in the group*. Before beginning the activities we asked the subjects to point out any members of the group they considered to be friends. At the group level, we used the mean number of friends per person.
- *Cognitive score*. The number of correct responses each individual gave in the three-question test administered along with the background questionnaire. For the group level, we used the mean cognitive score of the individuals in the group.

CALCULATING THE COMPETENCY SCORE

We used three cognitive questions, six memory questions, and crime scene questions to create a latent competency score. We asked an UNMIL police peacekeeper to postcode the crime scene questions based on the training the LNP receive in their academy. Crimes that matched a statutory crime were coded as correct. When the evidence matched the crime, each piece was coded as correct. If they correctly listed the immediate action on arrival (per their training), it was coded as correct. Correct answers were always coded as a 1, ensuring that the direction of the scale remained consistent. In the models with this index, we drop the cognitive score as a control variable because the cognitive tests are built into the index.

In total, fourteen manifest variables were used for the latent competency score. The statutory crime, evidence, and action questions were questions that all police officers should be able to answer based on their training. The memory questions were added for two reasons. First, memory is important for policing because officers are required to write detailed reports of investigations and are often called in jury trials to give testimonies about events. Police officers are required to remember physical details and names of criminals; names and physical locations of buildings, routes, and access points to parks and other public areas; and sections of the Criminal Code so that they can quickly prepare criminal charges. In places such as Liberia, where police may not be equipped with cameras to take pictures of crime scenes, it is particularly important to be able to recall details. Second, memory training is particularly important for operations. For example, snipers participate in reconnaissance and intelligence operations, where memory is vitally important to the mission. Thus, we included various measures of memory to capture different levels of difficulty inherent in the questions.

We use an item response model to better predict a latent score of competency. This allows us to take into consideration the differences among questions with respect to the level of difficulty. Simply adding scores does not take into consideration the varying level of difficulty of each question based on how many people got them correct. We also include prior information about sex and age as potentially influencing the level of competency. The specific notation is below:

$$Pr\left(y_{ij} = 1\right) = \text{logit}^{-1}\left(\beta_{0i} + \beta_{1j}\,\theta_i\right)$$
$$\theta_i \sim N(\mu_1, \tau)$$
$$\mu_1 = \lambda_0 + \lambda_1\left(\text{sex}_i\right) + \lambda_2(\text{age}_i)$$

The Pr (y_{ij} = 1) represents the probability of each individual (i) getting each of the fourteen individual questions (j) correct. The q_i parameter is the latent competency score for the individual. We assume that θ_i is normally distributed because a histogram of the questions answered correctly (added) demonstrates that the answers are normally distributed. The β_{0i} is the difficulty parameter for each question and the β_1 is the discrimination parameter for each question. The model estimates an individual competency score, θ_i.

MODEL RESULTS FOR LAB-IN-THE-FIELD EXPERIMENTS WITH LNP

The tables of coefficients for the models using data from the lab-in-the-field experiments with the LNP are presented in tables A4.1 and A4.2.

Table A4.1. MODEL RESULTS FOR FIREARMS
INSTRUCTOR SURVEY EXPERIMENT

Independent Variable	Estimate
Female, 2 f., 4 m.	0.131
	(0.571)
Female, 4 f., 2 m.	−0.335
	(0.518)
Male, 2 m., 4 f.	−0.0822
	(0.638)
Male, 4 m., 2 f.	−0.111
	(0.586)
Male, 6 m., 0 f.	−0.301
	(0.533)
Female, 2 f., 4 m. x vs. Patience	−1.033
	(0.703)
Female, 4 f., 2 m. x vs. Patience	−0.0494
	(0.612)
Male, 2 m., 4 f. x vs. Patience	0.595
	(0.829)
Male, 4 m., 2 f. x vs. Patience	−0.0153
	(0.682)
Male, 6 m., 0 f. x vs. Patience	0.0727
	(0.652)
vs. Patience	0.404
	(0.538)
Age range	−0.0836
	(0.114)
Education	0.0673
	(0.106)
Tenure	0.00351**
	(0.00173)
Rank	−0.0303
	(0.0646)
Friends	0.0598
	(0.0731)
Cognitive score	−0.132
	(0.164)
Constant	−0.0197
	(0.793)
Observations	612

Note: Values are coefficients with standard errors in parentheses.
Dependent variable: choosing Abraham as the firearms instructor.
*$p < 0.1$; **$p < 0.05$; ***$p < 0.01$.

Table A4.2. MODEL RESULTS OF LAB-IN-THE-FIELD EXPERIMENT ON GROUP COMPOSITION AND OUTCOMES

Independent variables	Vote for female	Talk tally proportion	Argue tally proportion	Matched answers proportion	Gender-related crime
Female, 2 f., 4 m.	0.779*	−0.0366	−0.0780	0.188	0.675
	(0.445)	(0.0724)	(0.337)	(0.140)	(0.519)
Female, 4 f., 2 m.		0.0600	0.100	0.0480	0.227
		(0.0665)	(0.315)	(0.147)	(0.474)
Male, 2 m., 4 f.	−0.471	0.211**	0.556	−0.104	0.566
	(0.477)	(0.0825)	(0.349)	(0.167)	(0.513)
Male, 4 m., 2 f.	−1.015***	0.0787	0.242	−0.214	0.101
	(0.349)	(0.0937)	(0.411)	(0.153)	(0.432)
Male, 6 m., 0 f.		0.0288	0.161	0.00609	0.228
		(0.0705)	(0.311)	(0.135)	(0.434)
Female, 2 f., 4 m. x competence differential		0.132	−0.462	−0.0652	1.485
		(0.111)	(0.434)	(0.196)	(0.952)
Female, 4 f., 2 m. x competence differential		0.0642	−1.549***	0.0296	0.617
		(0.0998)	(0.459)	(0.172)	(0.653)
Male, 2 m., 4 f. x competence differential		0.0437	−0.590	−0.0913	−0.482
		(0.115)	(0.464)	(0.203)	(0.599)
Male, 4 m., 2 f. x competence differential		0.0270	−0.413	0.125	−0.351
		(0.111)	(0.448)	(0.179)	(0.653)
Male, 6 m., 0 f. x competence differential		0.0901	−0.434	0.106	0.0533
		(0.0958)	(0.415)	(0.167)	(0.492)
Competence differential		0.108	1.048***	0.294**	1.536***
		(0.0849)	(0.382)	(0.132)	(0.436)
Age range	−0.282*	−0.00174	−0.135	−0.110**	−0.607***
	(0.154)	(0.0240)	(0.0924)	(0.0457)	(0.135)
Education	−0.0965	0.0643***	0.0276	−0.0110	0.106
	(0.166)	(0.0230)	(0.0822)	(0.0471)	(0.138)
Tenure	0.00210	−0.000387	0.000652	0.000407	−0.00612**
	(0.00276)	(0.000456)	(0.00162)	(0.000702)	(0.00292)
Rank	0.225**	0.0335**	0.0503	−0.0135	0.127*
	(0.109)	(0.0167)	(0.0643)	(0.0274)	(0.0772)
Friends	0.0144	0.0161	0.0231	−0.0329	0.0897
	(0.120)	(0.0108)	(0.0395)	(0.0315)	(0.106)

(continued)

Independent variables	Vote for female	Talk tally proportion	Argue tally proportion	Matched answers proportion	Gender-related crime
Cognitive score	−0.121				
	(0.241)				
Female leader assigned	−0.259				
	(0.308)				
Constant	0.697	−2.044***	−1.741***	0.835***	0.711
	(1.091)	(0.134)	(0.588)	(0.289)	(0.884)
Observations	300	612	444	612	612

Note: Values are coefficients with standard errors in parentheses.
***p < 0.01; **p < 0.05, *p < 0.1.

Table A4.3. MODEL RESULTS
OF PREFERENCE FOR POLICE
RESPONSE TO RAPE

Independent variable	Estimate
Number of contacts with police	0.29***
	(0.08)
Experienced wartime violence	−0.03
	(0.05)
Cognitive ability	0.20
	(0.13)
Armed group member	−0.0005
	(0.01)
Gender equality index	0.07*
	(0.04)
Crime victim	0.04
	(0.04)
Pay a bribe	−0.43***
	(0.15)
Female	−0.23*
	(0.13)
Live in West Point	0.31**
	(0.13)
Contact with police*war victim	−0.38***
	(0.09)
Constant	−1.41***
	(0.32)
Observations	1,264

Note: Values are coefficients with standard errors in parentheses. Dependent variable: prefer police only to respond to rape.
*p < 0.1; **p < 0.05; ***p < 0.01.

The tables of coefficients from the models using the survey data from West Point and Peace Island are presented in tables A4.3, A4.4, A4.5, A4.6, A4.7, and A4.8

Table A4.4. MODEL RESULTS OF PREFERENCES FOR THE POLICE
TO RESPOND TO SECURITY ISSUES, BY FEMALE CONTACT

Independent variables	Provide security	Armed violence	Riot	Rape	Beating
Contact with female officer only	0.23 (0.15)	0.26* (0.15)	0.35** (0.14)	0.28* (0.16)	0.43*** (0.15)
No contact with a police officer	0.01 (0.18)	−0.13 (0.19)	−0.10 (0.18)	−0.15 (0.19)	0.25 (0.18)
Female	−0.22* (0.12)	−0.27** (0.13)	0.24* (0.12)	−0.22* (0.13)	−0.46*** (0.13)
Age	0.01* (0.005)	0.01** (0.01)	0.01*** (0.005)	0.004 (0.01)	−0.001 (0.005)
Live in West Point	−0.03 (0.12)	0.07 (0.12)	0.15 (0.11)	0.31** (0.12)	0.28** (0.12)
Pay a bribe to police	−0.23 (0.15)	−0.24 (0.16)	−0.27* (0.15)	−0.50*** (0.16)	−0.46*** (0.15)
No UNMIL contact	−0.003 (0.19)	0.25 (0.20)	0.16 (0.18)	0.64*** (0.22)	0.79*** (0.21)
Female UNMIL contact	−0.45 (0.29)	0.18 (0.29)	−0.15 (0.27)	0.36 (0.31)	0.84*** (0.29)
Secret society	−0.04 (0.03)	0.02* (0.01)	0.01 (0.01)	−0.03 (0.02)	0.01 (0.01)
Muslim	0.25 (0.19)	0.29 (0.19)	0.13 (0.18)	−0.005 (0.20)	−0.61*** (0.20)
Crime victim	−0.15 (0.12)	−0.32** (0.13)	0.02 (0.02)	0.03 (0.03)	0.02 (0.02)
Constant	−0.52* (0.29)	−1.03*** (0.31)	−0.85*** (0.29)	−1.35*** (0.32)	−0.87*** (0.30)
Observations	1,276	1,276	1,276	1,276	1,276

Note: Values are coefficients with standard errors in parentheses.

*p < 0.1; **p < 0.05; ***p < 0.01.

Table A4.5. MODEL RESULTS OF PREFERENCES FOR THE POLICE TO RESPOND TO SECURITY ISSUES, BY MALE CONTACT

Independent variables	Provide security	Armed violence	Riot	Rape	Beating
Contact with male officer only	−0.23	−0.26*	−0.35**	−0.28*	−0.43***
	(0.15)	(0.15)	(0.14)	(0.16)	(0.15)
No contact with a police officer	−0.22	−0.39**	−0.44**	−0.43**	−0.18
	(0.18)	(0.18)	(0.17)	(0.18)	(0.17)
Female	−0.22*	−0.27**	0.24*	−0.22*	−0.46***
	(0.12)	(0.13)	(0.12)	(0.13)	(0.13)
Age	0.01*	0.01**	0.01***	0.004	−0.001
	(0.005)	(0.01)	(0.005)	(0.01)	(0.005)
Live in West Point	−0.03	0.07	0.15	0.31**	0.28**
	(0.12)	(0.12)	(0.11)	(0.12)	(0.12)
Pay a bribe to police	−0.23	−0.24	−0.27*	−0.50***	−0.46***
	(0.15)	(0.16)	(0.15)	(0.16)	(0.15)
No UNMIL contact	−0.003	0.25	0.16	0.64***	0.79***
	(0.19)	(0.20)	(0.18)	(0.22)	(0.21)
Female UNMIL contact	−0.45	0.18	−0.15	0.36	0.84***
	(0.29)	(0.29)	(0.27)	(0.31)	(0.29)
Secret society	−0.04	0.02*	0.01	−0.03	0.01
	(0.03)	(0.01)	(0.01)	(0.02)	(0.01)
Muslim	0.25	0.29	0.13	−0.005	−0.61***
	(0.19)	(0.19)	(0.18)	(0.20)	(0.20)
Crime victim	−0.15	−0.32**	0.02	0.03	0.02
	(0.12)	(0.13)	(0.02)	(0.03)	(0.02)
Constant	−0.29	−0.77**	−0.50*	−1.07***	−0.44
	(0.30)	(0.32)	(0.29)	(0.33)	(0.31)
Observations	1,276	1,276	1,276	1,276	1,276

Note: Values are coefficients with standard errors in parentheses.

*p < 0.1; **p < 0.05; ***p < 0.01.

Table A4.6. MODEL RESULTS OF PREFERENCES FOR THE POLICE
TO RESPOND TO SECURITY ISSUES, BY FEMALE AND MALE CONTACT

Independent variables	Provide security	Armed violence	Riot	Rape	Beating
Contact with male officer only	−0.01	0.13	0.10	0.15	−0.25
	(0.18)	(0.19)	(0.18)	(0.19)	(0.18)
Contact with female officer only	0.22	0.39**	0.44**	0.43**	0.18
	(0.18)	(0.18)	(0.17)	(0.18)	(0.17)
Female	−0.22*	−0.27**	0.24*	−0.22*	−0.46***
	(0.12)	(0.13)	(0.12)	(0.13)	(0.13)
Age	0.01*	0.01**	0.01***	0.004	−0.001
	(0.005)	(0.01)	(0.005)	(0.01)	(0.005)
Live in West Point	−0.03	0.07	0.15	0.31**	0.28**
	(0.12)	(0.12)	(0.11)	(0.12)	(0.12)
Pay a bribe to police	−0.23	−0.24	−0.27*	−0.50***	−0.46***
	(0.15)	(0.16)	(0.15)	(0.16)	(0.15)
No UNMIL contact	−0.003	0.25	0.16	0.64***	0.79***
	(0.19)	(0.20)	(0.18)	(0.22)	(0.21)
Female UNMIL contact	−0.45	0.18	−0.15	0.36	0.84***
	(0.29)	(0.29)	(0.27)	(0.31)	(0.29)
Secret society	−0.04	0.02*	0.01	−0.03	0.01
	(0.03)	(0.01)	(0.01)	(0.02)	(0.01)
Muslim	0.25	0.29	0.13	−0.005	−0.61***
	(0.19)	(0.19)	(0.18)	(0.20)	(0.20)
Crime victim	−0.15	−0.32**	0.02	0.03	0.02
	(0.12)	(0.13)	(0.02)	(0.03)	(0.02)
Constant	−0.51*	−1.16***	−0.95***	−1.50***	−0.62**
	(0.28)	(0.30)	(0.28)	(0.31)	(0.29)
Observations	1,276	1,276	1,276	1,276	1,276

Note: Values are coefficients with standard errors in parentheses.

*$p < 0.1$; **$p < 0.05$; ***$p < 0.01$.

Table A4.7. MODEL RESULTS OF PREFERENCES FOR POLICE
TO RESPOND TO A HALA HALA, BY FEMALE CONTACT

Independent variables	Model 1	Model 2	Model 3
Contact with female police	0.88**	1.06***	
	(0.38)	(0.30)	
Contact with male LNP	−0.25		−1.39***
	(0.31)		(0.33)
No contact with police		−0.08	−1.26***
		(0.29)	(0.38)
Displaced during war	−0.55**	−0.56**	−0.51*
	(0.28)	(0.28)	(0.28)
House burned during war	0.42*	0.43*	0.36
	(0.24)	(0.24)	(0.24)
Age	−0.004	−0.004	−0.004
	(0.01)	(0.01)	(0.01)
Female	0.07	0.04	0.06
	(0.24)	(0.24)	(0.24)
Can read	0.15	0.18	0.12
	(0.24)	(0.24)	(0.24)
Nimba	−0.79**	−0.78**	−0.68**
	(0.35)	(0.35)	(0.34)
River Gee	−0.27	−0.30	−0.25
	(0.30)	(0.30)	(0.30)
Grand Gedeh	−0.07	−0.06	−0.06
	(0.30)	(0.30)	(0.30)
Constant	−1.03**	−1.21***	0.14
	(0.50)	(0.44)	(0.51)
Observations	554	554	558

Note: Values are coefficients with standard errors in parentheses.
*p < 0.1; **p < 0.05; ***p < 0.01.

Table A4.8. MODEL RESULTS OF PREFERENCES FOR
POLICE TO RESPOND TO SECURITY ISSUES, BY FEMALE
CONTACT AND GENDER EQUALITY PERCEPTIONS

Independent variables	Rape	Provide security
Gender equality index	0.20***	0.19***
	(0.06)	(0.05)
Contact with female LNP	1.58**	2.52***
	(0.65)	(0.60)
No LNP contact	0.09	0.26
	(0.20)	(0.18)
Female	−0.29*	−0.27*
	(0.17)	(0.15)
Age	−0.01	0.01
	(0.01)	(0.01)
Victim of crime	0.26*	−0.02
	(0.15)	(0.04)
Victim of war violence	−0.13	0.02
	(0.15)	(0.01)
Contact with UNMIL	−0.25**	0.23**
	(0.11)	(0.10)
Positive perceptions of UNMIL	0.02***	−0.01
	(0.01)	(0.01)
Participated in armed group	0.004	0.01
	(0.01)	(0.01)
Number of children	0.25***	−0.10*
	(0.06)	(0.06)
Gender equality x contact with female LNP only	−0.16*	−0.29***
	(0.09)	(0.08)
Constant	−2.80***	−2.14***
	(0.58)	(0.50)
Observations	966	966

Note: Values are coefficients with standard errors in parentheses.
*p < 0.1; **p < 0.05; ***p < 0.01.

NOTES

CHAPTER 1

1. See the Swedish Government website, http://www.government.se/government-policy/feminist-foreign-policy/ (December 7, 2015). The statement of foreign policy explicitly affirms: "A feminist foreign policy is now being formulated, the purpose of which is to combat discrimination against women, improve conditions for women and contribute to peace and development. Women's participation in decision-making must be strengthened in countries at peace, countries in conflict and countries in which reconstruction is under way. This will also strengthen the sustainability of our societies. . . . A feminist foreign policy will be an integral part of activities throughout the Swedish Foreign Service, and aims to strengthen women's rights, improve women's access to resources and increase women's representation."
2. The United States follows at least sixteen other countries, including Canada, Romania, France, Germany, Denmark, Israel, the Netherlands, New Zealand, Poland, Sweden, and Australia, among others.
3. Studies in international politics, most prominently by Mary Caprioli and Valerie Hudson, have found a link between gender equality and reductions in violent armed conflict. For example, see Caprioli (2000, 2003, 2005, 2009), Caprioli et al. (2009), Hudson and Boer (2002), and Hudson, Ballif-Spanvill, Caprioli, and Emmett (2012). Erik Melander (2005a, 2005b) has also found links between measures of norms of gender equity and less conflict and human rights abuses. Melander's work with Erin Bjarnegård has also found that democratic societies are more peaceful only if there have been moves to gender equality (Bjarnegård and Melander, 2011).
4. As mentioned later in chapter 3, by "gender equality" we mean when women and men and the different roles they play enjoy the same rights and opportunities across all sectors of society, including economic participation and decision-making. Gender equality is the outcome of interest or the end goal for society and can be measured through both observable indicators such as the ratio of men and women in the labor force, as well as an examination of men and women's own experiences and feelings toward achieving equality. In this book, a "conflict-ridden country" refers to any country currently experiencing an intrastate armed conflict. A "post-conflict country" refers to any country that has experienced an intrastate armed conflict in the recent past.
5. Previous UN resolutions had treated women as victims of war, in need of protection. However, UNSCR 1325 also recognized women as agents in building peace and guaranteeing security (Pratt and Richter-Devroe, 2011).
6. By "gender reform" we mean changes that affect women and men's roles in and through peacekeeping missions so that there is a move toward equality between the sexes and among genders. Gender refers to the social attributes associated with being male or female that are learned through socialization and determine a person's position and authority in a given context (Egnell et al., 2014: 4).
7. Sexual and gender-based violence includes gender-based violence. The term "gender-based violence" is used to distinguish common violence from violence that targets

individuals or groups of individuals on the basis of their gender. Gender-based violence has been defined by The United Nations Committee on the Elimination of Discrimination against Women (CEDAW) as violence that is directed at a person on the basis of gender or sex. It includes acts that inflict physical, mental or sexual harm or suffering, threat of such acts, coercion, and other deprivations of liberty. Sexual violence is included in the definition. "Sexual violence" includes exploitation and abuse and refers to any act, attempt, or threat of a sexual nature that results or is likely to result in physical, psychological, or emotional harm (including rape).

8. The UN limits the discussion to sexual exploitation and abuse (SEA), but we include harassment and violence, because they differ conceptually.

9. Not to mention that due to the problem of SEAHV in missions, the UN's Office of Internal Oversight Services Inspection and Evaluation Division released an evaluation report, "Evolution of the Enforcement and Remedial Assistance Effort for Sexual Exploitation and Abuse by the United Nations and Related Personnel in Peacekeeping Operations," on May 15, 2015. The report documents widespread sexual transgressions committed by peacekeepers (Office of Internal Oversight Services Inspection, 2015).

10. Similarly, though not something that is widely explored in this book, men are often considered unfit for "women's work."

11. See the work of Tickner (1992), Enloe (1983, 1990, 2000, 2004, 2007, 2010), Sjoberg (2009, 2011), Wibben (2011), Cohn (1987, 1999, 2013), Shepherd (2008a), and Pettman (1996), among others.

12. See, for example, Fortna (2008), Gilligan and Sergenti (2008), Howard (2008), and Doyle Sambanis (2006).

13. See the work of Enloe (1984, 1990, 2000, 2007, 2010), Sjoberg (2009, 2011), Cohn (1987, 2000, 2010), Shepherd (2008a), and Whitworth (2007), among others.

14. See Ramazanoglu and Holland (2002).

CHAPTER 2

1. For a full assessment of the meaning of the all-female Indian FPU in Liberia, see Pruitt (2016).

2. See Basu (2010).

3. The recent Report of the High-Level Independent Panel on Peace Operations stresses these two areas with respect to the WPS agenda and PKOs. See in particular UN (2015: 59).

4. One of the main contributions from the 1992 "Agenda for Peace" was its introduction of postconflict peace-building, which was defined as "action to identify and support structures which will tend to strengthen and solidify peace in order to avoid a relapse into conflict." Peacekeeping mission did not have such a mandate previously.

5. For more on the taxonomy of peacekeeping missions, see Bellamy, Williams, and Griffin (2010) and Diehl and Druckman (2010).

6. See the Formed Police Units, UN Website http://www.un.org/en/peacekeeping/sites/police/units.shtml (accessed December 10, 2015).

7. See work by Charli Carpenter for examples of gendered violence.

8. For a detailed explanation of the process, see Anderlini (2007). Many of these challenges are still ongoing, as women have been notably absent in some high-profile peace negotiations, such as those to resolve the Colombian and Syrian crises.

9. The Declaration uses the term "gender balancing." Below, we refer to the policy of increasing women's representation in the security sector as "female ratio balancing."

10. For an evolution and evaluation of UNSCR 1325, see Olsson and Gizelis (2013, 2015), Pratt and Richter-Devroe (2011), and Shepherd (2008a, 2008b).

11. Previous UNSC resolutions had treated women as victims of war, in need of protection. However, UNSCR 1325 also recognizes women as agents in building peace and guaranteeing security (Pratt and Richter-Devroe, 2011).

12. Passed in 2008, UNSCR 1820 recognizes that conflict-related sexual violence is a tactic of warfare and calls for the training of troops in preventing and responding to sexual violence, the deployment of more women to peace operations, and the enforcement of zero tolerance policies for peacekeepers with regard to acts of sexual exploitation or abuse. Passed in 2009, UNSCR 1888 strengthens the implementation of UNSCR 1820 by calling for leadership to address conflict-related sexual violence, deployment of teams (military and gender experts) to critical conflict areas, and improved monitoring and reporting on conflict trends and perpetrators. Passed in 2009, UNSCR 1889 addresses obstacles to women's participation in peace processes and calls for development of global indicators to track the implementation of UNSCR 1325 and improvement of international and national responses to the needs of women in conflict and postconflict settings. Passed in December 2010, UNSCR 1960 calls for an end to sexual violence in armed conflict, particularly against women and girls, and provides measures aimed at ending impunity for perpetrators of sexual violence, including through sanctions and reporting measures. Passed in June 2013, UNSCR 2106 adds greater operational detail to previous resolutions on this topic, reiterates that all actors, including not only the Security Council and parties to armed conflict, but all Member States and UN entities, must do more to implement previous mandates and combat impunity for these crimes. Passed in October 2013, UNSCR 2122 puts in place stronger measures to enable women to participate in conflict resolution and recovery and puts the onus on the Security Council, the UN, regional organizations, and Member States to dismantle the barriers, create the space, and provide seats at the table for women. Passed in 2015, UNSCR 2242 improves implementation of the landmark WPS agenda, covering work on countering violent extremism and terrorism, improving working methods, and broadly taking up the gender recommendations of a global study completed in 2015.

13. For example, Shepherd (2008b) and Cohn (2008) argue that the problems inherent in military institutions cannot be solved by UNSCR 1325 because there is a contradiction in using soldiers to achieve the ends of the WPS agenda, when soldiers defend and in part constitute a system that perpetuates injustice. Peacekeeping missions in this sense may be considered "neocolonial." Also see Duncanson (2013: 23–42) and Cohn, Kinsella, and Gibbings (2004). Note that Duncanson only partially agrees with these critiques (Duncanson 2013: 46–51).

14. See UN (2010a).

15. See UN (2015: 78–81).

16. Other work by Pruitt (2012, 2013, 2016) and by Sion (2008), Whitworth (2007), Higate and Henry (2009), Higate (2003), Beber, Gilligan, Guardado, and Karim (2017), Bridges and Horsfall (2009), and others is explored in the rest of the book. For a comprehensive bibliography of scholarship on gender and peacekeeping, see Karim and Beardsley (2016b).

17. "Women UN Peacekeepers—More Needed," IRIN News, May 20, 2010, http://www. irinnews.org/feature/2010/05/20/women-un-peacekeepers-more-needed (accessed January 13, 2014).

18. See UN (2010b).

19. We should not overstate the value that NAPs will have in implementing UNSCR 1325. Without third-party enforcement provisions, NAP states might face repercussion for failing to implement their plans. We doubt that the 1325 initiative is so salient that this would generate widespread international or domestic condemnation against countries that fail to implement their NAPs. See also Basini and Ryan (2016) for a critique of NAPs.

20. We had two coders read the NAPs and evaluate whether the focus of the objectives was domestic or international.

21. These differences are statistically significant using a bivariate t-test ($p < 0.001$).

22. We are limited in doing a more comprehensive cross-national assessment of how peacekeeping relates to improvements in gender equality in the host country, in

part because observable improvements in gender equality are likely to take years to become manifested and in part because the cases with peacekeeping are so different from the cases without peacekeeping in terms of their baseline levels of factors related to good governance. That being said, Murdie and Davis (2010) analyzed whether peacekeeping missions improved downstream human rights performance and found that peacekeeping missions with a humanitarian purpose improved the protection of physical integrity rights.

23. The "zero tolerance policy" bans almost all sexual activity between UN peacekeeping personnel and local women in order to prevent "sexual exploitation." The bans not only prohibit any "exchange of money, employment, goods or services for sex" but also "strongly discourage sexual relationships between UN staff and beneficiaries of assistance since they are based on inherently unequal power dynamics."

24. For more details, see UN (2005), also known as the "Zeid Report." See Stern (2015) for an assessment of the Zeid Report.

25. See Ndulo (2009).

26. See Csaky (2008) and Jennings (2008).

27. See Gilligan and Stedman (2003) and Fortna (2008). Hultman (2013) similarly finds that peacekeeping missions go to the conflicts with larger civilian casualties.

28. Cohen and Nordås (2014) provide definitions for "no reports" and "some," "several/many," and "massive" reports of sexual violence. The conflict years and postconflict years are taken from the SSR Dataset (Karim, 2016a). The list of countries for the SSR Dataset are from the PRIO/UCDP conflict dataset.

29. See UN (2015: 23).

30. See, for example, Mazurana, Raven-Roberts, and Parpart (2005).

31. See p. v.

32. See p. 1.

33. See the website, "UN Resources on Gender Approaches to Gender Equality," http://www.un.org/womenwatch/resources/goodpractices/approach.html (accessed September 28, 2014).

34. See the website: "UN Women Good Practices Examples," http://www.un.org/womenwatch/osagi/goodpraexamples.htm (accessed September 28, 2014).

35. See p. 14.

36. See UN Women (2015: 146).

CHAPTER 3

1. We note that SEAHV does not only affect women. However, the focus of this book is on how it affects female peacekeepers and local women. We encourage a more thorough examination of SEAHV and peacekeeping missions as it relates to boys and men.

2. We recognize that this conventional definition is oversimplified because some individuals genetically do not fall into an x-x (female) or x-y (male) pairing on the twenty-third chromosome and because some individuals alter their congenital genitalia.

3. See, for example, Sjoberg and Via (2010).

4. See Detraz (2012).

5. See, for example, Sjoberg and Gentry (2007, 2011); Sjoberg and Via (2010); Carpenter (2005); Cohn (2013); Detraz (2012).

6. See Detraz (2012); Sjoberg and Gentry (2007).

7. See Sandberg (2013). While she describes numerous examples of gender inequality in the workforce, her manuscript is not meant to explore the underlying causes of gender power differentials. Thus, we cite this work to illustrate an example, not to highlight her contribution to a theoretical premise.

8. See Cohn (2013).

9. The type of institutionalism we refer to is based on work by March and Olsen (1989) that includes not only formal rules and practices but also the "symbol systems,

cognitive scripts and moral templates that provide the 'frames of meaning' guiding human behavior" (Hall and Taylor, 1996: 947). The sociological approach assumes that institutional actors are fundamentally social and act in habitual ways, following a "logic of appropriateness" that both prescribes and proscribes certain types of behavior.

10. For example, for an excellent account of how the U.S. Congress as an institution is gendered (and raced), see Hawkesworth (2003).
11. A notable example is the lack of women in the STEM (science, technology, engineering, and math) fields.
12. Peacekeeping missions are composed of military, police, and civilian units, but most peacekeeping is usually conceptualized as including military and police units (Bellamy and Williams, 2013).
13. We also expect gendered implications for men in peacekeeping missions that result from these gender imbalances, but for the purposes of this book we focus on the implications for women and femininity. The impact of gender power imbalances for male peacekeepers would be a fascinating area of new research.
14. See, for example, Easlea (1983), McAllister (1982), and Reardon (1993, 1996).
15. See Fox (2001).
16. See discussion by Carreiras (2006: 35–37).
17. See explanation by Carreiras (2006: 36).
18. See U.S. Marine Corp (2015).
19. See Hunter (2015).
20. See Yuval-Davis (1997).
21. See Carreiras (2006: 44–45) for a discussion on protection.
22. See Young (2003: 2).
23. See also DeGroot (2001), Hoffman and Hickey (2005), Love and Singer (1988), Boyce and Herd (2003), Carreiras (2006), Chrisler and McCreary (2010), Goldstein (2003), Herrnson, Lay, and Stokes (2003), and Williams and Best (1990).
24. The gendered protection norm has other implications that relate to race and colonialism. For an overview, see Duncanson (2013: 28–42).
25. See, for example, Cohn, Kinsella, and Gibbings (2004), Shepherd (2008b, 2011), Pratt and Richter-Devroe (2011).
26. See, among others, Michaels (2013), Fenner and deYoung (2001), MacCoun, Kier, and Belkin (2006), Quester (1977), Maginnis (2013), and Van Crevald (2000, 2001).
27. See, for example, Beardsley and Schmidt (2012), Fortna (2008), and Gilligan and Stedman (2003).
28. See Karim and Beardsley (2013, 2015).
29. For example, women receive disproportionate attention in the media when they are injured, as in the case of Private Jessica Lynch (Sjolander and Trevenen, 2010a, 2010b); Gartner (2008).
30. See Skaine (2011) for a discussion on women's exclusion from combat-oriented tasks.
31. Numerous scholars have critiqued the point that unit cohesion, military effectiveness, and masculinity are tied together. For example, MacCoun, Kier, and Belkin (2006) find that social cohesion does not have much support in the literature for military effectiveness and that task cohesion is perhaps more important. King (2013) reiterates the importance of task cohesion. Moreover, Segal and Kastenbaum (2002: 41–58) apply the concept of "imagined communities" to understand how cohesion may be formed, as cohesion may occur through common membership and experience, not necessarily the creation of out-groups. We return to implications of these critiques at the end of the chapter and in the conclusion of the book.
32. See Carreiras (2006) and Higate (2003). This idea is also similar to Connell's (1987) explanation of cathexis.
33. See Connell and Messerschmidt (2005) and Higate (2003).
34. See Goldstein (2003).

35. The existing scholarship has additionally discussed how militarized masculinity is supported by institutional power (Connell and Messerschmidt, 2005), has been widely used to enhance unit or group cohesion (Kronsell, 2012; Whitworth, 2007), and helps ensure that soldiers are able to kill members of the enemy group (Asken, Christensen, and Grossman, 2010).
36. See Higate (2003).
37. See Hudson and Boer (2002) and Tiger and Fox (1998).
38. See, for example, Van Creveld (2001), Fenner and deYoung (2001), Gutmann (2013), and Febbraro and McCann (2003).
39. See Rosen (1996).
40. See Van Creveld (2000, 2001).
41. See Enloe (2000) and Whitworth (2007).
42. For example, see Lehr (1999: 123), Enloe (2000), Harrison (2002), Sayers, Farrow, Ross, and Oslin (2009), Valente and Wight (2007).
43. See Meintjes, Turshen, and Pillay (2002).
44. See Novaco and Chemtob (2002) and Whitworth (2007).
45. See Harrison and Laliberté (1994), Harrison (2002), Sadler, Booth, Cook, and Doebbeling (2003), Harrison and Laliberté (2002), and Titunik (2000).
46. See Ellison (2011), Zeigler and Gunderson (2005), Murdoch and Nichol (1995), and Campbell et al. (2003).
47. See Kronsell (2012).
48. See DiTomaso (1989: 71).
49. It is important to note that we do not suggest that all or even most soldiers and police officers will exhibit such behavior, but simply that the socialization process contributes to creating a context where individuals become more prone to such tendencies. In addition, it is important to note that men and boys may also suffer from SEAHV.
50. See Martin (2005), Higate (2004, 2007), Higate and Henry (2004), Nordås and Rustad (2013), Bolkovac and Lynn (2011), Karim and Beardsley (2016a).
51. For example, see Enloe (1990, 2000) and Moon (1997).
52. See Enloe (1990), Moon (1997), and Beber et al. (2017).
53. See Dunkle et al. (2006).
54. See "Introduction" in Simm (2013).
55. Whitworth (2007) similarly ties this identity crisis to backlash against the local population.
56. See Martin (1999).
57. See Balko (2013).
58. See Hartz (1999).
59. Although this may be changing around the world, particularly in the United States. See Balko (2013).
60. See Greener (2009).
61. See also discussion by Carreiras (2006: 82).
62. See DeGroot (2001), Bridges and Horsfall (2009), Reardon (1993), Burguieres (1990), Boulding (1995), York (1998), and Salla (2001).
63. See UN Peacekeeping Website: "Gender and Peacekeeping," http://www.un.org/en/peacekeeping/issues/women/ (accessed March 12, 2013).
64. See "Women in Peacekeeping," UN Peacekeeping website, http://www.un.org/en/peacekeeping/issues/women/womeninpk.shtml (accessed March 12, 2013).
65. See "Women in Peacekeeping," UN Peacekeeping website, http://www.un.org/en/peacekeeping/issues/women/womeninpk.shtml (accessed March 12, 2013).
66. Jennings draws from the following sources: Bertolazzi (2010), UN DPKO (2000), UN DPKO (2004), UNIFEM (2007), Cordell (2009), Bridges and Horsfall (2009), and Olsson and Tryggestad (2001).
67. Such sentiment about women's representative capabilities is not new. It is echoed in the American politics literature. Women's representation is important to politics because of descriptive representation: women can serve as role models;

representation is important for normative reasons; and women can help crystallize trust with constituents and promote the status of underprivileged groups in communities. See Phillips (1998) and Mansbridge (1999).

68. See Jennings (2011).
69. Secretary-General Speech, "Far More Must Be Done to Involve Women in Conflict Prevention, Peace Talks," Ban Ki-Moon, June 19, 2008, DG/SM/11647, SC 9365, WOM 1685, see UN press release http://www.un.org/press/en/2008/sgsm11647.doc.htm (accessed September 15, 2016).
70. See Simić (2013) and Zeigler and Gunderson (2005).
71. See Keiser, Wilkins, Meier, and Holland (2002), Meier and Nicholson-Crotty (2006).
72. See also Kember (2010).
73. Conventionally, the "critical mass" argument posits that 30 percent women is the proportion needed to make a difference. For example, in summarizing his findings, Cary (2001: 53–54) notes that local women confide more in female peacekeepers, women negotiators understand and articulate the implications of processes for women better than do men, peace missions with higher percentages of women have been successful, and if 30 percent of mission personnel are female then local women are more quick to join peace committees. For more mixed reviews about critical mass theory, see Beckwith and Cowell-Meyers (2007), Bratton (2005), Childs and Krook (2006), Dahlerup (2006a), and Grey (2006).
74. See Kronsell (2012).
75. See Jennings (2008), Otto (2007), Simić (2010), and Henry (2012).
76. See also Baaz and Utas (2012).
77. According to Sjoberg and Gentry (2007), women engaged in violence are often portrayed either as a mothers, who are fulfilling their biological destinies, as monsters, who are pathologically damaged, or as whores, whose violence is inspired by sexual deviance. The authors demonstrate that this negates women's agency in committing violence because there must be a reason they do it, whereas for men committing violence is normalized.
78. See Sjoberg and Gentry (2007, 2011), Sjoberg and Via (2010), and McKelvey (2007).
79. See Tsjeard, Frerks, and Bannon (2005).
80. See Sion (2008), Simić (2010), Jeffreys (2007), Jennings (2008), Henry (2012), and Pruitt (2013, 2016).
81. On intersectionality, see Inayatullah and Blaney (2004), Crenshaw (1989), and Hancock (2007). Relatedly, some feminist scholars have argued that peacekeeping missions discount race and other intersectional approaches (Yuval-Davis, 2006; Razack, 2004).
82. Including a quota in peacekeeping missions is not feasible because contributing countries voluntarily provide troops and police. These countries have sole discretion over who they send, not the UN.
83. See Dahlerup and Freidenvall (2005), Dahlerup (2006b), Franceschet, Krook, and Piscopo (2012), Krook (2006, 2010), and Tripp and Kang (2008).
84. See Bhavnani (2009), Chen (2010), Dahlerup (2008), and Franceschet et al. (2012).
85. See Bush (2011).
86. On "seeing the uniform," see Simić (2010), Barth (2004), and Henry (2012).
87. See Valenius (2007), Sion (2008), Jennings (2008), and Simić (2010).
88. See also Jennings (2011), Kronsell (2012), Olsson (2009), and Olsson and Tryggestad (2001).
89. To be transparent, our macro-level quantitative analysis uses aggregate measures of gender equality, thereby falling into what Arat (2015) would claim as the liberal feminism trap. We do so because aggregate indicators that better measure gender equality are absent and because some measures do provide an indication of how well countries are doing relative to one another, which is important in identifying potential countries that are at least starting to take gender reforms seriously or that are failing in doing so.

90. Arat provides three central critiques: defining power as a quality possessed by individuals (1) treats gaining access to power as an increase in the power held, (2) assumes that gained power will lead to the exercise of power and change power relations, and (3) posits that targeting gender equality by providing access to power to some women will have a redistributive effect at the aggregate, macro level, thereby empowering all women. She argues that these are all misconceptions (Arat, 2015: 684). In addition, Kara Ellerby (2017, forthcoming) provides critiques of traditional understandings of gender equality as well.

91. Snapshots of progress along these dimensions can be measured through both observable indicators, such as the ratio of men and women in the labor force, and an examination of men and women's own experiences, feelings, and beliefs regarding achieving equality. For this reason, our macro-level analysis is accompanied and triangulated by individual female peacekeepers and locals. In addition, our measures of gender equality at the aggregate level are used as proxies to measure beliefs about gender equality or parity in belief systems, which we believe is an important aspect of equal opportunity peacekeeping.

92. There may be others, such as equality in relationships, but we highlight these as important for institutional change.

93. See March and Olsen (1989), Hall and Taylor (1996), and Olsen (2009).

94. See Finnemore and Sikkink (1998).

95. To some extent so has Great Britain; see Duncanson (2013: 76).

PART II

1. See UN Mission in Ethiopia and Eritrea (UNMEE).

2. See UN Integrated Mission in Timor-Leste (UNMIT); UNSCR 1704 (2006).

3. Contributor information is not available for UNSMIL, and it thus does not appear in our analyses.

4. See UN Operation in Côte d'Ivoire (UNOCI).

5. See UNDOF.

6. See UN Peacekeeping Force in Cyprus (UNFICYP).

7. See UN Interim Administration Mission in Kosovo (UNMIK).

CHAPTER 4

1. See Adebajo (2013), who writes about the implications for peacekeeping related to Nigeria's desire to be a regional hegemon and have influence in West Africa.

2. Much of the information in this chapter can also be found in Karim and Beardsley (2013, 2015).

3. It is worth pausing here to point out that we do not equate aggregate country-level indicators as the same as improving equal opportunity peacekeeping. However, we use levels of gender equality as a proxy for the likelihood that a country's norms about women participating in traditionally masculine spaces have improved.

4. For an overview, see Kathman and Melin (2014) and Koga-Sudduth and Karim (2015).

5. We excluded from the plots those countries that averaged less than one person contributed per year (which include thirty-two countries).

6. The analysis here parallels Carreiras's (2006) assessment of whether time affects the integration of women into NATO militaries. In other words, historical removals of barriers are expected to lead to more female integration over time. She does not find a relationship, however, in the sense that the year women entered the military did not correlate with the proportion of women later.

7. This information comes from e-mail exchanges with Susanne Axmacher, June 19, 2013.

8. See Pfalzer (2013).

9. See appendix 1 for a description of the data sources and coding. Note that the domestic female ratio balance information is missing for a number of countries.

10. We transform the proportions using a logit transformation, which accounts for the bounded nature of a ratio variable by fitting the curve for the expected proportion of women on an S-curve that ranges between 0 and 1. For the logit transformation, we added 0.001 (0.1 percent) to each of the values because a logit transformation of 0.000 is undefined.
11. This approach accounts for the potential for observations from the same contributing countries or to the same missions to be correlated with one another.
12. The other variables in the models are held at their means, with the exception that the total number of troops in the missions is set to 10,000 and the total number of police in the missions is set to 1,500.
13. While multiple imputation confirms the robustness of the other findings discussed in this chapter (details in appendix 1), the estimated relationship between the proportion of women in contributing countries' militaries and the proportion of women in peacekeeping contributions is not robust to the imputation.
14. We conducted interviews, focus groups, and a survey with the female contingents and peacekeepers in Monrovia, Buchanan, and Gbarnga (where the Ghanaian and Bangladeshi contingents were stationed) between May 2012 and June 2012. We also conducted a questionnaire of women in the mission, with ninety-four respondents. See chapter 6 for details on the data.
15. The force commander is the military head of the mission.
16. See "First UN Female Force Commander Takes Reins in Cyprus," UN News Centre, August 13, 2014, http://www.un.org/apps/news/story.asp?NewsID=48462#.VpgVr5MrK9Y (accessed January 13, 2016).
17. We use the term sexual violence as defined in Cohen and Nordås (2014).
18. For example, women receive disproportionate attention in the media when they are injured, as in the case of Private Jessica Lynch (Sjolander and Trevenen, 2010; Gartner, 2008).
19. E-mail interview, October 9, 2014.
20. In American politics, a similar argument is made about why there are so few female politicians. Research has shown that women even in the highest of tiers of professional accomplishment are substantially less likely than men to demonstrate ambition to seek elected office because of traditional sex socialization, as women do not think they are qualified to run for office (Lawless and Fox, 2010).
21. The mission in Kosovo has such a high number because there are so few personnel who serve in this observer mission. For this reason, it is important that we control for mission size.
22. UCDP Battle-Related Deaths Dataset v.5-2013, Uppsala Conflict Data Program, Uppsala University, www.ucdp.uu.se. We chose not to look at the violence in the most recent year because peacekeeping missions will tend to deploy as violence has attenuated, even if only briefly. We thus chose a measure that could capture the history of severe violence and thus the potential for PKOs to have to respond to major escalations in violent hostilities.
23. For missions deployed in multiple countries, we chose the per capita GDP of the poorest country because this better captures risk.
24. Again, we hold other variables at their means, with the exception that the total number of troops is set to 10,000, and the total number of police is set to 1,500.
25. The result is consistent with Carreiras (2006), who finds that higher GDP and the Gender-related Development Index (human development index indicators) correlate with higher proportions of women in domestic security forces in NATO countries.
26. Since sexual violence is likely an intervening variable between these other measures of insecurity and deployment decisions, rather than a confounding variable, it remains plausible that conflict severity and economic challenges help explain the composition of peacekeeping contributions.
27. See Kronsell (2012), Whitworth (2007), and Carreiras (2006).

28. Particularly, to describe social structure, she refers to women's roles in society, such as women's participation in the labor force.
29. But she was quick to mention that in UNMIL she experienced heavy discrimination in her role as a senior manager for UNPOL in Liberia.
30. See St. Pierre (2011) and Paxton, Hughes, and Green (2006).
31. See Banaszak (2003), Costain (1992), and McAdam (1999).
32. See Walsh (2008).
33. See also Hafner-Burton and Tsutsui (2005) and Hafner-Burton, Tsutsui, and Meyer (2008), who explore the domestic political incentives to decouple formal commitments to the human rights regime from compliance. See also Huber and Karim (2016) on compliance with gender balancing reforms in postconflict countries.
34. Carreiras (2006) makes and tests this argument. She does not find evidence, however, that either the higher percentage of women in the labor force or the gender empowerment index leads to higher proportions of women in the armed forces in NATO countries.
35. Crawford, Lebovic, and Macdonald (2015) use the Cingranelli-Richards Human Rights (CIRI) Data Set and annual gross enrollment ratio of girls to boys in secondary education to measure women's rights.
36. While the measure does not accurately capture the condition for all women (Arat, 2015), it does allow a basis for comparing a manifestation of gender power imbalances across countries.
37. By this we do not only mean measurable improvements in ratios of women in different sectors, such as education and the labor force, but take a broader interpretation, such as changing social values about gender equality, as suggested by Arat (2015).
38. However, we tested whether countries that have adopted NAPs tied to UNSCR 1325 send more female peacekeepers and found no evidence that they do. Full implementation of the NAPs is likely needed, and not just adoption, even if adoption can signal something about egalitarian intent.
39. See Aguayo et al. (2016).
40. See Paxton et al. (2006).

CHAPTER 5

1. The story comes from interviews done in Liberia in July 2014. We changed her name to protect her privacy.
2. See Ndulo (2009).
3. See, for example, Martin (2005) and Bolkovac and Lynn (2011).
4. See Csaky (2008).
5. Office of Internal Oversight Services (2015).
6. This builds off of earlier work, Karim and Beardsley (2016a).
7. See Hossain, Zimmerman, Abas, Light, and Watts (2010).
8. See Day, McKenna, and Bowlus (2005).
9. See Klot and DeLargy (2007).
10. See Frerichs, Keim, Barrais, and Piarroux (2012).
11. See Jennings and Nikolić-Ristanović (2009), Kronsell (2012), and Atwood (2011).
12. See Dunkle et al. (2006).
13. On a per capita basis, allegations against civilian personnel are actually higher than against military personnel.
14. See Csaky (2008) and Jennings (2008).
15. See Enloe (1993, 2000), Whitworth (2007), and Sjoberg and Via (2010).
16. See Sjoberg and Via (2010).
17. See UN (2000), or the "Brahimi Report."
18. See Carreiras (2010).
19. See Bolkovac and Lynn (2011) for an account of human trafficking in PKOs in Bosnia.

20. See Ndulo (2009).
21. See Allred (2006).
22. Note that our larger argument about militarization may pertain to civilians as well. However, we are unable to test whether the argument on UN civilians holds, due to lack of data.
23. See Smith, Hold, and Durch (2007).
24. See Jennings (2008).
25. For example, see Bridges and Horsfalls (2009) and Hull, Eriksson, MacDermott, Ruden, and Waleij (2009: 53). For critique of this position, see Simić (2010) and Jennings (2008, 2011).
26. See Dharmapuri (2012).
27. See also Crawford, Lebovic, and Macdonald (2015) and Karim and Beardsley (2013, 2015).
28. Quoted in Simić (2010: 193–194).
29. See Kronsell (2012: 105) and Valenius (2007: 517).
30. See Sjoberg and Gentry (2007).
31. See Kronsell (2012: 105–106).
32. See Lutz, Gutmann, and Brown (2009: 9).
33. See Kronsell (2012: 105) and Simić (2010: 188) for a similar critique.
34. Gender power imbalances are not fixed over time, as many societies are engaged in efforts to address the pernicious entrenchment of rigid gender norms. See Schuler, Ruth, Hashemi, Riley, and Akhter (1996). See examples of programs in Aguayo et al. (2016).
35. See Arat (2015).
36. Data on the representation of women in UN missions that are disaggregated by country are only available starting in 2009. The UN started collecting data on SEAHV allegations starting in 2007, which is why some descriptive statistics cover 2007–2013.
37. As mentioned in this chapter, we only look at military and police allegations.
38. For the counts of military allegations, we use a random effects negative binomial regression, because log-likelihood tests of the dispersion parameter indicate that a Poisson model would be inferior because of overdispersion. For the counts of police allegations, which are much less on average, the random effects negative binomial regression models failed to produce estimates. We thus use random effects Poisson models for the counts of SEAHV allegations against police personnel.
39. See the website of the UN Conduct and Discipline Unit, https://cdu.unlb.org/ (accessed January 12, 2015).
40. Our use of random effects will account for some of the mission-specific differences in propensities for offenses to be reported.
41. See Csaky (2008).
42. In addition, including a measure of the population sizes of the host countries—which might relate to access to the peacekeeping missions—does not show this to be a relevant variable in explaining the variation in SEAHV across missions.
43. We note that there are many different theories and indicators that may be used to measure the level of patriarchy in society. See for example Bjarnegård and Melander (2011), Caprioli (2005), Caprioli and Boyer (2001), Caprioli (2000, 2003), Melander (2005a, 2005b).
44. We use multiple measures of the practice of gender equality, allowing for multiple glimpses at the underlying societal norms and beliefs that should manifest themselves in the observed gender dynamics. Note that Melander (2005b) uses a higher-education attainment ratio and the proportion of women in parliament as alternative measures, but we choose not to use the former because a number of states with prima facie poor records on women's rights (Gulf states such as Saudi Arabia) are some of the best performers on this measure, and we choose not to use the latter because parliamentary quotas are likely to skew the ability for this

measure to represent day-to-day gender equality in the society. Regressions with these two measures indicate that the proportion of women in parliament does correlate negatively and significantly with SEAHV military allegations, but the association with higher-education attainment is not statistically significant.

45. Carreiras (2006) makes a similar argument. Data come from the World Bank.
46. See Htun and Weldon (2012).
47. This comes from the WomenStats Database of Hudson et al. (2012).
48. See the website of Peace Women. http://www.peacewomen.org/ (accessed March 27, 2013).
49. Information about the NAP adopters can be found at http://peacewomen.org/naps/ (accessed March 13, 2013).
50. We generate the weights by, for each month, dividing each contributing-country's contribution to a type of force (troop, UNPOL, FPU, experts, etc.) by the total size of that type of force for the mission. We then multiply those weights by the contributing-country's values for women's participation in the labor force, etc. Then we sum across all the contributing countries to the mission, to get the weighted averages at the monthly level. Then, we choose the month of each year in which there were the most peacekeepers (when the total size of the peacekeeping mission was largest) to represent the values for the mission-year.
51. See tables A1.2 and A1.3.
52. See Hartz (1999).
53. See Greener (2009).
54. On this latter point about NAPs, see Basini and Ryan (2016).
55. See Lynch (2004) and Gardiner (2005).
56. It is important to note that these may not be the only troop-contributing countries that received allegations. The ones listed are the ones that have been made public and reported by the media.
57. We collected the data by looking through media headlines from each country for the years 2007–2013. We searched media headlines in LexusNexus and searched for key terms such as "rape" and the name of the country's military. It was outside the scope of this study to collect these data for the entire dataset above. Future projects could collect these data on a wider scale.
58. See Sieff (2016) and Sengupta (2015).
59. See Jennings (2008).

PART III

1. Other missions, such as in the DRC and Haiti, have also included all-female FPUs since, but the Liberian case was the first effort.
2. See p. 5. In later years, the mandate added on more state building tasks such as: enabling the transition of full security responsibility to the Liberia National Police by strengthening its capabilities; promoting human rights; supporting national processes of reconciliation, constitutional reform and decentralization; enhancing support for security sector and rule of law reform; supporting the participation of women in conflict prevention, conflict resolution and peacebuilding; enhancing cooperation with the United Nations Mission in Côte d'Ivoire (UNOCI) for the stabilization of the border area; and coordinating and collaborating with the Peacebuilding Commission on its engagement in Liberia (UNSC, 2013). The mission has significantly drawn down since 2013.

CHAPTER 6

1. The objectives of the award is to "promote an understanding of police in peace operations throughout the world; highlight the efforts of female police in global peace operations; increase understanding of the roles of women officers in various countries; encourage participation in UN peace operations by all countries of the world; promote membership in the UN International Female Police Peacekeepers Network; increase international understanding and awareness of women in

international police peacekeeping and the UN International Female Police Peacekeepers Network; and recognize the outstanding accomplishments of a female police peacekeeper." See "Female Peacekeeping Award," http://www.un.org/en/peacekeeping/sites/police/award.shtml (accessed January 20, 2014).

2. We conducted interviews, focus groups, and a survey with the female contingents and peacekeepers in Monrovia, Buchanan, and Gbarnga (where the Ghanaian and Bangladeshi contingents are stationed) between May 2012 and June 2012. We also conducted a questionnaire of women in the mission, with ninety-five respondents. The authorities in UNMIL determined whether or not we conducted a focus group or interview. In some cases the UN organized focus groups, and in some cases they organized interviews. Focus groups included as few as four participants or as many as twenty. One set of interviews with the Norwegians was conducted with two interviewees at the same time. See appendix 3 for the breakdown of the interviews and focus groups. The focus group questions are included in appendix 3. We explicitly asked for access to female peacekeepers, but on many occasions we had the opportunity to speak with men as well, both formally and informally. Discussions with them (both formal and informal) are included in the tables.

3. The focus groups and interviews are not a representative sample of the UNMIL or UN missions in general, and they do not provide information in a dynamic context. The interviews and focus groups were all conducted during one period, not over time. While not all women were represented from missions around the world (or even the UNMIL mission), we did speak to women from many parts of the world, and the same themes surfaced in almost all the different conversations. This suggests that there are some similarities across female peacekeepers irrespective of their home country affiliations.

4. A shorter version of this chapter can be found in *International Interactions* (Karim, 2016b).

5. One of two sets of survey questions were randomly assigned to different female peacekeepers. In the first set of questions, respondents were asked: "on a scale of 1–5 (with 5 being the most important) how important do you think *male* peacekeepers are to promoting peace in the local community?"; "on a scale of 1–5 (with 5 being the most important) how important do you think *male* peacekeepers are to improving the quality of life in the local community?"; and "on a scale of 1–5 (with 5 being most important), how important do you think *male* peacekeepers are to improving the security of women in the local community?" In the second set of questions, the word "male" was replaced with "female."

6. The median time of service is eleven years.

7. By "full participation" we mean women's ability to participate in all the roles in the peacekeeping mission.

8. For a discussion of the depictions as gendered, see Henry (2012) and Pruitt (2013, 2016).

9. Sabrina watched a number of interactions between her and her superior (a male American military officer), and he treated her vastly differently from her male counterparts in the division. In many cases the treatment was, in our opinion, unwarranted.

10. The remaining barriers included no promotion, not getting to do the job they want to do, deployment is too long, difficult to get anything done in the UN, the workday/week is too long, corruption in the UN, bad behavior by UN peacekeepers, and no respect among Liberians. All of these potential answers were taken from suggestions by female peacekeepers in initial focus groups.

11. The initiative happened while Sabrina was present in Liberia and observed the entire process.

12. See Beber et al. (2017) for a comprehensive overview of the survey.

13. Specifically, the questions were "When was the last time you socialized with UNMIL PKO personnel?" and then, if the respondent had had some amount of social interaction, "was this a male or a female peacekeeper?"

14. Specifically, the question was "has the presence of UNMIL increased your own personal security? (agree, disagree)."
15. Full regression tables are in appendix 3.
16. The data for this study are used in chapter 7, where they are described more in detail.
17. See Karim (2016b) for full regression analysis.
18. It is possible that in the Monrovia sample, individuals had contact with both male and female peacekeepers and this is not reported. Nevertheless, 73 percent of the sample stated that they had never had contact with a peacekeeper.
19. These findings are statistically significant for police service but not for military service.
20. Most female respondents stated they would like to join the military and police because "it is a personal sacrifice to my country" and to "gain respect."

CHAPTER 7

1. The UN secretary-general, in 2008 report, referred to SSR as "a process of assessment, review and implementation as well as monitoring and evaluation of the security sector, led by national authorities, and that has as its goal the enhancement of effective and accountable security for the State and its peoples, without discrimination and with full respect of human rights and the rule of law" (see UN, 2008: 3). It is generally accepted that the security sector includes defense, law enforcement, corrections, intelligence services, and institutions responsible for border management, customs, and civil emergencies. Elements of the judicial sector responsible for the adjudication of cases of alleged criminal conduct and misuse of force are in many instances also included. Furthermore, the security sector includes actors who play a role in managing and overseeing the design and implementation of security, such as ministries, legislative bodies, and civil society groups. Other nonstate actors who could be considered part of the security sector include customary or informal authorities and private security services. See UN website "Security Sector Reform," https://unssr.unlb.org/ (accessed September 11, 2016).
2. See Karim, Gilligan, Blair, and Beardsley (2016) for an account of the full study.
3. We also recognize the neoliberal and neocolonial critiques about gender and development by such authors as Mohanty (1988), Mohanty, Russo, and Torres (1991), Chant (2008, 2012), Chant and Sweetman (2012), and Sylvester (2012), among others. Our interest is not to provide a critique similar to these authors, but rather to assess the implications of these reforms.
4. See Basini and Ryan (2016).
5. See the documentary *Pray the Devil Back to Hell*.
6. The UN's work on these issues can be found at the UN DPKO's website on security sector reform http://www.un.org/en/peacekeeping/issues/security.shtml (accessed September 11, 2016).
7. See Friedman (2011).
8. See Friedman (2011).
9. The requirements included good standing in the community, a high school diploma, physical fitness, no record of war crimes, and basic arithmetic and written skills (based on testing).
10. See Friedman (2011) for other reforms.
11. Again, we note that the focus on gender was not solely or even mainly due to the peacekeeping mission. As an extension of the Liberian women's peace movement, groups of female government officials and female civil society leaders addressed donors at the World Bank and called for penal reform that discriminated between gender and age, training for security forces to include trauma counseling, anticorruption measures that would target requests for sex and not just money, the use of women as full partners in creating security sector strategy, the increased involvement of women in the security sector at large, and the hiring of gender experts in the Governance Reform Commission (responsible for SSR). Some of these

received attention (Bastick, 2008; Geneva Centre for the Democratic Control of Armed Forces, 2011).

12. The UN International Research and Training Institute also had an important role in the NAP process. See also UNSCR 1509 (2003).

13. Liberia launched its NAP in March 2009.

14. See Republic of Liberia (2009: 7).

15. Though Basini (2013) provides a critique of the reintegration aspect of the DDR for women.

16. See also Nagelhus and Carvalho (2010).

17. For more on the role of UNMIL's influence on the LNP see Karim and Gorman (2016) and Bacon (2012). See also Nduka-Agwu (2009).

18. For an in-depth case study of the implementations of gender reforms in the LNP, see Bacon (2012).

19. In July 2010, the United Nations General Assembly created UN Women, the United Nations Entity for Gender Equality and the Empowerment of Women. The creation of UN Women came about as part of the UN reform agenda, bringing together resources and mandates for greater impact. It merged the following agencies: Division for the Advancement of Women (DAW); International Research and Training Institute for the Advancement of Women (INSTRAW); Office of the Special Adviser on Gender Issues and Advancement of Women (OSAGI); and United Nations Development Fund for Women (UNIFEM).

20. The Women and Children Protection Unit used the Sierra Leone model of "Family Support Units."

21. See also Karim (2016b).

22. This idea is supported cross-nationally in Huber and Karim (2016).

23. See also Karim and Gorman (2016).

24. See appendix 4 for coefficient tables.

25. See Dovidio, Brown, Heltman, and Keating (1988) for a similar finding in a different context.

26. These might include various domestic disputes within households, disputes between neighbors, or disputes between members of different communities (intercommunity disputes).

27. See p. 35.

28. See Bastick, Grimm, and Kunz (2007: 14).

29. See p. 42.

30. This paragraph was included in the Liberia profile that Sabrina Karim, Pamela Scully, and Erin Bernstein wrote for the website of the Women Under Siege Project, (http://www.womenundersiegeproject.org/).

31. See Cibelli, Hoover, and Krüger (2009).

32. See the Liberia Demographic and Health Survey for 2007 (conducted by the Liberia Institute of Statistics and Geo-Information Services, the Ministry of Health and Social Welfare, and the National AIDS Control Program, available at the website of http://dhsprogram.com/pubs/pdf/FR201/FR201.pdf [accessed August 25, 2014]); Liberia Institute of Statistics and Geo-Information Services (LISGIS) [Liberia] and Macro International, 2008.

33. See Sivakumaran (2010).

34. Liberia is split up into regional counties much like the United States is divided by states.

35. For details on this survey, see Karim (2016a).

36. This study was commissioned by the Swedish Police (Bilateral Program) in Liberia to better understand the nature of local security provision by the Liberia National Police (LNP), to better understand the general public's perceptions and attitudes towards the police in their communities, and to substantiate the need for input on necessities and opportunity for security sector reform.

37. In 2014, there were only nineteen police officers in all of Grand Kru County.

38. See Karim (2014).
39. For a detailed description of this survey, see Karim (2014).
40. These included AFL, police, UNMIL, religious leader, Liberian NGO, international NGO, women's group, council of elders, judicial system, township commissioner/community watch, other. These options are based on focus group answers about where people seek protection.
41. We recognize that rape is only one form of SGBV (Cohen, 2016).
42. Tables of the survey results can be found in appendix 4.
43. We used cognitive questions, memory questions, and crime scene questions to create a latent competency score. We asked an UNMIL Police peacekeeper to postcode the crime scene questions based on the training the LNP receive in their academy. Crimes that matched a statutory crime were coded as correct. When the evidence matched the crime, each piece was coded as correct. If they correctly listed the immediate action on arrival (per their training), it was coded as correct. Correct answers were always coded as a 1, ensuring that the direction of the scale remained consistent. The specific latent scale model can be found in appendix 4. In the models with this index, we drop the cognitive score as a control variable because the cognitive tests are built into the index.
44. The coefficient tables can be found in appendix 4.
45. The NGO program sought to strengthen the economic recovery of host communities via the provision of agricultural tools and training. It selected communities using multiple criteria: (high) experience hosting refugees, high to moderate levels of poverty, and previous exposure to NGOs.
46. The counties are spread out, and the capital city, Monrovia, where the previous survey was conducted, is not included in this sample.
47. See appendix 4 for coefficient tables.
48. A randomized controlled trial is a study in which subjects are allocated at random (by chance alone) to receive an intervention. One of these interventions is the standard of comparison or control group. Outcomes are then compared between the "treated" group and the control group. For more information on field experiments, see Gerber and Green (2012).
49. Appendix 4 provides the coefficient tables.

CHAPTER 8

1. Of course there are feminist critiques of this point as being postcolonial. See Jabri (1996) and Young (2007).
2. Some scholars see the move toward cosmopolitanism and peace-building masculinities in national militaries as evidence of feminization (Van Crevald, 2001, 2008: 395–401) suggests that such a move is working to break down gendered power asymmetries. There may be a backlash by some against this change, a point to which we return in the conclusion.
3. See Sylvester (1994: 96).
4. See website of Promundo "About Us." http://promundoglobal.org/about/ (accessed September 11, 2016).
5. See Duncanson (2013).
6. See Hooper (1998).
7. See World Bank website, "Mainstreaming Initiatives to Tackle Gender-Based Violence," April 14, 2014, http://www.worldbank.org/en/results/2014/04/14/mainstreaming-initiatives-to-tackle-gender-based-violence (accessed January 9, 2016).
8. See, for example, Wynes and Zahran (2011).
9. In the United States, we might say that the opposite is occurring—police forces are becoming more militarized and many recruits into the police forces are veterans of the military (Balko, 2013).

10. Such awards stand in stark contract to punishments that some peacekeepers have faced after being whistleblowers about SEAHV (Bolkovac and Lynn, 2011).
11. And if she had not faced a hostile work atmosphere by her male colleagues.
12. For training best practices, the Nordic Centre for Gender in Military Operations serves as a useful model.
13. See also King (2013).
14. See also Ben-Shalom, Lehrer, and Ben-Ari (2005).
15. For example, see the UN website "Allowances and Benefits," http://www.un.org/Depts/OHRM/salaries_allowances/allowanc.htm (accessed February 20, 2014).
16. See Karim and Gorman (2016).
17. Peacekeepers in UNMIL did not mention this particular challenge, perhaps due to the fact that they were working in an English-speaking country.
18. See Military Leadership Diversity Commission (2011).
19. See, for example, Mazurana, Raven-Roberts, and Parpart (2005).
20. See UN (2001).
21. Currently, there are not enough staff, funding, and resources for gender mainstreaming (UN Women, 2015).
22. See UN (2010c).
23. For example, see UN (2010c: 15–17, 26–28, 36–28).
24. These are also suggested by the High-Level Report (UN, 2015).
25. There is a long history of debate based on this trade-off. See Carreiras (2006: 86–96).
26. See Kronsell (2012).

REFERENCES

Acharya, Amitav. (2004). How ideas spread: Whose norms matter? Norm localization and institutional change in Asian regionalism. *International Organization,* 58(2): 239–275.

Acker, Joan. (1991). Hierarchies, jobs, bodies: A theory of gendered organizations. In *The social construction of gender*, ed. Judith Lorber and Susan A. Farrell, 162–179. London: Sage.

Adebajo, Adekeje. (2013). *UN peacekeeping in Africa: From the Suez crisis to the Sudan conflicts*. Boulder, CO: Lynne Rienner.

Aguayo, Francisco, Eduardo Kimelman, Pamela Saavedra, and Jane Kato-Wallace. (2016). *Engaging men in public policies for the prevention of violence against women and girls. Santiago: EME/CulturaSalud*. Washington, D.C.: Promundo-US. Panama City: UN Women and UNFPA.

Allred, Keith J. (2006). Peacekeepers and Prostitutes: How Deployed Forces Fuel the Demand for Trafficked Women and New Hope for Stopping It. *Armed Forces & Society,* 33(1): 5–23.

Anderholt, Charlotte. (2012, September). *Female participation in formed police units: A report on the integration of women in formed police units of peacekeeping operations*. PKSOI Papers, Army War College, Carlisle, PA. https://www.pksoi.org/document_repository/doc_lib/PKSOI_Paper_Females_in_Formed_Police_Units_(13-Sep-2012).pdf (accessed March 20, 2013).

Anderlini, Sanam. (2007). Women building peace: What they do, why it matters. Boulder, CO: Lynne Rienner.

Andersen, Hanne. (2014, January 15). *Report: Survey for PSU female officers*. Monrovia, Liberia: UNMIL.

Arat, Zehra F. (2015). Feminisms, women's rights, and the UN: Would achieving gender equality empower women? *American Political Science Review*, 109(4): 674–689.

Asken, Michael J., Loren W. Christensen, and Dave Grossman. (2010). *Warrior mindset: Mental toughness skills for a nation's defenders: Performance psychology applied to combat*. Millstadt, IL: Human Factor Research Group.

Atwood, Katherine A., Stephen B. Kennedy, Ernlee M. Barbu, Wede Nagbe, Wede Seekey, Prince Sirleaf, Oretha Perry, Roland B. Martin, and Fred Sosu. (2011). Transactional sex among youths in post-conflict Liberia. *Journal of Health, Population, and Nutrition*, 29(2): 113.

Baaz, Maria Eriksson, and Mats Utas. (2012). *Beyond gender and stir*. Policy Dialogues no. 9. Uppsala, Sweden: Nordic Africa Institute.

Bacon, Laura. (2012). *Building an inclusive, responsive national police service: Gender sensitive reforms in Liberia 2005–2011*. Innovations for Successful Society, Princeton University. http://www.princeton.edu/successfulsocieties (accessed November 16, 2016).

Balko, Radley. (2013). *Rise of the warrior cop: The militarization of America's police forces*. New York: PublicAffairs.

Barth, E. (2004). The United Nations mission in Eritrea/Ethiopia: Gender(ed) effects. In *Gender aspects of conflict interventions: Intended and unintended consequences*, ed. L. Olsson, I. Skejlebaek, E. Barth, and K. Hostens, 9–24. Oslo: International Peace Research Institute.

Banaszak, Lee Ann. (2003). *Women's movements facing the reconfigured state*. New York: Cambridge University Press.

Basini, Helen. (2013). Gender mainstreaming unraveled: The case of DDRR in Liberia. *International Interactions*, 39(4): 535–557.

Basini, Helen, and Caitlin Ryan. (2016). National Action Plans as an obstacle to meaningful local ownership of UNSCR 1325 in Liberia and Sierra Leone. *International Political Science Review*, 37(3): 390–403.

Bastick, Megan. (2008). *Integrating gender in post-conflict security sector reform*. Geneva: Geneva Centre for the Democratic Control of Armed Forces. http://dspace. cigilibrary.org/jspui/bitstream/123456789/27847/1/IntegratingGender in Post-ConflictSecuritySectorReform.pdf?1 (accessed October 30, 2013).

Bastick, Megan, Karin Grimm, and Rahel Kunz. (2007). *Sexual Violence In armed conflict: Global overview and implications for the security sector*. DCAF. http://www.essex. ac.uk/armedcon/story_id/sexualviolence_conflict_full%5B1%5D.pdf (accessed August 25, 2014)

Basu, Monu. (2010, March 2). Indian women peacekeepers hailed in Liberia. *CNN*, http:// www.cnn.com/2010/WORLD/africa/03/02/liberia.women/index.html (accessed August 14, 2014).

Beardsley, Kyle. (2011). Peacekeeping and the contagion of armed conflict. *Journal of Politics*, 73(4): 1051–1064.

Beardsley, Kyle, and Holger Schmidt. (2012). Following the flag or following the charter? Examining the determinants of UN involvement in international crises, 1945–2002. *International Studies Quarterly*, 56(1): 33–49.

Beber, Bernd, Michael Gilligan, Jenny Guardado Rodriguez, and Sabrina Karim. (2017). Peacekeeping, international norms, and transactional sex in Monrovia, Liberia. *International Organization* (Forthcoming).

Bellamy, Alex J., and Paul D. Williams. (2013). *Providing peacekeepers: The politics, challenges, and future of United Nations peacekeeping contributions*. Oxford: Oxford University Press.

Bellamy, Alex J., Paul Williams, and Stuart Griffin. (2010). *Understanding peacekeeping*. 2nd ed. Cambridge: Polity.

Beckwith, Karen, and Kimberly Cowell-Meyers. (2007). Sheer numbers: Critical representation thresholds and women's political representation. *Perspectives on Politics*, 5(3): 553–565.

Benedict, Helen. (2009). *The lonely soldier: The private war of women*. Boston: Beacon Press.

Ben-Shalom, U., Z. Lehrer, and E. Ben-Ari. (2005). Cohesion during military operations: A field study on combat units in the Al-Aqsa Intifada. *Armed Forces & Society*, 32(1): 63–79.

Bertolazzi, Francesco. (2010). Women with a blue helmet the integration of women and gender issues in UN peacekeeping missions. United Nations International Research and Training Institute for the Advancement of Women (UN-INSTRAW), Santo Domingo, Dominican Republic. http://www.peacewomen.org/assets/file/Resources/ UN/unbalpk_integrationwomengenderunpeacekeeping_instraw_aug_2010.pdf (accessed February 2, 2014).

Bhavnani, Rikhil R. (2009). Do electoral quotas work after they are withdrawn? Evidence from a natural experiment in India. *American Political Science Review*, 103(1): 23–35.

Bjarnegård, Elin, and Erik Melander. (2011). Disentangling gender, peace and democratization: The negative effects of militarized masculinity. *Journal of Gender Studies*, 20(2): 139–154.

Blair, Robert. (2015). *Four essays on peacebuilding and the consolidation of state authority*. Ph.D. dissertation, Yale University.

Boix, Carles. 2015. *Political order and inequality*. Cambridge: Cambridge University Press.

Bolkovac, Kathryn, and Cari Lynn. (2011). *The whistleblower: Sex trafficking, military contractors, and one woman's fight for justice*. New York: Palgrave Macmillan.

Boulding, E. (1995). Feminist inventions in the art of peacemaking. *Peace and Change* 20: 408–438.

Bove, Vincenzo, and Leandro Elia. (2011). Supplying peace: Participation in and troop contribution to peacekeeping missions. *Journal of Peace Research,* 48(6): 699 –714.

Boyce, Lisa A., and Ann M. Herd. (2003). The relationship between gender role stereotypes and requisite military leadership characteristics. *Sex Roles,* 49(7–8): 365–378.

Bratton, Kathleen A. (2005). Critical mass theory revisited: The behavior and success of token women in state legislatures. *Politics & Gender,* 1(1): 97–125.

Bridges, Donna, and Debbie Horsfall. (2009). Increasing operational effectiveness in UN peacekeeping. *Armed Forces & Society,* 36(1): 120.

Britton, Dana. (2000). The epistemology of gendered organizations. *Gender & Society,* 14(3): 418–434.

Burguieres, M. K. (1990). Feminist approaches to peace: Another step for peace studies. *Millennium,* 19:1–18.

Bush, Sarah Sunn. (2011). International politics and the spread of quotas for women in legislatures. *International Organization,* 65(1): 103–137.

Byrnes, James P., David C. Miller, and William D. Schafer. (1999). Gender differences in risk taking: A meta-analysis. *Psychological Bulletin,* 125(3): 367–83.

Campbell, J. C., M. A. Garza, A. C. Gielen, P. O'campo, J. Kub, J. Dienemann, and E. Jafar. (2003). Intimate partner violence and abuse among active duty military women. *Violence against Women,* 9(9): 1072–1092.

Caprioli, Mary. (2000). Gendered conflict. *Journal of Peace Research,* 37(1): 51–68.

Caprioli, Mary. (2003). Gender equality and state aggression: The impact of domestic gender equality on state first use of force. *International Interactions,* 29(3): 195–214.

Caprioli, Mary. (2005). Primed for violence: The role of gender inequality in predicting internal conflict. *International Studies Quarterly,* 49(2): 161–178.

Caprioli, Mary, and Mark A. Boyer. (2001). Gender, violence, and international crisis. *Journal of Conflict Resolution,* 45(4): 503–518.

Caprioli, Mary, Valerie M. Hudson, Rose Mcdermott, Bonnie Ballif-Spanvill, Chad F. Emmett, and S. Matthew Stearmer. (2009). The WomanStats project database: Advancing an empirical research agenda. *Journal of Peace Research,* 46(6): 839–851.

Carey, Henry F. (2001). Women, peacekeepers, and security: The politics of implementing gender sensitivity norms in peacekeeping. In *Women and international peacekeeping,* ed. Louise Olsson and Torunn L. Tryggestad, 49–68. Psychology Press.

Carpenter, R. Charli. (2003). "Women and children first": Gender, norms, and humanitarian evacuation in the Balkans 1991–95. *International Organization,* 57(4): 661–694.

Carpenter, R. Charli. (2005). "Women, children and other vulnerable groups": Gender, strategic frames and the protection of civilians as a transnational issue. *International Studies Quarterly,* 49(2): 295–334.

Carpenter, R. Charli. (2006a). *Innocent women and children: Gender, norms and the protection of civilians.* London: Ashgate.

Carpenter, R. Charli. (2006b). Recognizing gender-based violence against civilian men and boys in conflict zones. *Security Dialogue,* 27(1): 83–103.

Carreiras, Helena. (2006). *Gender and the military: Women in the armed forces of Western democracies.* London: Routledge.

Carreiras, Helena. (2010). Gendered culture in peacekeeping operations. *International Peacekeeping,* 17(4), 471–485.

Center for Action, Research, and Training (CART). (2016). *Public perceptions of security and policing in Monrovia, Liberia. Major survey findings.* Monrovia: Liberia.

Chant, Sylvia. (2008). The "feminisation of poverty" and the "feminisation" of anti-poverty programmes: Room for revision? *Journal of Development Studies,* 44(2): 165–197.

Chant, Sylvia. (2012). The disappearing of "smart economics"? The World Development Report 2012 on gender equality: Some concerns about the preparatory process and the prospects for paradigm change. *Global Social Policy*, 12(2): 198–218.

Chant, Sylvia, and Caroline Sweetman. (2012). Fixing women or fixing the world? "Smart economics," efficiency approaches, and gender equality in development. *Gender & Development*, 20(3): 517–529.

Chappell, Louise. (2010). Comparative gender and institutions: Directions for research. *Perspectives on Politics*, 8(1): 183-189.

Chen, Li-Ju. (2010). Do gender quotas influence women's representation and policies? *European Journal of Comparative Economics*, 7(1): 13–60.

Childs, Sarah, and Mona Lena Krook. (2006). Should feminists give up on critical mass? A contingent yes. *Politics & Gender*, 2(4): 522–530.

Chrisler, Joan C., and Donald R. McCreary, eds. (2010). *Handbook of gender research in psychology*. New York: Springer-Verlag.

Cibelli, Kristen, Amelia Hoover, and Jule Krüger. (2009). Descriptive statistics from statements to the Liberian Truth and Reconciliation Commission. Benetech. http://trcofliberia.org/resources/reports/final/descriptive-statistics-from-statements-to-the-liberian-trc-benetech.pdf (accessed August 25, 2013).

Ciment, James. (2013). *Another America: The story of Liberia and the former slaves who ruled it*. New York: Hill and Wang.

Cockburn, Cynthia. (2010). Gender relations as causal in militarization and war. *International Feminist Journal of Politics*, 12(2): 139–157.

Cockburn, Cynthia, and Meliha Hubic. (2002). Gender and the peacekeeping military: A view from Bosnian women's organizations. In *The postwar moment: Militaries, masculinities and international peacekeeping*, ed. Cynthia Cockburn and Dubravka Zarkov,. London: Lawrence and Wishart.

Cohen, Dara Kay. (2013). Explaining rape during civil war: Cross-national evidence (1980–2009). *American Political Science Review*, 107(3): 461–477.

Cohen, Dara Kay. (2016). *Rape during civil war*. Ithaca: Cornell University Press.

Cohen, Dara Kay, and Amelia Hoover Green. (2012). Dueling incentives: Sexual violence in Liberia and the politics of human rights advocacy. *Journal of Peace Research*, 49(3): 445–458.

Cohen, Dara Kay, Amelia Hoover Green, and Elisabeth Jean Wood. (2013, February). Wartime sexual violence: Misconceptions, implications, and ways forward. United States Institute of Peace.

Cohen, Dara Kay, and Ragnhild Nordås. (2014). Sexual violence in armed conflict: Introducing the SVAC dataset, 1989–2009. *Journal of Peace Research*, 51(3): 418–428.

Cohen, Dara Kay, and Ragnhild Nordås. (2015). Do states delegate shameful violence to militias? Patterns of sexual violence in recent armed conflicts. *Journal of Conflict Resolution*, 59(5): 877–898.

Cohn, Carol. (1987). Sex and death in the rational world of defense intellectuals. *Signs*, 12(4): 687–718.

Cohn, Carol. (1999). Wars, wimps, and women: Talking gender and thinking war. In *Gendering war talk*, ed. Miriam Cooke and Angela Woollacott, 227–246. Princeton, NJ: Princeton University Press.

Cohn, Carol. (2000). "How can she claim equal rights when she doesn't have to do as many push-ups as I do?" The framing of men's opposition to women's equality in the military. *Men and Masculinities*, 3(2): 131–151.

Cohn, Carol. (2008). Mainstreaming gender in UN security policy: A path to political transformation? In *Global governance: Feminist perspectives*, ed. Shirin M. Rai and Georgina Waylen, 185–206. Basingstoke: Palgrave Macmillan.

Cohn, Carol. (2013). *Women and wars*. Cambridge: Polity Press.

Cohn, Carol, Helen Kinsella, and Sheri Gibbings. (2004). Women, peace and Security Resolution 1325. *International Feminist Journal of Politics*, 6(1): 130–140.

Connell, Raewyn. (2005). *Masculinities*. Berkeley: University of California Press.

Connell, Robert. (1987). *Gender and power: Society, the person, and sexual politics*. Stanford, CA: Stanford University Press.

Connell, R. W. (2000a). Arms and the man: Using the new research on masculinities to understand violence and promote peace in the contemporary world. In *Male Roles, masculinities, and violence*, ed. I. Breines, R. W. Connell, and I. Eide, 21–33. Paris: UNESCO.

Connell, R. W. (2000b). The great illusion: Women in the military. *Millennium—Journal of International Studies*, 29(2): 429–442.

Connell, R. W. (2001). *Men, women, and war*. London: Cassell.

Connell, R. W., and James W. Messerschmidt. (2005). Hegemonic masculinity: Rethinking the concept. *Gender and Society*, 19(6): 829–859.

Cordell, Kristen. (2009). Gender-related best practices in peacekeeping operations in Liberia: 2003–2009, Mimeo.

Costain, Anne N. (1992). *Inviting women's rebellion: A political interpretation of the women's movement*. 1st ed. Baltimore: Johns Hopkins University Press.

Crawford, Kerry F., James H. Lebovic, and Julia M. Macdonald. (2015). Explaining the variation in gender composition of personnel contributions to UN peacekeeping operations. *Armed Forces & Society*, 41(2): 257–281

Crenshaw, Kimberle. (1989). Demarginalizing the intersection of race and sex: A black feminist critique of antidiscrimination doctrine, feminist theory and antiracist politics. *University of Chicago Legal Forum*: 139–168

Csaky, Corinna. (2008). *No one to turn to: The under-reporting of child sexual exploitation and abuse by aid workers and peacekeepers*. http://www.un.org/en/pseataskforce/docs/no_one_to_turn_under_reporting_of_child_sea_by_aid_workers.pdf (accessed June 28, 2014).

Dahlerup, Drude, and Lenita Freidenvall. (2005). Quotas as a "fast track" to equal representation for women. *International Feminist Journal of Politics*, 7(1): 26–48.

Dahlerup, Drude. (2006a). The story of the theory of critical mass. *Politics & Gender*, 2(4): 511–522.

Dahlerup, Drude. (2006b). *Women, quotas and politics*. London: Routledge.

Dahlerup, Drude. (2008). Gender quotas—controversial but trendy. *International Feminist Journal of Politics*, 10(3): 322–28.

Dai, Xinyuan. (2005). Why comply? The domestic constituency mechanism. *International Organization*, 59(2): 363–398.

D'Amico, Francine J., and Laurie L. Weinstein. (1999). *Gender camouflage: Women and the U.S. military*. New York: New York University Press.

Day, Tanis, Katherine McKenna, and Audra Bowlus. (2005). *The economic costs of violence against women: An evaluation of the literature expert brief compiled in preparation for the secretary-general's in-depth study on all forms of violence against women*. United Nations. http://www.un.org/womenwatch/daw/vaw/expert%20brief%20costs.pdf (accessed September 15, 2016).

DeGroot, Gerard J. (2001). A few good women: Gender stereotypes, the military and peacekeeping. *International Peacekeeping*, 8(2): 23–38.

Detraz, Nicole. (2012). *International security and gender*. Cambridge: Polity.

Dharmapuri, Sahana. (2012). *Not just a numbers game: Providing for peacekeeping no. 4*. New York: International Peace Institute.

Diehl, Paul F., and Daniel Druckman. (2010). *Evaluating peace operations*. Boulder, CO: Lynne Rienner.

DiTomaso, Nancu. (1989). Sexuality in the workplace: Discrimination and Harassment. In *The sexuality of organization*, ed. Jeff Hearn, Deborah L. Sheppard, Peter Tancred, and Gibson Burrell, 71–90. Newbury Park, CA: Sage.

Dovidio, John F. Clifford Brown, Karen Heltman, and Caroline Keating. (1988). Power displays between women and men in discussions of gender-linked tasks: A multichannel study. *Journal of Personality and Social Psychology*, 55(4): 580–587.

Doyle, Michael W., and Nicholas Sambanis. (2006). *Making war and building peace: United Nations peace operations*. Princeton, NJ: Princeton University Press.

Duncanson, Claire. (2013). *Forces for good? military masculinities and peacebuilding in Afghanistan and Iraq*. London: Palgrave Macmillan.

Dunkle, Kristin L., R. K. Jewkes, M. Nduna, J. Levin, N. Jama, N. Khuzwayo, M. P. Koss, and N. Duvvury. (2006). Perpetration of partner violence and HIV risk behaviour among young men in the rural Eastern Cape, South Africa. *AIDS*, 20(16): 2107–2114.

Easlea, Brian. (1983). *Fathering the unthinkable: Masculinity, scientists, and the nuclear arms race*. London: Pluto Press.

Egnell, Robert, Petter Hojem, and Hannes Berts. (2014). *Gender, military effectiveness, and organizational change: The Swedish model*. London: Palgrave Macmillan.

Ellerby, Kara. (2017). *The problem with gender equality: The politics of women's inclusion*. New York: New York University Press. (Forthcoming).

Ellison, Jesse. (2011, April 3). The military's secret shame. *Newsweek*.

Elshtain, Jean Bethke. (1995). *Women and war, with a new epilogue*. 1st ed. Chicago: University of Chicago Press.

Enloe, Cynthia H. (1983). *Does khaki become you?* London: Pluto Press.

Enloe, Cynthia H. (1990). *Bananas, beaches and bases: Making feminist sense of international politics*. Berkeley: University of California Press.

Enloe, Cynthia H. (2000). *Maneuvers: The international politics of militarizing women's lives*. 1st ed. Berkeley: University of California Press.

Enloe, Cynthia H. (2004). *The curious feminist searching for women in a new age of empire*. Berkeley: University of California Press.

Enloe, Cynthia H. (2007). *Globalization and militarism: Feminists make the link*. Rowman and Littlefield.

Enloe, Cynthia H. (2010). *Nimo's, Emma's war: Making feminist sense of the Iraq War*. 1st ed. Berkeley: University of California Press.

Erwin, Stephanie K. (2012). *The veil of kevlar: An analysis of the female engagement teams in Afghanistan*. Masters thesis, Naval Postgraduate School, Department of National Security Affairs, Monterey, CA.

Febbraro, Angela R., and Carol McCann. (2003). Demystifying the "feminine mythtique": Or, women and combat can mix. *Marine Corps Gazette*, 87(3): 1–5.

Fenner, Lorry, and Marie deYoung. (2001). *Women in combat: Civic duty or military liability?* Washington, DC: Georgetown University Press.

Finnemore, Martha, and Kathryn Sikkink. (1998). International norm dynamics and political change. *International Organization*, 52 (autumn): 887–917.

Fortna, Virginia Page. (2008). *Does peacekeeping work? Shaping belligerents' choices after civil war*. Princeton, NJ: Princeton University Press.

Fox, Mary Jane. (2001). The idea of women in peacekeeping: Lysistrata and Antigone. In *Women and international peacekeeping*, ed. Louise Olsson and Torunn L. Tryggestad, 9–22. London: Frank Cass Publishers.

Fox, Richard, and Jennifer Lawless. (2005). *It still takes a candidate: Why women don't run for office*. Cambridge: Cambridge University Press.

Franceschet, Susan, Mona Lena Krook, and Jennifer M. Piscopo, eds. (2012). *The impact of gender quotas*. Oxford: Oxford University Press.

Fréchette, Louise. (2012, April). *UN peacekeeping: 20 years of reform*. Ontario: Center for International Governance Innovation.

Frerichs, Ralph R., Paul S. Keim, Robert Barrais, and Renaud Piarroux. (2012). Nepalese origin of cholera epidemic in Haiti. *Clinical Microbiology and Infection*, 18(6): 158–163.

Friedman, Jonathan. (2011). *Building a civilian police capacity in post-conflict Liberia 2003–2011*. Innovations for Successful Societies. Princeton, NJ: Princeton University. http://successfulsocieties.princeton.edu/publications/building-civilian-police-capacity-post-conflict-liberia-2003-2011 (accessed September 15, 2016).

Fukuyama, Francis. (1998). Women and the evolution of world politics. *Foreign Affairs,* 77(5): 24–40.

Gardiner, Nile. 2005. The U.N. Peacekeeping Scandal in the Congo: How Congress Should Respond. The Heritage Foundation. http://www.heritage.org/research/lecture/the-un-peacekeeping-scandal-in-thecongo-how-congress-should-respond (accessed January 12, 2015).

Gartner, Scott Sigmund. (2008). Secondary casualty information: Casualty uncertainty, female casualties, and wartime support. *Conflict Management and Peace Science,* 25(2): 98–111.

Gates, Philippa. (2006). *Detecting men: Masculinity and the Hollywood detective film.* Albany: State University of New York Press.

Geneva Centre for the Democratic Control of Armed Forces. (2011). *Gender and security sector reform: Examples from the group.* http://www.dcaf.ch/Publications/Gender-and-Security-Sector-Reform-Examples-from-the-Ground (accessed September 22, 2012).

Gerber, Alan S., and Donald P. Green. (2012). *Field experiments: Design, analysis, and interpretation.* New York: WW Norton.

Gilligan, Michael J., and Ernest J. Sergenti. (2008). Do UN interventions cause peace? Using matching to improve causal inference. *Quarterly Journal of Political Science,* 3(2): 89–122.

Gilligan, Michael, and Stephen John Stedman. (2003). Where do the peacekeepers go? *International Studies Review,* 5(4): 37–54.

Gizelis, Theodora-Ismene. (2009). Gender empowerment and United Nations peacebuilding. *Journal of Peace Research,* 46(4): 505–523.

Gizelis, Theodora-Ismene. (2011). A country of their own: Women and peacebuilding. *Conflict Management and Peace Science,* 28(5): 522–542.

Goldstein, Joshua S. (2003). *War and gender: How gender shapes the war system and vice versa.* Cambridge: Cambridge University Press.

Grady, Kate. (2010). Sexual exploitation and abuse by UN peacekeepers: A threat to impartiality. *International Peacekeeping,* 17(2): 215–228.

Greener, B. K. (2009). UNPOL: UN police as peacekeepers. *Policing and Society,* 19(2): 106–118.

Grey, Sandra. (2006). Numbers and beyond: The relevance of critical mass in gender research. *Politics & Gender,* 2(4): 492–502.

Griffith, James. (2007). Further considerations concerning the cohesion-performance relation in military settings. *Armed Forces & Society* 34(1): 138–147.

Gruber, James E. (1998). The impact of male work environments and organizational policies on women's experiences of sexual harassment. *Gender & Society,* 12(3): 301–320.

Gutmann, Stephanie. (2013, January 24). Women in combat: The devil's in the details. *National Review.* http://www.nationalreview.com/corner/338699/women-combat-devils-details-stephanie-gutmann (accessed September 25, 2013).

Hafner-Burton, Emilie M. (2008). Sticks and stones: Naming and shaming the human rights enforcement problem. *International Organization,* 62(4): 689–716.

Hafner-Burton, Emilie M., and Kiyoteru Tsutsui. (2005). Human Rights in a globalizing world: The paradox of empty promises. *American Journal of Sociology,* 110(5): 1373–1411.

Hafner-Burton, Emilie M., Kiyoteru Tsutsui, and John W. Meyer. (2008). International human rights law and the politics of legitimation: Repressive states and human rights treaties. *International Sociology,* 23(1): 115–141.

Hall, Peter A., and Rosemary Taylor. (1996). Political science and the three new institutionalisms. *Political Studies,* 44(5): 936–957.

Hancock, Ange-Marie. (2007). When multiplication doesn't equal quick addition: Examining intersectionality as a research paradigm. *Perspectives on Politics,* 5(1): 63–79.

Harris, Mary B., and Kari C. Miller. (2000). Gender and perceptions of danger. *Sex Roles,* 43(11–12): 843–863.

Harrison, Deborah. (2002). *The first casualty: Violence against women in Canadian military communities.* Toronto: Lorimer.

Harrison, Deborah, and Lucie Laliberte. (1994). *No life like it: Military wives in Canada.* Toronto: Lorimer.

Hartz, H. (1999). CIVPOL: The UN instrument for police reform. *International Peacekeeping,* 6(4): 27–42.

Hathaway, Oona A. (2007). Why do countries commit to human rights treaties? *Journal of Conflict Resolution,* 51(4): 588–621.

Hawkesworth, Mary. (2003). Congressional enactments of race-gender: Toward a theory of raced-gendered institutions. *American Political Science Review* 97(4): 529–550.

Henry, Marsha. (2012). Peacexploitation? Interrogating labor hierarchies and global sisterhood among Indian and Uruguayan female peacekeepers. *Globalizations,* 9(1): 15–33.

Herbert, Melissa S. (2001). *Camouflage isn't only for combat: Gender, sexuality, and women in the military.* New York: New York University Press.

Herbert, Steve. (2001). "Hard charger" or "station queen"? Policing and the masculinist state. *Gender, Place & Culture,* 8(1): 55–71.

Herrnson, P. S., J. C. Lay, and A. K. Stokes. (2003). Women running "as women": Candidate gender, campaign issues, and voter-targeting strategies. *Journal of Politics,* 65(1): 244–255.

Higate, Paul. (2003). *Military masculinities: Identity and the state.* Westport, CT: Praeger.

Higate, Paul. (2004). *Gender and peacekeeping. Case studies: The Democratic Republic of the Congo and Sierra Leone.* ISS Monograph Series 91. Pretoria: Institute for Security Studies.

Higate, Paul. (2007). Peacekeepers, masculinities and sexual exploitation. *Men and Masculinities,* 10(1): 99–119.

Higate, Paul, and Marsha Henry. (2004). Engendering (in)security in peace support to operations. *Security Dialogue,* 35(4): 481–498.

Higate, Paul, and Marsha Henry. (2009). *Insecure spaces: Peacekeeping, power and performance in Haiti, Kosovo and Liberia.* New York: Zed Books.

Hoffman, Peter B., and Edward R. Hickey. (2005). Use of force by female police officers. *Journal of Criminal Justice,* 33(2): 145–151.

Hooper, C. (1998). Masculinist practices and gender politics: The operation of multiple masculinities in international relations. In *The Man Question in International Relations,* ed. M. Zalewski and J. Parpart, 28–53. Boulder, CO: Westview Press.

Hossain, Mazeda, Cathy Zimmerman, Melanie Abas, Miriam Light, and Charlotte Watts. (2010). The relationship of trauma to mental disorders among trafficked and sexually exploited girls and women. *American Journal of Public Health,* 100(12): 2442–2449.

Howard, Lise Morjé. (2008). *UN peacekeeping in civil wars.* 1st ed. Cambridge: Cambridge University Press.

Htun, M., and S. L. Weldon. (2012). The civic origins of progressive policy change: Combating violence against women in global perspective, 1975–2005. *American Political Science Review,* 1(1): 1–22.

Huber, Laura, and Sabrina Karim. (2016). *The Internationalization of Security Sector Gender Reform in Post-Conflict Countries.* Working Paper. Atlanta: Emory University.

Hudson, Valerie M., Bonnie Ballif-Spanvill, Mary Caprioli, and Chad F. Emmett. (2012). *Sex and world peace.* New York: Columbia University Press.

Hudson, Valerie M., and Andrea Den Boer. (2002). A surplus of men, a deficit of peace: Security and sex ratios in Asia's largest states. *International Security,* 26(4): 5–38.

Hudson, V. M., and P. Leidl. (2015). *The Hillary doctrine: Sex and American foreign policy.* New York: Columbia University Press.

Hull, Cecilia, Mikael Eriksson, Justin MacDermott, Fanny Ruden, and Amanda Waleij. (2009). *Managing unintended consequences of peace support operations.* Stockholm: FOI, Swedish Defense Research Agency.

Hultman, Lisa, Jacob Kathman, and Megan Shannon. (2013). United Nations peacekeeping and civilian protection in civil war. *American Journal of Political Science,* 57(4): 875–891.

Hultman, Lisa, Jacob Kathman, and Megan Shannon. (2014). Beyond keeping peace: United Nations effectiveness in the midst of fighting. *American Political Science Review,* 108(4): 737–753.

Hunnicutt, Gwen. (2009). Varieties of patriarchy and violence against women: Resurrecting "patriarchy" as a theoretical tool. *Violence against Women,* 15(5): 553–573.

Hunter, Kyleanne. (2015). Of methodology and men. Political Violence at a Glance, October 6, 2015. http://politicalviolenceataglance.org/2015/10/06/of-methodology-and-men/ (accessed January 21, 2016).

Inayatullah, Naeem, and David L. Blaney. (2004). *International relations and the problem of difference.* New York: Routledge.

International Alert. (2002, July). Gender mainstreaming in peace support operations: Moving beyond rhetoric to practice. http://www.international-alert.org/resources/publications/gender-mainstreaming-peace-support-operations-moving-beyond-rhetoric-practice#sthash.GpZTJmlk.dpbs (accessed November 12, 2016).

Jabri, Vivienne. 1996. *Discourses on violence.* Manchester: Manchester University Press.

Jeffreys, Sheila. (2007, January). Double jeopardy: Women, the US military and the war in Iraq. *Women's Studies International Forum,* 30(1): 16–25.

Jennings, Kathleen. (2008). *Protecting whom? Approaches to sexual exploitation and abuse in UN peacekeeping operations.* Oslo: Fafo Report.

Jennings, Kathleen. (2010). Unintended consequences of intimacy: Political economies of peacekeeping and sex tourism. *International Peacekeeping,* 17(2): 229–243.

Jennings, Kathleen. (2011). *Women's participation in UN peacekeeping operations: Agents of change or stranded symbols?* NOREF Report. Oslo: NOREF.

Jennings, Kathleen, and Vesna Nikolić-Ristanović. (2009). *UN peacekeeping economies and local sex industries: Connections and implications.* MICROCON Research Working Paper No. 17. Brighton, UK: . http://papers.ssrn.com/sol3/papers.cfm?abstract_id=1488842 (accessed November 12, 2016).

Johnson, Kirsten, and Jana Asher. (2008). Association of combatant status and sexual violence with health and mental health outcomes in postconflict Liberia. *Journal of the American Medical Association,* 300(6): 676–690.

Kanetake, Machiko. (2010). Whose zero tolerance counts? Reassessing a zero tolerance policy against sexual exploitation and abuse by UN Peacekeepers. *International Peacekeeping,* 17(2): 200–214.

Kanter, Rosabeth. (1993). *Men and women of the corporation.* New York: Basic Books.

Karamé, Kari H. (2001). Military women in peace operations: Experiences of the Norwegian battalion in UNIFIL 1978–98. *International Peacekeeping,* 8(2): 85–96.

Karim, Sabrina. (2014). *Evaluating the changing of the guards: Survey evidence from Liberia on security sector female ratio balancing policies.* Paper presented at UNSC 1325 Working Group, Folke Bernadotte Academy, London, October 21–22, 2013.

Karim, Sabrina. (2016a). *Finding the right security sector strategy: The Goldilocks problem in post-conflict states.* Ph.D. dissertation, Emory University.

Karim, Sabrina. (2016b). Re-evaluating peacekeeping effectiveness: Does gender neutrality inhibit progress? *International Interactions* (Forthcoming).

Karim, Sabrina, and Kyle Beardsley. (2013). Female peacekeepers and gender balancing: Token gestures or informed policymaking? *International Interactions,* 39(4): 461–488.

Karim, Sabrina, and Kyle Beardsley. (2015). Ladies Last: Peacekeeping and gendered protection. In *A Systematic understanding of gender, peace, and security: Implementing UNSC 1325,* ed. Ismene Gizelis and Louise Olsson, 62–96. Oxford: Routledge.

Karim, Sabrina, and Kyle Beardsley. (2016a). Explaining sexual exploitation and abuse in peacekeeping missions: The role of Female peacekeepers and gender equality in contributing countries. *Journal of Peace Research*, 53(1): 100–115.

Karim, Sabrina, and Kyle Beardsley. (2016b). Women and peacemaking/peacekeeping. In *Oxford Bibliographies in International Relations,* ed. Patrick James. New York: Oxford University Press <http://www.oxfordbibliographies.com/view/document/obo-9780199743292/obo-9780199743292-0146.xml> (accessed November 16, 2016).

Karim, Sabrina, and Ryan Gorman. (2016). Building a more competent security sector: The case of the Liberian National Police. *International Peacekeeping*, 23(1), 158–191.

Karim, Sabrina, Michael Gilligan, Robert Blair, and Kyle Beardsley. (2016). International interventions to empower women in post-conflict countries: Lab-in-the-field evidence from the Liberian National Police, Working Paper.

Koga Sudduth, Jun, and Sabrina Karim. (2015). *Running toward danger: Explaining peacekeeping contributing country decisions to send personnel to difficult cases.* Paper presented at the annual meeting of the American Political Science Association, San Francisco, CA, September 3–6, 2015.

Kathman, Jacob D., and Molly M. Melin. (2014, August). *Who keeps the peace? Understanding state contributions to UN peacekeeping operations.* Paper presented at the annual meeting of the American Political Science Association, Washington, D.C.

Keiser, Lael R., Vicky M. Wilkins, Kenneth J. Meier, and Catherine A. Holland. (2002). Lipstick and logarithms: Gender, institutional context, and representative bureaucracy. *American Political Science Review,* 96(3): 553–564.

Kember, Olivia. (2010). *The impact of the Indian formed police unit in the United Nations Mission in Liberia*. M.A. thesis, Georgetown University.

King, A. (2013). *The combat soldier: Infantry tactics and cohesion in the twentieth and twenty-first centuries*. Oxford: Oxford University Press.

Kirby, Paul, and Marsha Henry. (2012). Rethinking masculinity and practices of violence in conflict settings. *International Feminist Journal of Politics,* 14(4): 445–449.

Klot, J., and P. DeLargy. (2007). Sexual violence and HIV/AIDS transmission. *Forced Migration Review,* 27: 23–24.

Kronsell, Annica. (2012). *Gender, sex and the postnational defense: Militarism and peacekeeping*. Oxford: Oxford University Press.

Krook, Mona Lena. (2006). Reforming representation: The diffusion of candidate gender quotas worldwide. *Politics & Gender,* 2(3): 303–327.

Krook, Mona Lena. (2010). *Quotas for women in politics: Gender and candidate selection reform worldwide*. Oxford: Oxford University Press.

Lehr, Doreen Drewry. (1999). Military wives: Breaking the silence. In *Gender Camouflage: Women and the U.S. Military*, ed. Francine J. D'Amico and Laurie L. Weinstein, 117–131. New York: New York University Press.

Liberia Institute of Statistics and Geo-Information Services (LISGIS) [Liberia] and Macro International. (2008). *Liberia Demographic and Health Survey 2007: Key findings*. Calverton, MD: LISGIS and Macro International.

Love, Ken, and Ming Singer. (1988). Self-efficacy, psychological well-being, job satisfaction and job involvement: A comparison of male and female police officers. *Police Studies: The International Review of Police Development,* 11: 98.

Lutz, Catherine, Matthew Gutmann, and Keith Brown. 2009, October 19. *Conduct and discipline in UN peacekeeping operations: Culture, political economy and gender*. Report Submitted to the Conduct and Discipline Unit, Department of Peacekeeping Operations, United Nations.

Lynch, Colum. (2004, December 16). U.N. sexual abuse alleged in congo peacekeepers accused in draft report. *Washington Post*, page A26. http://www.washingtonpost.com/wp-dyn/articles/A3145-2004Dec15.html (accessed January 12, 2015).

MacCoun, Robert J., Elizabeth Kier, and Aaron Belkin. (2006). Does social cohesion determine motivation in combat? An old question with an old answer. *Armed Forces & Society* 32(4): 646–654.

Mackay, F., M. Kenny, and L. Chappell. (2010). New institutionalism through a gender lens: Towards a feminist institutionalism? *International Political Science Review*, 31(5): 573–588.

Maginnis, Robert L. (2013). *Deadly consequences: How cowards are pushing women into combat*. Washington, DC: Regnery.

Mansbridge, Jane. (1999). Should blacks represent blacks and women represent women? A contingent "yes." *Journal of Politics,* 61(3): 628–657.

Mansfield, Edward D., and Jack Snyder. (2002). Democratic transitions, institutional strength, and war. *International Organization,* 56(2): 297–337.

March, James G., and Johan P. Olsen. (1989). *Rediscovering institutions*. New York Simon and Schuster.

Marlowe, David H. (1983). The manning of the force and the structure of battle. Part 2: Men and women. In *Conscripts and volunteers: Military requirements, social justice and the all-volunteer force*, ed. R. K. Fullinwider, 189–199. Totowa, NJ: Rowman & Allanheld.

Marshall, Monty G., Ted Robert Gurr, and Keith Jaggers. (2016). *Polity IV Project: Political regime characteristics and transitions, 1800–2015*. http://www.systemicpeace.org/inscrdata.html (accessed February 19, 2016).

Martin, Sarah. (2005). *Must boys be boys? Ending sexual exploitation and abuse in UN peacekeeping missions*. Washington, DC: Refugees International.

Martin, Susan Ehrlich. (1999). Police force or police service? Gender and emotional labor. *Annals of the American Academy of Political and Social Science,* 561(1): 111–126.

Mazurana, Dyan, Angela Raven-Roberts, and Jane Parpart, eds. (2005). *Gender, conflict, and peacekeeping*. Lanham, MD: Rowman and Littlefield.

McAdam, Doug. (1999). *Political process and the development of black insurgency, 1930–1970,* 2nd ed. Chicago: University Of Chicago Press.

McAllister, Pam. (1982). *Reweaving the web of life: Feminism and nonviolence*. Philadelphia: New Society.

McDermott, Rose, and Jonathan A. Cowden. (2001). The effects of uncertainty and sex in a crisis simulation game. *International Interactions,* 27(4): 353–380.

McKelvey, Tara. (2007). *One of the guys: Women as aggressors and torturers*. Berkeley: Seal Press.

Meier, Kenneth J., and Jill Nicholson Crotty. (2006). Gender, representative bureaucracy, and law enforcement: The case of sexual assault. *Public Administration Review,* 66(6): 850–860.

Meintjes, Sheila, Meredeth Turshen, and Anu Pillay. (2002). *The aftermath: Women in post-conflict transformation*. New York: Zed Books.

Melander, Erik. (2005a). Gender equality and intrastate armed conflict. *International Studies Quarterly,* 49(4): 695–714.

Melander, Erik. (2005b). Political gender equality and state human rights abuse. *Journal of Peace Research,* 42(2): 149–166.

Michaels, Jim. (2013, February 3). Debate over women in combat shifts to physical strength. *USA Today*. http://www.usatoday.com/story/news/nation/2013/02/02/marines-army-standards-women-combat/1884141/ (accessed July 29, 2013).

Military Leadership Diversity Commission. (2011). From representation to inclusion: Diversity leadership for the 21st century military. Final Report. http://diversity.defense.gov/Portals/51/Documents/Special%20Feature/MLDC_Final_Report.pdf (accessed March 20, 2014).

Mohanty, Chandra Talpade. (1988). Under Western eyes: Feminist scholarship and colonial discourses. *Feminist Review* 30: 61–88.

Mohanty, Chandra Talpade, Ann Russo, and Lourdes Torres. (1991). *Third world women and the politics of feminism*. 4th ed. Bloomington: Indiana University Press.

Moon, Katharine H. S. (1997). *Sex among allies*. New York: Columbia University Press.

Murdie, Amanda, and David R. Davis. (2010). Problematic potential: The human rights consequences of peacekeeping interventions in civil wars. *Human Rights Quarterly,* 32(1): 49–72.

Murdoch, M., and K. L. Nichol. (1995). Women veterans' experiences with domestic violence and with sexual harassment while in the military. *Archives of Family Medicine,* 4(5): 411.

Nagelhus, Schia, and Benjamin Carvalho. (2010). *Nobody gets justice here! Addressing sexual and gender-based violence and the rule of law in Liberia.* Working Paper. Norwegian Institute of International Affairs (NUPI). http://dspace.cigilibrary.org/jspui/handle/123456789/27745 (accessed November 12, 2016).

Nduka-Agwu, Adibeli. (2009). "Doing gender" after the war: Dealing with gender mainstreaming and sexual exploitation and abuse in UN peace support operations in Liberia and Sierra Leone. *Civil Wars,* 11(2): 179–199.

Ndulo, Muna. (2009). The United Nations responses to the sexual abuse and exploitation of women and girls by peacekeepers during peacekeeping missions. *Berkeley Journal of International Law,* 27: 127.

Ní Aoláin, Fionnuala, and Dina Francesca Haynes. (2011). *On the frontlines: Gender, war, and the post-conflict process.* Oxford: Oxford University Press.

Nordås, Ragnhild, and Siri C. A. Rustad. (2013). Sexual exploitation and abuse by peacekeepers: Understanding variation. *International Interactions,* 39(4): 511–534.

Novaco, Raymond W., and Claude M. Chemtob. (2002). Anger and combat-related posttraumatic stress disorder. *Journal of Traumatic Stress,* 15(2): 123–132.

Office of Internal Oversight Services (OIOS). (2015, May 15). *Evolution of the enforcement and remedial assistance effort for sexual exploitation and abuse by the United Nations and related personnel in peacekeeping operations.* Assignment No.: IED-15-00. New York: United Nations.

Olsen, J. (2009). Change and continuity: An institutional approach to institutions of democratic government. *European Political Science Review,* 1(1): 3–32.

Olsson, Louise. (2009). *Gender equality and United Nations peace operations in Timor Leste.* Leiden: Brill.

Olsson, Louise, and Theodora-Ismene Gizelis, eds. (2015). *Gender, peace and security: Implementing UN Security Council Resolution 1325.* New York: Routledge.

Olsson, Louise, and Torunn L. Tryggestad. (2001). *Women and international peacekeeping.* London: Frank Cass.

Onekali, Catherine A. T. (2013). Women in peacekeeping: The emergence of the all-female uniformed units in UNMIL and MONUSC. *Conflict Trends, ACCORD,* Issue 2. https://www.pksoi.org/document_repository/Misc/ACCORD_Conflict_Trends_2013-2_(4-Jul-13)-CDR-832.pdf#page=43 (accessed September 15, 2016).

Otto, Dianne. (2007). Making sense of zero tolerance policies in peacekeeping economies. In *Sexuality and the law: Feminist engagements,* ed. Vanessa Munro and Carl Stychin, 259–282. London: GlassHouse Press.

Paris, Roland. (2004). *At war's end: Building peace after civil conflict.* New York: Cambridge University Press.

Paxton, Pamela, Melanie M. Hughes, and Jennifer L. Green. (2006). The international women's movement and women's political representation, 1893–2003. *American Sociological Review,* 71(6): 898–920.

Peterson, V. S., and A. S. Runyan. (2010). *Global gender issues: In the new millennium.* 3rd ed. Boulder, CO: Westview Press.

Pettman, Jan Jindy. (1996). *Worlding women: A feminist international politics.* New York: Routledge.

Pfalzer, Janina. (2013, August 21). Swedish army turned professional tempts more female recruits. *Bloomberg News.* http://www.bloomberg.com/news/2013-08-21/swedish-army-turned-professional-tempts-more-female-recruits.html (accessed September 28, 2014).

Phillips, Anne. (1998). *The politics of presence.* Oxford: Oxford University Press.

Pouligny, Béatrice.(2006). Peace operations seen from below: UN missions and local people. London: C. Hurst & Co.

Prokos, Anastasia, and Irene Padavic. (2002). "There oughtta be a law against bitches": Masculinity lessons in police academy training. *Gender, Work & Organization,* 9(4): 439–459.

Pratt, Nicola, and Sophie Richter-Devroe. (2011). Critically examining UNSCR 1325 on women, peace and security. *International Feminist Journal of Politics,* 13(4): 489–503.

Pruitt, Lesley. (2012). Looking back, moving forward: International approaches to addressing conflict-related sexual violence. *Journal of Women, Politics & Policy,* 33(4): 299–321.

Pruitt, Lesley. (2013). All-female police contingents: Feminism and the discourse of armed protection. *International Peacekeeping,* 20(1): 67–79.

Pruitt, Lesley. (2016). *The Women in Blue Helmets: Gender, Policing, and the UN's First All-Female Peacekeeping Unit.* Berkeley, CA: University of California Press.

Quester, George H. (1977). Women in combat. *International Security,* 1(4): 80–91.

Rabe-Hemp, C. E. (2008). POLICEwomen or PoliceWOMEN? Doing gender and police work. *Feminist Criminology,* 4(2): 114–129.

Ramazanoglu, Caroline, and Janet Holland. (2002). *Feminist methodology challenges and choices.* London: Sage.

Razack, S. (2004). *Dark threats and white knights: The Somalia affair, peacekeeping and the new imperialism.* Toronto: University of Toronto Press.

Reardon, Betty. (1993). *Women and peace: Feminist visions on global security.* Albany, NY: SUNY Press

Reardon, Betty. (1996). *Sexism and the war system.* Syracuse, NY: Syracuse University Press.

Reingold, Beth. (2000). *Representing women: Sex, gender, and legislative behavior in Arizona and California.* Chapel Hill: University of North Carolina Press.

Reingold, Beth, ed. (2008). *Legislative women: Getting elected, getting ahead.* Boulder, CO: Lynne Rienner.

Republic of Liberia (2009). The Liberia National Action Plan for the Implementation of UN Resolution 1325. http://www.peacewomen.o(2009)rg/assets/file/NationalActionPlans/liberia_nationalactionplanmarch2009.pdf (accessed September 28, 2016).

Rosen, Leora N. (1996). Cohesion and readiness in gender-integrated combat service support units: The impact of acceptance of women and gender ratio. *Armed Forces & Society,* 22(4): 537–553.

Sadler, Anne G., Brenda M. Booth, Brian L. Cook, and Bradley N. Doebbeling. (2003). Factors associated with women's risk of rape in the military environment. *American Journal of Industrial Medicine,* 43(3): 262–273.

Salla, M. E. (2001). Women and war, men and pacifism. In *Gender, peace and conflict,* ed. I. Skjelsbæk and D. Smith, 68–79. London: Sage.

Sandberg, Sheryl. (2013). *Lean in: Women, work, and the will to lead.* 1st ed. New York: Knopf.

Sayers, S. L., V. A. Farrow, J. Ross, and D. W. Oslin. (2009). Family problems among recently returned military veterans referred for a mental health evaluation. *Journal of Clinical Psychiatry,* 70(2): 163.

Schuler, Sidney Ruth, Syed M. Hashemi, Ann P. Riley, and Shireen Akhter. (1996). Credit programs, patriarchy and men's violence against women in rural Bangladesh. *Social Science & Medicine,* 43(12): 1729–1742.

Scully, Pamela. (2010). Expanding the concept of gender-based violence in peacebuilding and development. *Journal of Peacebuilding & Development,* 5(3): 21–33.

Segal, David R., and Meyer Kestenbaum. (2002). Professional closure in the military labour market: A critique of pure cohesion. In *The Future of the Army Profession,* ed. Don Snider and Gayle Watkins, 41–58. New York: McGraw Hill.

Segal, Lynne. (1997). *Slow motion: Changing masculinities, changing men.* 2nd ed. London: Virago.

Segal, Mady Wechsler. (1995). Women's roles cross nationally past, present, and future. *Gender & Society,* 9(6): 757–75.

Sengupta, Somini. (2015, May 25). Allegations Against French Peacekeepers Highlight Obstacles in Addressing Abuse. *New York Times.* http://www.nytimes.com/2015/05/26/world/europe/allegations-against-french-peacekeepers-highlight-obstacles-in-addressing-abuse.html?_r=0 (accessed February 20, 2016).

Shepherd, Laura J. (2008a). *Gender, violence and security: Discourse as practice.* London: Zed Books.

Shepherd, Laura J. (2008b). Power and authority in the production of United Nations Security Council Resolution 1325. *International Studies Quarterly,* 52(2): 383–404.

Shepherd, Laura J. (2011). Sex, security and superhero(in)es: From 1325 to 1820 and beyond. *International Feminist Journal of Politics,* 13(4): 504–521.

Sieff, Kevin. (2016, January 11). U.N. says some of its peacekeepers were paying 13-year-olds for sex. *Washington Post,* https://www.washingtonpost.com/world/africa/un-says-some-of-its-peacekeepers-were-paying-13-year-olds-for-sex/2016/01/11/504e48a8-b493-11e5-8abc-d09392edc612_story.html (accessed February 20, 2016).

Simić, Olivera. (2009). Rethinking "sexual exploitation" in UN peacekeeping operations. *Women's Studies International Forum,* 32(4): 288–95.

Simić, Olivera. (2010). Does the presence of women really matter? Towards combating male sexual violence in peacekeeping operations. *International Peacekeeping,* 17(2): 188–199.

Simić, Olivera. (2013). *Moving beyond the numbers: Integrating women into peacekeeping operations.* Policy Brief. Oslo: Norwegian Peacebuilding Resource Centre.

Simm, Gabrielle. (2013). *Sex in peace operations.* Cambridge: Cambridge University Press.

Simmons, Beth A. (2009). *Mobilizing for human rights: International law in domestic politics.* Cambridge: Cambridge University Press.

Sion, Liora. (2008, October 1). Peacekeeping and the gender regime: Dutch female peacekeepers in Bosnia and Kosovo. *Journal of Contemporary Ethnography,* 37(5): 565–585.

Sivakumaran, Sandesh. (2010). Lost in translation: UN responses to sexual violence against men and boys in situations of armed conflict. *International Review of the Red Cross,* no. 877. https://www.icrc.org/eng/resources/documents/article/review/review-877-p259.htm (accessed August 25, 2014).

Sjoberg, Laura. (2006). *Gender, justice, and the wars in Iraq.* Lanham, MD: Lexington Books.

Sjoberg, Laura, ed. (2009). *Gender and international security: Feminist perspectives.* 1st ed. New York: Routledge.

Sjoberg, Laura, and Sandra Via. (2010). *Gender, war, and militarism: Feminist perspectives.* 1st ed. Santa Barbara, CA: Praeger.

Sjoberg, Laura, and Caron E. Gentry. (2007). *Mothers, monsters, whores: Women's violence in global politics.* 1st ed. New York: Zed Books.

Sjolander, Claire Turenne, and Kathryn Trevenen. (2010a). Constructions of nation, construction of war: Media representation of Captain Nichola Goddard. In *Canadian security into the 21st century: (Re)articulations of security in the post-911 world,* ed. Bruno Charbonneau and Wayne S. Cox, 126–149. Vancouver: University of British Columbia Press.

Sjolander, Claire Turenne, and Kathryn Trevenen. (2010b). One of the boys? *International Feminist Journal of Politics,* 1(2): 158–176.

Skaine, Rosemarie. (2011). *Women in combat: A reference handbook.* 1st ed. Santa Barbara, CA: ABC-CLIO.

Smith, Joshua G., Victoria K. Holt, and William J. Durch. (2007). *Enhancing United Nations capacity to support post-conflict policing and rule of law.* Stimson Center Report No. 63. http://www.stimson.org/images/uploads/research-pdfs/Stimson_UNPOL_Report_Nov07.pdf (accessed July 14, 2015).

Smuts, Barbara. (1992). Male aggression against women. *Human Nature,* 3(1): 1–44.

Stern, Jenna. (2015, February). *Reducing sexual exploitation and abuse in UN peacekeeping: Ten years after the Zeid Report.* Civilians in Conflict, Policy Brief No. 1. Washington, D.C.: Stimson Center. http://www.stimson.org/images/uploads/research-pdfs/Policy-Brief-Sexual-Abuse-Feb-2015-WEB.pdf (accessed December 17, 2015).

Stiehm, Judith Hicks. (1982). The protected, the protector, the defender. *Women's Studies International Forum,* 5(3–4): 367–376.

Stiehm, Judith Hicks. (2001). Women, peacekeeping and peacemaking: Gender balance and mainstreaming. *International Peacekeeping,* 8(2): 39–48.

St. Pierre, Kristine. (2011). Implementing the women, peace, and security agenda, in peace operations: Overview of recent efforts and lessons learned. Pearson Centre. http://www.peacebuild.ca/St-Pierre-%20WPS%20in%20Peacekeeping.pdf (accessed September 26, 2016).

Swedish International Development Cooperation. (2011, October). *In-depth study on reasons for high incidence of sexual and gender based violence in Liberia: Recommendations on prevention and response.* https://www.concern.net/sites/www.concern.net/files/media/blog-post/5876-final_high_incidence_of_sgbv_15_may.pdf (accessed August 25, 2014).

Swiss, S., P. J. Jennings, G. V. Aryee, Peggy J. Jennings, Gladys V. Aryee, Grace H. Brown, Ruth M. Jappah-Samukai, Mary S. Kamara, Rosana D. H. Schaack, and Rojatu S. Turay-Kanneh. (1998). Violence against women during the Liberian civil conflict. *Journal of the American Medical Association,* 279(8): 625–629.

Sylvester, C. (1994). Empathetic cooperation: A feminist method for IR. *Millennium,* 23(2): 315–334.

Sylvester, C. (2012). *War as experience: Contributions from international relations and feminist analysis.* 1st ed. New York: Routledge.

The World Bank. (2014). *World development indicators.* http://datacatalog.worldbank.org/ (accessed January 27, 2015).

Tickner, Ann J. (1992). *Gender in international relations: Feminist perspectives on achieving global security.* New York: Columbia University Press.

Tickner, Ann J. (2001). *Gendering world politics.* New York: Columbia University Press.

Tiger, Lionel, and Robin Fox. (1998). *The imperial animal.* New Brunswick, NJ: Transaction.

Titunik, R. F. (2000). The first wave: Gender integration and military culture. *Armed Forces and Society,* 26: 229–257.

Tripp, Aili Mari, and Alice Kang. (2008). The global impact of quotas on the fast track to increased female legislative representation. *Comparative Political Studies,* 41(3): 338–361.

True, Jacqui, and Michael Mintrom. (2001). Transnational networks and policy diffusion: The case of gender mainstreaming. *International Studies Quarterly,* 45(1): 27–57.

Tsjeard, Bouta, George Frerks, and Ian Bannon. (2005). *Gender, conflict and development.* Washington, DC: International Bank for Reconstruction and Development, World Bank.

UN. (1995). Women 2000: The role of women in United Nations Peacekeeping, December 1995. Department for the Advancement of Women, Department for Policy Coordination and Sustainable Development.

UN. (2000). *Comprehensive review of the whole question of peacekeeping operations in all their aspects.* General Assembly Security Council, A/55/305–S/2000/809. http://www.un.org/en/ga/search/view_doc.asp?symbol=A/55/305&referer=/english/&Lang=E (adopted August 21, 2000; accessed February 13, 2013).

UN. (2001). Gender mainstreaming: Strategy for promoting gender equality. Office of the Special Adviser on Gender Issues and Advancement of Women. http://www.un.org/womenwatch/osagi/pdf/factsheet1.pdf (accessed February 18, 2014).

UN. (2002). Gender mainstreaming: An overview. Office of the Special Adviser on Gender Issues and the Advancement of Women. http://www.un.org/womenwatch/osagi/pdf/e65237.pdf (accessed February 18, 2014).

UN. (2003). Secretary-General's Bulletin Special Measures for Protection from Sexual Exploitation and Sexual Abuse, ST/SGB/2003/13. https://cdu.unlb.org/portals/0/documents/keydoc4.pdf (accessed February 13, 2013).

UN. (2005, March 24). *Comprehensive review of the whole question of peacekeeping operations in all their aspects.* General Assembly Security Council, A/59/710 (accessed February 13, 2013).

UN. (2010a). Ten year impact study on implementation of UN Security Council Resolution 1325 (2000) on women, peace and security in peacekeeping. Final Report to the United Nations Department of Peacekeeping Operations, Department of Field Support, New York. http://www.un.org/en/peacekeeping/documents/10year_impact_study_1325.pdf (accessed February 13, 2013).

UN. (2010b). *Policy on gender equality in peacekeeping operations,* 2010, UN DPKO Department of Field Support, Ref 2010.25, New York. http://www.un.org/en/peacekeeping/documents/gender_directive_2010.pdf (accessed February 13, 2013).

UN. (2010c). DPKO/DFS Guidelines: Integrating a Gender Perspective into the Work of the United Nations Military in Peacekeeping Operations. Office of the Military Adviser, Department of Peacekeeping Operations, New York. http://www.un.org/en/peacekeeping/documents/dpko_dfs_gender_military_perspective.pdf (accessed February 13, 2013).

UN. (2014). Conflict-related sexual violence: Report of the Secretary General, General Assembly Security Council S/2014/181. http://www.securitycouncilreport.org/atf/cf/%7B65BFCF9B-6D27-4E9C-8CD3-CF6E4FF96FF9%7D/s_2014_181.pdf (accessed: April 26, 2015).

UN. (2015). *Comprehensive review of the whole question of peacekeeping operations in all their aspects.* General Assembly Security Council, A/70/95–S/2015/446. http://www.un.org/sg/pdf/HIPPO_Report_1_June_2015.pdf (accessed December 10, 2015) (accessed November 12, 2016).

UN DPKO. (2000, July). Mainstreaming a gender perspective in multidimensional peace operations, United Nations. Lessons Learned Unit (accessed September 28, 2016).

UN DPKO. (2004). Gender resource package for peacekeeping operations. New York.

UNIFEM. (2007, October). Gender-sensitive police reform in post-conflict societies. http://www.unwomen.org/~/media/Headquarters/Media/Publications/UNIFEM/GenderSensitivePoliceReformPolicyBrief2007eng.pdf (accessed September 28, 2016).

UNMIL. (2010). Gender mainstreaming in peacekeeping operations Liberia 2003–2009 Best Practices Report, Office of the Gender Adviser (OGA). http://www.resdal.org/facebook/UNMIL_Gender_Mainstreaming_in_PKO_in_Liberia-Best.pdf Accra, Ghana (accessed September 11, 2016).

UN. (2008). Securing peace and development: The role of the UN in supporting security sector reform. Report of the Secretary-General, Sixty-seventh session A/67/970–S/2013/480. http://www.securitycouncilreport.org/atf/cf/%7B65BFCF9B-6D27-4E9C-8CD3-CF6E4FF96FF9%7D/s_2013_480.pdf (accessed September 11, 2016).

UN Women. (2010). Addressing conflict-related sexual violence an analytical inventory of peacekeeping practice. http://www.unwomen.org/~/media/Headquarters/Media/Publications/en/04DAnAnalyticalinventoryofPeacekeepingPracti.pdf (accessed September 28, 2016).

UN Women. (2015). *Preventing conflict, transforming justice, securing the peace: A global study on the implementation of UN Security Council Resolution 1325.* http://wps.unwomen.org/~/media/files/un%20women/wps/highlights/unw-global-study-1325-2015.pdf (accessed February 10, 2016).

UN Mission in Ethiopia and Eritrea (UNMEE). http://www.un.org/en/peacekeeping/missions/past/unmee/ (accessed September 30, 2014).

UN Integrated Mission in Timor-Leste (UNMIT). UN Integrated Mission in Timor-Leste Completes Its Mandate. http://www.un.org/en/peacekeeping/missions/past/unmit/documents/unmit_fact_sheet_11dec2012_2.pdf (accessed September 30, 2014).

UN Operation in Côte d'Ivoire (UNOCI). UNOCI United Nations Operation in Côte d'Ivoire. http://www.un.org/en/peacekeeping/missions/unoci/ (accessed September 30, 2014).

UN Disengagement Observer Force (UNDOF). http://www.un.org/en/peacekeeping/missions/undof/ (accessed September 30, 2014).

UN Peacekeeping Force in Cyprus (UNFICYP). http://www.unficyp.org/nqcontent.cfm?a_id=778&tt=graphic&lang=l1 (accessed September 30, 2014).

UN Interim Administration Mission in Kosovo (UNMIK). http://www.un.org/en/peacekeeping/missions/unmik/background.shtml (accessed September 30, 2014).

UN Security Council, Security Council Resolution 1325 (2000) [on women and peace and security], October 31, 2000, S/RES/1325 (2000). http://www.refworld.org/docid/3b00f4672e.html (accessed September 28, 2016).

UN Security Council. (2003). Security Council Resolution 1509 (2003). S/RES/1509 (2003). Adopted by Security Council on September 19, 2003.

UN Security Council, Security Council Resolution 1820 (2008) [on acts of sexual violence against civilians in armed conflicts], June 19, 2008, S/RES/1820 (2008). http://www.refworld.org/docid/485bbca72.html (accessed September 28, 2016).

UN Security Council, Security Council Resolution 1888 (2009) [on acts of sexual violence against civilians in armed conflicts], September 30, 2009, S/RES/1888 (2009). http://www.refworld.org/docid/4ac9aa152.html (accessed September 28, 2016).

UN Security Council, Security Council Resolution 1960 (2010) [on women and peace and security], December 16, 2010, S/RES/1960(2010). http://www.refworld.org/docid/4d2708a02.html (accessed September 28, 2016).

UN Security Council, Resolution 2116. (2013). Adopted by the Security Council at its 7033rd meeting, on September 18, 2013.

U.S. Marine Corp 2015. Marine Corps gender integration research executive summary. http://www.scribd.com/doc/280017557/Marine-Corps-gender-integration-research-executive-summary (accessed February 11, 2016).

Utas, Mats. (2005). Victimcy, girlfriending, soldiering: Tactic agency in a young woman's social navigation of the Liberian war zone. *Anthropological Quarterly*, 78(2): 403–430.

Uzonyi, Gary. (2015). Refugee flows and state contributions to post-Cold War UN peacekeeping missions. *Journal of Peace Research*, 52(6): 743–757.

Van Creveld, Martin. (2001). *Men, women and war: Do women belong in the frontline?*. London: Cassel.

Van Creveld, Martin. (2008). *The culture of war*. New York: Ballantine Books.

Valenius, Johanna. (2007). A few kind women: Gender essentialism and Nordic peacekeeping operations. *International Peacekeeping*, 14(4): 510–523.

Valente, Sharon, and Callie Wight. 2007. Military sexual trauma: Violence and sexual abuse. *Military Medicine*, 172(3): 259–265.

Walsh, Shannon D. (2008). Engendering justice: Constructing institutions to address violence against women. *Studies in Social Justice*, 2(1): 48–66.

Walsh, Shannon D. (2015). Advances and limits of policing and human security for women: Nicaragua comparative perspective. In Gender violence in peace and war: States of complicity, ed. Victoria Sanford, Katerina Stefatos, and Cecilia Salvi, 133–146. New Brunswick, NJ: Rutgers University Press.

Ward, Hugh, and Han Dorussen. (2016). Standing alongside your friends: Network Centrality and Providing troops to UN peacekeeping operations. *Journal of Peace Research*, 53(3): 392–408.

Whitworth, Sandra. (2007). *Men, militarism, and UN peacekeeping: A gendered analysis*. Boulder, CO: Lynne Rienner.

Wibben, Annick T. R. (2011). *Feminist security studies: A Narrative approach*. 1st ed. New York: Routledge.

Williams, Christine. (1989). *Gender differences at work: Women and men in non-traditional occupations*. Berkeley: University of California Press.

Williams, John E., and Deborah L. Best. (1990). *Measuring sex stereotypes: A multination study*. Rev. ed. New York: Sage.

Woodward, R., and P. Winter. *Sexing the soldier: The politics of gender and the contemporary British Army*. Abingdon, UK: Routledge.

Wynes, M. Deborah, and Mohamed Mounir Zahran. (2011). Transparency in the selection and appointment of senior managers in the United Nations Secretariat. Report of the United Nations: Joint Inspection Unit, JIU/REP/2011/2. https://www.unjiu.org/en/reports-notes/JIU%20Products/JIU_REP_2011_2_English.pdf (accessed February 18, 2016), 11.

York, J. (1998). The truth about women and peace. In *The women and war reader*, ed. L. A. Lorentzen and J. Turpin, 19–25. New York: New York University Press.

Young, Iris. (2003). Logic of masculinist protection: Reflections on the current security state. *Signs*, 29: 1.

Young, Iris. (2007). *Global challenges: War, self-determination and responsibility for justice*. Cambridge, MA: Polity.

Yuval-Davis, Nira. (1997). *Gender and nation*. Thousand Oaks, CA: Sage.

Yuval-Davis, Nira. (2006). Intersectionality and feminist politics. *European Journal of Women's Studies*, 13(3): 193–209.

Zarkov, Dubravka, and Cynthia Cockburn. (2002). *The postwar moment: Militaries, masculinities, and international peacekeeping*. London: Lawrence and Wishart.

Zeigler, Sara, and Gregory Gunderson. (2005). *Moving beyond GI Jane: Women and the US military*. Lanham, MD: University Press of America.

INDEX

Page numbers followed by *t* or *f* indicate tables or figures, respectively. Numbers followed by "n" indicate notes.

protection against, 17, 21–24
reform efforts, 24, 191–192
remedies to, 52
research on, 98–101, 101–105
in UN Mission in Liberia, 109–112, 113–164, 152f
women in military contributions and, 78–80, 78f, 80f
sexuality, male, 38–40, 93
sexual misconduct, 93. *See also* sexual exploitation, abuse, harassment, and violence (SEAHV)
sexual servants, 150
sexual violence, 39–44, 48, 52, 76, 79–81, 80f, 87, 92, 97, 133, 135, 140–141, 147, 149–152, 191, 201, 212, 226n7, 227n12, 228n28, 233n17, 233n26. *See also* sexual and gender-based violence (SGBV); sexual exploitation, abuse, harassment, and violence (SEAHV)
conflict-related, 22–24, 23f
prevention of, 140, 178
SGBV. *See* sexual and gender-based violence
Shannon, Megan, 37
Sierra Leone, 21, 81–82, 99t, 101t, 139, 196t, 238n20, 239n20
Simić, Olivera, 49
Simmons, Beth, 85
Sion, Liora, 51
Sirleaf, Ellen Johnson, 137, 140–141
sisterhood, 53
slavery, sexual, 22, 147
Slovakia, 70, 196t
Slovenia, 101t, 196t
Smuts, Barbara, 31
social cohesion, 39, 179, 229n31
social interactions, 118, 132, 185
social networking, 185. *See also* networking
societal gender equality, 83–87. *See also* gender equality
Sohel, Sade Uddin Ahmed, 76–77
soldiers, 32, 36, 38–43, 48, 56, 171, 176, 191, 227n13, 230n49. *See also* armed forces; military forces
bonds among, 179, 230n35 (*see also* unit cohesion)
British, 169, 172
South Africa, 14, 46–47, 69–70, 105–107, 106t
South Sudan, 62, 99t, 196t. *See also* United Nations Mission in the Republic of South Sudan (UNMISS)
Spain, 101t

special representatives of the secretary-general (SRSGs), 172–173, 175–176, 178, 184, 187, 191
SRSGs. *See* special representatives of the secretary-general
SSRs. *See* security sector reforms
standards, 5, 53–54, 56, 67, 69, 89, 100, 138, 164, 168, 170, 173–175, 177, 192–193
stereotypes, 51, 130. *See also* gender stereotypes
Stimson Center, 182
stripping, forced, 147
Sudan, 60, 62, 196t
UN-African Union Mission in Darfur (UNAMID), 61t, 62, 74, 98, 99t
UN Interim Security Force for Abyei (UNISFA), 61t, 62, 74–75
UN Mission in Sudan (UNMIS), 61t, 62, 74, 98, 99t
UN Mission in the Republic of South Sudan (UNMISS), 61t, 62, 98, 99t
Sudan People's Liberation Movement, 62
Sweden, 49, 54, 194, 225n2
feminist foreign policy, 1, 165, 225n1
military, 56, 69, 169, 179
National Action Plan (NAP), 101t
peacekeeping contingents, 69, 179
Switzerland, ix, 101t, 129, 196t, 206t
Syria, 63–64, 99t, 197t, 226n8
UN Disengagement Observer Force (UNDOF), 61t, 63–64, 99t
UN Truce Supervision Organization (UNTSO), 61t, 63

task cohesion, 108, 179, 181, 229n31
Taylor, Charles, 110–111, 138, 150
Ten-year Impact Study on Implementation of UN Security Council Resolution 1325 (2000) on Women, Peace and Security in Peacekeeping, 15
Thailand, 69, 197t
Tickner, Ann, 32, 38–39, 226n11
Tiger, Lionel, 31, 230n37
Timor-Leste, 16, 99t, 232n2. *See also* United Nations Integrated Mission in Timor-Leste (UNMIT)
token women, 49
Tolbert, William R., Jr., 110–111
training, 5, 12, 25, 33, 53, 56, 88, 136–137, 168, 170, 178–181, 185, 194, 209, 241n12
gender equality, 21, 25, 94, 98, 108, 141, 154, 178–181, 185, 188, 191
in-service, 25, 146, 180, 188
militarization and, 39, 43

Lightning Source UK Ltd.
Milton Keynes UK
UKHW021029070223
416524UK00018B/322

9 780190 093532